PETITIONS AND PETITIONING IN EUROPE AND NORTH AMERICA

For over 100 years the *Proceedings of the British Academy* series has provided a unique record of British scholarship in the humanities and social sciences. These themed volumes drive scholarship forward and are landmarks in their field. For more information about the series, please visit www.thebritishacademy.ac.uk/proceedings.

PROCEEDINGS OF THE BRITISH ACADEMY • 262

PETITIONS AND PETITIONING IN EUROPE AND NORTH AMERICA

FROM THE LATE MEDIEVAL PERIOD TO THE PRESENT

Edited by
RICHARD HUZZEY, MAARTJE JANSE,
HENRY MILLER, JORIS ODDENS,
AND BRODIE WADDELL

Published for THE BRITISH ACADEMY
by OXFORD UNIVERSITY PRESS

Oxford University Press, Great Clarendon Street, Oxford OX2 6DP

First edition published in 2024

British Library Cataloguing in Publication Data
Data available

Library of Congress Cataloguing in Publication Data
Data available

Typeset by Newgen Publishing UK

ISBN: 978-0-19-726772-1 (hardback)
ISBN: 978-0-19-893096-9 (epub)
ISBN: 978-0-19-893095-2 (UPDF)
ISBN: 978-0-19-893097-6 (online)
ISSN 0068-1202

In memory of

Malcolm Chase (1957–2020)
Aaron Graham (1984–2023)

Contents

List of Figures

List of Tables

Notes on Contributors

Maggie Blackhawk (Fond du Lac Band of Lake Superior Ojibwe) is Professor of Law at New York University. She researches and teaches in the fields of constitutional law, federal Indian law, and legislation. Her research has been published in *Harvard Law Review*, *Stanford Law Review*, *Yale Law Journal*, *Columbia Law Review*, and *Supreme Court Review*, among others. Her recent projects examine the ways that American democracy can and should empower minorities, and she is currently writing a book on the centrality of Native Nations, Native peoples, and American colonialism to the constitutional law and history of the United States.

Daniel Carpenter is Allie S. Freed Professor of Government and Chair of the Department of Government at Harvard University. He is the author of *Democracy by Petition: Popular Politics in Transformation, 1790–1870* (2021), and he has published numerous articles on petitions in journals including *American Political Science Review*, *Perspectives on Politics*, *Studies in American Political Development*, *Social Science History*, *Legislative Studies Quarterly*, and the *Journal of Politics*, among others. He has also led a series of digitisations of historic petitions from Massachusetts, supported by grants from the National Endowment for the Humanities and the Mellon Foundation.

Edurne De Wilde is a PhD candidate at the Leiden University Institute for History. She is currently working on her thesis concerning the afterlives of Francis Bacon's theory of the idols. This project is part of the NWO VICI project 'Scholarly Vices: A Longue Durée History' (2019–2024), which seeks to explain the persistence of early modern language of vice in modern scholarly discourse. Previously, during her Research MA (2017–19), she worked as a research trainee on the project 'Languages of Citizenship: Conceptions of Politics and Discursive Strategies in Petitions to Dutch Parliamentary Assemblies, 1796–1940' (Leiden University).

Gwilym Dodd is Associate Professor in the Department of History at the University of Nottingham. His research specialises in late medieval England. He is the author of *Justice and Grace: Private Petitioning and the English Parliament in the Late Middle Ages* (2007), and articles in *English Historical Review*, *Journal of Medieval History*, and *Speculum*, among others. He is co-editor of *Medieval Petitions* (2009), *Petitions to the Crown from English Religious Houses, c. 1272–c. 1485* (2010) and *Petitions from Lincolnshire, c. 1272–c. 1485* (2020).

Lara Douds is Assistant Professor of Russian History in the Department of Humanities at Northumbria University. She is a specialist in the history of state building, political practice, and political culture in the early decades of Soviet power. She is the author of *Inside Lenin's Government: Power, Ideology and Practice in the Early Soviet State* (2018) and co-editor of *The Fate of the Bolshevik Revolution: Illiberal Liberation, 1917–41* (2020).

Aaron Graham (1984–2023) was Lecturer in Early Modern British Economic History at University College London (UCL). He was previously a research associate on the ERC Horizon Project 'The European Fiscal-Military System, 1530–1870' at Oxford, and before that held Leverhulme and British Academy post-doctoral fellowships at UCL and Oxford. He published widely on politics, government, and finance in Britain and the British empire between 1660 and 1850. His second monograph, *Bills of Union: Money, Empire, and Ambitions in the Mid-Eighteenth Century British Atlantic*, was published in 2021, and his third book, *Tropical Leviathan: Slavery, Society, and State-Making in Jamaica, 1770–1840*, will be published posthumously.

Marta Gravela is Associate Professor in Medieval History at the University of Turin, where she is the PI of the ERC StG project 'Democracies of the Alps: Issues, Practices and Ideals of Politics in Mountain Communities, 1300–1500' (DEMALPS). Her research interests lie at the intersection of social, political, and economic history of late medieval Europe, with particular reference to northern Italy and France. In 2017 she published the book *Il corpo della città: Politica e parentela a Torino nel tardo Medioevo* (Rome: Viella).

Richard Huzzey is Professor of Modern British History at Durham University. He was Principal Investigator of the Leverhulme Trust project on 'Rethinking Petitions, Parliament, and People in the Long Nineteenth Century' (2016–19) and the AHRC-ESRC project on 'Petitioning and People Power in Twentieth-Century Britain' (2020–3). His first book and a range of scholarly essays focused on slavery and abolitionism in the British empire. He co-edited *The Suppression of the Atlantic Slave Trade* (2015) and edited *Pressure and Parliament: From Civil War to Civil Society* (2018).

Joanna Innes was, until her retirement, Fellow and Tutor at Somerville College and Professor of Modern History at the University of Oxford. She is currently Senior Research Fellow at Somerville College. Her work has been mainly concerned with 18th- and early-19th-century political culture. Her books include *Inferior Politics: Social Problems and Social Policies in Britain 1688–1800* (2009) and volumes on 'reimagining democracy' in America, France, Britain, and Ireland, 1750–1850 (2013); the Mediterranean, 1780–1860 (2018); and Latin America and the Caribbean, 1780–1870 (2023). She continues to research and publish on these themes.

Maartje Janse is Associate Professor of History at Leiden University. She jointly led the NWO-funded research group The Promise of Organization, and was Principal Investigator of the NWO-funded project 'Organizing the Masses'. She jointly led the project 'Languages of Citizenship'. She has published widely on political participation, including *De Afschaffers: Publieke opinie, organisatie en politiek in Nederland, 1840–1880* (2007) and articles in *Past & Present*, *European Review of History*, and *Social Science History*, among others. She co-edited the volume *Organizing Democracy* (2017) and is one of the editors of the Palgrave Studies in Political History book series.

Mark Knights is Professor of History at the University of Warwick. He has published extensively on petitioning in the early modern period, including in his monograph *Representation and Misrepresentation in Later Stuart Britain: Partisanship and Political Culture* (2005), as well as *Past & Present* and the *Historical Journal*, among other journals. His most recent work is *Corruption in Office in Britain and Its Empire, 1600–1850* (2021).

Cristina Leston-Bandeira is Professor of Politics at the University of Leeds. She is the Chair of the International Parliament Engagement Network and co-editor of the pioneering book *Exploring Parliament* (2018). She has served in several prestigious roles, such as Chair of the UK Study of Parliament Group (2019–22) and co-editor of *Parliamentary Affairs* (2017–21). Her research focuses on the relationship between parliaments and the public, particularly public and digital engagement, such as e-petitions. She has written extensively on the topic, including articles in *Political Studies*, *Journal of Legislative Studies*, *Parliamentary Affairs*, and *Policy & Politics*.

Elsa Miedema is a freelance researcher. She is currently conducting several research projects relating to political and military history. Her book on the history of the Dutch Military Rehabilitation Centre is forthcoming. Previously, during her History MA (2017–19), she worked as a research trainee on the project 'Languages of Citizenship: Conceptions of Politics and Discursive Strategies in Petitions to Dutch Parliamentary Assemblies, 1796–1940' at Leiden University.

Henry Miller is Vice Chancellor's Fellow at Northumbria Univerity. He was Principal Investigator of the AHRC Research Network on Petitions and Petitioning (2018–19), from which this volume is derived. He has edited a special issue of *Social Science History* (2019) on the comparative history of petitioning in the 19th century, and published articles on petitions in *Past & Present*, *English Historical Review*, *Historical Journal*, and the *Journal of British Studies*, among others. His second book, *A Nation of Petitioners: Petitions and Petitioning in the United Kingdom, 1780–1918*, was published in 2023.

Joris Oddens is Research Group Leader at the Huygens Institute for the History and Culture of the Netherlands, Royal Netherlands Academy of Arts and Sciences (KNAW). He has published widely on the history of petitioning in journals such as *European History Quarterly*, *Eighteenth Century Studies*, *National Identities*, and *Low Countries Historical Review*, as well as in multiple edited volumes. In 2023 he published a book on petitions and politics in the Netherlands in the 18th and 19th centuries: *Op veler verzoek: Inclusieve politiek in Nederland 1780–1860.*

Ismini Pells is a departmental lecturer at the University of Oxford's Department for Continuing Education. She is also project manager of the AHRC-funded Civil War Petitions project, investigating pensions awarded to maimed soldiers and war widows from the English Civil Wars. She previously worked as a postdoctoral researcher at the Universities of Leicester and Exeter, after obtaining her PhD from the University of Cambridge. Her publications include *Philip Skippon and the British Civil Wars: The 'Christian Centurion'* (2020) and 'Reassessing Frontline Medical Practitioners of the British Civil Wars in the Context of the Seventeenth-Century Medical World', *Historical Journal* (2019).

Anne Petterson is Assistant Professor in Political History at Radboud University Nijmegen. Her current research focuses on the culture of political debate in and beyond parliaments in the modern era. She jointly led the project 'Languages of Citizenship: Conceptions of Politics and Discursive Strategies in Petitions to Dutch Parliamentary Assemblies, 1796–1940' at Leiden University in 2018. Her PhD thesis on popular nationalism in 19th-century Amsterdam was published as *Eigenwijs vaderland* (2017) and awarded the prestigious Dirk Jacob Veegens Prijs of the Koninklijke Hollandsche Maatschappij der Wetenschappen.

Joris van den Tol is Assistant Professor of Economic History at Radboud University Nijmegen, having previously held fellowships at Harvard (2019–21) and Cambridge (2022–3). His first book, *Lobbying in Company* (2020), studies the importance of petitions in relation to the colony of Dutch Brazil (1630–54). His postdoctoral research focuses on transnational petitions between the Dutch Republic and the British Isles on the topic of international commerce and diplomacy in the 17th century. His research on petitions in the Atlantic World and in Asia has been published in journals and edited volumes in both Dutch and in English.

Brodie Waddell is Senior Lecturer in Early Modern History at Birkbeck, University of London. He was Principal Investigator on the AHRC-funded project 'The Power of Petitioning in Seventeenth-Century England' (2019–21). His interest in petitioning began with his first book, *God, Duty, and Community in English Economic Life, 1660–1720* (2012), and he edited *Addressing Authority: An Online Symposium on Petitions and Supplications in Early Modern Society* (2016). He has published widely on early modern history in *Past & Present*, *Journal of*

Social History, *History Workshop Journal*, and *English Historical Review*. He is co-editor of *Cultural and Social History*.

Hannah Worthen is a historian based at the University of Hull. Her research focuses on the lives of early modern women, as well as women's engagement with space in historical and contemporary contexts. Her PhD was awarded by the University of Leicester in 2018 and was titled 'The Experience of War Widows in Mid-Seventeenth Century England'. Her recent publications include 'Gender, Property, and Succession in the Early Modern English Aristocracy: The Case of Martha Janes and her Illegitimate Children', *Women's History Review*, 30 (2021), co-authored with Briony McDonagh and Amanda Capern.

Andreas Würgler is Full Professor of Early Modern History at the University of Geneva. Together with Cecilia Nubola (ISIG Trento, Italy) he led the European project on 'Supplications and Petitions' (four volumes, published 2002–10). His Swiss National Science Foundation project 'Petitions in Times of Change' (2007–13) is documented in *Grenzen des Zumutbaren: Erfahrungen mit der französischen Okkupation und der Helvetischen Republik (1798–1803)* (2011). His publications on petitions include 'Voices from among the "Silent Masses": Humble Petitions and Social Conflicts in Early Modern Central Europe', *International Review of Social History*, 46 (2001), Supplement 9.

David Zaret is Emeritus Professor of Sociology and History at Indiana University. His earlier work on petitioning explored links between the practice and development of a public sphere, mainly in Great Britain, in *Origins of Democratic Culture: Printing, Petitions, and the Public Sphere in Early Modern England* (Princeton: Princeton University Press, 2000). His more recent work is a comparative analysis of premodern petitioning across Eurasia, 'Petition-and-Response and Liminal Petitioning in Comparative/Historical Perspective,' *Social Science History*, 43 (2019), although he continues to pursue archival research on British petitioning, including a recent article in *Parliaments, Estates, and Representation* (2022).

Acknowledgements

This book was developed from an AHRC Research Network (AH/R008868/1). We would like to acknowledge the generous support of the AHRC that made the Network possible, and the contributions made by Durham University; Birkbeck, University of London; and Leiden University in support of the three workshops held in 2018 and 2019. We would also like to thank Research and Innovation Services at Durham, particularly Anna Hutchinson, for their assistance in developing the grant application. Next, we would like to thank the British Academy, Portia Taylor, and the Publishing Committee for their efficient management of the application and publication process; the two anonymous reviewers of our proposal; and Mike Braddick for writing a strong endorsement of the book. We are also indebted to those colleagues who kindly acted as independent reviewers of specific chapters, often at short notice, and around other commitments: Anna Bocking-Welch, Elaine Chalus, Sarah Davies, Christian Liddy, Diego Palacios Cerezales, Mark Stoyle, Henk te Velde, and Nick Vivyan. Informal discussions about petitions and petitioning with colleagues have also fed into our thinking and the final volume.

As is perhaps normal with edited books, this volume has had a long gestation period, so we would like to thank our contributors for their continued enthusiasm for this project and their patience. It has been a long game, but we think we can all be pleased with the outcome. We would also like to thank the other participants in the AHRC Network whose papers, interventions, reflections, and conversations shaped the content of the volume in numerous ways. In addition to those already mentioned, we would like to thank Benoît Agnès, Martin Almbjär, Yuval Ben-Bassat, Catherine Bochel, Jean-Gabriel Contamin, Miguel Dantas da Cruz, Stephen Fricker, Peter Hill, Andrew Hopper, Julian Hoppit, Sharon Howard, Robert Jones, Karen Lauwers, Philip Loft, Carrie Long, Ciara Stewart, Laura Stewart, Hannah Weiss Muller, Tim Verhoeven, and Quentin Verreycken.

We would like to dedicate the volume to two outstanding historians, Malcolm Chase and Aaron Graham, who sadly passed away before this book was published. As well as being a fine social historian, Malcolm, who was a participant at the first of our workshops, was always very encouraging to younger scholars and had a deep interest in petitions because of his expertise on Chartism. In his memorable contribution, he asked provocatively whether petitions in their modern digital form had essentially been 'tamed' of their disruptive and often subversive potential. It was a characteristically thought-provoking question.

Shortly before we submitted the first draft of the manuscript we learnt of the sudden passing of Aaron Graham, one of our contributors. In a short time, Aaron had already established himself as a brilliant scholar through his many publications, and held a string of prestigious postdoctoral fellowships before securing the permanent job he had long deserved. Aaron's chapter reflects his strengths as a researcher and also gives a tantalising glimpse of a future project on petitions in Jamaica that he had sketched out. We are grateful to Aaron's family and his colleague Jon Chandler for working with us to see Aaron's chapter through to publication.

Finally, the contributions of Joris Oddens to this volume have been made possible by the Dutch Research Council ('The Persistence of Civic Identities in the Netherlands, 1747–1848') and the Statesman Thorbecke Fund ('The Dutch Attitude towards Petitioning in a Comparative European Perspective'). Brodie Waddell's contribution is based partly on research funded by an AHRC Research Grant ('The Power of Petitioning in Seventeenth-Century England', AH/S001654/1).

Introduction: Petitions and Petitioning in Historical Perspective

RICHARD HUZZEY, MAARTJE JANSE, HENRY MILLER, JORIS ODDENS, AND BRODIE WADDELL

In 1852, following a public meeting, the women of Sheffield petitioned the UK House of Commons against a proposed plan to form militias. The petition bluntly informed MPs that 'we have for too long seen the demoralising effects of taking our children and husbands from their peaceful homes' before declaiming that 'war is detestable in any shape'. If Parliament assented to the government's scheme, it was tantamount to mounting 'an aggressive war on the people of this country', particularly their 'hearths and liberties'.[1] The petition, one of a million or so sent to the Commons from 1780 to 1918, was a powerful example of the ways in which petitioning enabled unenfranchised women to mobilise a potent gendered rhetoric that combined an emphasis on their role as custodians of the family, with an increasing appeal to rights and liberties.[2] Removed from its specific geographical and historical context, the petition stands as but one example of an important and ubiquitous practice with a long lineage, which is the subject of this volume.

From classical antiquity to the emergence of e-petitions in the early 21st century, petitions and petitioning have been ubiquitous practices in myriad societies and polities. Across many centuries and many territories, these practices have constituted a persistent channel of communication between rulers and ruled, monarchs and their subjects, representatives and the represented, and states and citizens. Petitions have proved to be a malleable tool for those subject to different forms of power, both formal and informal. The specific characteristics of petitions, as well as their ubiquity and longevity, mean that a broader study of this phenomenon is not just important in terms of particular periods, places, or polities. It is

[1] Select Committee on Public Petitions, *Reports* (1852), Appendix 214.

[2] H. Miller, *A Nation of Petitioners: Petitions and Petitioning in the United Kingdom, 1780–1918* (Cambridge, Cambridge University Press, 2023), pp. 147–52.

Proceedings of the British Academy, **262**, 1–30, © The British Academy 2024.

also crucial for scholars seeking to understand power and authority, representation and representative claims, collective action and repertoires of popular contention, popular politics, political culture, state formation, institutions, citizenship and participation, and democracy and democratisation. To explain the scope and objective of this volume, we will begin by outlining the body of research to which it contributes.

Research on petitioning published before the 1990s typically used petitions as source material or a theme to address particular questions within an existing field of study. Not surprisingly, given that these works addressed distinct regions and literatures, scholars isolated the specific, rather than the broader phenomenon of petitioning, and rarely drew comparisons to form a coherent body of scholarship on petitions.[3] Since then petitions and related genres have more often been studied as practices in their own right. The project led by Cecilia Nubola and Andreas Würgler on petitions in late medieval and early modern Europe produced a series of edited collections published in both German and Italian in the 2000s.[4] This project fed directly into a much-cited special issue of the *International Review of Social History* (2001), edited by Lex Heerma van Voss, on *Petitions in Social History*.[5] In the British context, in the same decade, the York Medieval Petitions project traced petitioning in the remaking of England's monarchy and Parliament, while Mark Knights and David Zaret examined the role of petitioning in forging a public sphere in the 17th century.[6]

[3] S. M. Stern, 'Petitions from the Ayyūbid Period', *Bulletin of the School of Oriental and African Studies*, 27 (1964), 1–32; S. M. Stern, 'Petitions from the Mamlūk Period', *Bulletin of the School of Oriental and African Studies*, 29 (1966), 233–76; E. R. Foster, 'Petitions and the Petition of Right', *Journal of British Studies*, 14 (1974), 21–45; J. E. Bradley, *Popular Politics and the American Revolution in England: Petitions, the Crown, and Public Opinion* (Macon, GA, Mercer University Press, 1986); H. Neuhaus, *Reichstag und Supplikationsausschuß: Ein Beitrag zur Reichsverfassungsgeschichte der ersten Hälfte des 16. Jahrhunderts* (Berlin, Duncker & Humblot, 1977); J. Talsma, *Het recht van petitie, verzoekschriften aan de Tweede Kamer en het ombudsmanvraagstuk* (Arnhem, Gouda Quint, 1989).

[4] C. Nubola and A. Würgler (eds), *Suppliche e gravamina: Politica, amministrazione, giustizia in Europa (secoli XIV–XVIII)* (Bologna, Società editrice il Mulino, 2002)/*Bittschriften und Gravamina: Politik, Verwaltung und Justiz in Europa (14.–18. Jahrhundert)* (Berlin, Duncker & Humblot, 2005); C. Nubola and A. Würgler (eds), *Formen der politischen Kommunication in Europa vom 15. bis 18. Jahrhundert: Suppliken, Gravamina, Brief* (Berlin, Duncker & Humblot, 2004)/*Forme della comunicazione politica in Europa nei secoli XV–XVIII: Suppliche, gravamina, lettere* (Bologna, Società editrice il Mulino, 2004); C. Nubola and A. Würgler (eds), *Operare la resistenza: Suppliche, gravamina e rivolte in Europa (1400–1800)* (Bologna, Società editrice il Mulino, 2006)/*Pratiken des Widerstandes: Suppliken, Gravamina und Revolten in Europa (1400–1800)* (Berlin, Duncker & Humblot, 2006).

[5] L. Heerma van Voss (ed.), *Petitions in Social History*, Supplement 9 of *International Review of Social History*, 46 (2001).

[6] G. Dodd, *Justice and Grace: Private Petitioning and the English Parliament in the Late Middle Ages* (Oxford, Oxford University Press, 2007); W. M. Ormrod, G. Dodd, and A. Musson (eds), *Medieval Petitions: Grace and Grievance* (Woodbridge, York Medieval Press, 2009); M. Knights, *Representation and Misrepresentation in Later Stuart Political Culture* (Oxford, Oxford University Press, 2005), Chapter 3; D. Zaret, *Origins of Democratic Culture: Printing, Petitions, and the Public Sphere in Early Modern England* (Princeton, NJ, Princeton University Press, 2000).

Meanwhile, Charles Tilly's historical sociology of popular contention in Europe highlighted petitions as part of a broader repertoire of tactics that forged the modern social movement.[7] Since the 1980s, scholars of constitutional law in the United States have become increasingly interested in the historical development of the Anglo-American right to petition, as they have sought to rehabilitate petitioning as 'a robust, essential, and institutionalized democratic practice'.[8]

Building on this earlier work, a burgeoning scholarly interest in petitions and petitioning has expanded in the last decade, in part thanks to major national research projects. Historical studies on petitions, or in which they have been central to the analysis, include important monographs on early modern England, Ireland, and Scotland;[9] early modern Dutch Brazil;[10] the early modern Mediterranean region centred on Venice and Istanbul;[11] 19th-century USA, UK, Mexico, Netherlands, and France;[12] early colonial India;[13] late Ottoman Palestine;[14] and East Germany;[15]

[7] C. Tilly, *Popular Contention in Great Britain, 1758–1834* (Cambridge, MA, Harvard University Press, 1995); C. Tilly, *Contentious Performances* (Cambridge, Cambridge University Press, 2008).

[8] C. Phillips, 'The Lost Democratic Institution of Petitioning: Public Employee Collective Bargaining as a Constitutional Right', *First Amendment Law Review*, 10 (2011–12), 652–91 (p. 672). See also R. Handley, 'Public Order, Petitioning, and Freedom of Assembly', *Journal of Legal History*, 7 (1986), 123–55; S. Higginson, 'A Short History of the Right to Petition Government for the Redress of Grievances', *Yale Law Journal*, 96 (1986–7), 142–66; G. A. Mark, 'The Vestigial Constitution: The History and Significance of the Right to Petition', *Fordham Law Review*, 66 (1998), 2163–75; and R. J. Krotoszynski, *Reclaiming the Petition Clause: Seditious Libel, 'Offensive Protest', and the Right to Petition Government for a Redress of Grievances* (New Haven, CT, Yale University Press, 2012), pp. 83–103.

[9] L. Stewart, *Rethinking the Scottish Revolution: Covenanted Scotland, 1637–1651* (Oxford, Oxford University Press, 2016); T. Vallance, *Loyalty, Memory and Public Opinion in England, 1658–1727* (Manchester, Manchester University Press, 2019); K. Bowie, *Public Opinion in Early Modern Scotland, c. 1560–1707* (Cambridge, Cambridge University Press, 2020); A. Whiting, *Women and Petitioning in the Seventeenth-Century English Revolution* (Turnhout, Brepols, 2015); R. A. Houston, *Peasant Petitions: Social Relations and Economic Life on Landed Estates, 1600–1850* (Basingstoke, Palgrave, 2014); C. Dennehy, *The Irish Parliament, 1613–89: The Evolution of a Colonial Institution* (Manchester, Manchester University Press, 2019).

[10] J. van den Tol, *Lobbying in Company: Economic Interests and Political Decision Making in the History of Dutch Brazil, 1621–1656* (Leiden, Brill, 2020).

[11] E. N. Rothman, *Brokering Empire: Trans-Imperial Subjects between Venice and Istanbul* (Ithaca, NY, Cornell University Press, 2012).

[12] D. Carpenter, *Democracy by Petition: Popular Politics in Transformation, 1790–1870* (Cambridge, MA, Harvard University Press, 2021); Miller, *A Nation of Petitioners*; B. Agnès, *L'appel au pouvoir: Les pétitions aux parlements en France et au Royaume-Uni (1814–1848)* (Rennes, Presses universitaires de Rennes, 2018); W. Fowler, *Independent Mexico: The 'Pronunciamiento' in the Age of Santa Anna, 1821–1858* (Lincoln, University of Nebraska Press, 2016); J. Oddens, *Op veler verzoek: Inclusieve politiek in Nederlands (1780–1860)* (Amsterdam, Boom, 2023).

[13] B. Raman, *Document Raj: Writing and Scribes in Early Colonial India* (Chicago, Chicago University Press, 2011), pp. 161–92.

[14] Y. Ben-Bassat, *Petitioning the Sultan: Protests and Justice in Late Ottoman Palestine* (London, I.B. Tauris, 2013).

[15] P. Betts, *Within Walls: Private Life in the German Democratic Republic* (Oxford, Oxford University Press, 2010), pp. 173–92.

as well as studies of contemporary China and earlier dynasties back to the Han.[16] Leading journals in history, law, and the political and social sciences have published articles on petitions and petitioning.[17] A spate of edited volumes and special issues have examined petitions within specific historical contexts, such as South Asia and colonial India, early modern Britain and Scandinavia, the Atlantic world, 19th-century western Europe and America, 19th-century Mexico, late medieval England, and the Holocaust.[18]

The dramatic growth of this field of research is only partly explained by the increasing accessibility of digitised historic petitions and related material. In many cases, the transcription or digitisation of these sources have been outputs that

[16] Q. Fang, *Chinese Complaint Systems: Natural Resistance* (London, Routledge, 2013); Ho-fung Hung, *Protest with Chinese Characteristics: Demonstrations, Riots, and Petitions in the Mid-Qing Dynasty* (New York, Columbia University Press, 2011).

[17] A by no means exhaustive list of key articles includes: G. Dodd, 'County and Community in Medieval England', *English Historical Review*, 134 (2019), 777–820; M. McKinley, 'Petitioning and the Making of the Administrative State', *Yale Law Journal*, 127 (2018), 1538–637; M. McKinley, 'Lobbying and the Petition Clause', *Stanford Law Review*, 68 (2016), 1131–205; R. Huzzey and H. Miller, 'Petitions, Parliament and Political Culture: Petitioning the House of Commons, 1780–1918', *Past & Present*, 248 (2020), 123–64; D. Coast, 'Speaking for the People in Early Modern England', *Past & Present*, 244 (2019), 51–88; N. Wheatley, 'Mandatory Interpretation: Legal Hermeneutics and the New International Order in Arab and Jewish Petitions to the League of Nations', *Past & Present*, 227 (2015), 205–48; D. Carpenter and C. D. Moore, 'When Canvassers Became Activists: Antislavery Petitioning and the Political Mobilization of American Women', *American Political Science Review*, 108 (2014), 479–98; J. Oddens, '"The Greatest Right of Them All": The Debate on the Right to Petition in the Netherlands from the Dutch Republic to the Kingdom (*c.* 1750–1830)', *European History Quarterly*, 47 (2017), 634–56; P. Gatrell, A. Ghoshal, K. Nowak, and A. Dowdall, 'Reckoning with Refugeedom: Refugee Voices in Modern History', *Social History*, 46 (2021), 70–95; H. Weiss Muller, 'From *Requête* to Petition: Petitioning the Monarch between Empires', *Historical Journal*, 60 (2017), 659–86; C. Bochel, 'Petitions Systems: Outcomes, "Success" and "Failure"', *Parliamentary Affairs*, 73 (2020), 233–52; T. Escher and U. Riehm, 'Petitioning the German Bundestag: Political Equality and the Role of the Internet', *Parliamentary Affairs*, 70 (2017), 132–54; P. Loft, 'Involving the Public: Parliament, Petitioning and the Language of Interest, 1688–1720', *Journal of British Studies*, 55 (2016), 1–23; and Y. Israeli, 'Petition and Response as Social Process: Royal Power, Justice, and the People in Late Medieval Castile (c. 1474–1504)', *Past & Present* (forthcoming).

[18] R. De and R. Travers (eds), *Petitioning and Political Cultures in South Asia, Modern Asian Studies*, special issue, 53:1 (2019); K. Bowie and T. Munck (eds), *Early Modern Political Petitioning and Public Engagement in Scotland, Britain and Scandanavia, c. 1550–1795* (London, Routledge, 2018); B. Waddell and J. Peacey (eds), *The Power of Petitioning in Early Modern Britain* (London, UCL Press, forthcoming); M. D. da Cruz (ed.), *Petitioning in the Atlantic World, c. 1500–1840: Empires, Revolutions and Social Movements* (Basingstoke, Palgrave, 2022); H. Miller (ed.), *The Transformation of Petitioning in the Long Nineteenth Century (1780–1914), Social Science History*, special issue, 43:3 (2019); W. Fowler (ed.), *Forceful Negotiations: The Origins of the 'Pronunciamiento' in Nineteenth-Century Mexico* (Lincoln, University of Nebraska Press, 2010); W. Fowler (ed.), *Celebrating Insurrection: The Commemoration and Representation of the Nineteenth-Century Mexican 'Pronunciamiento'* (Lincoln, University of Nebraska Press, 2012); W. Fowler (ed.), *Malcontents, Rebels, and 'Pronunciados': The Politics of Insurrection in Nineteenth-Century Mexico* (Lincoln, University of Nebraska Press, 2012); T. Smith and H. Killick (eds), *Petitions and Strategies of Persuasion in the Middle Ages: The English Crown and the Church, c. 1200–c. 1550* (Woodbridge, Boydell & Brewer, 2018); T. Kaplan and W. Gruner (eds), *Resisting Persecution: Jews and Their Petitions during the Holocaust* (Oxford, Berghahn, 2020).

have followed, rather than preceded, major research projects.[19] Broader intellectual reasons for the proliferation of work on petitions and petitioning include their utility, as social historians have long known, as a vital resource for recovering the voices of groups often marginalised within the historical record, such as women, refugees, indigenous or first peoples, and colonised peoples.[20] Examinations of petitions and petitioning have also been an attractive means to question established narratives and paradigms. For instance, dissatisfied with traditional narratives of the 'rise' of mass democracy centred on the ballot box, historians and social scientists have increasingly turned to examining the contested history of democracy, and of a much broader range of practices than voting, in challenging older accounts of political 'modernisation'.[21] A cultural turn in the humanities has encouraged scholars to broaden the concept of 'the political' by attending to languages, cultures, and rituals, bringing different forms of identity, including gender, to bear on their study of the past.[22]

Hence, rather than adopting a top-down or bottom-up approach, many recent studies have focused on the interactive, dynamic relationship between petitioners and authority. Petitions, French scholars have suggested, were a way of citizens 'facing' the state.[23] Medievalists as well as contemporary scholars of

[19] As in the case of the datasets produced by the York Medieval Petitions project, the petition in North America, the Civil War Petitions project, and the Power of Petitioning in Seventeenth-Century England project.

[20] P. Gatrell, A. Ghoshal, K. Nowak, and A. Dowdall, 'Reckoning with Refugeedom: Refugee Voices in Modern History', *Social History*, 46 (2021), 70–95; A. Irfan, 'Petitioning for Palestine: Refugee Appeals to International Authorities', *Contemporary Levant*, 5 (2020), 79–96; M. Blackhawk, D. Carpenter, T. Resch, and B. Schneer, 'Congressional Representation by Petition: Assessing the Voices of the Voteless in a Comprehensive New Database, 1789–1949', *Legislative Studies Quarterly*, 46 (2021), 817–49; R. Huzzey and H. Miller, 'Colonial Petitions, Colonial Petitioners and the Imperial Parliament, c. 1780–1918', *Journal of British Studies*, 61 (2022), 261–89; S. Connors, 'Mass Petitioning, Education Reform, and the Development of Political Culture in Madras, 1839–1842', *Historical Journal*, 65 (2022), 393–414; A. Masters and B. Dixon, 'Indigenous Petitioning in the Early Modern British and Spanish New World', in Da Cruz, *Petitioning in the Atlantic World*, pp. 105–36.

[21] E. Avril and J. Neem (eds), *Democracy, Participation, and Contestation* (London, Routledge, 2015); J. Innes and M. Philp (eds), *Re-Imagining Democracy in the Age of Revolutions: America, France, Britain, Ireland, 1750–1850* (Oxford, Oxford University Press, 2013); J. Innes and M. Philp (eds), *Re-Imagining Democracy in the Mediterranean, 1780–1860* (Oxford, Oxford University Press, 2018); Carpenter, *Democracy by Petition*; Huzzey and Miller, 'Petitions, Parliament, and Political Culture', pp. 160–3; Miller, *A Nation of Petitioners*, pp. 7–8, 45–9.

[22] *The Rebirth of Political History*, *Australian Journal of Politics & History*, special issue, 56 (2010); 'Forum: The Contours of the Political', *German History*, 33 (2015), 255–73; C. Carpenter, 'Introduction: Political Culture, Politics, and Cultural History', in L. Clark and C. Carpenter (eds), *Political Culture in Late Medieval Britain* (Woodbridge, Boydell & Brewer, 2004), pp. 1–19; D. Craig, '"High Politics" and the "New Political History"', *Historical Journal*, 53 (2010), 453–75; J. Lawrence and A. Campsie, 'Political History', in H. Feldner, K. Passmore, and S. Berger (eds), *Writing History: Theory and Practice* (London, Bloomsbury, 2020), pp. 323–42.

[23] F. Moret and P. Grandemange, '"Les Français face à l'Etat, les pétitions adressées aux assemblées de 1815 à 1940": Objectifs et méthodologie d'un nouveau projet de recherche', *L'individu face au pouvoir: Les pétitions aux assemblées parlementaires*, *La revue administrative*, special issue (2008), 39–46.

e-petitions have identified 'processes' as crucial for understanding the relationship between petitioners, authority, and political culture.[24] Writing of the 19th-century United States, Daniel Carpenter has suggested that petitions allow us to rethink institutions as 'encounters' between citizens and government.[25] The interactions between petitioners and authority might also be conceptualised as a form of ongoing negotiation. In his study of early modern Scandinavia, Thomas Munck has observed that petitions reveal the 'complicated negotiation of power within an absolute monarchy'.[26] Scholars studying e-petitions have noted that they provide a form of 'linkage' between citizens and representative institutions.[27] However conceptualised, the point is that studying petitionary interactions allows us to cut across different categories (such as elite politics and histories of protest), fields (such as political history and social history), and topics (such as institutions and social movements) in ways that provide fruitful new perspectives on the past and present.

In shaping the workshops that forged this volume, we sought to consolidate and develop comparison over the *longue durée* by confining the contributions to roughly 700 years and to a certain portion of the world, namely Europe and North America. These chronological and geographical limits mean that the following chapters share antecedents in petitions of the Graeco-Roman-Mediterranean world, imparting derivative traditions and etymologies, as well as later cross-fertilisation, between European states.[28] However, as this introductory chapter and its footnotes make clear, we have sought to learn from research into forms of petitioning outside the scope of the volume. Our geographical focus provides coherent and related case studies to trace comparative developments across time, in fields with a concentration of researchers studying petitions. At the same time, this risks isolating them from a broader family of petitioning traditions and innovations. Incorporating work on Jamaica, Canada, and the United States of America allows some of the following chapters to trace the descent of petitioning in societies formed from the European

[24] G. Dodd and S. Petit-Renaud, 'Grace and Favour: The Petition and Its Mechanisms', in C. Fletcher, J.-P. Genet, and J. Watts (eds), *Government and Political Life in England and France, c. 1300–c. 1500* (Cambridge, Cambridge University Press, 2015), pp. 240–78 (p. 240); C. Bochel, 'Process Matters: Petitions Systems in Britain's Legislatures', *Journal of Legislative Studies*, 22 (2016), 368–84; see Leston-Bandeira chapter in this volume.

[25] D. Carpenter, 'Representation at a Visual Interface: Institutions as Encounters between Early American Government and Its Citizens', in P. Chatterjee and I. Katznelson (eds), *Anxieties of Democracy: Tocquevillean Reflections on India and the United States* (Oxford, Oxford University Press, 2012), pp. 50–78 (p. 55).

[26] T. Munck, 'Petitions and "Legitimate" Engagement with Power in Absolutist Denmark, 1660–1800', *Parliaments, Estates and Representation*, 38 (2018), 378–91.

[27] C. Leston-Bandeira, 'Parliamentary Petitions and Public Engagement: An Empirical Analysis of the Role of E-Petitions', *Policy & Politics*, 47 (2019), 415–36 (pp. 419–20).

[28] T. Hauken, *Petition and Response: An Epigraphic Study of Petitions to Roman Emperors, 181–249* (Bergen, Norwegian Institute at Athens, 1998); S. Connolly, *Lives behind the Laws: The World of the Codex Hermogenianus* (Bloomington, Indiana University Press, 2010); B. Kelly, *Petitions, Litigation, and Social Control in Roman Egypt* (Oxford, Oxford University Press, 2011); F. S. Naiden, *Ancient Supplication* (Oxford, Oxford University Press, 2006).

colonisation of North America. However, we hope that this volume will stimulate further comparisons, incorporating systems of petitioning developed in other regions, such as East Asia, West Africa, and South Asia, as much as their influence on subsequent colonial regimes. The chronological and geographical scope of this volume may then provide a foundation, not the definition, of further comparison of petitions and delineation of influences between societies, including the exchange within continental and intercontinental empires.[29]

Beyond opening up new approaches to the historical exercise and contest of power in European and North American polities, the further significance of this volume lies in addressing important topics within social and political science, as two specific examples demonstrate. First, given the focus on the impact of technology on politics, and the trend towards declining turnouts and party memberships in many mature democracies, scholars of contemporary politics have increasingly focused on e-petitions as a form of public engagement and participation.[30]

[29] For further examples to those in other footnotes of this chapter, see: A. Masters, *We, the King: Creating Royal Legislation in the Sixteenth-Century Spanish New World* (Cambridge, Cambridge University Press, 2023); B. Premo, 'Before the Law: Women's Petitions in the Eighteenth-Century Spanish Empire', *Comparative Studies in Society and History*, 53 (2011), 261–89; Y. Silva, 'Letters from the Rio de La Plata: Agency and Identity in Colonial Women's Petitions', in M. Díaz and R. Quispe-Agnoli (eds), *Women's Negotiations and Textual Agency in Latin America, 1500–1799* (London, Routledge, 2017), pp. 153–76; F. Cody, 'Inscribing Subjects to Citizenship: Petitions, Literacy, Activism, and the Performativity of Signature in Rural Tamil India', *Cultural Anthropology*, 24 (2009), 347–80; J. Wang, 'Shifting Boundaries between State and Society: Village Cadres as New Activists in Collective Petition', *The China Quarterly*, 211 (2012), 697–717; R. Travers, 'Indian Petitioning and Colonial State-Formation in Eighteenth-Century Bengal', *Modern Asian Studies*, 53 (2019), 89–122; J. Elyachar, 'Upending Infrastructure: *Tamarod*, Resistance, and Agency after the January 25th Revolution in Egypt', *History and Anthropology*, 25 (2014), 452–71; T. Iwaki, 'Petitioning by Clerks and the Colonial State in Late Nineteenth-Century Burma', *South East Asia Research*, 29 (2021), 348–64; J. van den Tol, 'Chinese Petitions to the Dutch East India Company: Gambling on Formosa', in T. Westeijn (ed.), *Foreign Devils and Philosophers: Cultural Encounters between the Chinese, the Dutch, and other Europeans, 1590–1800* (Leiden, Brill, 2020), pp. 132–47; R. Nedostup and L. Hong-ming, '"Begging the Sages of the Party-State": Citizenship and Government in Transition in Nationalist China, 1927–1937', in Heerma van Voss, *Petitions in Social History*, pp. 185–208; A. Slemian, 'Petitions to the Courts of Appeal in Portuguese America and the Protection of Rights (c. 1750–1808)', in Da Cruz, *Petitioning in the Atlantic World*, pp. 65–84; L. Kopytoff, '"We Are All French": Race, Religion, and Citizenship in Petitions from Senegal, 1760s–1840s', in Da Cruz, *Petitioning in the Atlantic World*, pp. 157–76; A. Caso Bello, 'Petitions to Correct Revolutionary Rumours: The City Council of Santafé Bogotá and Madrid's *Agentes de Indias*, c. 1780–1795', in Da Cruz, *Petitioning in the Atlantic World*, pp. 85–104; H. Sabato, 'Citizenship, Politcal Participation, and the Formation of the Public Sphere in Buenos Aires, 1850s–1880s', *P&P* (1992), 139–63 (p. 153); and J. Sanders, 'Indigenous Citizens and Black Republicans: Continuities and Evolutions of Subalterns' Political Visions and Repertoires in Post-Independence Columbia and Mexico', in J. Pollman and H. te Velde (eds), *Civic Continuities in an Age of Revolutionary Change, c. 1750–1850: Europe and the Americas* (Basingstoke, Palgrave, 2023), pp. 171–96.

[30] In addition to works already cited, key interventions include C. Bochel, 'Petitions Systems: Contributing to Representative Democracy?', *Parliamentary Affairs*, 66 (2013), 798–815; R. Lindner and U. Riehm, 'Broadening Participation through E-Petitions? An Empirical Study of Petitions to the German Parliament', *Policy & Internet*, 3 (2011), 1–23; and S. Rosenberger, B. Seisl, J. Stadlmair, and E. Dalpra, 'What Are Petitions Good For? Institutional Design and Democratic Functions', *Parliamentary Affairs*, 75 (2022), 217–37.

Consolidating and distilling a broad literature, this volume provides a necessary historical context to recent accounts of e-petitions, in particular, by drawing attention to the wider uses of petitioning beyond the formal, institutional settings that have been the typical unit of analysis in such studies. Second, social scientists studying collective action have tended to categorise petitioning as merely one activity within a wider repertoire of contention,[31] or presented it as a rather conventional and low-risk one.[32] A historical perspective suggests that these assumptions need revising because petitions and petitioning have often underpinned and facilitated many other forms of collective action, including more direct forms of protest. For these reasons, this volume will have important implications for social and political scientists, as well as historians.

The significance of this collection lies in developing a new definitional clarity, longer chronological frameworks, and detailed studies with the ambition of consolidating and advancing this vibrant field. Making the topic accessible to scholars across the humanities and social sciences may support further research on these polities and also offer a platform for comparison with other portions of the globe with distinct practices analogous to petitioning. Largely adopting a historical perspective, this book is divided into three sections that probe why, when, and in what circumstances petitions and petitioning mattered, in chapters offering conceptual, chronological, and contextual studies. Mirroring this structure, the rest of our introduction seeks first to define petitions, then to outline key trends over the *longue durée*, and finally to examine the effects of petitions and petitioning.

Definitions

One of the challenges of conceptualising petitions is crafting a definition that is both inclusive and distinctive enough. As Miguel da Cruz has put it, it is important to acknowledge the 'variations by which people have petitioned through time, from secretive court appeals and poor relief requests to modern, public, political mass petitions', while also identifying 'common features and historical continuities'.[33]

[31] S. Tarrow, *Power in Movement: Social Movements and Contentious Politics* (Cambridge, Cambridge University Press, 2011), pp. 47–51; D. della Porta and M. Diani, *Social Movements: An Introduction*, 3rd edn (Hoboken, NJ, Wiley, 2020), pp. 164, 168; M. Guigni and T. Grasso, *Street Citizens: Protest Politics and Social Movements in an Age of Globalization* (Cambridge, Cambridge University Press, 2019), pp. 87–94.

[32] S. Tarrow, *Power in Movement: Social Movements and Contentious Politics*, 2nd edn (Cambridge, Cambridge University Press, 1998), pp. 38–9; W. A. Samson and D. S. Meyer, 'Framing Political Opportunity', in D. McAdam, J. D. McCarthy, and M. N. Zald (eds), *Comparative Perspectives on Social Movements: Political Opportunities, Mobilizing Structures, and Cultural Framings* (Cambridge, Cambridge University Press, 1996), pp. 275–90 (pp. 293–4).

[33] M. D. da Cruz, 'Introduction: Atlantic Petitionary Traditions and Developments', in Da Cruz, *Petitioning in the Atlantic World*, pp. 1–18 (pp. 4–5).

Table 0.1 Five definitions of petitions

Lex Heerma van Voss (2001)	Demands for a favour, or for the redressing of an injustice, directed to some established authority.
Cecilia Nubola (2001)	Letters (or documentation) that single citizens, or organised and recognised groups, sent to the state authorities requesting grace, favours, or privileges, or calling attention to injustices and abuses.
Gwilym Dodd (2007)	Written entreaties presented in a formal manner to a higher authority.
Griet Vermeesch (2012)	A wide variety of letters, written by (groups of) subjects to rulers or administrative bodies, describing certain needs and soliciting certain actions.
Jean Gabriel Contamin (2013)	Protest texts that are intended to be signed by a number of persons, at least one of whom has not the opportunity to amend it.

Sources: L. Heerma van Voss, 'Introduction', in L. Heerma van Voss, *Petitions in Social History*, Supplement 9 of *IRSH*, 46 (2001), 1–10 (p. 1); C. Nubola, 'Supplications between Politics and Justice: The Northern and Southern Italian States in the Early Modern Age', in Heerma van Voss, *Petitions in Social History*, pp. 35–56, (p. 35); G. Dodd, *Justice and Grace: Private Petitioning and the English Parliament in the Late Middle Ages* (Oxford, Oxford University Press, 2007), p. 1; G. Vermeesch, 'Professional Lobbying in Eighteenth-Century Brussels: The Role of Agents in Petitioning the Central Government Institutions in the Habsburg Netherlands', *Journal of Early Modern History* 16 (2012), 95–119 (p. 99); J.-G. Contamin, 'Petitions', in D. A. Snow, D. Della Porta, B. Klandermans, and D. McAdam (eds.), *The Wiley-Blackwell Encyclopedia of Social and Political Movements*, published online, 14 January 2013, https://onlinelibrary.wiley.com/doi/abs/10.1002/9780470674871.wbespm151 (accessed 17 January 2024).

If we imagine possible definitions to be on a spectrum, the most inclusive definition would be simply that (1) petitions are appeals to power-holders. At the other extreme of the spectrum, a much more distinctive definition would be that (2) petitions are written, signed, addressed and submitted, deferential, standardised requests, to established authorities. Other scholars have provided a host of different definitions (Table 0.1) that highlight particular elements of a petition. Most present-day petitions and many historical petitions do not meet all the criteria dictated by the second definition above, but this definition is valuable in clarifying the broader phenomenon with which this volume is concerned. Accordingly, we will separately discuss the different elements of the second definition with reference to historical and contemporary petitioning practices.

Written

Most contemporary scholars understand petitions as written texts. Yet many examples from medieval and early modern contexts emphasise that petitioning (or supplicating) could be understood as appearing before an authority and performing a sequence of ritual (speech) acts.[34] One such act may have been to present a written request in order for the authority to have documentary evidence of this encounter with the petitioner, but this was not a compulsory element, and many requests were made only in verbal form. In later periods, orally transmitted requests to authorities continued, but in many cases we seem to have stopped thinking of these requests as petitions.

Signed

A quintessential feature of contemporary petitions is that they bear the names or signatures of the petitioners. Petitions are collective, and the very point is to collect as many names as possible. In many languages other than English, versions of the word 'petition' are reserved for such collective petitions.[35] However, a multiplicity of subscribers is certainly no requirement for a document to be a petition. On the contrary, in the historical record, petitions with only one or a few signatures probably make up the majority. They may only bear the names of the persons making a request, or of an intermediary writing the petition on their behalf, with no canvassing for additional signatures having taken place.

While the submission of written petitions seems to be almost as old as writing itself, signatures have only become a standard feature in the early modern period. Before the 17th century, when literacy levels were much lower, petitions were not as a rule undersigned by the petitioner. Instead, the identity of the petitioner appeared from the text of the petition – which was often written by a scribe[36] – or from the fact that they presented it in person. Without the names of the petitioners written onto the petition or appended to it, authorities did not always know who had petitioned them. This could be to the advantage of petitioners, who thus could claim to be a larger group than they actually were, or make bold demands for which they could not be held personally accountable. It was for this reason, and for reasons of bureaucratic efficiency, that authorities might choose to make signatures mandatory, requiring those unable to write their name to place a mark and have it countersigned by someone else. Although the sign manual (or a substitute mark) gradually displaced the aristocratic seal as the legal personification of an individual, some forms of petitioning still permitted names to be printed or added on the remote authority of another person.[37]

[34] G. Koziol, *Begging Pardon and Favor: Ritual and Political Order in Early Medieval France* (New Haven, CT, Yale University Press, 1992); see also the chapters by Zaret, Oddens, and Dodd in this volume.
[35] See chapter by Oddens in this volume.
[36] H. Killick, 'The Scribes of Petitions in Late Medieval England', in T. W. Smith and H. Killick (eds), *Petitions and Strategies of Persuasion in the Middle Ages* (Woodbridge, Boydell & Brewer, 2018), pp. 64–82; F. Dabhoiwala, 'Writing Petitions in Early Modern England', in M. Braddick and J. Innes (eds), *Suffering and Happiness in England 1550–1850: Narratives and Representations. A Collection to Honour Paul Slack* (Oxford, Oxford University Press, 2017), pp. 127–48.
[37] E. Higgs, *Identifying the English: A History of Personal Identification, 1500 to the Present* (London, Continuum, 2011), pp. 58–71; *Leven Advertiser & Wemyss Gazette*, 10 April 1924, p. 5; *The Poultry World*, March 1880, pp. 88–9.

Deferential

Petitions typically reflect a vertical relationship between the petitioner and the addressee. When a petition contains a request – as most petitions do – this implies a hierarchical, unequal relationship: the addressee is in a position to grant something to the petitioner.[38] Moreover, historically, petitions have emphasised the difference in power between petitioner and addressee: the petitioner appeals to the authority – or, as has been argued, to the jurisdiction[39] – of the addressee, and in exchange hopes for their request to be favourably considered.[40]

The vertical relationship between an authority and petitioners has often been expressed through deferential forms, such as the submissiveness of those physically presenting their petitions to its recipient or, more often, expressed in the formulaic language of the petition, such as 'your humble petitioners'. Formulaic expressions of deference have often become standard elements: in many historic collections of petitions, every one contains the same, or similar phrases. When this happens, the original meaning of such phrases is diluted through repetition and they are more of a formality. Paradoxically, the formulaic phrases that imply a minimum degree of deference can thus lower the threshold for transgressive or even subversive content.[41]

Because formulaic expressions of deference are often clichés of the genre, it becomes all the more significant when they are omitted, such as during moments of revolution.[42] At such junctures, new formulaic phrases, in which the petitioner(s) addressed authority on more egalitarian terms, were coined. Even so, the underlying unequal power relations between petitioner(s) and authority did not change, and nor usually did the bureaucratic procedure by which the petition was handled. When revolutionary regimes were short-lived, traditional expressions of deference usually returned. Contemporary petitions typically lack expressions of deference, and tend to be commanding rather than submissive.

[38] G. Held, 'Supplica la mia parvidade ... Petitions in Medieval Society: A Matter of Ritualised or First Reflexive Politeness?', *Journal of Historical Pragmatics*, 11 (2010), 194–218 (p. 195).

[39] S. Cerutti, 'Archaeology of Rights: Petitions and Mercy in Early Modern Societies', Columbia University, Italian Academy for Advanced Studies in America, published online, 18 April 2018, https://italianacademy.columbia.edu/paper/archaeology-rights-petitions-and-mercy-early-modern-societies (accessed 16 January 2024).

[40] Dodd and Petit-Renaud, 'Grace and Favour', p. 245.

[41] W. Te Brake, 'Petitions, Contentious Politics, and Revolution in Early Modern Europe', in Nubola and Würgler, *Operare la resistenza*, pp. 17–28; M. Almbjär, 'The Problem with Early-Modern Petitions: Safety Valve or Powder Keg?', *European Review of History*, 26 (2019), 1013–39 (p. 1026).

[42] A. Würgler, 'Kontinuität und Diskontinuität zwischen Ancien Régime und Helvetischer Republik am Beispiel der Bittschriften', in D. Schläppi (ed.), *Umbruch und Beständigkeit: Kontinuitäten in der Helvetischen Revolution von 1798* (Basel, Schwabe Verlag, 2009), pp. 49–64; Y. Ben-Bassat, 'The Ottoman Institution of Petitioning when the Sultan No Longer Reigned: A View from Post-1908 Ottoman Palestine', *New Perspectives on Turkey*, 56 (2017), 87–103.

Addressed and Submitted

A universal characteristic of a petition may be that it has, like other epistolary forms, an addressee. Petitions in standardised formats typically mention the addressee at the top of the text. Informal petitions sometimes lack a formal statement of the addressee, but instead the addressee may be directly addressed, in the second person, in the body of the text. Historically, most petitions were submitted to their addressee: by handing the document to the addressee in person; through an official; by sending by post; or, latterly, through e-petition websites. Petitions can also be submitted making use of the services of an intermediary; in some times and places this was even made obligatory by the authorities.[43]

Over time, it is possible to detect the growth of the expressive and representative function of petition-signing, as some petitions circulated primarily to reach a wider audience, or increasingly expressed the signatories' beliefs, with the addressee's response itself of secondary importance.[44] In such cases, these petitions can appear as standalone publications, such as pamphlets, or appear in newspapers, in which case they have much in common with open letters.[45] At the same time, individual and collective appeals on questions of policy have often taken the form of letters addressed and submitted to politicians. Appeals with private requests for redress, as well as public concerns on law-making, are sometimes termed 'citizen letters' when directed to individual legislators rather than formally to a legislature as an institution.[46] In fact, the boundaries between petitioning and the letters addressed or forms submitted to authorities may be the hardest to identify. Amongst social historians of England, paupers' petitions are sometimes distinguished from the familiar salutation and genre of personal letters that contained substantively identical requests for relief.[47] It is very difficult to draw a sharp border between petitioning and other

[43] Talsma, *Het recht van petitie*, pp. 101–3; Munck, 'Petitions and "Legitimate" Engagement', p. 380.

[44] Zaret, *Origins*, pp. 240–65; M. Janse, *De afschaffers: Publieke opinie, organisatie en politiek in Nederland 1840–1880* (Amsterdam, Wereldbibliotheek, 2007), pp. 115–16.

[45] H. Miller, 'Introduction: The Transformation of Petitioning in the Long Nineteenth Century (1780–1914)', *Social Science History*, 43 (2019), 409–29 (p. 416); Whiting, *Women and Petitioning*, pp. 69–76.

[46] M. Fenske, *Demokratie erschreiben: Bürgerbriefe und Petitionen als Medien politischer Kultur 1950–1974* (Frankfurt, Campus Verlag, 2013); H. Kaal and V. van de Griend, 'Postwar Popular Politics: Integrating the Voice of the People in Postwar Political History', in H. Kaal and D. Slootjes (eds), *New Perspectives on Power and Political Representation from Ancient History to the Present Day: Repertoires of Representation* (Leiden, Brill, 2019), pp. 124–43; K. Lauwers, *Ordinary Citizens and the French Third Republic: Negotiations between People and Parliament, c. 1900–1930* (Basingstoke, Palgrave, 2022); see also chapter by Huzzey and Miller in this volume.

[47] T. Sokoll, *Essex Pauper Letters, 1731–1837* (Oxford, Oxford University Press, 2001); P. Jones and S. King, 'From Petition to Pauper Letter: The Development of an Epistolary Form', in P. Jones and S. King (eds), *Obligation, Entitlement and Dispute under the English Poor Laws* (Newcastle, Cambridge Scholars, 2016), pp. 53–77; P. Jones and S. A. King, *Navigating the Old English Poor Law: The Kirkby Lonsdale Letters, 1809–1836* (Oxford, Oxford University Press for the British Academy, 2020); S. King, *Writing the Lives of the English Poor, 1750s–1830s* (Montreal, McGill-Queen's University Press, 2019); S. King, P. Carter, N. Carter, P. Jones, and C. Beardmore, *In Their Own Write: Contesting the New Poor Law, 1834–1900* (Montreal, McGill-Queen's University Press, 2022).

forms of 'writing upwards', as the wider genre of the weak writing to the powerful has been termed, and they often adopted the purposes, and sometimes acquired the designation, of petitions.[48]

Standardised

Petitions have often been characterised as formal texts with a standardised format, following the structure of ancient oratory and containing formulaic expressions and other conventions, such as the use of the third person.[49] Besides their content, the material form of petitions can also be standardised: in certain times, places, or archival collections, for instance, all petitions have been written onto stamped paper or have a uniform layout. Whereas stamped paper for taxation purposes has sometimes been a requirement for petitions,[50] official rules for how petitions should be drawn up have historically been rarer. However, even where authorities did not officially impose a standard format for petitions, conventional formats emerged nonetheless for reasons of scribal and bureaucratic efficiency. In many countries, writing manuals were available that provided model petitions.[51]

The extent to which a document needs to meet certain formal characteristics before we can consider it a petition is more a matter of historiographical convention than of legal requirements. Many written requests from the poor blurred different forms and genres.[52] In archival collections we may find formal petitions alongside informal requests written in the first person or using idiosyncratic language. In many cases, authorities considered all legible requests, including informal petitions that lacked formulaic phrases but remained standardised in other respects.[53] Archival series of informal petitions often have many features in common, which implies

[48] M. Lyons, 'Writing Upwards: How the Weak Wrote to the Powerful', *Journal of Social History*, 49 (2015), 317–30.

[49] See e.g. S. Grosse, M. Grimberg, T. Hölscher, and J. Karweick (eds), *'Denn das Schreiben gehört nicht zu meiner täglichen Beschäftigung': Der Alltag kleiner Leute in Bittschriften, Briefen und Berichten aus dem 19. Jahrhundert. Ein Lesebuch* (Bonn, Dietz Bonn, 1989), pp. 29–32; Houston, *Peasant Petitions*, pp. 73–107.

[50] M. Almbjär, 'The Voice of the People? Supplications Submitted to the Swedish Diet in the Age of Liberty, 1719–1772', PhD thesis (Umea University, 2016), p. 82; J. van der Poel, *De geschiedenis van het Nederlands fiscaal-zegel, 1624–1954* (Deventer, Davo, [1954]).

[51] B. Agnès, 'Le "Pétitionnaire universel": Les normes de la pétition en France et au Royaume-Uni pendant la première moitié du XIXe siècle', *Revue d'histoire moderne & contemporaine*, 58 (2011), 45–70; Y. Ben-Bassat and F. Sachs, 'Correspondence Manuals in Nineteenth-Century Greater Syria: Between the *Arzuhalci* and the Advent of Popular Letter Writing', *Turkish Historical Review*, 4 (2013), 1–25.

[52] S. Broomhall, 'Identity and Life Narratives of the Poor in Later Sixteenth-Century Tours', *Renaissance Quarterly*, 57 (2004), 439–65; C. Hämmerle, 'Requests, Complaints, Demands: Preliminary Thoughts on the Petitioning Letters of Lower-Class Austrian Women, 1865–1918', in C. Bland and M. Cross (eds), *Gender and Politics in the Age of Letter-Writing, 1750–2000* (Abingdon, Ashgate, 2004), pp. 115–33.

[53] S. Karlgren, 'Informal Petitions: Problems and Possibilities of Interpreting Letters of Petition Directed to Swedish High Noble Women', *Frühneuzeit-Info*, 23 (2012), 86–91.

that even if such documents were not drawn up by experienced scribes, petitioners still had access to networks in which new informal conventions developed, were transmitted, and crystallised.[54]

Over the course of the modern era, petitions have gradually lost their formulaic features and adopted freer forms of expression, especially in publicly representing opinions. The e-petition of the 21st century is standardised less by political custom than by the requirements of the websites on which it is published, whether hosted by a state or private providers.[55] By contrast, states and bureaucracies have channelled many instrumental requests, such as for welfare, into application forms that were historically articulated in petitions.[56]

Request

To petition implies making a request. The very word 'petition', which is derived from the Latin verb *petere* ('seek', 'beg'), seems to suggest as much.[57] While many historic petitions contain recognisable requests, there are also less clear-cut cases. As mentioned above, a petition may have all the formulaic conventions of a deferential request, but its illocutionary meaning may be that of a demand or a command. Indeed, on occasion petitioners may only thinly mask the fact that their petition is meant to be imperative rather than supplicatory.

A request and a demand at least have in common that the goal is for their addressee to take action, but what if this is not the main aim of petitioners? Petitions can serve many purposes other than triggering policy decisions, such as setting the political agenda, informing or mobilising the public, recruiting supporters, or obtaining the personal details of the subscribers.[58] Often petitioners did not expect their requests to be granted, but most of these petitions were still formulated as requests. There are, however, forms of subscriptional (or name-signing) culture, such as 'loyal' addresses, that express support for an authority rather than make formal requests, and in some cases were actively solicited by governments seeking popular endorsement (or the appearance of it).[59] Historians have usually considered

[54] J. Oddens, 'So Close and Yet So Far: Degrees of Emotional Proximity in Pauper Letters to Dutch National Power Holders around 1800', in A. Stynen, M. Van Ginderachter, and X. Manoel Núñez Seixas (eds), *Emotions and Everyday Nationalism in Modern European History* (Abingdon, Routledge, 2020), pp. 34–50.

[55] S. Wright, 'E-Petitions', in S. Coleman and Deen Freelon (eds), *Handbook of Digital Politics* (Cheltenham, Edward Elgar, 2015), pp. 136–50.

[56] R. Huzzey and H. Miller, 'The Politics of Petitioning: Parliament, Government, and Subscriptional Cultures in the United Kingdom, 1780–1918', *History*, 106 (2021), 221–43.

[57] See chapter by Oddens in this volume.

[58] D. Carpenter, 'Recruitment by Petition: American Antislavery, French Protestantism, English Suppression', *Perspectives on Politics*, 14 (2016), 700–23; Leston-Bandeira, 'Parliamentary Petitions and Public Engagement', pp. 419–20; Miller, 'Introduction', pp. 421–4.

[59] See chapter by Oddens in this volume; D. Palacios Cerezales, 'Petitioning for Empire in Napoleonic Europe', *Journal of Modern European History*, 18 (2020), 96–114 (pp. 104–8); and Vallance, *Loyalty, Memory, and Public Opinion.*

addresses as petitions, or at least a closely related genre, because in practice it is difficult to distinguish between both types of texts: addresses have often followed the petitionary format and in such cases were considered and archived by authorities as such. In the present, e-petitions are sometimes used to convey gratitude or political support. In this sense, addresses or expressions of support can be regarded as requests for action in terms of maintaining the status quo or continuing with current policies. Historically, there were also related forms of subscriptional culture such as covenants, bonds, or declarations, in which signatories were bound together in common cause, but which were unattached to a request to authority.[60]

Established Authority

Today, some non-governmental websites allow individuals and groups to publish petitions online without (directly) submitting them to the recipients they address. This is the digital equivalent of an open public letter or a declaration containing a signatory list but not directed to a particular authority. Individuals starting e-petitions on third-party web platforms such as change.org or 38degrees.org.uk can address them to corporations and non-governmental organisations, as well as to formal political institutions, or may not specify the immediate target of the demand.

While petitions without a specific addressee seem to be mostly a recent phenomenon, there are many historical examples of petitions addressed to bodies other than formal political institutions. In early modern times, the boards of many semi-public corporations such as churches and guilds, as well as trading companies, received petitions.[61] Moreover, large numbers of petitions have been addressed to individual power-holders, ranging from great kings to small lords. While individual office-holders can of course be established authorities, many people supplicated these power-holders as potential patrons or leaders of political factions, rather than in their official capacity.[62] A key difference between the petition and other forms of interaction or communication between people and power-holders is perhaps the expectation of a response, or what has been called the 'norm of receptivity' shared by petitioners and petitioned alike.[63]

[60] See chapter by Knights in this volume; T. Vallance, 'Protestation, Vow, Covenant, and Engagement: Swearing Allegiance in the English Civil War', *Historical Research*, 75 (2002), 408–24; and K. Bowie, 'Gathering Hands: Political Petitioning and Participative Subscription in Post-Reformation Scotland', in Waddell and Peacey, *The Power of Petitioning*.

[61] W. Pettigrew and E. Smith, 'Corporate Management, Labor Relations, and the East India Company's Blackwall Dockyard, 1600–1657', *Journal of Social History*, 53 (2019), 133–56.

[62] T. Filer, 'Letters to the President: Participation beyond the Public Sphere, 1989–1999', *Journal of Iberian and Latin American Studies*, 23 (2017), 317–39; J. Judge and J. Oddens, 'Father Figures and Faction Leaders: Identification Strategies and Monarchical Imagery among Ordinary Citizens of the Northern and Southern Low Countries (c. 1780–1820)', *BMGN – Low Countries Historical Review*, 133 (2018), 72–97.

[63] Carpenter, *Democracy by Petition*, p. 31; D. Zaret, 'Petition-and-Response and Liminal Petitioning in Comparative/Historical Perspective', *Social Science History*, 43 (2019), 431–52 (p. 440).

Ultimately, what makes petitions challenging to define is that they have changed over time, but so gradually that they can still be regarded as one phenomenon, even if following distinct heritages within particular European societies or their North American offshoots. Yet petitions have also changed so profoundly that a highly deferential, ritualised appeal that was orally transmitted to a medieval ruler, and a bold one-sentence statement with a list of signatures published on an e-petitions website and addressed to 'all of us', would seem to have little in common. Finally, petitions are both formal and fixed, regulated by the official or institutional petition systems that receive them, but they also exist as social and political practices outside these contexts. This explains why petitions have been an ambiguous, mutable, and unstable form of interaction between authority and those who address it.

Continuities and Transitions

The changing nature of how 'petitions' have been defined was merely part of a series of shifts in their role in society since the late medieval period. Petitioning practices and the genre itself were shaped by well-known social and political developments across this period.[64] Moreover, petitions also contributed to many of these broader changes as people used them in a vast range of ways to attempt to gain redress, shape policy, or change opinion. As this volume demonstrates, looking across different periods that are usually studied in isolation allows us to chart these transformations more clearly, while acknowledging the deep continuities in petitioning that are often missed when we privilege disruption and change.

Traditional narratives of 'the rise of democracy' paid little attention to petitioning apart from studies of campaigns that could be linked directly to debates about suffrage and constitutional matters, such as those, in the British context, of the 17th-century Levellers and the 19th-century Chartists. However, more recently historians have shown that petitioning was a vital part of broader changes in the nature of 'representation' and 'public opinion' over the last 700 years. In England, for example, it contributed to new conceptions of 'the commons' in 14th-century parliaments and helped to broaden public debates about political issues in the 17th century.[65] Likewise, in his study of 19th-century North America, Daniel Carpenter has shown how the process of democratisation was closely associated with, and driven by, an explosion of petitioning.[66] Historians have also begun to integrate petitioning into histories of 'state formation', demonstrating that it could be crucial to the evolution and expansion of institutions of governance from antiquity

[64] For examples of studies of the 'practice' of petitioning in particular periods, see H. Worthen, 'The Process and Practice of Petitioning in Early Modern England', in Waddell and Peacey, *The Power of Petitioning*; and Miller, *A Nation of Petitioners*, pp. 179–202.

[65] Dodd, *Justice and Grace*, pp. 126–55; Zaret, *Origins*, pp. 217–65.

[66] Carpenter, *Democracy by Petition*.

onwards.[67] It was, for instance, a valuable tool for strengthening the authority of the state in both early modern Italy and revolutionary Russia.[68] A recent survey of early modern Scandinavia has commented that petitioning contributed to a process of 'state building from below'.[69] Our grand narratives of social and political change may gain, therefore, from considering petitions as drivers of large-scale transformations rather than as merely indicators of that change.

While this intervention within broader national and international historiographies is important, it also poses a risk for scholars of petitioning. The danger of simply adding petitioning to broader histories of change is that its distinctive features are elided and its particular chronologies are obscured. Given its importance to these sweeping histories, it is vital to understand better the specific chronologies of petitioning itself. Few previous studies have attempted to examine such developments over long periods, but the suggestive existing work, when combined with the new research in this volume, makes it possible to begin to trace these threads. David Zaret has offered a valuable starting point by suggesting that 'the premodern petition was primarily an instrument of state' that subsequently developed into a 'liminal' mode of political action in the early modern period before becoming an accepted tool of protest in contemporary society.[70]

Zaret's model, which echoes Tilly's notion of a shift in repertoires of contention, offers a convenient way to conceptualise how the character of petitioning changed across time rather than assuming a static, all-encompassing definition by suggesting that there was a shift from one petition archetype to another, bridged by an era of overlap and transition. Specifically, for Zaret, each archetype has features that fit with the underlying norms of its associated period. The 'premodern' petition, which was ubiquitous across Europe until at least the 17th century, came from an individual or corporate body; was submitted privately and directly; and was expressed in humble, deferential language. By contrast, the 'modern' petition, which was common in England at least by the early 19th century, came from masses of individual subscribers, was created and presented publicly, and adopted an assertive or even 'insurgent' tone.[71] According to Zaret, the

[67] P. Blickle (ed.), *Gemeinde und Staat im Alten Europa* (Munich, De Gruyter, 1998); W. Blockmans, A. Holenstein, and J. Mathieu (eds), *Empowering Interactions: Political Cultures and the Emergence of the State in Europe, 1300–1900* (Farnham, Ashgate, 2009); W. He, *Public Interest and State Legitimation: Early Modern England, Japan, and China* (Cambridge, Cambridge University Press, 2023); B. Waddell, 'Shaping the State from Below: The Rise of Local Petitioning in Early Modern England', in Waddell and Peacey, *The Power of Petitioning*.

[68] C. Nubola, 'Supplications between Politics and Justice: The Northern and Southern Italian States in the Early Modern Age', in Heerma van Voss, *Petitions in Social History*, pp. 35–56; Douds chapter in this volume.

[69] K. Dørum, M. Hallenberg, and K. Katajala (eds), *Bringing the People Back In: State Building from Below in the Nordic Countries, c. 1500–1800* (London, Routledge, 2021).

[70] Zaret, 'Petition-and-Response'.

[71] For another analysis of petitions that examines how 'the collapse of communal restraints on political discourse had opened new avenues for self-assertive engagement', see D. Luebke, 'Signatures and Political Culture in Eighteenth-Century Germany', *Journal of Modern History*, 76 (2004), 497–530 (p. 518).

shift from one to the other included a 'liminal' stage that emerged in England in the mid-17th century and elsewhere in western Europe in the 18th century, when the legitimacy of different types of petitioning was constantly debated and many individual examples exhibited a 'paradoxical combination of deference and defiance'. The transition was, he notes, 'an extended, uneven process' that happened at different times in different places, yet this overall narrative of modernisation is still useful as an attempt to provide a coherent chronology of petitioning that accounts for change across many centuries rather than confining analysis to a single period.[72]

Although the phases of petitioning described by Zaret are much better than the static portrait found in some earlier scholarship, we can go further still by examining how these practices often changed in ways that do not fit into a model of linear development and by foregrounding the importance of long-term continuities. Moreover, we need to attend to the way that some changes in petitioning were sudden, dramatic shifts that contemporaries noticed and commented upon, whereas others were gradual long-term transitions that were barely perceived by the people involved in the process and which are only visible in hindsight. Looking at even just a few of the key features of petitions discussed in this volume from a chronological perspective reveals some of the commonalities, and complexities, of how this worked in practice across time and geography.

One apparent continuity in the history of petitioning is the fact that almost anyone could – in theory – submit a formal petition. From the medieval period, if not before, it seems to have been widely accepted that there were virtually no categories of people who were officially excluded from this process, and we have many examples of individuals who would normally have no lawful 'voice' in the polity using petitions to attempt to secure redress or advancement. Immigrant craftsmen in medieval Genoa, convicted murderers in 16th-century France, impoverished war widows in 17th-century England, enslaved people in 18th-century Jamaica and New Orleans, indigenous groups in the early United States, serfs in pre-emancipation Bohemia and Russia – all were able to petition even if they had no other legal route for addressing state authorities.[73] Here, then, is an obvious example of a long-term continuity despite major changes in political and social structures.

Yet, the widespread lack of formal exclusions from petitioning masks the many ways that the profile of petitioners changed in practice. Unfortunately, until the late 20th century we lack the sorts of social surveys that can show us, for example, that three in five Canadians reported signing petitions in the early 1980s.[74] But in many

[72] Zaret, 'Petition-and-Response', pp. 443–4.

[73] N. Z. Davis, *Fiction in the Archives: Pardon Tales and their Tellers in Sixteenth-Century France* (Stanford, CA, Stanford University Press, 1987); chapters by Gravela, Waddell and Worthen, and Graham in this volume; J. M. Johnson, *Wicked Flesh: Black Women, Intimacy, and Freedom in the Atlantic World* (Philadelphia, PA, University of Pennsylvania Press, 2020), pp. 155–65; Blackhawk et al., 'Congressional Representation by Petition'; T. Dennison and S. Ogilvie, 'Serfdom and Social Capital in Bohemia and Russia', *Economic History Review*, 60 (2007), 513–44.

[74] See chapter by Huzzey and Miller in this volume.

places the proportion of the population involved in petitioning appears to have been increasing over time, meaning that more people of low social status were able and willing to use this tool in later than in earlier periods. Sometimes this happened very quickly, as in the oft-cited example of England in the 1640s, when political turmoil and civil war spurred tens of thousands of individuals to subscribe to mass petitions about religious policy and 'affairs of state'.[75] In other cases, the change was more gradual, as in Scotland, where we find petitioning initially dominated by groups of nobles in the late 16th century but widening to include more and more ordinary people over the course of subsequent centuries.[76] Still, we should not assume that the number of people involved in petitioning simply grew ever larger. More than one regime attempted to reverse such trends by imposing restrictions on collective subscriptions and discouraging direct appeals about certain issues or from certain groups. While they rarely succeeded in fully suppressing these practices, governments could narrow the range of people comfortable adding their name to a list of signatures.[77]

The main recipients of petitions also changed, though this has received rather less attention from historians, despite the fact that identifying who received petitions can be a very effective way of tracking shifts in political and administrative power over time. For instance, medievalists have long studied the central role of the papacy as the target of petitioners from across western Christendom and, while this continued to be important in Catholic countries into the early modern period, there was a sharp shift towards petitioning royal or more local ecclesiastical authorities in northern Europe during the Reformation.[78] This necessitated severing many centuries-old long-distance supplicatory practices that had previously connected churchmen and laypeople to Rome.[79] In a much more gradual way, the slow decline in the volume of petitions addressed to landlords speaks to a substantial reconfiguration of social and economic power as customary forms of tenancy gave way to more commercialised arrangements.[80] Meanwhile, the appearance of novel institutions – whether Republican Clubs in late-18th-century France, legislatures in the 19th century, or international bodies in the 20th century – provided new targets

[75] M. Knights, 'Participation and Representation before Democracy: Petitions and Addresses in Premodern Britain', in I. Shapiro, S. Stokes, E. Wood, and A. Kirshner (eds), *Political Representation* (Cambridge, Cambridge University Press, 2009), pp. 35–57 (pp. 39–40, 45).

[76] K. Bowie, 'From Customary to Constitutional Right: The Right to Petition in Scotland before the 1707 Act of Union', *Parliaments, Estates and Representation*, 38 (2018), 279–92; L. Stewart, 'Petitioning in Early Seventeenth-Century Scotland, 1625–51', *Parliaments, Estates and Representation*, 38 (2018), 307–22.

[77] M. Knights, '"The Lowest Degree of Freedom": The Right to Petition Parliament, 1640–1800', in R. Huzzey (ed.), *Pressure and Parliament: From Civil War to Civil Society* (Oxford, Wiley, 2018), pp. 18–34; Miller, 'Introduction', pp. 415, 419–20.

[78] Smith and Killick, *Petitions and Strategies of Persuasion.*

[79] It is worth noting that one of the most important Parliamentary Acts of the English Reformation was the Statute in Restraint of Appeals (1532) which forbade seeking redress from the pope and, in so doing, established the monarch as the supreme sovereign in both temporal and spiritual matters.

[80] Houston, *Peasant Petitions*, pp. 50–2, 207.

for those seeking relief, redress, or policy change.[81] We need, therefore, to be very attentive to changes in the flow of petitions. As Huzzey and Miller argue later in this volume, if we only focus on national political institutions then our sense of the chronology of petitioning will be fundamentally skewed. Moreover, acknowledging continuities is equally important. Royal – or presidential – individuals remained popular targets for petitions even when their formal political power was limited or diminished, partly owing to the symbolic importance of their roles. Even without much influence on national policy, modern monarchs and their republican equivalents still retained a reputation as potential sources of gracious intervention in the lives of individual subjects.[82]

The form and rhetoric found in petitions could remain similar over extremely long periods of time, but sometimes changed very quickly to adapt to new political contexts. For many centuries petitions tended to follow a fairly simple structure – a humble address, an explanatory narrative, an actionable request, a prayerful conclusion – and, as noted already, in some spheres scribal practice gradually standardised this into something approaching a formula. Indeed, some types of petitions became so formulaic that enterprising printers had them typeset with blank spaces for the names of the petitioner and other key information. On the other hand, we can also trace a countervailing trend towards vernacularisation and personalisation, as less literate individuals became involved in writing them. In 18th-century England, both trajectories are visible, as imprisoned debtors turned to printed petitions to submit their fully standardised requests while at the same time growing numbers of paupers wrote highly individualised letters to parish overseers seeking relief on their own behalf.[83]

The specific rhetoric used in petitions was even more changeable. Over the long term, it would be difficult to deny that there was a shift from meek supplications asking for mercy or patronage to assertive demands claiming legal or civic rights. In moments of revolution, this gradual trend could accelerate, leading to sudden, jarring changes in how petitioners justified themselves, whether in England in the 1640s or in the short-lived Helvetic Republic in the 1790s.[84] Yet a sudden change of regime did not always lead to novelty in petitioning.[85] Moreover, even when it did,

[81] D. Briscoe, 'Representing Poverty in Petitions for Assistance in Revolutionary Bordeaux, 1791–95', *French History and Civilization*, 10 (2021), 148–61, accessible from h-france.net/rude/category/volume/ (accessed 16 January 2024); Miller, 'Introduction', pp. 411–12; chapter by Huzzey and Miller in this volume; K. Nowak, '"To Reach the Lands of Freedom": Petitions of Polish Displaced Persons to American Poles, Moral Screening, and the Role of Diaspora in Refugee Resettlement', *Cultural and Social History*, 16 (2019), 621–42.

[82] See chapter by Douds in this volume; and C. Reed, *Royal Tourists, Colonial Subjects, and the Making of a British World, 1860–1911* (Manchester, Manchester University Press, 2016), pp. 165–74.

[83] 'Worcestershire Quarter Sessions: 1720s', in B. Waddell (ed.), *Petitions to the Worcestershire Quarter Sessions, 1592–1797*, *British History Online*, www.british-history.ac.uk/petitions/worcs-quarter-sessions/1720s (accessed 9 October 2021); Sokoll, *Essex Pauper Letters*.

[84] See chapters by Waddell and Worthen, and Würgler.

[85] Muller, 'From *Requête* to Petition'.

this should not be seen as a simple shift from 'premodern' to 'modern' petitionary forms, because so many exceptions undermine any attempt to impose such categories. In 14th-century England, for instance, the 'commons' petitions presented to the king could contain aggressive complaints rather than humble pleas.[86]

The aims of petitioners – much like their form and rhetoric – were often remarkably stable across vast periods of time, though this continuity ran alongside a long-term rise in appeals for substantive policy changes. In the late medieval period, most supplicants sought judicial mercy, material relief, or career advancement. Even collective petitions often focused on exceptions from taxation or other special consideration. These issues remained popular throughout the early modern and well into the modern period, as seen in the thousands of appeals about pensions submitted to the United States Congress in the late 19th and early 20th centuries, or the individual requests for aid sent by Polish refugees in postwar Germany.[87]

However, in most jurisdictions, there was a decline in the number of people using petitions for such purposes in the modern era, as both state institutions and administrative agencies tried to impose a depersonalised system of restrictive printed forms to handle such claims.[88] Meanwhile, more and more activists and lobbyists used petitions to push for broader changes in government policy or general (rather than specific) legislation on matters ranging from religion to slavery to suffrage. Sometimes this happened only gradually, but often newly organised campaigns or political instability provoked an upsurge in large-scale petitioning on these issues. While the Chartist mass petition drives of the 1830s and 1840s were perhaps the most well-known British example, the same aim of policy change can also be seen in the 4.5 million subscribers to a petition defending ambulance drivers in 1989, or 6.1 million for the anti-Brexit e-petition of 2019.[89] Yet we cannot ignore the many ways that this apparent trajectory away from specific exemptions or exceptions to more 'political' goals aimed at changing general policy misses important alternative developments. For instance, the flurry of petitions and counterpetitions about the rights of mestizos in late-16th-century Spanish America were undoubtedly focused on 'policy' but far too 'early' to fit easily into this narrative.[90] Likewise, according to Joanna Innes, petitioning about 'contentious matters' relating to church and state became less common in early 18th-century Britain despite its importance in the preceding and subsequent periods.[91]

[86] See chapter by Dodd.

[87] McKinley, 'Petitioning and the Making of the Administrative State', pp. 1590–3; Nowak, 'To Reach the Lands of Freedom'.

[88] McKinley, 'Petitioning and the Making of the Administrative State'; Huzzey and Miller, 'The Politics of Petitioning', pp. 240–1.

[89] Jenny Crane, 'Petitions and the NHS', *People's History of the NHS*, https://peopleshistorynhs.org/encyclopaedia/petitions-and-the-nhs/ (accessed 16 January 2024); chapter by Leston-Bandeira in this volume.

[90] A. Masters, 'A Thousand Invisible Architects: Vassals, the Petition and Response System, and the Creation of Spanish Imperial Caste Legislation', *Hispanic American Historical Review*, 98 (2018), 377–406.

[91] See chapter by Innes in this volume.

We are left, then, with a chronology of petitioning that aligns relatively well with a story of broader political and social modernisation, in some polities, but which constituted more than merely a symptom of these long-term trends. Petitioners adapted quickly and vigorously in moments of sudden political change, sometimes anticipating or accelerating them rather than simply reacting to institutional shifts. Moreover, the typically 'vertical' nature of the practice meant that it is easy to find continuities in form and function across many centuries, wherever inequalities in power made such appeals attractive to both authorities and petitioners alike. While these are sometimes obscured by shifts in jurisdictional remits or official ideologies, by broadening our lens to encompass many different types and targets of petitioning, the resilient and adaptable nature of this practice over the *longue durée* is revealed.

Petitions and Petitioning in Context

Scholars of contemporary politics have all too frequently evaluated the effectiveness of petitions and e-petitions in terms of whether they achieve policy change or their impact on officials and politicians.[92] The problem with such a narrow, instrumental view is that it fails to explain adequately why people petition,[93] and have petitioned throughout history, when, typically, their demands have rarely been granted. While there are plenty of historic examples of petitions that have led to important changes, such as the abolition of feudal tenure in 19th-century North America, the outcomes for specific requests usually disappointed petitioners.[94] To put it another way, why then do petitions and petitioning matter, and why have they mattered for centuries? Part III focuses on specific studies of petitions and petitioning in context, but here we reflect upon the broader reasons why these practices have mattered to petitioners and authorities, as well as their wider consequences. Rather than judging petitions and petitioning on the success or failure rate of particular requests, we should consider them in the round.

Historically, petitions have always been vehicles for making individual as well as collective claims. Petitioners have addressed authority to negotiate their status, and claim rights, privileges, and exemptions as citizens or subjects.[95] In

[92] R. Hough, 'Do Legislative Petitions Systems Enhance the Relationship between Parliament and Citizen?', *Journal of Legislative Studies*, 18 (2012), 479–95; F. Matthews, 'The Value of "Between-Election" Political Participation: Do Parliamentary E-Petitions Matter to Political Elites?', *British Journal of Politics and International Relations*, 23 (2021), 410–29.

[93] S. Wright, '"Success" and Online Political Participation: The Case of Downing Street E-Petitions', *Information, Communication, and Society*, 19 (2016), 843–57.

[94] Carpenter, *Democracy by Petition*, pp. 384–414.

[95] N. Ota, 'Private Matters: Family and Race and the Post-World War II Translation of "American"', in Heerma van Voss, *Petitions in Social History*, pp. 209–34; H. Weiss Muller, 'Bonds of Belonging: Subjecthood and the British Empire', *Journal of British Studies*, 53 (2014), 29–58; J. Shaw, 'Writing to the Prince: Supplications, Equity, and Absolutism in Sixteenth-Century Tuscany', *P&P*, 215 (2012), 51–83. See also the chapter by Gravela in this volume.

the English context, through the genre of pauper petitions or letters, supplicants sought to access welfare.[96] At other times and in other places too, petitions have been a mechanism to claim entitlements, such as military pensions.[97] Petitions from widows, and war widows specifically, have allowed scholars to recover women's experiences of legal processes generally, and war in particular.[98] Petitions have always been an important way for individuals to seek dispute resolution or arbitration, make patronage requests, and advance other personal interests through appeals to power.[99]

Petitions have been an important 'weapon of the weak' for individuals or groups lacking legal or political rights and material resources, or who were otherwise marginalised.[100] As a diverse number of studies have found, at times petitions have been a useful, if limited, tool for indigenous and colonised peoples,[101] peasants,[102]

[96] S. King, *Writing the Lives of the English Poor, 1750s–1830s* (Montreal, McGill-Queen's University Press, 2019); P. Jones and S. King, 'Voices from the Far North: Pauper Letters and the Provision of Welfare in Sutherland, 1845–1900', *Journal of British Studies*, 55 (2016), 76–98; P. Jones and N. Carter, 'Writing for Redress: Redrawing the Epistolary Relationship under the New Poor Law', *Continuity and Change*, 34 (2019), 375–99.

[97] Carpenter, *Democracy by Petition*, p. 43; chapter by Pells in this volume.

[98] K. Collins, '"Petitions without Number": Widows' Petitions and the Early Nineteenth-Century Origins of Public Marriage-Based Entitlements', *Law and History Review*, 31 (2013), 1–60; H. Worthen, 'Supplicants and Guardians: The Petitions of Royalist Widows during the Civil Wars and Interregnum, 1642–1660', *Women's History Review*, 26 (2017), 528–40; S. Beale, '"Unpittyed by Any?": Royalist Widows and the Crown, 1660–70', *Historical Research*, 92 (2019), 737–53; E. Mahir Metinsoy, *Ottoman Women during World War I: Everyday Experiences, Politics and Conflicts* (Cambridge, Cambridge University Press, 2017), pp. 75–84.

[99] J. Baldwin, 'Petitioning the Sultan in Ottoman Egypt', *Bulletin of the School of Oriental and African Studies*, 73 (2012), 499–524; J. Jaffe, 'The Languages of Petitioning in Early Colonial India', *Social Science History*, 43 (2019), 581–98; J. K. Johnson, '"Claims of Equity and Justice": Petitions and Petitioners in Upper Canada, 1815–1840', *Histoire Sociale/Social History* (1995), 219–40 (pp. 225–6); Israeli, 'Petition and Response'.

[100] J. Scott, *Weapons of the Weak: Everyday Forms of Peasant Resistance* (New Haven, CT, Yale University Press, 1985).

[101] R. De Costa, 'Identity, Authority, and the Moral Worlds of Indigenous Petitions', *Comparative Studies in Society and History*, 48 (2006), 669–98; Blackhawk et al., 'Congressional Representation by Petition'; K. O'Brien, *Petitioning for Land: The Petitions of First Peoples of Modern British Colonies* (London, Bloomsbury, 2018); J. R. Miller, *Reflections on Native–Newcomer Relations* (Toronto, University of Toronto Press, 2004), pp. 215–41; B. Owensby, *Empire's Law and Indian Justice in Colonial Mexico* (Stanford, CA, Stanford University Press, 2008); M. Valerio, 'The Spanish Petition System, Hospital/ity, and the Formation of a Mulato Community in Sixteenth-Century Mexico', *The Americas*, 78 (2021), 415–37; J. van den Tol, 'Non-Dutch Petitions in the Seventeenth-Century Dutch Atlantic', *Early Modern Low Countries*, 4 (2020), 158–80; Carpenter, *Democracy by Petition*, pp. 117–63, 415–38.

[102] A. Verner, 'Discursive Strategies in the 1905 Revolution: Peasant Petitions from Vladimir Province', *Russian Review*, 54 (1995), 65–90; Houston, *Peasant Petitions*; A. Brewer, 'Russian Peasant Petitions in the Late 18th Century: Perceptions of Law, Justice, and a "Just Authority"', *Cahiers du monde russe*, 53 (2012), 41–64; A. Engelst Norgaard, 'Speaking through Petitions: Peasant Farmers in the Nascent Democracy, Denmark 1830s', *Journal of Modern European History*, 21 (2023), 90–109.

and women, to give just three examples.[103] Writing of the last group, one scholar has commented: 'Petitions provide historians with one of the few opportunities to "hear" non-elite women voice their concerns', although as in other cases the voices of petitioners were usually mediated.[104]

Collective petitioning, too, had many uses for historical actors, regardless of the response of authorities, as a hefty body of recent scholarship has made clear. Petitions were and are a way to promote legislation, influence policy, and push specific issues up the political agenda.[105] While this volume focuses on petitionary practices, we should not isolate petitioning from a wider repertoire of collective action, with which it was closely, and in some cases inseparably, associated, including strikes, associations, meetings, assemblies, riots, and demonstrations.[106] The mutability and flexibility of petitioning as a tool that was connected and, to an extent, underpinned other forms of activity, was part of its appeal. Through petitions, signatories forged political communities, made representative claims on behalf of wider groups, and catalysed collective identities.[107]

In the modern era, petitioning has been an essential tool for political recruitment and organisation, building social movements, mobilising popular support,

[103] S. Richardson, *The Political Worlds of Women: Gender and Politics in Nineteenth-Century Britain* (London, Routledge, 2013), pp. 109–25; R. Blickle, 'Peasant Protest and the Language of Women's Petitions: Christina Vend's Supplications of 1629', in U. Rublack (ed.), *Gender in Early Modern German History* (Cambridge, Cambridge University Press, 2002), pp. 177–99; D. Carpenter, Z. Popp, T. Resch, B. Schneer, and N. Topich, 'Suffrage Petitioning as Formative Practice: American Women Presage and Prepare for the Vote, 1840–1940', *Studies in American Political Development*, 32 (2018), 24–48; L. Schmugge, 'Female Petitioners in the Papal Penitentiary', *Gender & History*, 12 (2002), 685–703; W. M. Ormrod, *Women and Parliament in Later Medieval England* (Basingstoke, Palgrave, 2020), pp. 63–73; J. Beatty, *In Dependence: Women and the Patriarchal State in Revolutionary America* (Chapel Hill: University of North Carolina Press, 2023); T. Verhoeven, '"My how I have walked and worked to get those names": Petitioning and the Women's Suffrage Movement in the United States, 1908–1920', *Women's History Review* (forthcoming); B. Waddell and J. Peacey, 'Introduction: Power, Processes, and Patterns in Early Modern Petitioning', in Waddell and Peacey, *The Power of Petitioning*.

[104] M. Schmidt Blaine, 'The Power of Petitions: Women and the New Hampshire Provincial Government, 1695–1770', in Heerma van Voss, *Petitions in Social History*, pp. 57–77 (p. 57); Whiting, *Women and Petitioning*, pp. 25–8; Houston, *Peasant Petitions*, pp. 24, 77, 85–6; Dodd, *Justice and Grace*, pp. 211–15; C. Stewart, 'The Ulster Women's Declaration and the Passion of Women in the Campaign against Home Rule, c. 1886–1912', *Parliamentary History*, 42 (2023), 129–47.

[105] B. Kümin and A. Würgler, 'Petitions, *Gravamina*, and the Early Modern State: Local Influence on Central Legislation in England and Germany (Hesse)', *Parliaments, Estates and Representation*, 17 (1997), 39–60; Leston-Bandeira, 'Parliamentary Petitions and Public Engagement', pp. 430–1.

[106] J. Haemers and C. Liddy, 'Popular Politics in the Late Medieval City: York and Bruges', *English Historical Review*, 128 (2013), 771–805; D. Palacios Cerezales, 'Re-Imagining Petitioning in Spain (1808–23)', *Social Science History*, 43 (2019), 487–508. See chapters by Würgler, and Huzzey and Miller. See also Worthen, 'The Process and Practice', on other forms of early modern justice-seeking that existed alongside petitions.

[107] Miller, *A Nation of Petitioners*, pp. 132–53; M. Saward, *The Representative Claim* (Oxford, Oxford University Press, 2010); Z. Haaparinne, 'Voice of the People or Raving of the Rabble? Petitions and Disputes on Political Representation in Britain, 1721–1776', PhD thesis (University of Jyväskylä, 2021); S. Zaeske, *Signatures of Citizenship: Petitioning, Antislavery, and Women's Political Identity* (Chapel Hill, University of North Carolina Press, 2003).

raising public awareness, and creating networks.[108] Petitioners have often used the petitioning process to promote their cause to a wide range of audiences, including the public, the media, and potential signatories, as much as the authority to which the petition is nominally addressed – hence the emphasis placed by 20th-century campaigners on turning the public presentation of petitions at sites of authority, such as 10 Downing Street in the United Kingdom, into photo opportunities intended to be communicated to wider audiences through the modern mass media.[109] By such means petitions could also reach international as well as domestic audiences. Commenting on the (typically unsuccessful) petitions sent to the League of Nations Permanent Mandates Commission, Susan Pedersen has perceptively observed that the petitioners 'persisted, rather, because of what petitioning offered: exposure, contacts, credibility, publicity, voice'.[110] Even if their requests had no impact in the corridors of power, petitioners' dogged commitment to petitioning is much more understandable when we consider the range of uses to which these practices could be put.

For states, institutions, or rulers, petitions have always been an instrument of rule because the very act of petitioning requires petitioners to submit to and recognise their authority and jurisdiction within a given territory. For this reason, the petition 'played a critical role in facilitating royal authority in the broader context of late medieval English government'.[111] To cite another example, Karin Sennefelt has observed of 18th- and early-nineteenth-century Scandinavia that petitions were 'an informational channel for the absolute ruler which … legitimized the political system'.[112] In the 20th century, the reception of petitions reinforced the authority of new international bodies. Commenting on Jewish and Arab petitions from Palestine to the League of Nations, Natasha Wheatley has written that 'petitions enacted a jurisdictional hierarchy with the League at its apex'.[113]

The utility of petitions as a mechanism for confirming authority was such that even if requests were not granted, the considerable bureaucratic resources that have been expended on receiving, considering, and archiving petitions testify to how seriously they have been taken in many polities.[114] Similarly, while authorities may have occasionally circumscribed the right of petition, the value of petitions as an instrument of rule explains why few thought it politic to close it off entirely.[115]

[108] Miller, *A Nation of Petitioners*, pp. 203–28; Miller, 'Introduction', pp. 422–4; Carpenter, 'Recruitment by Petition'.

[109] H. Miller, 'The British Women's Movement and the Practice of Petitioning, 1780–1918', *Historical Journal*, 64 (2021), 332–56 (pp. 338–42); Miller, *A Nation of Petitioners*, pp. 265–6.

[110] S. Pedersen, *The Guardians: The League of Nations and the Crisis of Empire* (Oxford, Oxford University Press, 2015), pp. 93–4.

[111] Dodd and Petit-Renaud, 'Grace and Favour', p. 259.

[112] K. Sennefelt, 'The Shifting Boundaries of Political Participation', in P. Ihalainen, M. Bregnsbo, K. Sennefelt, and P. Winton (eds), *Scandinavia in the Age of Revolution: Nordic Political Cultures, 1740–1820* (Abingdon, Routledge, 2011), pp. 269–78 (p. 271).

[113] Wheatley, 'Mandatory Interpretation', p. 211.

[114] Zaret, 'Petition-and-Response', pp. 439–43.

[115] Miller, 'Introduction', pp. 418–19; M. Janse, '"What Value Should We Attach to All These Petitions?": Petition Campaigns and the Problem of Legitimacy in the Nineteenth-Century Netherlands', *Social Science History*, 43 (2019), 509–30 (pp. 513–14).

For expanding empires, receiving petitions had the additional benefit of incorporating supplicants as subjects.[116] Historical examples also demonstrate the correlation between petitions and state formation: new bureaucratic bodies developed out of the petitioning process and have subsequently spawned separate administrative structures, while other branches of states have been reshaped through the interaction with petitioners.[117]

Petitions have historically been a legitimation tool for authorities. Writing of early colonial America, Da Cruz has observed that petitions 'were a legitimating factor for distant governments that were otherwise unable to ensure the obedience of scattered overseas communities of settlers'.[118] The same logic applied closer to home. This explains why new institutions or rulers seeking to establish their legitimacy, such as the Cromwellian protectorate of the 1650s, national legislatures founded during the 'age of revolutions' (1789–1848), or the German Democratic Republic, have welcomed petitions and frequently codified the right to petition as one of their first acts.[119] Petitions could thus be foundational to a regime's legitimacy, but states and authorities also had instrumental reasons to receive petitions. Petitions were a valuable source of local information for political elites, such as 18th-century British MPs.[120] For legislatures more generally, petitions have been a mechanism for representation, including that of non-voters.[121] In authoritarian contexts, where political expression was restricted to varying extents, petitions have offered states valuable intelligence about popular opinion and dissatisfaction.[122] Petitions could also function as 'useful complaints' for central authorities, serving as a tool for checking and disciplining subordinate officials.[123]

[116] Muller, 'From *Requête* to Petition'; J. Vernet, 'Petitions from the Peripheries of Empire: Louisiana and Quebec', *American Review of Canadian Studies*, 38 (2008), 495–512; G. Dodd, 'Law, Legislation, and Consent in the Plantagenet Empire: Wales and Ireland, 1272–1461', *Journal of British Studies*, 56 (2017), 225–49; Palacios Cerezales, 'Petitioning for Empire'.

[117] M. Ailes, 'Wars, Widows, and State Formation in 17th-Century Sweden', *Scandinavian Journal of History*, 31 (2006), 17–34; Huzzey and Miller, 'The Politics of Petitioning'; McKinley, 'Petitioning and the Administrative State'.

[118] Da Cruz, 'Introduction', p. 6.

[119] D. Hirst, 'Making Contact: Petitions and the English Republic', *Journal of British Studies*, 45 (2006), 26–50; Miller, 'Introduction', p. 420; Oddens, 'The Greatest Right', pp. 639–40; Betts, *Within Walls*, p. 175.

[120] J. Hoppit, *Britain's Political Economies: Parliament and Economic Life, 1660–1800* (Cambridge, Cambridge University Press, 2017), pp. 150–62; P. Loft, 'Involving the Public: Parliament, Petitioning, and the Language of Interest, 1688–1720', *Journal of British Studies*, 55 (2016), 1–23.

[121] Knights, 'Participation and Representation'; Miller, *A Nation of Petitioners*, pp. 229–52; J. D. Griffin and G. Sager, 'Democratic Representation of All "the People": Antislavery Petitions in the U.S. Senate', *Studies in American Political Development*, 34 (2020), 269–91; P. Chaney, I. Rees Jones, and R. Fevre, 'Exploring the Substantive Representation of Non-Humans in UK Parliamentary Business: A Legislative Functions Perspective of Animal Welfare Petitions, 2010–2019', *Parliamentary Affairs*, 75 (2022), 813–42.

[122] Betts, *Within Walls*, p. 180; H. Lueders, 'Electoral Responsiveness in Closed Autocracies: Evidence from Petitions in the Former German Democratic Republic', *American Political Science Review*, 116 (2022), 827–42.

[123] J. Chen, *Useful Complaints: How Petitions Assist Decentralized Authoritarianism in China* (Lanham, MD, Lexington, 2016); S. Fitzpatrick, 'Editor's Introduction: Petitions and Denunciations in Russian and Soviet History', *Russian History*, 24 (1997), 1–9 (pp. 6–7).

So far we have focused on why petitions and petitioning have been important for both petitioners and authority. There are broader reasons why petitionary practices have been historically significant. We have already noted the relationship of petitions and petitioning with important historical processes such as the emergence of the public sphere, state formation, and democratisation, for example. As well as contributing to such developments over the *longue durée*, petitions and petitioning could be a catalyst for more unpredictable and sudden upheavals, even if these proved to be short-lived.

Petitions are an inherently unstable and ambiguous form of interaction between subjects and authority because of their dual character. As Prashant Kidambi has put it in his study of colonial Bombay, 'petitioning was both a routine reinscription of power relations and a potential "event" that could unsettle them'.[124] Because petitions were addressed to authority, often in superficially deferential or loyal language, they could be used to make coded criticisms and question the legitimacy of rulers. The 'hidden transcripts' of petitions may even contain 'an implicit threat of violence' or rebellion, clothed in a 'deferential tone of address', as James C. Scott has written.[125] This explains why petitioning has been intimately linked to revolts and rebellions, or the threat thereof, in numerous polities, including monarchies and republics across medieval and early modern Europe, as well as colonial societies such as mid-19th-century Jamaica.[126] Another example of this broader phenomenon would be the *pronunciamiento* that flourished in 19th-century Mexico, which has been defined as an 'extra-constitutional political practice that soldiers and civilians used to negotiate or petition forcefully for political change, both at a national and at a local level, in the absence of a clearly established constitutional order'.[127] Less dramatically, petitions could lead to slow-burning ruptures in the relationship between governors and governed, as in East Germany, by gradually exposing the gap between official rhetoric and the lived experiences of citizens.[128]

We are not claiming that petitions inevitably trigger revolutions or regime change. But there are enough historical examples to suggest the potential of petitions to disrupt and destabilise established authority, and thereby engender sudden and unpredictable political change. On this basis, then, regardless of the outcome of specific requests, the effects of petitions and petitioning in the short term could be significant. It is tempting to conclude that the emergence of e-petitions contained within institutional petitions systems has tamed the unruly potential that has long been a latent characteristic of petitions and petitioning. Yet, given the long and

[124] P. Kidambi, 'The Petition as Event: Colonial Bombay, circa 1889–1914', *Modern Asian Studies*, 53 (2019), 203–39 (p. 206).

[125] J. C. Scott, *Domination and the Arts of Resistance: Hidden Transcripts* (New Haven, CT, Yale University Press, 1990), pp. 96–101 (p. 96).

[126] Ibid., p. 95; Nubola and Würgler, *Operare*; Huzzey and Miller, 'Colonial Petitions'.

[127] W. Fowler, 'Preface', in Fowler, *Forceful Negotiations*, pp. vii–ix (p. viii).

[128] Betts, *Within Walls*, pp. 185–90.

chequered history of petitions and related forms over the *longue durée*, and because these forms have always existed outside, as well as within, formal institutional systems, such a conclusion would be premature.

Scope and Structure

In covering a broad, diverse phenomenon across North America and Europe over several centuries, inevitably this volume has had to focus its scope on certain areas and not others. While many chapters recover and show the importance of petitions and petitioning to women, the book as a whole does not offer an extended account of the relationship between these practices and gender, although a number of excellent studies already exist.[129] While scholars have noted the similarity between rituals of petition and prayer,[130] and the historical relationship between religious communities and petitioning has been a feature of recent work,[131] the book does not provide an overarching analysis of the interaction between petitions and religion, nor the phenomenon of petitions to religious authorities, such as the papacy.[132] As already noted, the book's geographic focus means that it does not offer a global history of petitions, nor does it examine the culture of petitioning within colonial and imperial contexts in South America, Asia, Africa, or Australasia and the Pacific. While not running themes in this volume, these, and other areas for future research, are discussed in the conclusion.

Turning to the content of the book, the chapters in Part I address definitional questions. In his chapter, David Zaret argues that rather than being defined by their formal qualities, petitions must be understood as shaped by the practice of reception: this distinguishes petitions from related practices. Providing a comparative etymology of petition, supplication, and related terms across Germanic and Romance languages, Joris Oddens argues that a historical understanding of the semantics of these terms is crucial to understanding the extraordinarily diverse nature of petitions, supplications, and related forms, albeit that he notes the increasing adoption of 'petition' across a number of languages from the late 18th century onwards. Surveying early modern Britain, Mark Knights explores the interrelationship between petitions and similar, but different, forms of 'subscriptional'

[129] Schmidt Blaine, 'The Power of Petitions'; Zaeske, *Signatures of Citizenship*; Blickle, 'Peasant Protest'; Beatty, *In Dependence*; A. Bocking-Welch, R. Huzzey, C. Leston-Bandeira, and H. Miller, 'Women's Campaigning, Petitioning, and Grassroots Activism, 1945–1997', *Women's History Review* (forthcoming).

[130] D. Nicholls, 'Addressing God as Ruler: Prayer and Petition', *British Journal of Sociology*, 44 (1993), 125–41.

[131] Miller, *A Nation of Petitioners*, pp. 140–7, 160–5.

[132] P. Zutshi, 'Petitions to the Pope in the Fourteenth Century', in W. Ormrod, G. Dodd, and A. Musson (eds), *Medieval Petitions: Grace and Grievance* (Woodbridge, York Medieval Press, 2009), pp. 82–98; D. Palacios Cerezales, 'Catholic Transnational Repertoires in the Nineteenth Century: Signatures, Newspapers, and Organisation', in D. Palacios Cerezales and O. Luján (eds), *Popular Agency and Politicisation in Nineteenth-Century Europe: Beyond the Vote* (Cham, Palgrave, 2022), pp. 235–58.

practices, including associations, covenants, addresses, and remonstrances. In her chapter, Joanna Innes emphasises the fuzzy boundaries and hybridity of petitions as a genre, and importantly clarifies the different mechanisms for change through a study of late-18th- and early-19th-century England. Evaluating the growth of e-petitions, Cristina Leston-Bandeira outlines the key differences between digital and traditional forms, before arguing that e-petitions must be defined by the 'petition system', or the formal institutional processes that receive them.

The chapters in Part II examine petitioning within specific historical contexts over long stretches of time to examine and complicate our understanding of cycles of continuity and change within this ancient practice. In their contribution, Brodie Waddell and Hannah Worthen demonstrate that the famous outbursts of 'political' or 'radical' petitioning in 17th-century England were preceded by a surge in petitioning on local and quotidian topics, pointing to deeper continuities even in a period of political upheaval. The Dutch experience over three centuries, Maartje Janse, Joris Oddens, Anne Petterson, Joris van den Tol, Edurne de Wilde, and Elsa Miedema suggest, reveals that rather than there being a linear development from traditional to modern forms of representation through petitioning, petitioners continually shifted between different types of representative claims. In his study of Jamaica, 1664–1834, Aaron Graham shows that trends in petitioning were closely associated with patterns of legislation within the colony, and that petitions enabled a limited degree of participation for particular groups, such as free people of colour and Jews, who were otherwise excluded from direct political representation. Andreas Würgler's detailed study of Switzerland over the *longue durée* shows that the marked continuities in petitioning were partly obscured by the regime changes during the 'age of revolutions' before the practice was superseded by the adoption of referendums and initiatives in the later 19th century. Examining North America and Europe from the mid-19th century to the early 21st century, Richard Huzzey and Henry Miller chart the shift away from petitioning legislatures to other institutions, including new international authorities, while showing that petitions remained critical to fostering collective action locally, nationally, and globally.

Part III offers a series of detailed analyses to address the question of when, why, and in what contexts petitions and petitioning have mattered. Examining 14th-century England, Gwilym Dodd chronicles how the 'common' petition that claimed to speak on behalf of the wider community came to be a powerful tool to exert pressure on the king, not least because it shielded the real sponsors from reprisals. Marta Gravela highlights the historical importance of petitions for claiming citizenship and, crucially, fiscal exemptions, through a study of 15th-century Genoa. The key significance of petitions as a mechanism for claiming welfare – in this case, pensions for soldiers wounded during the English Civil Wars of the mid-17th century – is the subject of Ismini Pells's chapter. Based on a database of 500,000 petitions to Congress, 1789–1950, Maggie Blackhawk and Daniel Carpenter provide a ground-breaking account of the way that petitioning provided a means of representation that operated independently of the electoral process and partisanship.

The utility of receiving petitions to authoritarian states for consolidating their power and gauging the public mood is revealed in Lara Douds's study of the early Soviet era.

Collectively, the chapters in this book consolidate and distil an emergent and dynamic field of scholarship. They aim to open up new approaches, understandings, and questions for historians, as well as social and political scientists, by addressing challenges relating to definition, chronology, and why people have petitioned and received petitions in historical and contemporary contexts. By such an undertaking we can begin to understand why petitions and petitioning have been ubiquitous in human societies, past and present.

Part I

Definitions

1

What is a Petition?

DAVID ZARET

KARL MARX'S FAMOUS remark on the modern commodity applies to the premodern petition: it is 'at first sight, a very trivial thing, and easily understood. Its analysis shows that it is, in reality, a very queer thing, abounding in metaphysical subtleties and theological niceties.'[1] I explore this point and suggest how a 'first sight' definition of premodern petitions, in otherwise meticulous historical scholarship, misconstrues the general practice that generated the petitions.

This problem is illuminated by insights from perspectives on genre as practice. Originally a literary concept, genre in ethnographic work by linguistic anthropologists refers to speech genre and discursive production but still pertains to written texts, including documentary texts.[2] Unlike perhaps more prominent social science theories of power,[3] this work is most helpful for thinking about premodern petitioning. Similar to speech genre, petitioning is not merely a generic classification used by scholars (e.g. archivists), but is an orienting framework for petitioners and respondents. As practice, genre generates endlessly diverse outcomes in specific situations, with complex intertextual relationships. Speech genre 'transcends the bounded, locally produced speech event' but is not static.[4] The same holds for petitionary genre that guides production of petitions. Its

[1] K. Marx, *Capital*, Vol. I (New York, Modern Library, 1906), p. 81.

[2] W. F. Hanks, *Converting Words: Maya in the Age of the Cross* (Berkeley and Los Angeles, CA, University of California Press, 2010), especially Chapters 4 and 10, which examine petitions.

[3] E.g. by Pierre Bourdieu, Margaret Levi, Michael Mann, James Scott, and Charles Tilly, whose perspectives on premodern power relations either deny the existence of petitioning or badly misconstrue it; see p. 50.

[4] R. Bauman, *A World of Others' Words: Cross-Cultural Perspectives on Intertextuality* (Oxford, Blackwell, 2004), p. 5. See also R. Bauman, 'Genre', *Journal of Linguistic Anthropology*, 9 (1999), 84–7; W. F. Hanks, 'Discourse Genres in a Theory of Practice', *American Ethnologist*, 14 (1987), 668–92 (pp. 668–9); and W. F. Hanks, 'Pierre Bourdieu and the Practices of Language', *Annual Review of Anthropology*, 34 (2005), 67–83, which criticises Bourdieu's reductionist account of language and practice.

Proceedings of the British Academy, **262**, 33–50,

orienting framework can shift precisely because it is transposable, easily adapted to new contexts, where deployments often create petitions with innovative structural and rhetorical elements.[5]

Hence, multiple accounts of premodern petitioning as practice easily are inferred from surviving petitions and their responding residues in other documentary texts, such as charters and warrants. Research on medieval European petitions seizes on deferential rhetoric and supplicatory imagery, which suggest that the matrix for the practice was Catholic doctrine on intercession and papal administrative practice.[6] What, then, explains similarities between these petitions and many key aspects of petitions in occidental antiquity and in Asia? Comparable problems arise in explanations that refer to a subset of requests in petitions. Select those similar to a papyri petition, two millennia ago, to a powerful official (a strategus) in Ptolemaic Egypt, from two brothers, beekeepers, who complain that a hostile local official 'ruined' many of their hives: 'by the agency of the gymnasiarch Sarapion … and those he brought with him secretly at night, all the hives … had been blocked up for several days'.[7] A 'first sight' observation concludes that petitions were instruments of protest by subjects with grievances against officials. Select petitions with requests such as those for promotion to senatorial rank in the Roman Empire, where 'elevation of various functionaries was as much the result of petition from below as of imperial intervention'.[8] Petitions now appear to be devices used by subjects to get desiderata from the state. Petitions in the 16th century to the Ottoman sultan Selim II from Sultan Alauddin in south-east Asian Aceh (now part of Indonesia), requesting military assistance against Portuguese attacks on Muslims, display the petition as a device used by non-subjects for diplomatic communication.[9]

[5] Transposition is an implicit theme running through meticulous archival research on medieval petitioning that describes intertextual relations among different documentary (decrees, petitions, reports), epistolary, and narrative genres. See M. Rustow, *The Lost Archive: Traces of a Caliphate in a Cairo Synagogue* (Princeton, NJ, Princeton University Press, 2020); and W. Scase, *Literature and Complaint in England* (Oxford, Oxford University Press, 2007).

[6] G. Koziol, 'The Early History of Rites of Supplication', in H. Millet (ed.), *Suppliques et requêtes: Le gouvernement par la grâce en Occident (XIIe–XVe siècle)* (Rome, École française de Rome, 2003), pp. 21–36.

[7] R. D. Sullivan, 'A Petition of Beekeepers at Oxyrhynchus', *The Bulletin of the American Society of Papyrologists*, 10 (1973), 5–13 (p. 6).

[8] J. N. Dillon, 'The Inflation of Rank and Privilege', in J. Wienand (ed.), *Contested Monarchy: Integrating the Roman Empire in the Fourth Century AD* (Oxford, Oxford University Press, 2015), pp. 42–66 (p. 63).

[9] İ. H. Kadi (ed.), *Ottoman–Southeast Relations: Sources from the Ottoman Archives*, 2 vols (Leiden, Brill, 2020), Vol. I, p. 55. For petitioning by other non-subjects, see R. M. Savory, 'Relations between the Safavid State and Its Non-Muslim Minorities', *Islam and Christian–Muslim Relations*, 14 (2003), 435–58. For diplomatic petitioning elsewhere, see Koziol, 'The Early History', pp. 21–3; and J. Ma, *Antiochos III and the Cities of Western Asia Minor* (Oxford, Oxford University Press, 2000).

A vast literature amply documents the ubiquity and prominence of the petitions (however defined) across premodern Eurasia.[10] There were floods of petitions – the metaphor frequently appears in studies of the practice. State archives hold tens, even hundreds of thousands, of petitions. In this broader context the 17,000 petitions to late medieval English parliaments appears unexceptional. For example, the early modern imperial divan annually received at least 4,000 Ottoman petitions, 900,000 petitions are listed in papal registers from 1471 to 1527, while more than 50,000 went to late medieval Royal Councils under the reign of Isabel and Fernando in Castile.[11] The petition, as genre, is an important archival category for cuneiform, papyrus, epigraphic, parchment, and paper records of premodern states, comparable to decrees, edicts, proclamations, warrants, and other types of documentary writing for imperative commands.[12]

Case studies with thick description of petitions in different times and places prompt some historians to conclude that petitioning was 'a general practice', 'more or less from time immemorial', 'ubiquitous across time and space', 'a global phenomenon, stretching back in time almost as far as writing'.[13] Petitioning flourished in empires, kingdoms, and city-states with diverse structures of governance, and in diverse cultural systems: in early Near Eastern cuneiform traditions, Persian Zoroastrianism, Hellenic and Roman cultures of benefaction, Christianity, Islam, Taoism, Confucianism, and the syncretic mix of Shinto and Buddhism in Japan. Current historical scholarship attests but does not adequately explain the ubiquity

[10] Before European conquest there is no evidence of glyphic petitions in Mesoamerica; I am indebted to William F. Hanks for this information. Later, vibrant petitioning in Nahuatl, Mextec, and Mayan scripts followed Spanish formularies.

[11] B. Tuğ, *Politics of Honor in Ottoman Anatolia* (Leiden, Brill, 2017), p. 81; H. Millet, 'Introduction', in Millet *Supplique et requêtes*, pp. 1–14 (p. 1); Y. Israeli, 'Petition and Response as Social Process: Royal Power, Justice, and the People in Late Medieval Castile (c. 1474–1504)', *Past & Present*, 262 (2024), 3–44 (p. 16).

[12] For papyrus records, petitions are a type of documentary (non-literary) text, one of the few with 'any claim to be typical, represented to some degree in all parts of the millennium from Alexander to the Arabs'; R. Bagnall, *Reading Papyri, Writing Ancient History* (London, Routledge, 1995), p. 18. In England, petitions 'are one of the commonest types of English-language documents to survive from the period before 1460'; G. Dodd, 'The Rise of English, the Decline of French: Supplications to the English Crown, c. 1420–1450', *Speculum*, 86 (2011), 117–50 (pp. 118–19).

[13] L. Heerma van Voss, 'Introduction', in L. Heerma van Voss (ed.), *Petitions in Social History* (Cambridge, Cambridge University Press, 2001), pp. 1–10 (p. 2); M. Vale, *Henry V: The Conscience of a King* (New Haven, CT, Yale University Press, 2016), p. 19; W. M. Ormrod, 'Introduction: Medieval Petitions in Context', in W. M. Ormrod, G. Dodd, and A. Musson (eds), *Medieval Petitions: Grace and Grievance* (York, York Medieval Press, 2009), pp. 1–11 (p. 5); A. Würgler, 'Voices from among the "Silent Masses": Humble Petitions and Social Conflicts in Early Modern Central Europe', in Heerma van Voss, *Petitions in Social History*, pp. 11–34 (p. 16). For nearly identical claims to those made in the last quotation, see M. D. da Cruz, 'Introduction: Atlantic Petitionary Traditions and Developments', in M. D. da Cruz (ed.), *Petitioning in the Atlantic World, c. 1500–1840: Empires, Revolutions and Social Movements* (Basingstoke, Palgrave, 2022), pp. 1–20 (p. 3); and N. P. Sahai, *Politics of Patronage and Protest: The State, Society, and Artisans in Early Modern Rajasthan* (Oxford, Oxford University Press, 2006), p. 29.

and prominence of premodern petitions. Instead, it offers divergent, contradictory accounts of the practice that generated these texts.

(a) The least satisfactory account comes from anachronism with modern notions of petitioning as a basic expressive freedom. Since it gained legal protection from the 17th century onwards,[14] petitioning has become a near-universal right (albeit unevenly upheld in practice). But that narrative is irrelevant for nearly all premodern petitioning, which contemporaries understood neither as a right nor as a device for contentious political claims. This anachronism is in outdated historical studies and pervades current legal scholarship that portrays Magna Carta as an embryonic version of the modern right.[15]

(b) A widespread definition refers to popular unrest, notably in research on social movements, by Charles Tilly and others, who link premodern and modern petitioning to different repertoires for political contention before and after the late 18th century.[16] A similar definition among social historians highlights requests with individual and collective complaints, often construed as 'demands', for petitioning in Europe,[17] the Middle East,[18] western antiquity,[19]

[14] E.g. Britain's 1689 Act Declaring the Rights and Liberties of the Subject and Settling the Succession of the Crown. For an earlier ordinance in May 1648 that asserts 'the right and privilege' to send petitions to Parliament, see C. H. Firth and R. S. Rait (eds), *Acts and Ordinances of the Interregnum, 1642–1660*, 3 vols (London, HMSO, 1911), Vol. I, p. 1139. This ordinance and the 1689 Act restricted the right by banning 'tumultuous' petitioning. For the 1683 *Dansk Lov* on a right to petition, based on a 1643 decree, see T. Munck, 'Petitions and "Legitimate" Engagement with Power in Absolutist Denmark', *Parliaments, Estates and Representation*, 38 (2018), 378–91.

[15] After 1215, 'petitioning began to take significance as a means of asserting political power against the state'. R. J. Krotoszynski, Jr, *Reclaiming the Petition Clause* (New Haven, CT, Yale University Press, 2012), p. 84, and see p. 16. A. Bhagwat, 'The Democratic First Amendment', *Northwestern University Law Review*, 110 (2016), 1097–124 (pp. 1109–10); G. Lawson and G. Seidman, 'Downsizing the Right to Petition', *Northwestern University Law Review*, 93 (1999), 739–66 (p. 740); J. M. Spanbauer, 'The First Amendment Right to Petition Government for a Redress of Grievances: Cut from a Different Cloth', *Hastings Constitutional Law Quarterly*, 21 (1993), 5–69 (pp. 19–20).

[16] C. Tilly, *Durable Inequality* (Berkeley, CA, University of California Press, 1998), pp. 216, 221–2; C. Tilly, *Regimes and Repertoires* (Chicago, IL, University of Chicago Press, 2006), pp. 53, 184; C. Tilly, *Contentious Performances* (Cambridge, Cambridge University Press, 2008), pp. 7, 44, 69–72. See also S. Tarrow, *Power in Movement: Social Movements, Collective Action, and Politics* (Cambridge, Cambridge University Press, 1994), pp. 19–20, 41–2.

[17] For 'voicing demands' and 'grievance' as 'the principal purpose of a petition', see Heerma van Voss, 'Introduction', p. 7; and C. Nubola, 'Supplications between Politics and Justice: The Northern and Central Italian States in the Early Modern Age', in Heerma van Voss, *Petitions in Social History*, pp. 35–56 (p. 35). For a subset of petitions with a 'demand', see K. Bowie and T. Munck, 'Early Modern Political Petitioning and Public Engagement in Scotland, Britain and Scandinavia, c. 1550–1795', *Parliaments, Estates and Representation*, 38 (2018), 271–8 (p. 271).

[18] Petitioning was 'a device by which the weak demanded justice from the strong'; L. T. Darling, *A History of Social Justice and Political Power in the Middle East* (London, Routledge, 2013), p. 7. See also K. Barkey, *Empire of Difference: The Ottomans in Comparative Perspective* (Cambridge, Cambridge University Press, 2008), p. 101.

[19] S. Connolly, 'Petitioning in the Ancient World', in Ormrod et al., *Medieval Petitions*, pp. 47–63 (pp. 48, 62–3); T. Hauken, 'Structure and Themes in Petitions to Roman Emperors', in D. Feissel and J. Gascou (eds), *La pétition à Byzance* (Paris, Association des Amis du Centre d'Histoire et Civilisation de Byzance, 2004), pp. 11–22 (p. 11).

and the Far East.[20] This definition leads to a concise explanation for the practice: 'petitions were used by subjects ... in various cultures and political settings to voice their demands. Their ubiquity suggests that petitions are responsive to a need felt by ... human societies across cultural boundaries, perhaps something as fundamental as the need for justice.'[21]

(c) Many studies highlight deferential rhetoric and, sometimes, imagery of intercession and supplication. Such homologies for petitions to worldly rulers and petitionary prayer to deities are commonplace across Eurasia and cited as evidence that the practice of petitioning mimicked religious prayer.[22] This contradicts (b) to the extent that deference and demand are antonyms.

(d) Another perspective on premodern petitioning relies on thick descriptions with typologies of requests. This incorporates complaints, as in (b), but adds requests denominated as favours, e.g. for appointments, charters, exemptions, pensions, privileges, and other desiderata. In Tudor England, Imperial China, and Tokugawa Japan, petitioners complained about local officials and requested tax relief, famine assistance, and infrastructural improvements.[23] Petitions from occupational associations in early modern Istanbul and Jodhpur requested economic privileges and complained about competitors.[24]

(e) Dictionaries supply the broadest definition, which obscures the historical specificity of premodern petitioning by conflating it with other generic practices that deferentially request assistance: appealing, begging, praying, and supplicating.

Even a brief survey of comparative/historical evidence on premodern petitioning undermines these definitions: (a) is patently unsatisfactory, (b) is loaded with 'presentist assumptions' from our intuitive association of petitioning and protest.[25] Most premodern petitioning sought favours, and those with grievances are misconstrued as 'demands'. From Tokugawa Japan to Tudor England, deferential petitions represented grievance as apolitical information on local conditions directly experienced by petitioners. This petitionary etiquette harbours no lexicons of rights, avoids even intimations of *vox populi*, and was not animated by contention against authorities. Complaints about officials are only

[20] L. Roberts, 'The Petition Box in Eighteenth Century Tosa' *Journal of Japanese Studies*, 20 (1994), 423–58; Sahai, *Politics of Patronage*; H. Sang-kwŏn, 'The Development of the Petition System in the Age of Chosŏn', *Seoul Journal of Korean Studies*, 11 (1998), 107–25; S. Vlastos, *Peasant Protests and Uprisings in Tokugawa Japan* (Berkeley, CA, University of California Press, 1990).

[21] Heerma van Voss, 'Introduction', p. 10; see also Hauken, 'Structure and Themes', p. 11; Nubola, 'Supplications', pp. 36–7.

[22] For references, see pp. 46–8.

[23] For compelling comparative analysis of the three cases, see W. He, *Public Interest and State Legitimation: Early Modern England, Japan, and China* (Cambridge, Cambridge University Press, 2023).

[24] Sahai, *Politics of Patronage*; E. Yi, *Guild Dynamics in Seventeenth Century Istanbul* (Leiden, Brill, 2004).

[25] See Ormrod, 'Introduction', p. 2: 'the medieval petition was not a modern e-petition in waiting'. Cf. Da Cruz, 'Introduction', p. 3.

a subset of grievances. There were many such complaints, but that was the tip of a much larger iceberg. Quarrels among subjects, within or between families, neighbours, and villages animated as many, if not more, petitions than subjects with complaints against authorities. Moreover, all types of grievances are still only a subset of requests in petitions. Requests were as infinitely diverse as commodities. If Marx explained the practice of buying and selling in this manner, he would describe use-values of important commodities, perhaps textiles and foods, instead of analysing the duality of use- and exchange-value that makes commodities 'a very queer thing'. Attributes of a subset of commodities or petitions conceal more than they reveal about general practices that generate those things.

The account in (c) of the general practice gains credibility from compelling homologies between petitioning and praying in specific times and places, specifically in medieval Europe. This is hardly surprising, given the transposability of genres and the 'complex intertextual relations that underlie genre'.[26] An intertextual relationship in one context conceals more than it reveals about a genre practice in other contexts. Variation in tropes and practices for religious prayer across Eurasia hardly explains the relative uniformity of petitioning. Moreover, we will see that (c) also overlooks evidence for petitioning to worldly rulers as the template for liturgical developments of petitionary prayer.

Thick description in (d) avoids anachronism with a simple but useful taxonomy that distinguishes between requests for favours and justice. But this addresses neither the coherence nor specificity of the general practice, and it omits other uses of petitions, notably as a convention for diplomatic communication by non-subjects and an administrative device for officials who provide reports and request authorisation for official actions.[27] Even for only European petitioning, no precise taxonomy is feasible for requests that 'ranged very widely and accordingly [are] hard or cumbersome to define' (Ancient Rome), were a 'vast and chaotic jumble of subjects' (early modern Venice), or were 'remarkably eclectic' and 'too varied for detailed description' (early modern England).[28] In the oldest attested petitions, requests on ancient Mesopotamian cuneiform tablets 'were clearly the vehicle for expressing a variety of human needs',

[26] C. L. Briggs and R. Bauman, 'Genre, Intertextuality, and Social Power', *Journal of Linguistic Anthropology*, 2 (1992), 131–72 (p. 132).

[27] For the diplomatic practice, see n. 9; for the administrative device in Fatimid regimes, see H. Halm, *Empire of the Mahdi* (Leiden, Brill, 1996), p. 354.

[28] Hauken, 'Structure and Themes', p. 11; R. C. Davies, *Shipbuilders of the Venetian Arsenal: Workers and Workplace in the Pre-Industrial City* (Baltimore, MD, Johns Hopkins University Press, 1991), p. 183; J. Hart, *Justice upon Petition* (London, HarperCollins, 1991), p. 19; Historical Manuscripts Commission, *Report on the Manuscripts of His Grace the Duke of Portland*, Vol. VIII (London, HMSO, 1907), p. v. See also B. Waddell, *God, Duty, and Community in English Economic Life 1660–1720* (Woodbridge, Boydell & Brewer, 2012), p. 137.

e.g. protection, 'preferment to a higher post', relief from debt slavery, and confirmation of a patrimony.[29]

The coherence and specificity of petitioning are also obscured in (e) by making them a synonym for other practices that deferentially request assistance. Petitioning was not begging. In early modern England, no one begged for a licence to petition, but victims of misfortune petitioned for a licence to solicit funds. Petitioning closely resembles supplication (deferential oral requests in face-to-face interaction), but, as I explain later, conflating these practices obscures their historical connection.

The upshot of these observations is that 'What is a petition?' is not a trivial question, even after distinctions are drawn among premodern, modern, and liminal practices for petitioning.[30] For the premodern practice, I suggest it was a documentary genre whose deployment generated texts with requests for assistance that traversed up power gradients and followed administrative protocols for managing power relations. The practice's context was fields of power (epitomised by premodern states) in which centres had only limited capacity to monitor peripheries and forcibly coerce them. In this context, petitioning was a remedy for limitations of despotic power, a source of infrastructural power[31] that more effectively penetrated local communities and managed power relations. This point explains why some types of petitioning in Tokugawa Japan, though illegal, 'were nevertheless widely practiced and informally permitted' by authorities, 'appearing to act out of benevolence': petitioning was indispensable for managing power relations at local and provincial levels.[32] The practice could be helpful to petitioners but it also satisfied and advanced important dominant interests. It not only legitimated power but also was a source of power, a practice for monitoring officials and regulating the balance of power at local and provincial levels. The practice easily coexisted with brutal deployments of premodern power.

Viewing petitioning as genre sheds light not only on problems in extant accounts of the practice but, more importantly, on historical and intertextual relationships between petitioning and three closely related genres: supplication, religious prayer, and legal plaints that initiate litigation. Although there is a vast literature with meticulous descriptions of connections between petitioning and the three other

[29] W. W. Hallo, 'Individual Prayer in Sumerian: The Continuity of a Tradition', *Journal of the American Oriental Society*, 88 (1968), 71–89 (pp. 78–9).

[30] D. Zaret, 'Petition-and-Response and Liminal Petitioning in Comparative/Historical Perspective', *Social Science History*, 43 (2019), 431–52.

[31] See pp. 49–50.

[32] L. S. Roberts, *Performing the Great Peace: Political Space and Open Secrets in Tokugawa Japan* (Honolulu, University of Hawai'i Press, 2012), p. 130. For other references to petitioning as a source of power, see F. Hasan, *Paper, Performance, and the State: Social Change and Political Culture in Mughal India* (Cambridge, Cambridge University Press, 2021), pp. 111–13; Israeli, 'Petition and Response'; and Rustow, *The Lost Archive*, p. 59.

practices, there are opportunities for untangling synchronic intertextuality from diachronic historical links. If successful, this yields a clearer portrait of the origins and subsequent genesis of premodern petitioning.

Writing, Administration, and Protocols for Petition-and-Response

Petitions exemplify the central place of writing in the administration of power relations among rulers, officials, and subjects. Like warrants, decrees, and other instruments of state, petitions are documentary texts that follow protocols for formulaic, redacted writing. As genre for a practice that produced documentary texts, hedged in by written protocols, petitioning most probably was less malleable than speech genres studied by linguistic anthropologists. In ancient Mesopotamian palace administration, cuneiform writing had conventions for deferential requests in 'letter prayers' as well as for commands in 'letter orders'.[33] Ancient writers used Græco-Phoenician alphabetic scripts to 'petition authority' and 'to answer petitions', as well as 'to give instructions to a subordinate' and 'issue an edict'.[34] Merovingian clerks had templates for 'responses to petitions' as well as for requisitions and other commands; a millennium later, so did clerks in Elizabethan Privy Councils.[35] There were comparable chancery practices in medieval and early modern Islamic regimes. Fatimid administrators in Shi' Egypt had handbooks that devoted 'a whole section to the procedure of delivering, answering and storing answers to petitions'. There and in Sunni states practice corresponded closely though not perfectly to such formal rules: another hallmark of genre.[36]

The baseline protocol across Eurasia was putting requests in writing. Of course, many requests came forward orally, by supplicating subjects and, less formally, by those with special access to corridors of power. Putting them in writing was necessary for nearly all inhabitants of premodern societies who did not have the ear of rulers and high officials. As elsewhere, medieval Muslim rulers and officials routinely received oral requests but also advice on the necessity

[33] Hallo, 'Individual Prayer in Sumerian', pp. 78–9; cf. A. Lenzi, *Reading Akkadian Prayers & Hymns* (Atlanta, GA, Society of Biblical Literature, 2011), p. 54, on 'letter prayer' as a misnomer.

[34] W. V. Harris, *Ancient Literacy* (Cambridge, MA, Harvard University Press, 2009), pp. 26–7.

[35] I. Wood, 'Administration, Law, and Culture in Merovingian Gaul', in T. F. X. Noble (ed.), *From Roman Provinces to Medieval Kingdoms* (New York, Routledge, 2006), pp. 299–313 (p. 301); *Formulary for a Clerk of the Privy Council c. 1572*, London, British Library, Additional MS 48150.

[36] P. M. Sijpesteijn, 'The Archival Mind in Early Islamic Egypt: Two Arabic Papyri', in P. M. Sijpesteijn, L. Sundelin, S. Torallas Tovar, and A. Zomeño (eds), *From al-Andalus to Khurasan: Documents from the Medieval Muslim World* (Leiden, Brill, 2007), pp.163–86 (p. 164). See also P. Fodor, 'The Grand Vizieral Telhis: A Study in the Ottoman Central Administration 1566–1656', *Archivum Ottomanicum*, 15 (1997), 137–88 (pp. 140–3); A. Minkov, *Conversion to Islam in the Balkans: Kisve Bahasi Petitions and Ottoman Social Life, 1670–1730* (Leiden, Brill, 2004), pp. 11–12; and S. M. Stern, 'Petitions from the Mamlūk Period', *Bulletin of the School of Oriental and African Studies*, 29 (1966), 233–76 (p. 241).

of formal petitions if the issue was 'comparatively important'.[37] A petition was not the only written text for requesting benevolent deployments of power. But, as genre, it was the root metaphor when transposed to other types of written texts, such as epistolary correspondence.[38] This use of letters was a privilege of powerful subjects and lesser ones with close connections to patrons. In Tudor England, such letters echoed deferential rhetoric in petitions and indexed themselves as petitions.[39] For 'the specifically curial variant' of requests that went to medieval European chanceries and parliaments, 'the petition is the encompassing genus'.[40] Another transposition is in eulogies that Islamic authors sent to patrons, in prefaces to their poetry, and in learned treatises that advanced the same wide range of requests, for 'favors, employment, and protection', as in petitions.[41] Other sources of mutability in petitionary requests are intertextual relationships to other documentary genres. Fatimids devised a formulary for petitions, widely followed by later Islamic regimes, which reinvented simple petitions that were similar to letters but now more closely resembled elaborate decrees.[42] Other intertextual relationships bridged documentary and literary genres, in Graeco-Roman Egypt and in medieval England, where petitionary genre pervaded a flourishing literature of poetic complaint.[43]

Protocols for composing requests generated the distinctive form of mature petitions comprising compact writing in structured sequences, with wide margins, usually on one side of paper, papyrus, or parchment. These protocols were 'essentially products of bureaucratic expedience', designed to meet 'needs of developing

[37] H. Darke (trans.), *The Book of Government or Rules for Kings: The Siyar Al-Muluk or Siyasat-Nama of Nizam al-Mulk* (London, Routledge, 2002), p. 13; and see S. M. Stern, 'Three Petitions of the Fatimid Period', *Oriens*, 15 (1962), 172–209 (pp. 195–8). For similar protocols in ancient Egypt and medieval France, see G. Dodd and S. Petit-Renaud, 'Grace and Favour: The Petition and Its Mechanisms', in C. Fletcher, J.-P. Genet, and J. Watts (eds), *Government and Political Life in England and France, c. 1300–1500* (Cambridge, Cambridge University Press, 2015), pp. 240–78 (p. 252); and G. P. F. van den Boorn, *The Duties of the Vizier: Civil Administration in the Early New Kingdom* (London, Kegan Paul, 1988), pp. 193, 198–9.

[38] For the reverse relationship, when florid register in letters transposed to opening lines of petitions, see G. Dodd, 'Kingship, Parliament and the Court: The Emergence of "High Style" in Petitions to the English Crown, c. 1350–1405', *English Historical Review*, 129 (2014), 515–45 (pp. 527, 530–1).

[39] J. Daybell, *Women Letter-Writers in Tudor England* (Oxford, Oxford University Press, 2006), pp. 229–64; B. J. Harris, 'The View from My Lady's Chamber: New Perspectives on the Early Tudor Monarchy', *Huntington Library Quarterly*, 60 (1997), 215–47.

[40] Koziol, 'The Early History', p. 21.

[41] B. Gruendler and L. Marlow, 'Preface', in B. Gruendler and L. Marlow (eds), *Writers and Rulers: Perspectives on Their Relationship from Abbasid to Safavid Times* (Wiesbaden, Reichert Verlag, 2004), pp. v–xi (p. v).

[42] Rustow, *The Lost Archive*, pp. 88, 96, 207–21. Intertextuality complicates analysis of partially preserved documents. The text of one on an ostracon (shard of pottery) from ancient Egypt is 'difficult to follow … it could be a draft of a petition, but it could also be a letter'; B. Kelly, *Petitions, Litigation, and Social Control in Roman Egypt* (Oxford, Oxford University Press, 2011), p. 302.

[43] J. Luc-Fournet, 'Archives and Libraries in Greco-Roman Egypt', in A. Bausi, C. Brockmann, M. Friedrich, and S. Kienitz (eds), *Manuscripts and Archives: Comparative Views on Record-Keeping* (Berlin, De Gruyter, 2018), pp. 171–99 (pp. 194–5); Scase, *Literature and Complaint*, pp. 83–136.

administrative monarchies'[44] for control and efficiency in processing floods of petitions. Ancient Greek and Roman scribes 'weeded out the trivia' and fitted requests to the compact form of a petition, sometimes with abbreviations used in other documents.[45] The petition's sequential structure concisely expressed requests. Typical sequences in European and Near Eastern petitions were receiver/sender/narrative/request/formulaic closing. By contrast, East Asian petitions put the sender at the end. Writing on recto sides with wide margins left room for annotations that were crucial to the response side of the practice.

Responding was an extended bureaucratic procedure, with investigation, assessment, decision, orders for action, and archiving all or part of the process. Seldom could requests, upon reception, be assessed, so they were delegated to others for investigation, which often required subdelegation. Officials, with or without formal duties related to petitioning, were delegates who investigated, assessed, and sometimes decided requests. Lower-level scribes were subdelegates who checked the records when these were relevant to requests. Even for simple ones, there was more work after a decision. It had to be recorded as a warrant for performance of the action that responded to a request and archived with the petition, or as a summary in a roll or register. Much of this activity appears in concise annotations in margins and on the reverse sides of petitions. With annotations, petitions became dossiers that exemplify Max Weber's ideal type for bureaucratic administration but undermine his claim that this is a uniquely 'modern' practice:

> Administrative acts, decisions, and rules are formulated and recorded in writing, even in cases where oral discussion is the rule or is even mandatory. This applies at least to preliminary discussion and proposals to final decisions … The combination of written documents and a continuous operation by officials constitutes the 'office' (*Bureau*) which is the central focus of all types of modern organized action.[46]

Two nearly invariant protocols were receptivity to petitioners and effusively deferential rhetoric in petitions. A pervasive norm of receptivity to petitioners underpinned petition-and-response across Eurasia.[47] Diverse dominant ideologies obliged rulers and officials to receive, though not necessarily grant, deferential requests for deployments of power. The norm's enactment consumed immense time and resources. Emperors, kings, shahs, sultans, caliphs, strategoi, satraps, municipal councils, viziers, prefects, and swarms of subaltern officials spent as much time responding to petitions as issuing commands. In medieval England, 'petitions

[44] Koziol, 'Early Rites of Supplication', p. 34; G. Dodd, 'Thomas Paunfield, the "heye Court of rightwisnesse" and the Language of Petitioning in the Fifteenth Century', in Ormrod et al., *Medieval Petitions*, pp. 222–41 (p. 239); and G. Dodd, *Justice and Grace* (Oxford, Oxford University Press, 2007), pp. 279–80, 314.

[45] Hauken, 'Structure and Themes', p. 14. See also Connolly, 'Petitioning', p. 53; and N. Lewis, *Greeks in Ptolemaic Egypt* (Oxford, Oxford University Press, 1986), p. 59.

[46] M. Weber, *Economy and Society* (Berkeley, CA, University of California Press, 1978), p. 219.

[47] Equally important was agency among subjects who, when confronted by problems or opportunities, habitually sought assistance for writing and sending petitions – a most important point but one beyond the scope of this chapter.

played a significant part in the exercise of lordship', not only by kings but also by queens and magnates throughout the realm.[48] From the ancient to early modern periods, advice literature strongly commended receptivity, as did positive and negative stories and legends about rulers and officials who were receptive or hostile to petitioning.[49]

Protocols for deferential rhetoric maintained four components of petitionary genre's distinctive register. First, it denoted humility and distance in contrast to personal letters.[50] As elsewhere, petitions in medieval Islamic regimes avoided 'all form of grammatical expression of instruction to the addressee',[51] anticipating positive responses by projecting them as acts of grace that magnified the power of addressees. A pervasive trope for this projection was the 'poor' petitioner, implicating positive responses as charity and denoting the sender's ostensibly hapless condition in contrast to the receiver's power for rendering assistance.[52] Second, it justified requests by invoking formal enunciations of power as a source of benevolent assistance to subjects, which was a key intertextual aspect of petitions that transformed rulership's pretentions to power into support for a subject's request. Third, it maintained the protected status of petitioning as a privileged communicative pathway for requests and complaints – another instance of petitioning's 'subtleties'.[53] Fourth, it tactfully alluded to reciprocal relationships, as an implicit '"covenant" of mutual obligations' between rulers and subjects, notably in the Circle of Justice motif in Near Eastern political thought, where, as elsewhere, there were no intimations of *vox populi*.[54] Instead, the rhetoric signalled that positive responses to requests would satisfy and advance the interests of responders,[55]

[48] A. Musson, 'Queenship, Lordship, and Petitioning in Late Medieval England', in Ormrod et al., *Medieval Petitions*, pp. 156–72 (p. 166).

[49] D. S. Fajardo, *The Royal Politician* (London, 1700 [1640]), pp. 283–4; R. P. Saller, *Personal Patronage under the Early Empire* (Cambridge, Cambridge University Press, 2002), pp. 62–3; N. Shupak, 'A New Source for the Study of the Judiciary and Law of Ancient Egypt: "The Tale of the Eloquent Peasant"', *Journal of Near Eastern Studies*, 51 (1992), 1–18 (p. 14); Stern, 'Three Petitions', 187–8; D. J. Steward, 'The First Shaykh al-Islam of the Safavid Capital Qazvin', *Journal of the American Oriental Society*, 116 (1996), 387–405 (p. 400).

[50] Separate departments in the Roman imperial chancellery issued responses to letters and petitions.

[51] G. Khan, 'The Historical Development of the Structure of Medieval Arabic Petitions', *Bulletin of the School of Oriental and African Studies*, 53 (1990), 8–30 (p. 20).

[52] Scase, *Literature and Complaint*, pp. 88–9; Dodd, 'Thomas Paunfield', p. 230. See also S. Connolly, *Lives behind the Laws: The World of the 'Codex Hermogenianus'* (Bloomington, Indiana University Press, 2010), pp. 21–2; and H. W. Dewey and A. M. Kleimola, 'The Petition (*Čelobitnaja*) as an Old Russian Literary Genre', *Slavic and East European Journal*, 14 (1970), 284–301 (p. 285).

[53] For Tokugawa Japan, see Roberts, *Performing the Great Peace*, p. 60.

[54] W. W. Kelly, *Deference and Defiance in Nineteenth-Century Japan* (Princeton, NJ, Princeton University Press, 1985), p. 20. See also Koziol, *Begging Pardon and Favor*, pp. 55–6. For the Circle of Justice, see Darling, *A History of Social Justice*.

[55] E.g. the claim that remediation of abusive behaviour by landlords and officials would prevent peasant petitioners from fleeing and enhance their ability to pay taxes. See Hallo, 'Individual Prayer in Sumerian', 79; Hauken, 'Structure and Themes', p. 17; T. Hauken, *Petition and Response: An Epigraphic Study of Petitions to Roman Emperors 181–249* (Bergen, Norwegian Institute at Athens, 1998), pp. 41, 95–6; Kelly, *Petitions, Litigation, and Social Control*, p. 37; and Vlastos, *Peasant Protests*, pp. 34–5.

in formulaic promises to be loyal and to pray for them, as at the end of British petitions: 'And your petitioner shall ever pray & etc.'. Similar promises mark the end of Mesopotamian letter prayers and medieval Near Eastern petitions.[56]

Daily drudgery in responding to petitions prompted adjustments in the practice. Early Roman imperial administrations returned petitions with annotated responses to petitioners. Under Hadrian, direct delivery ceased: subscribed petitions were publicly displayed for petitioners who made copies, then stored in archives where they were compiled in rolls. Similar procedures existed for petitions to provincial authorities.[57] Other recording practices enrolled decisions and summaries of petitions on parchment or compiled registers with this information – the latter is the source for Chinese petitions. Fatimid petitions, with subscriptions, were returned to petitioners. Other Islamic regimes did this but also gave petitioners decrees and retained annotated petitions.[58]

Some protocols were variable and had endogenous sources of change. Most important was pressure to process relentless streams of petitions, which promoted structural change. From the late 13th century, English petitions evolved from brief requests in a single block of Anglo-Norman text, with inconsistent use of Latin, to consistent address and sequenced sections in French. English displaced French by the mid-15th century.[59] Many cross-cultural similarities in protocols arose from exogenous sources of change. After the introduction of Confucian scribal practices by the Chosŏn dynasty (1392–1910), Korean petitioning resembled Chinese practice; Japanese petitioning also adopted many precedents from China, such as petition boxes.[60] Conquest was an important exogenous source of change, although language shift in petitions was not necessarily imposed via coercion. After Ptolemaic rulers displaced pharaohs, Greek quickly replaced Demotic in petitions because it afforded new opportunities for resolving conflicts within the indigenous

[56] Hallo, 'Individual Prayer in Sumerian',77; Khan, 'The Historical Development', 8–9, 12–13.

[57] W. Clarysse, 'Tomoi Synkollēsimoi', in M. Brosius (ed.), *Ancient Archives and Archival Traditions: Concepts of Record-Keeping in the Ancient World* (Oxford, Oxford University Press, 2003), pp. 344–59 (pp. 345–6, 349–50); E. A. Meyer, *Legitimacy and Law in the Roman World: Tabulae in Roman Belief and Practice* (Cambridge, Cambridge University Press, 2004), p. 196; W. Williams, 'The *Libellus* Procedure and the Severan Papyri', *Journal of Roman Studies*, 64 (1974), 86–103 (pp. 98–100).

[58] M. R. al-Din Ansari, *Dastur al-Moluk: A Safavid State Manual*, trans. W. Floor and M. H. Faghfoory (Costa Mesa, CA, Mazda, 2007), p. 88; J. S. Nielsen, *Secular Justice in an Islamic State: Maẓālim under the Baḥrī Mamlūks 662/1264–789/1387* (Leiden, Nederlands Historisch-Archaeologisch Instituut, 1985), pp. 71–2; Stern, 'Three Petitions', p. 195, Stern, 'Petitions from the Mamlūk Period', pp. 245, 254, 263, 267; M. Ursinus, *Grievance Administration (Şikayet) in an Ottoman Province* (London, Routledge, 2005), p. 2.

[59] P. Brand, 'Petitions and Parliament in the Reign of Edward I', *Parliamentary History*, 23 (2004), 14–38 (pp. 24–7); Dodd, *Justice and Grace*, pp. 20, 288–9. See Rustow, *The Lost Archive*, pp. 88, 96, 207–21, on elaboration of formulary for Fatimid petitions that previously resembled simple letters.

[60] Q. Fang, 'Hot Potatoes: Chinese Complaint Systems from Early Times to the Late Qing', *Journal of Asian Studies*, 68 (2009), 1105–35 (p. 1107); J. Koo, 'The Origins of the Public Sphere and Civil Society: Private Academies and Petitions in Korea, 1506–1800, *Social Science History*, 31 (2007), 381–409 (pp. 392–3); Sang-kwŏn, 'The Development of the Petition System'; Roberts, 'The Petition Box'.

population. Another prominent example is the expansion and consolidation of East India Company rule over South Asia, as British conventions for petitioning 'became the most ubiquitous means to appeal for redress, resolve disputes, or stake claims to resources'.[61]

Petitioning and Related Genre I: Supplication

Petitioning and supplication often appear as interchangeable labels, especially in studies of medieval European petitions. However, supplication and petitioning were not identical: their apparent similarity conceals differences between these practices in terms of their intertextual and historical connections. Confusion over this point arises from local (European) usage: petition and supplication, petitioner and supplicant were interchangeable words, deriving from the Latin *supplicatio*. Petitioners were sometimes called supplicants, for example, in the early modern Dutch Republic, even though they 'were never allowed to present their case in person'.[62]

This conflation is problematic if the practice of supplication is construed precisely as highly stylised gestures and deferential oral requests in face-to-face interaction.[63] Supplication preceded petitioning as an archaic practice for deferential requests. Its hallmark is 'demonstrative submission' that, in animal behaviour, deters aggressors and, in human action, conveys submissive requests for mercy or other vital assistance.[64] Archaeological and literary evidence displays a related set of gestures for ancient supplicants, such as prostration and kissing the hands of recipients. The supplicatory act in face-to-face interaction was as pervasive in power relations as the subsequent practice of petition-and-response, and both coexisted to nearly the end of the early modern era.

Petitioners supplicated when they directly presented petitions to rulers and high officials, notably in spectacular public ceremonies that now provoke scholarly debate over naïve and not-so-naïve monarchism. But the vast bulk of petitions entered the apparatus of petition-and-response via unspectacular, bureaucratic encounters between petitioners and receiving officials. There are many intertextual connections between the practices, in petitionary rhetoric that refers to supplicatory gestures. Formularies in Fatimid and later Islamic petitioning refer to Sasanian and Byzantine prostration: petitioners are slaves who kiss the ground.[65] Old Russian

[61] B. Raman, *Document Raj: Writing and Scribes in Early Colonial South India* (Chicago, IL, University of Chicago Press, 2012), p. 161.
[62] H. F. K. van Nierop, 'Popular Participation in Politics in the Dutch Republic', in P. Blickle (ed.), *Resistance, Representation, and Community* (Oxford, Oxford University Press, 1997), pp. 272–90 (p. 285).
[63] Here I follow F. S. Naiden, *Ancient Supplication* (Oxford, Oxford University Press, 2006), p. 24.
[64] W. Burkert, *Creation of the Sacred: Tracks of Biology in Early Religions* (Cambridge, MA, Harvard University Press, 1996), pp. 85–6.
[65] Khan, 'The Historical Development', 24–6; Stern, 'Three Petitions', 190–2.

petitioners were 'forehead knockers', employing the prevailing obeisance gesture.[66] The suggestion that petitionary genre derived from supplication as it was adapted to documentary culture in premodern administration gains support from many other common elements between the practices.[67] Supplication ritual established protected communicative spaces for requests, secured in petitions by effusively deferential rhetoric. Other common elements are receptivity to supplicants; discretion by recipients in responding; intimations of reciprocity that tactfully invoke past, present, or future loyalty and service; and the amount of time consumed by the activity.[68]

Petitioning and Related Genre II: Prayer

Relationships between these genres are more complex than connections between petitioning and supplication. Petitioning unambiguously derived from supplication. That historical connection does not hold for petitioning and prayer, despite other evident links between the practices in many times and places. Examples include the same word for petitions to Chinese rulers and those to supernatural officials in the Taoist celestial bureaucracy, and, in the ancient Near East, words that 'referred both to entreating deities and to asking favors from mortals'.[69] Nonetheless, connections between petition-and-response and religious prayer are nearly the opposite of what is suggested by observing that 'petitions to rulers have the structure of a prayer', followed 'protocols of the heavenly court', and 'were essentially prayers'.[70] They were so understood by contemporaries, but it is misleading to treat this intertextuality as evidence for a historical link between the practices. The reverse claim is more accurate.

Petitionary prayer in religious liturgies drew on conventions for deferential requests in worldly affairs as a key precedent. In this context, the salience of petition-and-response for development of petitionary prayer arose from

[66] Dewey and Kleimola, 'The Petition', 285; T. Keirstead, 'The Theatre of Protest: Petitions, Oaths, and Rebellion in the Shōen', *Journal of Japanese Studies*, 16 (1990), 357–88 (p. 385).

[67] F. B. Knutson, 'Cuneiform Letters and Social Conventions', *Semeia*, 22 (1981), 15–23 (pp. 16–20).

[68] Naiden, *Ancient Supplication*, pp. 31, 79, 220. Cf. an influential account of supplication ritual as contact magic that forces positive responses to requests: J. Gould, 'Hiketeia', *Journal of Hellenic Studies*, 93 (1973), 74–103.

[69] M. I. Gruber, *Aspects of Non-Verbal Communication in the Ancient Near East* (Rome, Biblical Institute Press, 1980), p. 84. See also P. R. Katz, 'Indictment Rituals and the Judicial Continuum in Late Imperial China', in R. E. Hegel and K. Carlitz (eds), *Writing and Law in Late Imperial China* (Seattle, University of Washington Press, 2007), pp. 161–88 (pp. 162–5); and P. R. Katz, *Divine Justice: Religion and the Development of Chinese Legal Culture* (Abingdon, Routledge, 2009), pp. 12, 192.

[70] Connolly, *Lives behind the Laws*, p. 2; Koziol, 'Early Rites of Supplication', pp. 29, 31. See also Dodd, *Justice and Grace*, pp. 284–85; Würgler, 'Voices', pp. 15–16; Dodd and Petit-Renaud, 'Grace and Favour', p. 244; and Raman, *Document Raj*, p. 164.

'a scribal view of bureaucratic rule'.[71] This holds for Mesopotamian 'letter prayers', developed by scribes who applied the format of letter orders to deferential requests to rulers and deities: 'both were petitioned in similar terms'.[72] More than a millennium later, an Aramaic template for petitions 'was present in the intellectual repertoire of the scribes at least from Neo-Assyrian times on', and reappears in biblical prayers.[73] The template was Roman petitioning when St Augustine thought about intercession and compared Christ's mediating role in prayer to the assistance of scribes in getting good responses to properly framed petitions to emperors.[74]

Elsewhere, petition-and-response as a template for petitionary prayer is well documented, for example, in the transition from shamanic practices to the Celestial Master lineage of Taoism in the late Han era.[75] Its central ritual, the Great Petition, replaced magical 'bargaining' in Shang ancestor worship, which conceived 'ancestral powers as occupying a hierarchy of negotiability'.[76] This liturgical practice composed petitions that were imaginatively sent to diverse offices and functionaries in a celestial bureaucracy. These petitions, 'like any genre of court communication, followed a closely regulated format', with sequenced sections and deferential rhetoric. A priestly manual, the *Petition Almanac of Master Red Pine*, contains many model petitions with requests as diverse as those in worldly petitions. Some were a defence against sepulchral plaints by the dead that caused worldly misfortune. Others include a *Petition for Keeping away Robbers*, another *for Stopping Officials*, and a *Petition for Preventing Locusts and Rats from Eating Seedlings*. The liturgy's 'thoroughgoing bureaucratism' also appears in *Master Red Pine's* instructions for sending heavenly petitions to the appropriate office in *Protocol of the Twelve*

[71] L. K. Handy, *Among the Host of of Heaven: The Syro-Palestinian Pantheon as Bureaucracy* (Winona Lake, IN, Eisenbrauns, 1994), p. 177.

[72] Hallo, 'Individual Prayer', 75–7; and see K. V. D. Toorn, *Family Religion in Babylonia, Ugarit and Israel* (Leiden, Brill, 1996), pp. 133–4.

[73] F. M. Fales, 'Aramaic Letters and Neo-Assyrian Letters: Philological and Methodological Notes', *Journal of the American Oriental Society*, 107 (1987), 451–69 (p. 467). See also T. Mullins, 'Petitions as a Literary Form', *Novum testamentum*, 5 (1962), 46–54; and F. R. Magdalene, 'Trying the Crime of Abuse of Royal Authority', in A. Mermelstein and S. E. Holtz (eds), *The Divine Courtroom in Comparative Perspective* (Leiden, Brill, 2015), pp. 167–245 (pp. 187, 198–9).

[74] C. Humfress, *Orthodoxy and the Courts in Late Antiquity* (Oxford, Oxford University Press, 2007), p. 79.

[75] P. Nickerson, 'The Great Petition for Sepulchral Plaints', in S. R. Bokenkamp, *Early Daoist Scriptures* (Berkeley, University of California Press, 1997), pp. 230–74. See also G. Raz, *The Emergence of Daoism* (New York, Routledge, 2012), p. 34, for other Taoist lineages with the 'bureaucratic petitioning model of ritual'.

[76] D. N. Keightley, 'The Making of Ancestors: Late Shang Religion and Its Legacy', in J. Lagerwey (ed.), *Religion and Chinese Society* (Hong Kong, Chinese University of Hong Kong Press, 2004), pp. 3–64 (pp. 9–11). The Great Petition rite provided 'a structural framework to functions that it took over from the exorcists and shamans'; Bokenkamp, *Early Daoist Scriptures*, p. 5.

Hundred Officials, 'an inventory of the bureaucracy with the names of lords presiding over each office, their residences and their subordinate staff'.[77]

These, and other examples,[78] should dispel any simple notion of religious prayer as an overarching template for petition-and response, even though robust homologies between the practices are reasonably regarded as mutually reinforcing practices at any point in time.

Petitioning and Related Genre III: Plaints

Before states had specialised legal systems with formal law codes, petitions with plaints about unjust acts received responses that indexed general notions of equity.[79] In East Asia, where there was no legal profession, 'the distinction between petitions or requests and what we would call suits or legal action is not at all clear'.[80] Petitions as formal legal devices for initiating litigation arose in systems of law that hived off petitioning as a general practice. In this development, organisational preceded doctrinal changes, driven by the growing scale of empire. Long before law codes and jurisprudence, there were protocols pertaining to venue and appeal for petitions with plaints. Ancient Egyptian viziers directed some petitions to local authorities and adjudicated others, notably those about official misconduct. By the middle of the 2nd millennium BCE there were multiple routes for petitions with different types of complaint.[81] In China, a rudimentary appeal system in the Han era evolved into the medieval Censorate, whose officials sent appeal petitions to emperors or local officials for reconsideration.[82] The development of Roman law codes that regulated adjudication was a natural extension of petitioning rulers with the expectation that they would refer matters to others for investigation.[83] Jurists compiled law codes from responses (rescripts) to petitions to Roman emperors that sought clarification, correction, or expedition of legal proceedings, selecting

[77] F. Verellen, 'The Heavenly Master Liturgical Agenda According to Chisong Zi's Petition Almanac', *Cahiers d'Extrême-Asie*, 14 (2004), 291–343 (pp. 297–9, 309, 311); Nickerson, 'The Great Petition', 234.

[78] Egyptian letters to the dead in the Late Kingdom have a petitionary format and refer to litigation in underworld courts.

[79] R. VerSteeg, *Early Mesopotamian Law* (Durham, NC, Carolina Academic Press, 2000); R. VerSteeg, *Law in Ancient Egypt* (Durham, NC, Carolina Academic Press, 2002).

[80] H. Ooms, *Tokugawa Village Practice: Class, Status, Power, Law* (Berkeley, University of California Press, 1996), p. 8. See also Kelly, *Petitions, Litigation, and Social Control*, p. 87; and C. F. Minzer, 'Xinfang: An Alternative to Formal Chinese Legal Institutions', *Stanford Journal of International Law*, 42 (2006), 103–79 (pp. 109–14).

[81] Shupak, 'A New Source'; Van den Boorn, *Duties of the Vizier*, pp. 147–8, 165–70, 190–91, 316–7; VerSteeg, *Law in Ancient Egypt*, p. 110–13.

[82] J. Ocko, 'I'll Take It All the Way to Beijing: Capital Appeals in the Qing', *Journal of Asian Studies*, 47 (1988), 291–315 (pp. 291, 294–5).

[83] J. Harries, *Law and Empire in Late Antiquity* (Cambridge, Cambridge University Press, 2001), pp. 104–5; Humfress, *Orthodoxy and the Courts*, pp. 41–3; W. Turpin, 'Imperial Subscriptions and the Administration of Justice', *Journal of Roman Studies*, 81 (1991), 101–18 (p. 117).

responses (probably drafted by jurists) with general implications and compiling them in eponymous codes such as *Codex Theodosianus*.[84]

In the medieval evolution of increasingly autonomous legal systems, complex connections persisted between legal systems and petition-and-response. The latter was adapted as a remedy for defects in legal systems, e.g. miscarriages of justice, problems with no legal remedies, and inconsistencies or contradictions in law.[85] In Islamic civilisation, Mazalim courts dispensed equitable remedies and operated alongside courts that followed Sharia; in England, chancery and other courts of equity provided such remedies, initially with far more flexible procedures than those by writ in common law courts.[86] According to a medieval chancellor, there was no requirement that pleadings 'should be in every point certain … after the solemnity of common law, for here there is only petition'.[87]

Conclusion

Across premodern Eurasia, petition-and-response originated and figured prominently in fields of power, where it was as generic as its inverse twin, command-and-obey. Both were indispensable for regulating transactions among rulers, officials, and subjects. Two principal premises for an adequate definition of the premodern petition are, first, its status as an instrument of state, framed by the administrative context for receiving, investigating, and responding to it, and, second, the precedence of petitioning practice as genre for analysing petitions. Deployments of the genre produced endlessly diverse petitions, while the genre mutated as it transposed to new situations and became entangled with other generic practices.

As much as orders flowing down chains of command, the reverse flow of deferential requests moving up was indispensable to premodern governance. It enabled the limited capacity of political centres to penetrate peripheries by a mechanism other than actual or imagined brute force, by what Michael Mann calls 'infrastructural power'.[88] Historical research on petitioning amply documents this point, which

[84] *Codex Gregorianus* and *Codex Hermogenianus* are earlier codes compiled from imperial rescripts.

[85] In medieval England, the complex connection also moved in the opposite direction, as common law procedure by writ developed as an alternative to cumbersome procedures for plaints in petitions to kings and their councils in Parliament; A. Harding, *Medieval Law and the Foundations of the State* (Oxford, Oxford University Press, 2001), pp. 186–9.

[86] Ibid., pp. 182–4; T. S. Haskett, 'The Medieval English Court of Chancery', *Law and History Review*, 14 (1996), 245–313; A. H. Hershey, 'Justice and Bureaucracy: The English Royal Writ and "1258"', *English Historical Review*, 113 (1998), 829–51; Nielsen, *Secular Justice*, pp. 23–6, 76–7; Stern, 'Three Petitions', p. 188; There were no Mazalim courts in the Ottoman Empire, where petitioning the sultan provided equitable remedies.

[87] I. S. Leadam and J. F. Baldwin (eds), *Select Cases before the King's Council, 1243–1482* (Cambridge, MA, Harvard University Press, 1918), p. xxxvi. Tudor regimes created the Court of Requests, which also proceeded by petition-and-response.

[88] M. Mann, *The Sources of Social Power: A History of Power from the Beginning to A.D. 1760* (Cambridge, Cambridge University Press, 1986). Ironically, premodern localities used petitioning to acquire infrastructural improvements (riverine and harbour projects, roads, bridges, city walls).

Mann and other leading theorists of power overlook.[89] An area for further enquiry is the disconnection between meticulous historical studies of petitioning and leading social science theories of power that have been applied to premodern societies by sociologists including Pierre Bourdieu, Charles Tilly, and Michael Mann, political scientists such as Margaret Levi, and anthropologist James Scott. In their extensive work on premodern social worlds, the near complete absence of petition-and-response is astounding.[90] Different disciplines, intellectual sources, and political and metatheoretical commitments make their theories of power a mixed bag of ideas, nonetheless united by the presumption, thought to be self-evident, that deployments of power invariably harm those subject to them – completely so by predatory premodern states. Of course, treating a proposition as self-evident does not validate it, especially if it violates massive evidence from a mountain of historical studies of petitioning across premodern Eurasia.

[89] For comparable criticism, see He, *Public Interest and State Legitimation*, 3, 7, 9–13, 186–7.

[90] A very partial exception is scattered remarks by Charles Tilly (see p. 36) that misconstrue premodern petitions as instruments of protest. See J. C. Scott, *Domination and the Arts of Resistance* (New Haven, CT, Yale University Press, 1990), pp. 63, 95, 158, for a bad caricature of 'the desperate act of petitioning', which supposedly was a capital crime in Tokugawa Japan. Violation of rules for petitioning was a crime, but illicit petitioning nonetheless was widely practised and tolerated in Japan (p. 39).

2

Petitions and Petitioning through the Ages: Etymology and Historical Semantics

JORIS ODDENS

MUCH HAS BEEN written, in this volume and elsewhere, about what petitions are and how they can be defined. This chapter aims to provide a missing piece of this puzzle by addressing a fresh set of questions. Which words have been used to describe petitionary practices since Roman antiquity? What are the etymological origins of these words? For which types of petitions have these terms been used and how have different synonyms for 'petition' semantically related to one another? If we want to be able to give a historical answer to the more general question of what petitions are, we need to be aware of the different words people had at their disposal to refer to petitionary instruments in different historical contexts and places. The meanings of these instruments could be prescribed by legal definitions, but such definitions always left room for interpretation and were often departed from, if they existed at all. To petitioners and authorities alike, what mattered at least as much in actual petitionary practice was the relative meaning and connotation of different words for petitionary texts within a given lexical field.

It is crucial to adopt a comparative perspective in choosing this approach, as this enables us to identify broader patterns and trends as well as instances of political transfer, but also to appreciate the specificity of developments in singular linguistic and political contexts. This chapter compares some of the most widely spoken languages of the Germanic and Romance families, namely English, German, Dutch, Swedish, Danish, French, Italian, Spanish, and Portuguese, which have historically made use of words that derived from Latin and older Germanic languages. The choice of these languages was dictated by the assumption that the political entities where they were spoken had related petitioning cultures, and therefore constitute a coherent unit of analysis.

Proceedings of the British Academy, **262**, 51–67, © The British Academy 2024.

Of course the historical practice of petitioning stretches far beyond the Germanic- and Romance-speaking regions. It is certainly desirable also to consider other language families in future study of this type, but this is a task for which others are better equipped.[1]

Ancient and Medieval Latin

In ancient Latin, written petitions were initially called *preces*, *libellus*, *querella*, or *supplicatio/supplicium*. *Preces* is the plural form of *prex* ('prayer'). In liturgical worship, the plural form has been used since ancient times to refer to the versicles sung by the officiant, which required a response from the congregation. *Libellus*, a diminutive of *liber* ('book'), could be used for any short, written document: a booklet, a pamphlet, an official government-issued document, or indeed a petition. The adjective *supplex* ('suppliant', 'humble') was usually added if those using the term wanted to make sure the document was understood as a petition. During the Roman Republic, administrators received *libelli* about judicial matters. After the fall of the Republic, emperors too became chief recipients of *libelli* because they held supreme legal authority. During the reign of Hadrian (117–38 CE), the practice of petitioning the emperor was formalised and a system of petition and response (*libellus–subscriptio*) was developed.[2] The word *querella* was specifically used for protests or complaints presented to Roman emperors by local communities.[3]

The noun *supplicatio* and its cognate *supplicium* are derived from the verb *supplicare* ('pray', 'supplicate'), which in turn derives from *supplex*.[4] This adjective *supplex* is thought to be made up of the prefix *sub-* (under') and either *plicare* ('bend') or *placare* ('appease').[5] A *supplicatio* originally referred not to a written

[1] See, for a broad overview of literature on petitioning in other linguistic contexts, D. Zaret, 'Petition-and-Response and Liminal Petitioning in Comparative/Historical Perspective', *Social Science History*, 43 (2019), 431–51.

[2] T. Hauken, *Petition and Response: An Epigraphic Study of Petitions to Roman Emperors 181–249* (Bergen, Norwegian Institute at Athens, 1998); A. J. B. Sirks, 'Making a Request to the Emperor: Rescripts in the Roman Empire', in L. de Blois (ed.), *Administration, Prosopography, and Appointment Policies in the Roman Empire* (Leiden, Brill, 2001), pp. 121–35; S. Connolly, 'Petitioning in the Ancient World', in W. M. Ormrod, G. Dodd, and A. Musson (eds), *Medieval Petitions: Grace and Grievance* (York, York Medieval Press, 2009), pp. 47–63.

[3] T. Hauken, 'Structure and Themes in Petitions to Roman Emperors', in D. Feissel and J. Gascou (eds), *La pétition à Byzance* (Paris, Association des Amis du Centre d'Histoire et Civilisation de Byzance, 2004), pp. 11–22 (p. 12).

[4] C. Février, *Supplicare deis: La supplication expiatoire à Rome* (Turnhout, Brepols, 2009), pp. 18–20.

[5] G. Freyburger, 'Supplication grecque et supplication romaine', *Latomus*, 47 (1988), 501–25 (p. 515).

document but to a series of related but different ritual acts. The ritual meanings that could be conveyed by performing these acts were individual offerings to the gods, worship, public prayer, thanksgiving, or supplication. In this last meaning, a *supplicatio* is a ritualistic combination of gestures and words that is much older than Roman antiquity. The gestures used in this ritual act vary across cultures, but they often include the clasping of the knees or the kissing of the hand of the *supplicandus* (the object of the act of supplication). Jews and Romans also prostrated themselves at the feet of the *supplicandus*. In Roman antiquity, suppliants communicated their intent to supplicate with the word *supplico* (first person singular of *supplicare*), but they may also have used its synonyms *obsecrare* ('entreat') or *deprecare* ('beseech').[6]

Suppliants in antiquity had the choice between supplicating to a person (or a group of persons) or a god. The more powerful a deity, the more supplications it received.[7] According to F. S. Naiden, ancient Greeks and Romans distinguished supplication, in the sense that concerns us here, from the ritual of prayer, even if they used, among other synonyms, the same word for both rituals (in Greek *hiketeia*, in Latin *supplicatio*):

> In prayer, the gods are the addressees. In supplication, a human being [the priest of the altar] is the addressee, or, if the suppliant goes to an altar, and persons controlling the altar respond to him in a god's name, they and the god are joint addressees … The addressee in a prayer is absent. In supplication, the addressee is present.[8]

In Naiden's view, there was no fundamental difference between supplicating to persons and supplicating to gods. Suppliants may have chosen a god over a person because the powerful ruler they aimed for was not within their reach, in which case they chose the more accessible option of a powerful god at a nearby altar instead.[9] Another possibility was for an individual or a group to supplicate a distant ruler by sending them an epistolary supplication. Such petitions could also be handed to a ruler in person.[10]

Both oral and written supplications survived into postclassical times. We do not have any extant petitions from Romance and Germanic writing cultures during the early Middle Ages, but we have the written acts that kings issued in response to them.[11] According to Geoffrey Koziol, the verbs used to describe the request in these acts were usually *petere* ('seek', 'beg') or *suggere* ('advise', 'suggest') until

[6] F. S. Naiden, *Ancient Supplication* (Oxford, Oxford University Press, 2006), pp. 42–50.
[7] Ibid., pp. 29–37.
[8] Ibid., p. 7.
[9] Ibid., pp. 36–8.
[10] Ibid., pp. 385–8; Sirks, 'Making a Request', p. 122.
[11] G. Koziol, 'The Early History of Rites of Supplication', in H. Millet (ed.), *Suppliques et requêtes: Le gouvernement par la grâce en Occident (XIIe–XVe siècle)* (Rome, École française de Rome, 2003), pp. 21–36 (p. 25).

the end of Charlemagne's reign (814) – in his view words that belonged to the language of Roman imperial transcripts. 'Thereafter', Koziol writes,

> the petition was increasingly assimilated to prayer, as the petitioner was said to 'beseech', 'implore', or 'supplicate' the king (*deprecare*, *obsecrare*, *supplicare*). Appropriate for entreaties to God, such words were also appropriate for entreaties addressed to God's ruler. *Suggere*, though still appropriate, became much rarer; *petere*, however, remained common because it too had an important place in the liturgy.[12]

If both Naiden and Koziol are right, the various meanings of the word *supplicatio* (prayer and supplication), which were distinguished from one another in Roman antiquity, became more conflated in the Middle Ages on account of the rise of the doctrine of the divine right of kings: a petition, in Koziol's words, was 'a prayer to a king who ruled on behalf of God, took his authority from God, modelled his authority on God's, and therefore, like God, received humble petitions from his faithful'.[13] Specific types of petitions for which in the Middle Ages other words were used, such as the *clamor*, a plea for the redress of wrongs, and the *deditio*, with which a defeated rebel begged for mercy, were also modelled on religious rituals.[14]

In the *Codex Justinianus* (529 CE), where the word for written petition was *supplicatio*, petitionary procedure was regulated in detail. In postclassical Roman civil procedure, the word *supplicatio* also came to be used, together with *appelatio*, to describe an instrument of appeal that could be employed to challenge legal decisions.[15] During the later Middle Ages, the term *supplicatio* met with increasing competition from *petitio*, derived from *petere*, which in the Roman Empire had been in use at least as early as the 4th century.[16] In the papal curia, which from the early Middle Ages onwards became a very important recipient of oral supplications and (ever more) written petitions, both *supplicatio* and *petitio* were used to describe the latter.[17] In the 13th century, intermediaries that assisted in drawing up petitions to the pope were known as *petitionarii*.[18]

In England, *petitio* came to be used alongside *billa*. Although both words were interchangeable, *billa* was more often used in legal contexts, such as the institutions of the general eyre, the common law courts, and the chancery; while *petitio* had the connotation of royal grace, so this term was more customary in the context of appealing to the king or Parliament.[19] The French chancery, which

[12] G. Koziol, *Begging Pardon and Favor: Ritual and Political Order in Early Medieval France* (Ithaca, NY, Cornell University Press, 1992), pp. 25–6.

[13] Koziol, 'The Early History', p. 29. Cf. D. Nicholls, 'Addressing God as Ruler: Prayer and Petition', *British Journal of Sociology*, 44 (1991), 125–41.

[14] Koziol, 'The Early History', p. 33.

[15] H. Neuhaus, *Reichstag und Supplikationsausschuß: Ein Beitrag zur Reichsverfassungsgeschichte der ersten Hälfte des 16. Jahrhunderts* (Berlin, Duncker & Humblot, 1977), pp. 77–8.

[16] R. W. Mathisen, '*Adnotatio* and *Petitio*: The Emperor's Favor and Special Exceptions in the Early Byzantine Empire', in Feissel and Gascou, *La pétition à Byzance*, pp. 23–32.

[17] P. Zutshi, 'Petitions to the Pope in the Fourteenth Century', in Ormrod et al., *Medieval Petitions*, pp. 82–98 (p. 82).

[18] Ibid., p. 86.

[19] G. Dodd, *Justice and Grace: Private Petitioning and the English Parliament in the Late Middle Ages* (Oxford, Oxford University Press, 2007), p. 1 n. 2.

modelled its petitionary administration on the papal curia, mainly used *petitio*, but in France *supplicatio* continued to be common as well.[20] In addition, other synonyms made their appearance: in the papers of two councillors of King Philip the Fair (r. 1285–1314), for instance, a distinction is made among *supplicationes*, *petitiones*, *querimonie*, and *gravamina*.[21]

Querimonie, or also *querelae* ('plaints'), were words that were used to refer to complaints about the misconduct of royal officials.[22] *Gravamina* ('grievances'), which is the plural form of *gravamen* ('burden'), usually refers to a petitionary document that lists multiple demands or complaints. *Gravamina* originated as (initially mostly ecclesiastical) protests that were submitted by estates to their lord on the occasion of a meeting of a representative assembly.[23] The word gradually came to be used more generally for petitions listing multiple complaints throughout late medieval Europe. The earliest documented occurrence of the word dates to the thirteenth century.[24] *Gravamina* was sometimes used interchangeably with other words, such as *desideria* ('wishes').[25]

Late Medieval and Early Modern Vernaculars

In England, *petitio* became *petition* (initially spelled more commonly as *peticion*) when French started to replace Latin during the reign of Edward I (1272–1307), and it remained *petition* when French was in turn replaced by English in the early 15th century.[26] *Supplication* was rarer in the meaning of written petition, although petitioners often called themselves *suppli(c)ants*. The English equivalent of *billa*

[20] C. V. Langlois, 'Lettres missives, suppliques, pétitions, doléances', in *Histoire littéraire de la France*, Vol. XXXVI (Paris, Imprimerie nationale, 1927), pp. 531–76 (p. 549).

[21] Ibid.

[22] A. Harding, *Medieval Law and the Foundations of the State* (Oxford, Oxford University Press, 2002), pp. 155–61.

[23] A. Würgler, 'Voices from among the "Silent Masses": Humble Petitions and Social Conflicts in Early Modern Central Europe', in L. Heerma van Voss (ed.), *Petitions in Social History*, Supplement 9 of *International Review of Social History*, 46 (2001), 11–34 (p. 14).

[24] W. R. Jones, 'Bishops, Politics, and the Two Laws: The *Gravamina* of the English Clergy, 1237–1399', *Speculum*, 41 (1966), 209–45; P. A. Linehan, 'The *Gravamina* of the Castilian Church in 1262–3', *English Historical Review*, 85 (1970), 730–54.

[25] B. Kümin and A. Würgler, 'Petitions, *Gravamina*, and the Early Modern State: Local Influence on Central Legislation in England and Germany (Hesse)', *Parliaments, Estates and Representation*, 17 (1997), 39–60 (p. 41).

[26] G. Dodd and S. Petit-Renaud, 'Grace and Favour: The Petition and Its Mechanisms', in C. Fletcher, J.-P. Genet, and J. Watts (eds), *Government and Political Life in England and France, c. 1300–c. 1500* (Cambridge, Cambridge University Press, 2015), pp. 240–79 (p. 243); P. Brand, 'Petitions and Parliament in the Reign of Edward I', *Parliamentary History*, 23 (2004), 14–38 (p. 24); G. Dodd, 'The Rise of English, the Decline of French: Supplications to the English Crown, c. 1420–1450', *Speculum*, 86 (2011), 117–50; G. Dodd, 'Blood, Brains, and Bay-Windows: The Use of English in Fifteenth-Century Parliamentary Petitions', in T. W. Smith and H. Killick (eds), *Petitions and Strategies of Persuasion in the Middle Ages: The English Crown and the Church, c. 1200–c. 1550* (York, York Medieval Press, 2018), pp. 11–39.

was *bill*. As mentioned, *petition* and *bill* were often used interchangeably in the Middle Ages; this continued until well into the 17th century.[27] From the 15th century onwards, however, the distinction between the two began to be more sharply drawn. Parliamentary clerks started to consider documents with a petitionary (in effect supplicatory) opening phrase as *petitions*, while they considered documents without such a phrase, which were already drafted in the way the petitioners wanted to have them enacted by the king, as *bills*.[28] Such *bills* could be concerned both with public and with private matters.[29]

Another distinction that had existed in the parliamentary context of late medieval England was that between 'private' and 'common' *petitions*. The petitions of the first category could be presented to the king and his council personally by individuals or groups, but more often petitioners commissioned their representative in Parliament to present it for them. From the 1370s and more commonly in the course of the 15th century, such petitions began to be addressed to the Commons rather than to the king directly.[30] Common *petitions* were petitions presented by the Commons to the king, on their own behalf or on the behalf of a group of subjects.[31] By the end of the 16th century, *bills* had almost wholly displaced common *petitions*, although Parliament continued occasionally to use the petitionary format in addressing the Crown.[32] While individuals and groups had over time come to prefer proceeding by private *bills* over proceeding by private *petitions*, a legislative crisis in the 1620s again led to a sharp increase of petitioning at the cost of presenting *bills*.[33]

Henceforth, *petition* was to remain the dominant term in the British parliamentary context.[34] However, in the 17th century new words entered the English vocabulary to describe new types of petitions. As Mark Knights states elsewhere in this volume, *remonstrances* (med. Latin: *remonstrare*, 'demonstrate') – and

[27] R. W. Hoyle, 'Petitioning as Popular Politics in Early Sixteenth-Century England', *Historical Research*, 75 (2002), 365–89 (p. 367); E. R. Foster, 'Petitions and the Petition of Right', *Journal of British Studies*, 14 (1974), 21–45 (p. 26).

[28] Dodd, *Justice and Grace*, p. 1 n. 2; G. R. Elton, 'The Rolls of Parliament, 1449–1547', *Historical Journal*, 22 (1979), 1–29 (p. 16).

[29] A. Thrush, 'Legislation and Petitions', in A. Thrush and J. P. Ferris (eds), *The History of Parliament: The House of Commons 1604–1629* (Cambridge, Cambridge University Press, 2010), available at www.historyofparliamentonline.org/volume/1604-1629/survey/xi-legislation-and-petitions (accessed 20 January 2024).

[30] A. R. Myers, 'Parliamentary Petitions in the Fifteenth Century: Part I. Petitions from Individuals or Groups', *English Historical Review*, 52 (1937), 389–91 (pp. 398–40).

[31] A. R. Myers, 'Parliamentary Petitions in the Fifteenth Century: Part II. Petitions of the Commons and Common Petitions', *English Historical Review*, 52 (1937), 690–13; Dodd, *Justice and Grace*, pp. 126–55. See also Gwilym Dodd's chapter in this volume.

[32] Foster, 'Petitions and the Petition of Right', 27–8.

[33] Thrush, 'Legislation and Petitions'.

[34] Philip Loft found that between 1660 and 1788, all petitioners to the Westminster Parliament described their documents as *petitions*, except in four cases. I am indebted to Philip Loft for this information. See also P. Loft, 'Petitioning and Petitioners to the Westminster Parliament, 1660–1788', *Parliamentary History*, 38 (2019), 342–61.

representations (Latin: *repraesentare*, 'make present') were documents that did not have the supplicatory form of *petitions* but adopted a plainer, sometimes more confrontational style; both of these terms had entered the English language from French.[35] *Memorial* (Latin: *memorare*, 'bring to remembrance', 'recount'), originally a word with a different meaning in English, came to be used to describe lengthy documents that were usually presented by merchants and other sectional groups, typically to the executive branch of government.[36]

A very common type of petition became the (*humble* or *loyal*) *address*. The noun *address* emanated from the verb *to address* (*oneself*) *to* (*someone*), under the influence of French, where this nominalisation had taken place earlier. In a published text written in French by King James I of England and VI of Scotland, and translated into English in 1616, mention is made of 'remonstrances and addresses', but here *address* probably means orally delivered speech.[37] The meaning of petitionary document, which did not exist in French, seems to have become established in the 1640s, when such speeches began to be printed.[38] Over the course of the century, the term *address* came to be used for formal communications that could contain a subtle request, but did not necessarily do so, and usually deployed a panegyrical or acclamatory form. They could serve the function of 'acclaiming, congratulating, thanking, assuring the addressee of allegiance and loyalty, or abhorring something done by others', but they could also be 'vehicles for expressing more subversive opinions'.[39] *Addresses* were typically addressed by official bodies to the monarch or, during the Commonwealth, to the Lord Protector.[40] In practice, the distinction among address, petition, and other terms was not always upheld: in 1661 the restored monarchy passed an 'Act against Tumultuous Petitioning' that applied to 'any petition, complaint, remonstrance, declaration, or other addresses' presented to the monarch or Parliament.[41]

35 See the contribution by Mark Knights in this volume.

36 P. Gauci, *The Politics of Trade: The Overseas Merchant in State and Society, 1660–1720* (Oxford, Oxford University Press 2001), pp. 127–35; R. Huzzey and H. Miller, 'The Politics of Petitioning: Parliament, Government and Subscriptional Cultures in the United Kingdom, 1780–1918', *History*, 106 (2021), 221–43.

37 James I, *A Remonstrance of the Most Gratious King Iames I ... For the Right of Kings* (Cambridge, Cantrell Legge, 1616), p. 96; cf. *Oxford English Dictionary*, www.oed.com, s.v. 'address' (accessed 20 January 2024).

38 The two earliest printed *addresses* in the English Short Title Catalogue both date to 1647: *The Humble Petition and Address of Divers Young Men* (London, n.p., 1647); and *The Humble Address of the Agitators of the Army to His Excellency Sir Thomas Fairfax* (London, J. Harris, [1647]).

39 M. Knights, *Representation and Misrepresentation in Later Stuart Britain: Partisanship and Political Culture* (Oxford, Oxford University Press), pp. 112, 118; Huzzey and Miller, 'The Politics of Petitioning', 235.

40 E. Vallance, 'Petitioning, Addressing and the Historical Imagination: The Case of Great Yarmouth, England 1658–1784', *Parliaments, Estates and Representation*, 38 (2018), 364–77 (pp. 365–6); E. Vallance, *Loyalty, Memory and Public Opinion in England, 1658–1727* (Manchester, Manchester University Press, 2019).

41 Quoted in J. Innes, 'Legislation and Public Participation, 1760–1830', in D. Lemmings (ed.), *The British and Their Laws in the Eighteenth Century* (Woodbridge, Boydell Press, 2005), pp. 102–32 (p. 105).

In other places and institutional contexts in the anglophone world, the terminology was different. In 17th-century Scotland, for instance, petitions were much more often called *supplication* than *petition*.[42] In the American colonies, *memorial* seems to have been more common than in Britain, and it was used 'almost interchangeably' with *petition* and *address*.[43] An anti-taxation protest issued by the House of Burgesses of the Colony of Virginia in 1768, which anticipated the American Revolution, was named *Petition to His Majesty, Memorial to the House of Lords, Remonstrance to the House of Commons*.[44] This example suggests that terms were chosen not based on the type of petition but on the authority it addressed, and that the petitioners had an idea of which word was appropriate for which recipient. Petitions to local authorities in early modern England (which seem to have been modelled after petitions in equity courts)[45] were sometimes untitled, but petitioners used, besides (*humble*) *petition*, words such as *complaint*, *appeal*, *supplication*, or *address*.[46]

Whereas *petition* was the French word for petition used in medieval Britain, *requête* (Latin: *requirere*, 'ask') became the dominant term in continental France. *Demande* (Latin: *demandare*, 'entrust', 'hand over'), *plainte* (Latin: *plangere*, 'lament'), and *placet* (Latin: *placere*, 'please') were sometimes used as well. The word *supplique* was also used, but more specifically to refer to petitions to the pope.[47] *Doléance* (Latin: *dolere*, 'suffer') and *remon(s)trance* functioned as the French equivalents of *querimonia* and *gravamina*: both words were used for collective petitions listing (multiple) grievances and demanding redress. A *représentation* was also a collective petition, but had a more respectful connotation. *Mémoire* was the French equivalent of the English *memorial*.[48]

In early modern Portugal, *petição* was the word most frequently used for petitions to the king, but petitions to the Cortes (the Representative Assembly) could also be called *capítulos* (Latin: *capitulum*, 'chapter'). Collective petitions expressing grievances were called *representações*. As in French, *súpplica* was

[42] J. Finlay, 'The Petition in the Court of Session in Early Modern Scotland', *Parliaments, Estates and Representation*, 38 (2018), 337–49 (pp. 337–8); A. R. MacDonald, 'Neither inside nor outside the Corridors of Power: Prosaic Petitioning and the Royal Burghs in Early Modern Scotland', *Parliaments, Estates and Representation*, 38 (2018), 293–306 (p. 296).

[43] H. Weiss Muller, 'From *Requête* to Petition: Petitioning the Monarch between Empires', *Historical Journal*, 60 (2017), 659–86 (p. 660).

[44] H. M. Gladney, *No Taxation without Representation: 1768 Petition, Memorial, and Remonstrance* (n.p., Xlibris, 2014).

[45] See L. Flannigan, 'Litigants in the English "Court of Poor Men's Causes", or Court of Requests, 1515–25', *Law and History Review*, 38 (2020), 303–37.

[46] See the 'English Petitions' collection on the *British History Online* database, created by B. Waddell, S. Howard, and J. Peacey, www.british-history.ac.uk/search/series/petitions (accessed 20 January 2024).

[47] ARTFL Project, *Dictionnaires d'autrefois: Dictionnaires des 17ème, 18ème, 19ème et 20ème siècles*, https://portail.atilf.fr/dictionnaires/, s.vv. 'requete', 'demande', 'plainte', 'supplique' (accessed 20 January 2024).

[48] Weiss Muller, 'From *Requête* to Petition', p. 61.

mostly reserved for papal petitions.[49] Its cognate *suplicação* was not used to refer to written requests, but its Roman civil law meaning of 'appeal' lived on in the name of the Casa da Suplicação, the royal court of justice. In old and early modern Spanish, *petición* was the dominant word, but there was much local and regional variation, and the terms *suplica, suplicación, demanda, pedimento* (another descendant of the Latin *petere*), *memorial, representacíon,* and *exposición* (Latin: *exponere*, 'set out') could all be found to describe written requests.[50] In Catalan the most current term became *greuges* ('grievances', from Latin: *aggravare*, 'make heavier').[51]

In Italian, there was relatively more uniformity in petitionary terminology. While *supplicazione* was reserved for the act of supplication, *supplica* (pl. *suppliche*) became the catch-all term for most types of written petitions.[52] This is not to say that no other words gained any currency. *Memoriale*, used in a way similar to that in other languages, became perhaps the most common alternative.[53] *I(n)stanze* ('urgent request', from Latin: *instare*, 'stand upon') were petitions of a less deferential kind. *Richiesta* and *domanda* typically referred to oral requests, but could informally serve to describe written petitions as well.[54]

In the German-speaking world, the most current vernacular form emanated from *supplicatio*. From the 15th century onwards we find the word *Supplikation* and its shortened form *Supplika(t)z* in the sources. By the end of the 17th century, under the influence of French, this became *Supplik*. A petitioner was called a *Supplikant*.[55] A Germanic alternative for these forms was offered by the word *Bitte* ('petition'). Like its cognate *Bete* ('prayer'), *Bitte* descends from the Gothic verb *bidjan*.[56] Related to *Bitte* are *Bittschrift, Bittbrief, Bittschreiben, Bittzettel*, and *Bittgesuch*.

[49] I am indebted to Pedro Cardim for this information. D. Palacios Cerezales, 'Embodying Public Opinion: From Petitions to Mass Meetings in Nineteenth-Century Portugal', *E-Journal of Portuguese History*, 9 (2011), 1–19 (p. 3); R. Bluteau, *Vocabulario portuguez e latino* … (Coimbra, Collegio das Artes da Companhia de Jesus, 1728), p. 792, s.v. 'súpplica'.

[50] D. Palacios Cerezales, 'Re-Imagining Petitioning in Spain (1808–1823)', *Social Science History*, 43 (2019), 487–508 (pp. 488–9). See also the various lemmata in the *Diccionario de la lenguia española*, http://dle.rae.es (accessed 20 January 2024).

[51] O. Oleart i Piquet, 'Els greuges de cort a la Catalunya del segle XVI', PhD thesis (University of Barcelona, 1992), pp. 36–7.

[52] C. Nubola, 'La "via supplicationis" negli stati italiani della prima età moderna (secoli XV–XVIII)', in C. Nubola and A. Würgler (eds), *Suppliche e 'gravamina': Politica, amministrazione, giustizia in Europa (secoli XIV–XVIII)* (Bologna, Il Mulino, 2002), pp. 21–63 (p. 22).

[53] P. Repetti, 'Scrivere ai potenti. Suppliche e memoriali a Parma (secoli XVI–XVIII): Lo Stato, la giustizia, la supplica', *Scrittura e civiltà*, 24 (2000), 295–358; I. Fosi, '"Beatissimo Padre …": Suppliche e memoriali nella Roma barocca', in Nubola and Würgler, *Suppliche e 'gravamina'*, pp. 343–65.

[54] C. D'Elia, 'Supplicanti e vandali: Testi scritti, testi non scritti, testi scritti dagli storici', *Quaderni storici*, 31 (1996), 459–85 (p. 461); Accademia della Crusca, *Lessicografia della Crusca in rete*, www.lessicografia.it/ (accessed 22 January 2024), s.vv. 'instanza', 'domanda', 'richiesta'.

[55] Neuhaus, *Reichstag und Supplikationsausschuß*, pp. 87–8; R. Fuhrmann, B. Kümin, and A. Würgler, 'Supplizierende Gemeinden: Aspekte einer vergleichenden Quellenbetrachtung', in P. Blickle (ed.), *Gemeinde und Staat im Alten Europa* (Munich, De Gruyter, 1997), pp. 267–323 (pp. 287–8).

[56] *Deutsches Wörterbuch von Jacob Grimm und Wilhelm Grimm*, http://woerterbuchnetz.de/cgi-bin/WBNetz/wbgui_py?sigle=DWB, s.vv. 'bitten' (accessed 20 January 2024).

In addition, early modern German had a great variety of other terms with a Germanic origin.[57] *Ansuchen/Ansuchung*, *Ersuchen/Ersuchung*, and *Gesuch* can all be considered equivalents of *petition*. *Beschwerde* (from the verb *beschweren*: 'burden') is the most literal German translation of *gravamina*, which remained in use in German as well. *Klage* and its cognates *Klagebrief*, *Klagschrift*, *Klagezettel* (from *klagen*: 'complain') can be seen as equivalents of *querimonia/querela*; while *Begehren* (from *begehren*: 'desire') is a German counterpart of *desideria*. The synonyms *Vorstellung*, *Anbringen*, *Antrag*, and *Eingabe* have a less supplicatory connotation and are in that sense more similar to Latin derivatives such as *demande*, *remonstrance*, and *representation*. The use of the word *Ansprache* predates that of its English equivalent *address*.[58] The ubiquitous *Memorial* could also be found in German.

The dominant term in the late medieval and early modern Low Countries was *request* (also spelled as *rek(w)est*, from the French *requête*).[59] The form *supplicatie* also existed, but was less common. The word petitioners used when they referred to themselves depended on the type of petition. Petitioners called themselves *rek(w)estrant* or *suppliant*, and in legal cases *rekwirant*.[60] Other words that were used in Dutch had either Germanic or Romance origins. *Verzoek* (cf. German *Gesuch*) means 'request' more generally. A written request can be called a *verzoekschrift*. Like the more supplicatory form *smeekschrift* (from *smeken*: 'beg', 'supplicate'), the word *verzoekschrift* originates in the 17th century, but both words were to gain currency only later. For collective, less deferential petitions, the French derivatives *memorie*, *remonstrantie*, and *doleantie* were used.[61]

Swedish, too, made use of a variety of Romance and Germanic forms that are by now familiar to us. *Supplik* became the standard term during the early modern period. *Memorial*, *gravamen*, *besvär*, *begäran*, and eventually also *ansöken* (cf. German *Beschwerde*, *Begehren*, *Ansuche*) also described (types of) petitions.[62] A synonym that we only find in the Scandinavian languages is *böneskrift*. This term descends, like the English word *boon*, from the Old Norse *bœn*, which could

[57] See also Würgler, 'Voices', p. 15 n. 16.

[58] A. Würgler, 'Suppliche, istanze e petizioni alla Dieta della Confederazione svizzera nel XVI secolo', in Nubola and Würgler, *Suppliche e 'gravamina'*, pp. 147–75 (p. 159).

[59] J. Haemers, '*Ad petitionem burgensium*: Petitions and Peaceful Resistance of Craftsmen in Flanders and Mechelen (13th–16th Centuries)', in J. Á. Solórzano Telechea, B. Arízage Bolumburu, and J. Haemers (eds), *Los grupos populares en la ciudad medieval Europea* (Logroño, Instituto de Estudios Riojanos, 2014), pp. 371–94 (p. 376).

[60] M. Ch. Le Bailly, *Procesgids: Staatse Raad van Vlaanderen te Middelburg (1599–1795). De hoofdlijnen van het procederen in civiele zaken voor de Staatse Raad van Vlaanderen zowel in eerste instantie als in hoger beroep* (Hilversum, Verloren, 2007), p. 25.

[61] Instituut voor de Nederlandse Taal, *Historische woordenboeken: Nederlands en Fries*, www.wnt.inl.nl, s.vv. 'verzoek', 'verzoekschrift', 'smeekschrift', 'memorie', 'remonstrantie', 'doleantie' (accessed 21 January 2024).

[62] M. Almbjär, 'The Voice of the People? Supplications Submitted to the Swedish Diet in the Age of Liberty, 1719–1772', PhD thesis (Umeå University, 2016).

mean both 'request' and 'prayer'. The Danish version of *böneskrift* is *bønskrift*. Other Danish terms were *begæring*, *ansøgning*, and *klageskrift*, although *supplik* or *supplikation* was the standard form in early modern Danish.[63]

The Age of Revolutions and After

The drawing up of the *cahiers de doléances* that took place everywhere in France in 1789 was firmly rooted in an age-old European tradition of compiling *gravamina*, even if the revolutionary circumstances were themselves unique. *Cahiers de doléances* is the name by which these documents have historically become known, but the terminology used by the corporations creating them was much more varied: the *cahiers* were also full of *demandes*, *plaintes*, *griefs*, *remontrances*, *représentations*, *réclamations*, *vœux* ('wishes'), *pouvoirs* ('powers'), *mandats*, *instructions*, and *pétitions*.[64]

Of these various terms, *pétition* was not the most common one, but as a French old regime term it was not exceptional either. It has been suggested, however, that it took a conscious act of political transfer for *pétition*, used in the English sense of *petition*, to get introduced to France. In December 1788 the physician Joseph-Ignace Guillotin drew up a *Pétition des citoyens domiciliés à Paris*, which also appeared in print. In this petition, which requested the doubling of the representation of the Third Estate, Guillotin explicitly refers to petitionary practices in the anglophone sphere.[65] The text of the petition was made available for Parisians to come and sign it around the city. Unlike the *cahiers*, this 'Pétition Guillotin' could not be considered an 'officially solicited petition' of one of the three estates.[66]

In the early days of the French Revolution, this terminological heterogeneity persisted. The National Assembly's standing order of July 1789 speaks of the possibility of presenting 'pétitions, demandes, lettres, requêtes ou adresses'.[67] In December 1789 the Assembly issued a law on municipal government in which the right to petition was codified for the first time on the European continent; the number of synonyms mentioned in this law was now reduced to two: *adresses* and *pétitions*. *Adresse* was – in this meaning – a neologism borrowed from English.

[63] M. Bregnsbo, *Folk skriver til kongen: Supplikerne og deres funktion i den dansk-norske enevælde i 1700–tallet* (Copenhagen, Selskabet for Udgivelse af Kilder til Dansk Historie, 1997); Det Danske Sprog- og Litteraturselskab, *Ordbog over det danske Sprog*, https://ordnet.dk/ods (accessed 21 January 2024). I am also grateful to Thomas Munck for information regarding this point.

[64] See for example Centre d'Étude des Documents de La Révolution française de l'Université SENSHU, 'La liste des cahiers de doléances de 1789 conservés dans la Collection des Documents de Michel Bernstein', https://core.ac.uk/display/151086624?recSetID= (accessed 21 January 2024).

[65] Y. A. Durelle-Marc, 'Nature et origines du droit de pétition', *La revue administrative*, 61 (2008), 47–60 (pp. 51–2).

[66] Cf. G. Shapiro and J. Markoff, 'Officially Solicited Petitions: The *Cahiers de doléances* as a Historical Source', in Heerma van Voss, *Petitions in Social History*, pp. 79–106.

[67] Durelle-Marc, 'Nature et origines', p. 55.

After having established itself, the National Assembly had immediately started to receive large numbers of *adresses d'adhésion*, which were modelled on the English *loyal address*.[68] In a special supplement to the 1798 edition of the *Dictionnaire de l'Académie française*, containing words that had been in use since the revolution, *adresse* was defined as a 'lettre de respect, de félicitation, d'adhésion ou de demande, adressée à une autorité supérieure'.[69] French *adresses* were by no means always panegyrical; on the contrary, their novel character and freer form allowed petitioners to be bolder than they would have been in an old-regime petition.

Over the course of its existence, the National Assembly attempted to create more legal and procedural clarity on the matter of the right to petition by attributing specific terms to different petitionary functions. From December 1791 onwards, it tried to distinguish between *pétitions* and *adresses*. Interestingly, the term *pétition* was now used for 'réclamations individuelles' – that is petitions on private affairs – which were to be considered directly by the Assembly, while *adresse* was reserved to petitions on public affairs, which were first to be sent to one of the Assembly's committees for review. It was left to petitioners to decide whether their petition was a *pétition* or an *adresse*, but as Adrian O'Connor points out, the distinction 'was constantly being blurred or ignored by petitioners, or by deputies themselves when it suited their interests or inclinations'.[70] Over time, *pétition* was to become the favoured term in France.[71]

Elsewhere, too, the age of revolutions brought a reconfiguration of petitionary terminology. During most of the 18th century, the word *adres* in its meaning of petition only appeared in Dutch in newspapers reporting on British politics. However, from the early 1780s onwards, the (*dank*)*adres* emerged as a new petitionary genre that was introduced by the revolutionary 'Patriot' movement.[72] While initially borrowed from English, the fact that the Dutch Constituent Assembly of 1798 received *adressen van adhaesie* (a direct translation of *adresse d'adhésion*) shows that later, in the Batavian Revolution of the 1790s, the French nomenclature served as a source of inspiration as well.

For the time being, *request* remained the preferred term in Dutch for both individual and collective petitions; *memorie* continued to have some currency but

[68] Ibid., 54.

[69] Académie française, *Dictionnaire de l'Académie françoise*, 5th edn (Paris, Smits, 1798), 'Supplément, contenant les mots nouveaux en usage depuis la Révolution', p. 766, s.v. 'adresse'.

[70] A. O'Connor, 'Action at a Distance: Petitions and the Debate over Political Representation in Revolutionary France', unpublished paper (2019), quoted with the author's permission; published (without the quotation) as A. O'Connor, 'Action at a Distance: Petitions and Political Representation in Revolutionary France', in M. D. da Cruz (ed.), *Petitioning in the Atlantic World, c. 1500–1840: Empires, Revolutions and Social Movements* (Basingstoke, Palgrave, 2022), pp. 199–217.

[71] B. Agnès, 'Pétitions françaises, pétitions britanniques: Des sources incomparables?', *La revue administrative*, 61 (2008), 77–86.

[72] The first Dutch *dankadres* seems to have been 'Dank-adres van de kooplieden der stad Amsterdam …', in A. Loosjes, *Gedenkzuil, ter gelegenheid der vry-verklaring van Noord-America* (Amsterdam, W. Holtrop, 1782), pp. 68–74.

other terms, such as *remonstrantie*, were no longer used. Unlike in France, Dutch revolutionaries did not legally distinguish between different types of petitions, but attempts to provide conceptual clarity could be found nonetheless. A 'constitutional' dictionary published in 1800, for instance, claimed that an *adres* was a type of petition concerned with matters of general interest.[73] From a formal point of view, *requesten* were mostly written in the third person and included a petitionary opening phrase, while *adressen* were in the first person and lacked such a phrase. The word *petitie*, which in the early modern Dutch Republic was reserved for authorities' requests for taxes, was not widely used to describe petitions until the time of the restoration monarchy.[74] In the bilingual United Kingdom of the Netherlands founded in 1815, the constitutional right to petition was commonly referred to as the *regt van petitie/droit de pétition*.[75]

The Dutch adoption of *petitie* was part of a much wider trend, in which the constitutional codification of the right to petition seems to have played an important role. In the German-speaking parts of Switzerland, *Bittschriften*, *Gesuche*, and *Suppliken* were increasingly called *Petitionen* from the Helvetic Revolution of 1798 onwards.[76] During the Napoleonic era, *Petition* also became established elsewhere the Germanophone sphere. In the Italian revolutionary republics, *petizione* became the official term.[77] In Spain, *petición* was in itself an old-regime word, but in the 18th century *representación* had been the preferred word for collective petitions. When the idea of a positive *derecho de petición* ('right to petition') gained ground in the early 19th century, *representación* made way for *petición*, even if initially the expression *derecho de representar* could also be found occasionally.[78] In Swedish *petition* was used to refer to British and French petitions from the 1790s onwards, but it wasn't until the 1830s that it began to be used for Swedish petitions.[79] Forms of *petition/pétition* spread beyond the Romance and Germanic languages as well: in Slavic languages (e.g. Russian: пети́ция [*petitsiya*]; Polish: *petycja*), as well as European languages belonging to other families (e.g. Estonian: *petitsioon*; Georgian: პეტიცია [*petitsia*]), or in the languages spoken in colonial empires

[73] J. Greeven, *Beredeneert constitutioneel woordenboek, waarin ... gevonden word alles wat een burger ... nodig heeft te weten tot verstand van zijne rechten en plichten* (Dordrecht, A. Blussé en zoon, 1800), p. 2.

[74] Instituut voor de Nederlandse Taal, *Historische woordenboeken*, s.v. 'petitie'.

[75] J. Talsma, *Het recht van petitie, verzoekschriften aan de Tweede Kamer en het ombudsmanvraagstuk: Nederland, 1795–1983* (Arnhem, Gouda Quint, 1989), pp. 20–7.

[76] A.Würgler, 'Kontinuität und Diskontinuität zwischen Ancien Régime und Helvetischer Republik am Beispiel der Bittschriften', in D. Schläppi (ed.), *Umbruch und Beständigkeit: Kontinuitäten in der Helvetischen Revolution von 1798* (Basel, Schwabe, 2009), pp. 49–64 (p. 50).

[77] See for instance art. 365 of the constitution of the Cisalpine Republic (1797) on the right to petition: 'Tutti i cittadini hanno la libertà di dirigere alle autorità pubbliche delle petizioni', www.dircost.unito.it/cs/docs/cisalpina1797.htm (accessed 21 January 2024).

[78] Palacios Cerezales, 'Re-Imagining Petitioning in Spain', p. 491. In various Latin American countries *peditorio* became the standard term.

[79] As can be seen in Swedish newspapers of this period; National Library of Sweden, Svenska tidningar database, https://tidningar.kb.se/ (accessed 21 January 2024).

(e.g. Punjabi: ਪਟੀਸ਼ਨ [*paṭīśana*]; Indonesian: *petisi*) they usually serve to describe collective petitions.[80] In Finnish, by contrast, one of the synonyms for petition is not a form of *petition* but *adressi*.

In the 19th century, new terms were invented to highlight the exceptional nature of certain petitions. The term *monster petition*, which draws on older connotations of the people as a 'many-headed monster', was first given to a series of three petitions of the British Chartist movement, addressed to Parliament in the 1830s and 1840s, each with between 1 and 3 million subscribers.[81] The Dutch noun (*volks*)*petitionnement* was borrowed from French (*pétitionnement* originally refers to the act of petitioning). In the late 1820s it was first used to describe the mass petitioning campaign that erupted in the Belgian half of the United Kingdom of the Netherlands.[82] Revolutionaries in Vienna in 1848 invented the word *Sturmpetition* ('storm petition') for a petition that they presented to Emperor Ferdinand I after having stormed his Hofburg palace.[83]

While originally intended for a specific petition or petition drive, such terms could gain a wider usage and were used to describe later, but sometimes also earlier, petitions. Petitions now known as *monster petitions* include one in 1891 for female suffrage submitted to the Parliament of the Australian state of Victoria, and London's *monster petition* of 1680, presented to King Charles II during the Exclusion Crisis.[84] *Volkspetitionnement* came to serve as the Dutch equivalent of *monster petition* and was employed to describe a number of mass petitions ranging from the *volkspetitionnement* of 1853 against the re-establishment of the episcopal hierarchy to the 1985 *volkspetitionnement* against nuclear armament.[85] A petition that Archduke Ferdinand II of Austria received in the Hofburg palace in 1619 is now known as *Sturmpetition* by analogy with the 1848 petition presented to his namesake in the same place.[86]

Words for petition, then, could travel back in time. In doing so, they sometimes contributed to a false sense of continuity between past and present political cultures. Where there was discontinuity, this could be the result of a word for

[80] See Google Translate, https://translate.google.co.uk/ (accessed 21 January 2024).

[81] P. Pickering, '"And Your Petitioners &c": Chartist Petitioning in Popular Politics 1838–48', *English Historical Review*, 116 (2001), 368–88. I am also grateful to Mark Knights for information regarding this point.

[82] F. Magnette, 'Le pétitionnement belge pour le redressement des griefs (1828–1830)', *Revue belge de philologie et d'histoire* (1933), 1061–76.

[83] *Deutsches Wörterbuch von Jacob Grimm und Wilhelm Grimm*, s.v. 'Sturmpetition'.

[84] B. Callahan, 'The "Monster Petition" and the Women of Davis Street', *Provenance*, 7 (2008), 96–104; M. Knights, 'London's "Monster" Petition of 1680', *Historical Journal*, 36 (1993), 39–67.

[85] M. Janse, '"What Value Should We Attach to All These Petitions?": Petition Campaigns and the Problem of Legitimacy in the Nineteenth-Century Netherlands', *Social Science History*, 43 (2019), 509–30; B. Klandermans, *Tekenen voor vrede: Het volkspetitionnement tegen de kruisraketten* (Assen, Van Gorcum, 1988).

[86] H. Kretschmer, *Sturmpetition und Blockade Wiens im Jahre 1619* (Vienna, Österreichischer Bundesverlag, 1978).

petition that had instead travelled across linguistic and political borders. This in turn could result in a deceiving sense of synchronic similarity: many European languages adopted forms of the English word *petition*, but no European state came anywhere near copying the British political culture in which this word had acquired a specific meaning in a process that spanned many centuries.[87]

Conclusion

It is fruitless to try and identify any essentialist meaning for the terms that have been used for petitions through the ages. Words do of course have etymological meanings, but their historical meanings have been shaped by the socio-political and socio-linguistic contexts in which they were used. Words that are derived from the Latin word *supplicatio* may now 'feel' more deferential than other terms because this word is both etymologically and ritualistically associated with supplicatory gestures. Yet, already in Roman antiquity *supplicatio* began to be used as a legal term for written documents, and while some descendants of the word preserved a supplicatory connotation (e.g. the French *supplique*), others inherited the more legalistic overtones (e.g. the German *Supplik*). In a few limited cases, the meaning of words has proved relatively stable across languages: the various forms of *mémoire/memorial*, for instance, usually seem to have described longer petitionary documents without a strict petitionary form.

The number of available terms for petitions was probably highest in the early modern period because of the fragmented and decentralised nature of the political and linguistic landscapes: language was less standardised, and within language areas, different levels of government and institutions used different sets of terms. As the example of the *cahiers* in prerevolutionary France suggests, this situation made it unproductive for language users to distinguish too sharply among the various terms: given the terminological variation in the *cahiers* as a whole, subtle semantic differences that may have existed within French regions were probably lost on the central authorities.

The decades around 1800 were characterised by more reflection on the meaning of petitioning and by terminological change that marks the transition of the right to petition from a customary to a codified right. In most European states, the political practices of this period were indebted to Britain and France; as a result, terms used in English and French found their way into many European languages. These terms were not always altogether new, but they assumed new meaning. States that experienced a less sharp political rupture also saw a less profound or delayed reconfiguration of petitionary terminology. In Britain itself, where the right to petition was codified in the 17th century and no political revolution occurred, petitionary

[87] Cf. also Agnès, 'Pétitions françaises, pétitions britanniques'.

terminology remained more stable, even to the point where it may have obscured actual changes in petitionary practices.[88]

In most languages, the terminology that became established over the course of the 19th century is, by and large, the terminology that we still use today. The number of available synonyms tends to be somewhat smaller than in the early modern period. This does not mean that there is now in all cases a one-to-one correspondence between terms and meanings. To illustrate this I will end this chapter with a description of the present-day situation in Dutch, the language I know best.

In modern Dutch, the umbrella term for petition, and thus the most direct equivalent of the English word *petition*, is *verzoekschrift*. In actual usage, however, *verzoekschrift* is mostly reserved for legal contexts and for individual requests to political authorities: the instrument of the *verzoekschrift* as institutionalised by the Dutch Parliament, for instance, serves only to file complaints about lower government bodies. The term *petitie* is understood, by the Parliament and in society at large, as any type of collective petition, even if legally a *petitie* can also be signed by one person.[89]

When historians write about petitioning in the Dutch Republic in Dutch, they rarely use the words *verzoekschrift* or *petitie*, but they use *rekest*, in line with early modern usage. This distinction is entirely conventional. There is nothing intrinsically different between 18th- and 19th-century Dutch petitions, and in fact the word *rekest* continued to be used into the 19th century.[90] Other terms are exclusively employed when referring to specific historical petitions. The term *remonstrantie* brings to mind, if anything at all, a petition presented to the States of Holland in 1610 by a group of Dutch Reformed dissenters. Some years later these dissenters founded the Remonstrant Brotherhood, an allusion to their petition. They started calling themselves Remonstrants, while their religious opponents, who had drawn up a *contra-remonstrantie*, became known as Contra-Remonstrants. The word *smeekschrift* is now only ever used to describe the *Smeekschrift der Edelen*, a petition (in fact one of a series of petitions) against the Spanish Inquisition submitted by some 200 nobles to Margaret of Parma in 1566.

Even if some synonyms have fallen entirely out of use, the Dutch language still has, then, a substantial number of words for historical and modern petitions. All of these words have their own connotations, developed over time. Of all Dutch synonyms, *smeekschrift* is most supplicatory in an etymological sense because, like *supplicatio*, it brings to mind the ritual act of supplication. Historically, however,

[88] See R. Huzzey and H. Miller, 'Petitions, Parliament and Political Culture: Petitioning the House of Commons, 1780–1918', *Past & Present*, 248 (2020), 123–64; and H. Miller, *A Nation of Petitioners: Petitions and Petitioning in the United Kingdom, 1780–1918* (Cambridge, Cambridge University Press, 2023).

[89] The Dutch Parliament also distinguishes a third type of petitionary document, the *burgerinitiatief* ('citizens' initiative'), which is a type of collective petition that needs to meet certain additional criteria, such as a minimum number of subscribers.

[90] On this, see J. Oddens, *Op veler verzoek: Inclusieve politiek in Nederland* (Amsterdam, Boom, 2023).

the word *smeekschrift* has become connected to what was, in a performative sense, one of the least supplicatory petitions in early modern Dutch history.

Calling the *Smeekschrift der Edelen* anything other than *smeekschrift* sounds strange to modern Dutch speakers, because it seems to ignore the uniqueness of what is considered a founding event in Dutch history. Yet, from the point of view of petitionary practice, the *Smeekschrift* was hardly unique in its own time.[91] Moreover, the word *smeekschrift* is a purist neologism invented by the 17th-century historian P. C. Hooft, and did not exist when the *Smeekschrift der Edelen* was submitted.[92] The actual word used by the petitioners was *remonstrantie* (or *remonstrance* in the original French version of the petition).

The example of the *Smeekschrift der Edelen* serves as a reminder that the choice for one term over another may be driven by ideological considerations. In English, which unscrupulously translates most foreign terms to 'petition', the *Smeekschrift der Edelen* is usually called 'Petition of the Nobles'. This more generic name makes it easier to think of the *Smeekschrift* as in the same ballpark with contemporaneous petitions such as the Huguenot petition presented to King Francis II of France in 1560; the Puritan 'Millenary Petition' presented to King James I of England and VI of Scotland in 1603; or the just-mentioned *Sturmpetition* of 1619, which was submitted to Ferdinand II by a group of Protestant Austrian aristocrats. While something is often lost in translation when we write about petitioning in another language, it can also help us to strip historical petitioning events from their mythological connotations.

Acknowledgements

This analysis is based on my own research experience, the available literature, historical dictionaries, and the help of others. I would like to thank Benoît Agnès; Yuval Ben-Bassat; Karin Bowie; Pedro Cardim; Miguel Dantas da Cruz; Gwilym Dodd; Marjolein 't Hart; Pasi Ihalainen; Joanna Innes; Ton van Kalmthout; Beat Kümin; Mark Knights; Philip Loft; Thomas Munck; Adrian O'Connor; Diego Palacios Cerezales; Ismini Pells; Sanne Steen; Henk te Velde; Quentin Verreycken; Andreas Würgler; and my co-editors Henry Miller, Richard Huzzey, Maartje Janse, and Brodie Waddell, as well as the anonymous reviewers for answering my many questions, suggesting literature, and commenting on previous versions of this chapter.

[91] F. Deen, 'Moorddam: Publiek debat en propaganda in Amsterdam tijdens de Nederlandse opstand (1566–1578)', PhD thesis (University of Amsterdam 2012), pp. 27–80.

[92] Instituut voor de Nederlandse Taal, *Historische Woordenboeken*, s.v. 'smeekschrift'.

3

Alike but Different: Varieties of Subscriptional Practices and Communities

MARK KNIGHTS

WHAT, IF ANYTHING, distinguished petitions from other forms of subscriptional texts such as addresses, associations, engagements, covenants, remonstrances, protestations, instructions, declarations, and agreements?[1] These were all genres common within early modern Britain that could be signed by one or more people in order to make a public statement or request, thereby creating subscriptional communities, so what they had in common may seem far more important than what divided them. Indeed, it might seem pedantic to disaggregate these different forms when contemporaries sometimes used them synonymously. *The Armies Petition: Or a New Engagement* (1648) ran the 'petition' and 'engagement' together;[2] and *Panarmonia, or, The Agreement of the People Revived* (1659) contained 'The humble Address and Petition of Several [of] the Justices of Peace, Gentlemen and others of the County of Glo[u]cester', thereby combining three forms: 'agreement', 'address', and 'petition'.[3] There was, as these examples suggest, some overlap between the forms. The 1662 Act that sought to restrain the tumultuous petitioning also referred to 'any Petition, Complaint, Remonstrance, Declaration, or other Address to the King, or both or either Houses of Parliament' in its desire to proscribe 'tumultuous and other disorderly soliciting and procuring of Hands by private Persons'.[4] One genre could even be used to support another: in 1796, in the wake of two repressive Acts against

[1] The chapter by Joris Oddens in this volume explores the different terminology for petition-like texts.

[2] *The Declaration and Engagement of the Officers and Souldiers of Col. Ingoldsbies Regiment for the Present Government* (London, B. A., 1649) similarly fused the 'declaration' and 'engagement' together.

[3] *Panarmonia* (London, printed for Livewell Chapman, 1659), p. 2.

[4] 13 Charles II, c. 5, s. 1. The act was still an issue of concern for petitioners in the early 19th century when the 'Blanketeers' in 1817 were advised by Major Cartwright to march in groups of 10, each carrying a petition: K. Navickas, *Protest and the Politics of Space and Place 1789–1848* (Manchester, Manchester University Press, 2016), p. 68; R. Poole, 'Petitioners and Rebels: Petitioning for Parliamentary Reform in Regency England', *Social Science History*, 43 (2019), 553–79 (p. 557).

Proceedings of the British Academy, **262**, 68–85, © The British Academy 2024.

petitioning and assembly, a Whig club was formed to uphold the right to petition and issued a declaration/association.[5] Indeed, in the early 18th century Daniel Defoe believed that differences between the genres had collapsed and that there were no longer material differences between a petition and an address: 'custom has now brought these things together, the address is call'd a petition and the petition an address; and as the age makes no distinction neither do I'.[6]

Yet Defoe's remarks also made clear that there *had* been 'essential differences between them' in the past 'which used to be observed by the People: petitioning being applied to Requests only and Addressing to every thing, congratulating or otherwise summary in representing the subject it is upon'.[7] Even in Defoe's day the genres had different usages, and petitions and addresses diverged again, especially from the later 18th century, when the petition became a principal vehicle of protest and the address returned to its loyalist core, often with a club or society to promote subscriptions to it.[8] There were subtle but important distinctions between associations and addresses, and between panegyrical addresses and instructions to MPs, differences that played a part in contemporary decisions about which genre to deploy.

Drawing mostly on evidence from the 17th and 18th centuries, this chapter seeks to set out the ways in which petitions and cognate genres were both alike and different. It aims to consider what overall functions the genres within the general category of subscriptional texts performed, as well as to identify the varieties within it and some of their distinguishing characteristics. Rather than focusing on petitioning, the contours of which are ably explored elsewhere in this volume, much of the discussion that follows examines its cognate forms. By highlighting the features of other subscriptional genres it is possible to see the elasticity of some of the boundaries between them – the result of overlapping functions and styles, as well as 'hybridisation' – but also that they were subtly and sometimes starkly different.[9]

Shared Characteristics

Petitions, addresses, associations, remonstrances, instructions, declarations, and agreements shared common characteristics. They all were genres that attracted multiple signatures to endorse and validate the explanatory text at their head.[10]

[5] *Declaration of, and Form of Association Recommended by the Whig Club* (n.p., 1796).

[6] [Daniel Defoe], *Two Great Questions Considered* ([Edinburgh, n.p., 1707), p. 3. 'Memorial' was also sometimes used alongside petition and address (e.g. *To the King's Most Excellent Majesty, the Lords Spiritual and Temporal, and the Commons of Great Britain, in Parliament assembled, the Address, Petition, and Memorial, of the Representatives of the Freeholders of the Province of Nova Scotia, in General Assembly* (n.p., 1775)), but was more often used in legal cases or summaries of other texts and information.

[7] [Defoe], *Two Great Questions Considered* (1707), p. 4.

[8] For early-19th-century examples of the dichotomy, see Navickas, *Protest*, pp. 70–1.

[9] Joanna Innes's chapter in this volume provides a very useful parallel discussion.

[10] The focus of what follows is on public texts from groups rather than private petitions from individuals.

The latter set out the collective position of the subscribers – and these texts articulated grievances and sentiments, but also helped to disseminate, consolidate, or mobilise support. Subscriptional texts were often a routine way of interacting with higher authorities but could also be ideological statements setting out demands, requests, instructions, and reasons for gratitude and other shared views. In terms of content, the genres were incredibly flexible, capable of representing almost any subject matter – political, religious, social, economic, and moral – both locally and nationally. The texts could be one-offs or part of a wider campaign that saw multiple texts being signed within days or weeks of each other. Texts could be promoted at a very local level but also at a national and colonial level – the latter is worth emphasising, since Britons took petitioning with them as colonists, such as in the Atlantic world, as well as sometimes finding kindred cultures, such as in India.[11] Subscriptional texts were important vehicles for dialogue not only within the state but also between domestic and colonial agencies, such as imperial assemblies and mercantile communities. Non-local subscriptions stimulated increasing amounts of co-ordination: by the second half of the 18th century, 'corresponding' between interest groups became common, such as occurred with the anti-popery and reformist groups from 1778 to 1780 and in radical circles in the 1790s.[12] In the case of a national campaign, the texts could appear quite formulaic when they repeated phrases used by others, but there was usually a degree of variation in the wording of texts from different locales – indeed, part of the drafter(s) art was to make each contribution distinctive while chiming with the general thrust.[13] Contemporaries therefore grew adept at reading the nuances and subtleties of wording.

The act of signing ideological or supplicatory or congratulatory statements bound the subscriber into agreement with a position that they may *already* have held or to which they had been converted by *the process of the circulation* of the text. Signing (even if it was only with a mark) was thus not a passive act – it incurred a personal obligation and actively testified a view or witnessed an oath, giving it a legalistic colour – though some subscribers did retrospectively complain that they did not understand what they had signed. Signing thus produced conscientious anxieties when successive texts seemed to conflict or be in tension with each other,[14] or when they were reinforced with oaths, as was commonly the case throughout the early modern period when the British state sought to test allegiances. Oaths

[11] R. Huzzey and H. Miller, 'Colonial Petitions, Colonial Petitioners, and the Imperial Parliament, ca. 1780–1918', *Journal of British Studies*, 61 (2022), 261–89; R. De and R. Travers, *Petitioning and Political Cultures in South Asia*, special issue of *Modern Asian Studies*, 53:1 (2019).

[12] In 1780 the Protestant Association and the Association movement pressing for economical reform both sought to co-ordinate the activities of regional groups and committees. The London Corresponding Society co-ordinated activity in the 1790s.

[13] For the employment of scriveners to draft private petitions, see F. Dabhoiwala, 'Writing Petitions in Early Modern England', in M. Braddick and J. Innes (eds), *Suffering and Happiness in England 1550–1850: Narratives and Representations. A Collection to Honour Paul Slack* (Oxford, Oxford University Press, 2017), pp. 147–68.

[14] See, for example, J. Oldmixon, *The History of Addresses*, 2 vols (London, n.p., 1709–11).

in particular, but also signing more generally, provoked debates about the legality and moral probity of a subscription. Thus, the 'engagement' to the Commonwealth regime in the mid-17th century created crises of conscience, resulting in pamphlets arguing the case.[15] Signing was thus a mark of commitment that was often taken very seriously. It had an emotional impact, helping to create an 'emotional community' of the like-minded – it was the excess of this emotion that propelled the 1780 'Gordon Riots', for example.[16] Some subscribers even recorded their enthusiasm alongside their signatures: subscribers of the Protestation were observed, for example, to sign it 'w[i]th much willingnesse and chearfullnesse';[17] and in Hawton parish in Nottinghamshire were said to have taken it 'freely & heartily'.[18] But texts could equally well promote outrage and disgust. One minister, Nathaniel Ward, said he would 'far rather submit to torture' than swear an oath against his conscience.[19] Texts could thus promote and reflect alarm and fear, whilst others could swell pride and gratitude.

A signature both indicated a recognition that a text represented the subscriber's views and, where multiple signatures were appended, was an attempt to show the intended recipient that there was support – sometimes extensive popular pressure – for a requested outcome. The number of signatories varied considerably, depending on the nature of the text and the calculations and strategy of its promoters. Subscriptional texts could be both open (accessible to a wide variety of people, across the social scale, including women, and to institutions that were not part of the parliamentary representative system) or closed (legitimated only by the members of a formal institution or group). While petitions could come from individuals (for personal requests), the subscriptional genres were flexible enough to accommodate small groups of subscribers and, on occasion, much larger ones, extending to many thousands.

When subscriptional texts appealed to a wider public, they could quickly become vehicles for mass subscriptions and could swell to huge proportions. Petitions, in particular, could be very large. The 1817 reform petitions may have had the support

[15] *Conscience Puzzel'd, about Subscribing the new Engagement* (n.p., 1650); J. Dury, *Considerations concerning the Present Engagement, whether it may Lawfully be Taken Yea or No?* (London, R[obert] L[eyborn] for Richard Wodenothe, 1650); J. M. Wallace, 'The Engagement Controversy 1649–52', *Bulletin of the New York Public Library*, 68 (1964), 384–405; Q. Skinner, 'Conquest and Consent: Thomas Hobbes and the Engagement Controversy', in G. Aylmer (ed.), *The Interregnum: The Quest for Settlement, 1646–60* (Hamden, CT, Archon, 1972), pp. 79–98; E. Vallance, 'Oaths, Casuistry and Equivocation: Anglican Responses to the Engagement Controversy', *Historical Journal*, 44 (2001), 59–77.

[16] I. Haywood and J. Seed (eds), *The Gordon Riots: Politics, Culture and Insurrection in Late Eighteenth-Century Britain* (Cambridge, Cambridge University Press, 2012).

[17] Staffordshire Record Office, D868/2/30, cited by J. Walter, *Covenanting Citizens: The Protestation Oath and Popular Political Culture in the English Revolution* (Oxford, Oxford University Press, 2016), p. 125.

[18] Nottinghamshire Archives, PR/8812/1, cited by Walter, *Covenanting Citizens*, p. 136; see also Walter, *Covenanting Citizens*, pp. 192–3.

[19] Walter, *Covenanting Citizens*, p. 145.

of about a quarter of the adult male population – about double the size of the electorate.[20] The 1839 Chartist petition was almost three miles long, with 1.2 million signatures, and as many as 3.3 million signed the 1842 Chartist petition – though the number of signatures was often a matter of dispute, since counting such huge numbers was a very inexact science. In 1848 the Chartists claimed 5.75 million but the Commons Committee on Public Petitions found just under 2 million, though the latter may also have been an incorrect figure.[21] But other genres could also attract thousands of names. Addresses were often endorsed by official or semi-official bodies, such as corporations and societies, but these often indicated the scale of support they had received and some addresses did attract numerous signatures.[22] Associations (and, in the mid-17th century, engagements and covenants) were intrinsically expressions of a large number of people bonding together, either to form a commercial or social company, or to form a public league when there was a national danger or threat. Some 426 association rolls, for example – each full of many thousands of signatures – were presented to William III in 1696 in response to an alleged attempt to assassinate him. A 1649 Leveller remonstrance claimed the support of '98064 hands and more to be added daily'.[23] Texts could also be much vaguer about the extent of support, with simply an indication that a 'major part' of a group had signed; others simply invoked 'the People' as supporting them or claimed to speak for many thousands (we might call these 'implied subscriptions' to distinguish them from actual signatures made to a document).[24] Mass signing, whether implied or actual, sought to confer solidarity, popular legitimacy, and/or an implied popular pressure to act.

Subscriptional texts, particularly when printed, claimed to give the 'sense' or 'voice' of the people, but such claims frequently provoked contest, leading to a

[20] Poole, 'Petitioners and Rebels', p. 567; F. O'Gorman, *Voters, Patrons, and Parties: The Unreformed Electoral System of Hanoverian England, 1734–1832* (Oxford, Clarendon Press, 1989), Chapter 4; J. Phillips, 'Popular Politics in Unreformed England', *Journal of Modern History*, 52 (1980), 599–625 (pp. 624–5).

[21] P. W. Slosson, *The Decline of the Chartist Movement* (New York, Columbia University Press, 1916), pp. 100–1. On mass petitioning in the 19th century, see R. Huzzey and H. Miller, 'Petitions, Parliament, and Political Culture: Petitioning the House of Commons, 1780–1918', *Past & Present*, 248 (2020), 123–64 (pp. 140–4); and H. Miller, *A Nation of Petitioners: Petitions and Petitioning in the United Kingdom, 1780–1918* (Cambridge, Cambridge University Press, 2023).

[22] M. Knights, *Representation and Misrepresentation in Later Stuart Britain: Partisanship and Political Culture* (Oxford, Oxford University Press, 2005), pp. 137–8. For the scale of 19th-century addresses to the monarch, see R. Huzzey and H. Miller, 'The Politics of Petitioning: Parliament, Government and Subscriptional Cultures in the United Kingdom, 1780–1918', *History*, 106 (2021), 221–43.

[23] *The Remonstrance of Many Thousands of the Free-People of England. Together with the Resolves of the Young-men and Apprentices of the City of London, in Behalf of Themselves, and those called Levelers* (London, 1649).

[24] The so-called 'Legion Memorial' of 1701 thus claimed to have the support of 'two hundred thousand Englishmen; *Mr. S—r, The Enclosed Memorial you are Charg'd with, in the Behalf of Many Thousands of the Good People of England* (London, 1701), p. 1. It concluded with a promise to provide a version 'sign'd with our Names' if needed (p. 8). The piece was attacked as an 'Impudent Remonstrance'; *The Memorial, alias Legion, Answered* (n.p., 1701), p. 2.

representational struggle over who best or legitimately represented the people. That struggle was among subscriptional, informal, and other more formal modes of representation, such as the corporation, assizes, or Parliament.[25] The numbers of petitioners could exceed that of voters (as they did in the Chartist era), but even if fewer than the electorate they could still mobilise huge numbers, sometimes of the unenfranchised. James Bradley estimated that petitions opposing the American war involved almost as many as those who voted in elections, and that about a half of the subscribers were not voters.[26]

Subscriptional texts could provoke contests and polarise opinion. In 1795 Joseph Cawthorne (in the pay of the government) argued that 'to talk of the rights of the people in general to assemble and petition the Legislature for supposed grievances is talking like a madman',[27] but at least 130,000 petitioners that year sought to defend the right to petition against governmental legislation curbing it.[28] Ironically, although bent on creating united communities of expression, subscriptional texts often proved divisive. They could even be used to count or identify opponents – in 1641 the City of London ordered books to be provided to record those who signed the Protestation, but explicitly stated that the names of those who refused were also to be noted down.[29] Similarly, those who refused to sign the Covenant (the 1643 agreement between the English and the Scots pushing for further religious reform) were 'declared uncapable' of holding a variety of civil and religious posts.[30]

Subscriptional texts had a life-cycle shaped by their performative nature and every stage required tactical and strategic decisions. Each genre could be drawn up in manuscript or (as will be discussed shortly) printed. There was then a choice of ways of promoting subscriptions: blank sheets ready for signatures could be hawked from door to door, parish to parish;[31] made available in public places, such as taverns and inns;[32] promoted by societies or semi-official bodies; fostered by

[25] Knights, *Representation and Misrepresentation*, pp. 109–62; M. Knights, 'Participation and Representation before Democracy: Petitions and Addresses in Premodern Britain', in I. Shapiro, S. Stokes, E. J. Wood, and A. Kirshner (eds), *Political Representation* (Cambridge, Cambridge University Press, 2009), pp. 35–57.

[26] J. Bradley, *Religion, Revolution, and English Radicalism: Nonconformity in Eighteenth-Century Politics and Society* (Cambridge, Cambridge University Press, 1990), pp. 319, 330.

[27] J. Cawthorne, *A Letter to the King* (London, printed for the author, 1796), p. 30, cited by G. Green, *The Majesty of the People: Popular Sovereignty and the Role of the Writer in the 1790s* (Oxford, Oxford University Press, 2014), p. 44.

[28] M. Knights, '"The Lowest Degree of Freedom": The Right to Petition Parliament, 1640–1800', in R. Huzzey (ed.), *Pressure and Parliament: From Civil War to Civil Society* (Oxford, Wiley-Blackwell, 2018), pp. 18–34 (pp. 26–7).

[29] Walter, *Covenanting Citizens*, p. 117.

[30] K. MacKenzie, *The Solemn League and Covenant and the Cromwellian Union, 1643–1663* (London, Routledge, 2018), p. 15.

[31] M. Knights, 'London's "Monster" Petition" of 1680', *Historical Journal*, 36 (1993), 39–67 (pp. 63–4); Poole, 'Petitioners and Rebels', p. 563.

[32] Navickas, *Protest*, pp. 55–6, recounts how rival petitions were left for subscription at nearby inns in Manchester.

reports in print; and, by the end of the 18th century, collected at meetings that included motivational speeches and debate. The practice of promoting subscriptions at a public meeting seems to have become common in the late 1760s during the Wilkesite agitation, and in the 1770s in the controversy over war with America, though there were already tavern meetings in the 1730s in Middlesex.[33] The growth of local newspapers meant that advertisements could give wide publicity to such meetings. Requisitions to the authorities for approval to meet were themselves a form of subscriptional community, since they were usually signed by a coterie of those seeking an assembly and set out the reasons why they should be allowed to meet.[34] Some of the meetings could themselves be very large – the Gordon Riots in 1780 followed a huge gathering of perhaps 20,000 signatories in St George's Fields, and in 1795 the London Corresponding Society organised a large meeting of 'several thousands' around the Copenhagen House tavern in Islington that duly produced petitions demanding universal suffrage.[35] Indeed, although until the mid-18th century meetings were called to support subscriptional texts, increasingly the public meeting became almost as important.[36] The 1795 Seditious Meetings Acts recognised this shift by simultaneously banning unauthorised meetings *and* 'any Petition, Complaint, Remonstrance, or Declaration, or other Address to the King, or to both Houses or either House of Parliament'.[37] Once signed, subscribed parchments or papers were collected and joined together, while preparations were made for their presentation: to any person or institution of authority with an ostensible power to remedy the grievance motivating subscribers and, when printed, also appealed to the public.

How the texts were presented to the authorities required another decision. They might be carried in procession and presented with the support of either crowds or dignitaries whose status gave legitimacy and attracted attention. But large crowds, either carrying subscriptional texts or trying to present them, risked slipping out of control, as seems to have happened to petitions being presented in 1641, 1780 (when the Gordon Riots created the largest damage to property of any 18th-century

[33] See *Reports from Committees of the House of Commons*, Vol. II (n.p., 1737), p. 16; C. Tilly, 'The Rise of the Public Meeting in Great Britain, 1758–1834', *Social Science History*, 34 (2010), 291–9.

[34] R. Huzzey, 'Public Meetings, Respectable Requisitions, and Popular Politics in Great Britain and Ireland, c. 1769–1850', *English Historical Review*, 138:590–1 (2023), 185–221. See Poole, 'Petitioners and Rebels', p. 558, for how disputes over the requisitions could lead in turn to further subscriptional action to defend the call for meetings.

[35] *An Account of the Resolutions Passed at a Meeting held November 12th, 1795, in the Neighbourhood of Copenhagen House* (London, 1795), broadside. James Gillray satirised the crowd in *Copenhagen House*; see F. G. Stephens and M. D. George, *BM Satires/Catalogue of Political and Personal Satires in the Department of Prints and Drawings in the British Museum*, 11 vols (London, British Museum Press, 1870–1954), no. 8685.

[36] 'Resolutions' were often the written outcome of physical meetings, either of institutions or of more informal gatherings; R. G. Thorne, 'Introductory Survey', in R. G. Thorne (ed.), *The History of Parliament: The House of Commons, 1790–1820*, 5 vols (London, Secker & Warburg, 1986), Vol. I, pp. 1–356 (p. 19).

[37] 36 Geo. III, c. 8 s. 1.

disturbance), and 1839. When presented to Parliament or the monarch, a further decision had to be made about who might sponsor and make the presentation, and further drama could ensue, since the recipient of the text could decide either to welcome or to reject it, a choice that was publicly watched and reported. When enthusiastically accepted, the presenters of subscriptional texts (particularly addresses) were rewarded; but they might also be treated with indifference, or even outright hostility and rejection.[38] Subscriptional texts also had an afterlife: they were often designed either to start an administrative or political process (inquiry, review, gathering of information, debate), or to contribute to one, and could in turn spark new subscriptional responses when these objectives were thought not to have been met. After the rise of public partisanship, texts could also often be seen as interventions in election campaigns, mobilising voters to rally behind the governing party or to critique it.

As David Zaret has shown, the decision to print subscriptional texts became far more frequent from the 1640s onwards.[39] Publication could take a variety of forms: the text might be published as a standalone document, or it might appear (either whole or in summary form) in a newspaper or periodical; and such documents were sometimes collected together and published as a bundle of associated texts.[40] Publication, as Zaret argued in relation to petitions (and the point can be extended to other subscriptional forms), changed the nature of the document. First, it created an implicit new audience or secondary umpire – the public – that was being asked (alongside the ostensible recipient) to judge the request or demand, thereby invoking and helping to create 'public opinion', which operated at a national (and even pan-colonial) rather than a local level. Second, publication frequently began a dialogic process in which rival groups of subscribers drew up countertexts that in turn prompted further subscriptions or declarations, an exchange that was sometimes very difficult to close down and often spilled over into wider printed exchanges among petitioners, pamphleteers, and newswriters. Third, publication undermined conventions of a language of deference that operated in most manuscript texts. Printing subscriptional texts thus had unintended consequences, creating an appeal to the public that provoked on ongoing dialogue within the state. Print ensured that subscriptional texts became part of, and helped to constitute, the national discourse. Print fed off the subcriptional texts and the controversies they engendered, such as

[38] See, for example, George III's responses to London petitions and addresses in the wake of the Wilkes affair and crises in the 1770s; *Addresses, Remonstrances, and Petitions; commencing the 24th of June 1769: Presented to the King and Parliament, from the Court of Common Council* ([London], printed by Henry Fenwick, [1778?]), pp. 14, 18–19, 26, 32, 38, 84, 115, 151.

[39] D. Zaret, *The Origins of Democratic Culture: Printing, Petitions, and the Public Sphere in Early Modern England* (Princeton, NJ, Princeton University Press, 2000).

[40] See, for example, *A Collection of the Addresses which have been Presented to the Queen, since the Impeachment Of the Reverend Dr. Henry Sacheverell* (London, printed and sold by John Morphew, 1710); *The Voice of the People: a Collection of Addresses to His Majesty, and Instructions to Members of Parliament by their Constituents, Upon the Unsuccessful Management of the Present War both at Land and Sea* (London, printed for J. Payne, 1756).

pamphlets and newspapers, creating a broader arena for public debate that in turn could foster further subscriptional activity.

The collection and presentation of subscriptional texts thus reflected and created 'subscriptional communities', bound together or even generated by a shared commitment and a common interest in an outcome. These rendered private individuals part of a larger community and incorporated them to give a public voice. The subscriptional genres were thus *representational*, but also *constitutive*, of communities: the act of gathering signatures could give voice to communities, a form of informal representation, but also be part of the process by which a community was strengthened or even came into being. As the 1795 associations cited earlier suggest, subscriptions could also generate formal or semi-formal institutions or groups that were initiated in order to promote and foster the subscriptional activity. Appeals for mass subscription also widened the political nation – both socially and in terms of gender.[41] And they were highly ritualised. John Walter observes that 'The [1641–2] Protestation drew on and created its own symbolically charged ritual. Preceded by a sermon, it was taken in the parish church and commonly on a day or date with significance in the calendars of Protestant worship and anti-popery ... To take the Protestation was to enact the nation.'[42]

Differences

The similarities across genres are important, but so are the differences between them, especially as these became pronounced at different times and in different contexts. Tactical and strategic decisions had to be made by promoters and signatories about how best they might achieve their ends, and promoters of text often consciously deployed different genres, fully cognisant of their varying impact and resonances.[43] The following analyses each in turn.

[41] P. Higgins, 'The Reactions of Women with Special Reference to Women Petitioners', in B. L. Manning (ed.), *Politics, Religion, and the English Civil War* (London, Edward Arnold, 1973), pp. 179–224. A. Button, 'Royalist Women Petitioners in South-West England, 1655–62', *Seventeenth Century*, 15 (2000), 53–66; A. J. Whiting, *Women and Petitioning in the Seventeenth-Century English Revolution: Deference, Difference and Dissent* (Turnhout, Brepols, 2015); S. Zaeske, *Signatures of Citizenship: Petitioning, Antislavery, and Women's Political Identity* (Chapel Hill, NC, University of North Carolina Press, 2003). Michael Braddick and John Walter talk of a negotiated state with brokers of internal dialogues (M. Braddick and J. Walter, 'Introduction. Grids of Power: Order, Hierarchy, and Subordination in Early Modern Society', in M. Braddick and J. Walter (eds), *Negotiating Power in Early Modern Society: Order, Hierarchy, and Subordination in Britain and Ireland* (Cambridge, Cambridge University Press, 2001), pp. 1–42); petitions formed part of that dialogue.

[42] Walter, *Covenanting Citizens*, pp. 194–5; see also D. Cressy, 'The Protestation Protested, 1641 and 1642', *Historical Journal*, 45 (2002), 251–79.

[43] On 25 July 1687 the mayor of Thetford wrote that addressing the king with thanks for his declaration of indulgence 'will run through the kingdom and [I] am not willing but to do as other corporations do'; *Calendar of State Papers, Domestic*, 3 vols (London, 1687–9), Vol. III, p. 33.

Addresses

Often thought of as 'loyal' to the prevailing or incoming power, or as vehicles to 'give thanks' for military victories or royal successions, and primarily aimed at monarchs and rulers rather than parliamentarians, addresses began to be promoted in the late 1650s (to bolster Richard Cromwell's 'accession' as Lord Protector) and were mostly deployed as a *panegyrical* rather than a *supplicatory* form.[44] This meant that addresses had a different set of textual conventions from petitions: they were more formulaic in their wording, and often sought to outdo each other both in their rhetoric and in the speed of their presentation, as addressers hurried to appear the most loyal. As such, they were often open to the accusation that they were procured by, or even written by, those in authority. Those promoted in 1763 to celebrate the prime minister Lord Bute's peace treaty with France, for example, were said to be 'in general, devised and dictated by some favourite tool of administration'.[45]

But even if they were often orchestrated by those with social and political capital, many found support from local official or semi-official bodies and institutions, such as corporations, companies, societies, assizes, and colonial assemblies. Subscriptional communities thus did not need to be radical and could be strongly loyalist, with the address as the preferred genre. Since they came largely from institutions, the number of individual subscriptions to addresses was less important than the number promoted across the country, though signatures were still often sought in large numbers. Addressing campaigns, though promoted locally, thus became national and colonial in nature, with many hundreds of addresses flooding in – and these were often published in the *London Gazette*, a periodical that recorded Court and government news. This was in part because the address was primarily aimed at the monarch rather than Parliament, and the presentation of an address at Court could offer a moment of political theatre at which the attitude of the monarch to the address could be publicly gauged.

In the late 17th and early 18th century addresses became a common way of mobilising loyalist support for the regime and for its government. Indeed, they could feed into, and sometimes shape, electoral campaigns when they coincided with them or even prefigured them, as they did for example in 1710, when 92 addresses helped to mobilise Tory opinion and force an election. To some extent, then, addresses could mobilise forces loyal to a regime in a way that a petition

[44] Knights, *Representation and Misrepresentation*, Chapter 3; M. Knights, 'The Loyal Address: Prose Panegyric, 1658–1715', in P. Kewes and A. McRae (eds), *Stuart Succession Literature: Moments and Transformations* (Oxford, Oxford University Press, 2019), pp. 319–35; E. Vallance, *Loyalty, Memory, and Public Opinion in England, 1658–1727* (Manchester, Manchester University Press, 2019). It is worth noting that not all addresses were loyalist: it was the genre adopted by the Revolution Societies in the early 1790s to express their views (see, for example, *A Collection of Addresses Transmitted by Certain English Clubs and Societies* (London, printed for J. Debrett, 1793).

[45] John Almon, *The History of the Minority, during the Years 1762, 1763, 1764, and 1765* (London, 1765), p. 33, quoted by H. Jephson, *The Platform: Its Rise and Progress*, 2 vols (London, Macmillan, 1892) Vol. I, p. 14.

could mobilise them against one. The two genres were at times in conflict with one another: during the succession crisis of 1679–81, for example, petitioners pressing for the king to allow Parliament to sit were criticised by a spate of addresses 'abhorring' the petitions, leading to a subsequent parliamentary investigation into the abhorrers that was critical of their activities.[46]

Instructions

A significantly different variant of the address was the 'instruction' presented to an electoral candidate or to a sitting MP to communicate the sentiments of constituents. Although, like the addresses just discussed, such addresses (they were sometimes also described as 'Letters') were often endorsed by corporations and other bodies, they had a radically different tone: rather than being panegyrical, an address from electors was far more assertive about the rights of the people, so much so that such texts often sparked debate about the independence of MPs to 'represent' rather than being sent as 'delegates' to Westminster.[47] This type of address was thus more like a petition combined with a declaration.

'Instructions', as a national tool, began to be used during the succession disputes of 1681 as a means of trying to secure candidates to standing by the 'exclusion' from the succession of the future James II, though they had been used as a much more limited, local tactic long before then, and could also be used out of election time as part of the routine interaction between constituents and representatives.[48] Instructions often functioned like a pre-emptive, extra-sessional petition for or against a certain legislative measure. Thus, in early 1733 the excise scheme provoked 51 such texts.[49] One of these, from Gloucester, purported to come from 'a great Number of the principal Inhabitants of the City': it was published in the opposition periodical, *The Craftsman*, though without specifying how many had signed. Another letter, 'from the inhabitants of Hindon, in Wilts', was published in the *Daily Post*.[50] Such activity paved the way for a more devastating petitioning attack that came after the bill had been introduced into Parliament and which (combined with 'outrageous and dangerous' unruliness at Westminster)[51] forced the

[46] M. Knights, *Politics and Opinion in Crisis, 1678–1681* (Cambridge, Cambridge University Press, 1994), pp. 258–305.

[47] P. Kelly, 'Constituents' Instructions to Members of Parliament', in C. Jones (ed.), *Party and Management in Parliament, 1660–1784* (Leicester, Leicester University Press, 1984), pp. 169–89.

[48] D. Hirst, *The Representative of the People? Voters and Voting under the Early Stuarts* (Cambridge, Cambridge University Press, 1975); G. Yerby, *People and Parliament: Representative Rights and the English Revolution* (Basingstoke, Palgrave Macmillan, 2008).

[49] *Excise: Being a Collection of Letters, &c. Containing, The Sentiments and Instructions of the Merchants, Traders, Gentry, and Inhabitants of the principal Cities, Counties, Towns, and Boroughs, in England, to their Representatives in Parliament, against a New Excise* (London, printed for W. Mears, 1733).

[50] *Excise*, pp. 14–16; *The Craftsman*, 17 February 1733; *Daily Post*, 7 March 1733.

[51] *Journals of the House of Commons*, 22 (1732–7), p. 115.

government to abandon it.[52] More 'instructions' followed, to help both to precipitate and to follow up on the fall of the prime minister Sir Robert Walpole in 1742, with over 40 texts urging the reinstatement of frequent elections as a means of restoring the voice of the people.[53] The earl of Egremont believed the instructions had drawn support from 'Numbers who had no Right to vote and la[id] hold of every Man they could draw in', and condemned them as having been promoted by a 'faction'.[54] The Jew Bill of 1753 also provoked a dozen instructions.[55] Attempts in 1763 to pass a Cider Act, imposing a duty, provoked opposition in apple-growing Gloucestershire, where an address signed by a 'large number' of the county town's constituents urged MP Charles Barrow to oppose it.[56]

In the late 18th century, instructions were explicitly used to assert the subordination of MPs to their constituents. Radicals in London held frequent meetings to vote instructions to Members, so effectively that in March 1790 James Martin declared that as a result he would vote against the repeal of the Test and Corporation Acts, contrary to his own views.[57] Yet instructions delegating MPs to act in certain ways provoked condemnation from those who, as *The Times* put it in 1802, thought this 'degraded the British senator to the condition of a Dutch deputy'.[58] Instructions, then, were used at certain points to put additional pressure on MPs, but they were also a niche tool that particularly appealed to radical groups, and their success was limited. For example, in 1792 Henry Grattan, sitting in the Irish Parliament, refused to listen to the instructions of a 'few' of his constituents against the Catholic relief bill.[59]

Associations and Covenants

The next subscriptional category, associations and covenants, varied in form, but all bound signatories together in a way that forged them as a united and strong body with more permanence than the sometimes temporary community created

[52] R. Turner, 'The Excise Scheme of 1733', *English Historical Review*, 165 (1927), 34–57; P. Langford, *The Excise Crisis: Society and Politics in the Age of Walpole* (Oxford, Oxford University Press, 1975).
[53] *The Champion*, 371 (1742), 1, 6, 8, 10, 22, and 24 April; 18 May.
[54] John Perceval, earl of Egremont, *Faction Detected, by the Evidence of Facts* (London, printed for J. Roberts, 1742), pp. 96–7. He thought that 'Parliaments have never allowed the Right of Instructing to lie in the People' (p. 101).
[55] T. Perry, *Public Opinion, Propaganda, and Politics in Eighteenth Century England: A Study of the Jew Bill of 1753* (Cambridge, MA, Harvard University Press, 1962), pp. 111–15.
[56] *Public Advertiser*, 14 April 1763, quoted in Jephson, *The Platform*, Vol. I, p. 26.
[57] J. Brooke, 'Introductory Survey', in L. Namier and J. Brooke (eds), *The History of Parliament: The House of Commons, 1754–1790*, 3 vols (London, Secker & Warburg, 1964), Vol. I, pp. 1–204 (p. 201) .
[58] *The Times*, 16 July 1802, p. 2. Lord North in 1784 thought instructions were 'directly repugnant to the constitution of Parliament', since MPs were 'trustees for the whole kingdom'; William Cobbett, *Parliamentary History of England* (London, 1812–20), Vol. XXIV, p. 988.
[59] *The Parliamentary Register* (Dublin, 1792), Vol. XI, p. 163, cited by G. O'Brien, 'The Unimportance of Public Opinion in Eighteenth-Century Britain and Ireland', *Eighteenth-Century Ireland/Iris an dá chultúr*, 8 (1993), 115–27 (p. 119).

by a petition or address.[60] While they could be more like 'articles of association', setting out parameters of agreement within a group,[61] they achieved more national prominence when uniting subscribers in the face of a common enemy, doing so in a stronger way than other forms of subscriptional community.[62] Associations and covenants deployed oaths, declarations, engagements, and protestations as a way of deepening the ties created by the signing process with which it coincided: an oath added a religious dimension that bound the conscience of the subscriber and was used by the state, from the Reformation onwards, to inculcate loyalty.[63] An oath was thought to have additional force, since only God could end its obligations. Subscription to a later oath that ran counter to an earlier one was thus deemed dangerous to the conscience and soul.[64] Oath-reinforced subcriptions thus had long afterlives: in 1663 'all persons in publick Trust' in Scotland were to sign a renunciation of all 'Leagues and Covenants' to take up arms against the king, and specifically the 1638 Covenant and the 1643 Solemn League and Covenant.[65] As this suggests, oaths could also foster loyalty amongst opponents of a regime. The Protestation Oath of 1641–2 thus became a loyalty oath that required those who took it – 'all inhabitants' – to defend the church, Parliament, and English liberties as well as the king, and hence helped confer legitimacy on the raising of Parliament's armed forces. Whether supporting or undermining the government, an association was capable of generating vast numbers of signatures, since promoters often aimed at universality. The 1584 association (when Elizabeth I's life was thought to be in danger) was a relatively modest affair, signed by those of high social status; a century later the 1696 associations, responding to an assassination attempt on William III, were signed *en masse*, including by illiterate people. In Norwich, which had two rival versions, nearly every adult male seems to have signed.[66] And in 1723 an association renouncing the exiled Stuarts

[60] D. M. Jones, *Conscience and Allegiance in Seventeenth Century England: The Political Significance of Oaths and Engagements* (Rochester, NY, University of Rochester Press, 1999); E. Vallance, *Revolutionary England and the National Covenant: State Oaths, Protestantism, and the Political Nation, 1553–1682* (Woodbridge, Boydell Press, 2005); E. Vallance, 'Protestation, Vow, Covenant, and Engagement: Swearing Allegiance in the English Civil War', *Historical Research*, 75 (2002), 408–24; D. Cressy, 'Binding the Nation: The Bonds of Association, 1584 and 1696', in D. J. Guth and J. W. McKenna (eds), *Tudor Rule and Revolution* (Cambridge, Cambridge University Press, 1982), pp. 217–34; Cressy, 'The Protestation Protested', pp. 255–6.

[61] A subgenre of association developed when counties joined together, as they did with the Association movement of the early 1780s, to petition collectively – here the signatories were implied rather than real. This prompted the Solicitor-General to condemn 'associations, delegations and committees' because they created a dangerous national ferment; Cobbett, *Parliamentary History*, Vol. XXII, p. 191.

[62] There was thus sometimes a military aspect to them or at least a threat of united force.

[63] Walter, *Covenanting Citizens*, p. 174.

[64] [E. Gee], *A Plea for Non-Scribers* (London, 1650), pp. 41, 43–4.

[65] *Additional Act Concerning the Declaration to be Signed by All Persons in Publick Trust* (Edinburgh, Evan Tyler, 1663).

[66] Knights, *Representation and Misrepresentation*, pp. 156–9.

(who had threatened an invasion), and making an oath of allegiance to George I, included mass subscriptions by women.[67]

Although oath-enforced associations declined after the defeat of Jacobitism in 1745, the notion of an association endured into the later 18th century in America. In 1774, the American crisis produced, in response to the bill to block up Boston harbour (in retaliation for the Tea Party), a document that was known at the time as the 'solemn League and Covenant'. Boston's Committee of Correspondence encouraged inhabitants in other towns to sign a solemn covenant binding them to suspend all commerce with Britain. Although it lacked the religious dimension of its 17th-century precedent, it retained something of the genre's earlier capacity to sort sheep from goats: the names of anyone refusing were to be published 'to the world'.[68] The strong wording – which prompted a public proclamation accusing the signatories of treason to dissuade further signing – provoked disquiet.[69] A Committee of Correspondence in Worcester noted that many thought the proposed covenant 'can answer no valuable end', and a significant number of inhabitants signed a protest against it; 'scruples' against signing were evident, too, in Braintree, which resolved to alter the wording 'in such manner as they might think proper'. Boston's merchants produced a loyal address to the out-going governor Thomas Hutchinson that more moderately condemned the Harbour bill, warning of the 'Miseries and Distresses' into which it would plunge the city.[70] Such tensions underlined the importance of the wording of all subscriptional texts to maximise support.

Declarations

A declaration – aping a royal or official pronouncement – was a formal statement authorised by its subscribers; it could also state loyalty to a cause. It often fulfilled the function of an association but without a sacred oath.[71] Not necessarily aiming to be presented to those in authority, the declaration, particularly as it developed in the 19th century, could challenge authority, or express support for a rival authority, and thus often lacked the submissiveness of the address, though it shared the latter's concern to attract publicity. Thus, in 1645, 34 inhabitants of Brecknockshire in

[67] Ibid., pp. 140–1. See also E. Vallance, 'Women, Politics, and the 1723 Oaths of Allegiance to George I', *Historical Journal*, 59 (2016), 975–99.

[68] A. Matthews, 'The Solemn League and Covenant, 1774', *Colonial Society of Massachusetts*, 18, 'Transactions, 1915–1916', 103–20, www.colonialsociety.org/node/394 (accessed 25 January 2024).

[69] N. York, 'Imperial Impotence: Treason in 1774 Massachusetts', *Law and History Review*, 29 (2011), 657–701 (pp. 681–2); *Massachusetts Gazette*, 30 June 1774.

[70] *Massachusetts Gazette*, 2 June 1774. The names of the subscribers were published in the 7 July edition and separately as a broadside: *Whereas a Great Number of People have Express'd a Desire that the Names of the Addressers to the late Gov. Hutchinson, and Protesters against the Solemn League and Covenant Might be made Publick, the Following is a True List of the Same* ([Boston], 1774).

[71] And for this reason was used by Quakers, who scrupled at oath-taking.

Wales signed a published declaration outlining their support for the parliamentary cause and acknowledging an 'Engagement' to stand with other counties; and Lancashire issued a similar 'engagement or declaration' of principles in 1648.[72] And in 1792 'a considerable number of signatures' were appended to the declaration made by the Belfast Volunteers in support of the French revolutionaries.[73] Declarations in the premodern period *could*, however, be pro-monarchical. The restoration of the monarchy in 1660 was in part ushered in by declarations by counties in favour of a free Parliament through the recall of the royalists excluded in 1648. *The Declaration of the County of Oxon to His Excellency the Lord General Monck* (1660) claimed to be signed by 'above five thousand considerable Inhabitants'.[74] *A Letter and Declaration of the Nobility and Gentry of the County of York* (1660) similarly protested that although its promoters had not been 'sollicitous to multiply Subscriptions, trusting more to the weight of the Proposalls than to the number of Subscribers; yet we may safely affirm this to be the sense of the Generallity of the County, as your Lordship sees it is of others'.[75] Declarations were again forthcoming at another moment of crisis, in the second revolution of the 17th century: in 1690, 28,000 in Lancashire signed a 'humble Declaration' of their readiness to risk their lives in defence of William and Mary, on news of a possible French invasion and a tract explicitly compared this with the wording of an 'association' made by MPs at Westminster.[76] Declarations were thus often the product of times of emergency and/or ideological crisis when statements of principle were felt to be required.

Remonstrances

The verb 'to remonstrate' was of early-17th-century coinage, meaning to declare, make clear, or to protest, disagree, and complain.[77] Remonstrances were generally neither supplicatory nor panegyrical, and adopted a plain, sometimes confrontational, challenging, and critical style that could be criticised as importunate and

[72] *A Declaration of the Gentlemen and Inhabitants of the County of Brecknock* (London, printed for Edward Husband, 1645); *The Engagement or Declaration of the Officers and Souldiers of the County Palatine of Lancaster* ([London], 1648)

[73] *A Collection of Addresses*, p. 5.

[74] *The Declaration of the County of Oxon to His Excellency the Lord General Monck* (London, printed for John Starkey, 1660). Cf. *A Concurrent Declaration of the Inhabitants of the City and Liberty of Westminister, with the Declaration of the People of England for a Free Parliament* (London, 1660).

[75] *A Letter and Declaration of the Nobility and Gentry of the County of York* (London, Tho. Leach, 1660). See also *A Declaration of the People of England for a Free-Parliament* (London, 1660); and *The Declaration of the Gentrie of the King's Party in the County of Devon* (London, Roger Norton, 1660). Worcestershire, Shropshire, Hertfordshire, Dorset, London, and Kent also made declarations.

[76] *The Necessity of Altering the Present Oath of Allegiance Made Evident also the Declaration Signed by above 28000 in Lancashire, when they Expected a late French Invasion, Compared with the Association Signed in this Present Parliament* (London, printed for John Salusbury, 1690), pp. 3–4.

[77] *Oxford English Dictionary*, www.oed.com, s.v. 'remonstrate' (accessed 25 January 2024).

dictatorial. Defoe thought that both petitions and addresses were different from 'representations or remonstrances', which were more peremptory claims of right.[78] The Grand Remonstrance of 1641, in which Parliament set out its grievances, helped legitimise the genre;[79] and the Levellers used the word quite frequently, as in *A Remonstrance of Many Thousand Citizens* (1646) and *The Remonstrance of Many Thousands of the Free-People of England* (1649).[80] Sometimes assertive petitioning was described as a remonstrance: a graphic satire of 1770 depicted 'The Effects of Petitions and Remonstrances',[81] and in 1795 the right to petition was attacked as merely 'the licence of seditious remonstrance'.[82] From the mid-18th century onwards, a remonstrance was often urged when petitioning failed. We can see this, for example, in 1779, when John Jebb explained the difference in genres to the Middlesex freeholders. Jebb likened a remonstrance to a petition but thought it more of a 'declaration of opinion, in the strongest language'.[83] He castigated the 'ill calculated' tactic of petitioning a corrupt body such as Parliament for its own reform and suggested that every framer of a petition had to ask whether, if their request was rejected, they had 'power to manifest such resentment, as may induce the rejectors to pay greater attention to a second application'.[84] He argued that 'remonstrating in combination' would have much greater weight than a series of individual county petitions, though in doing so he moved beyond individual subscriptions as the solution for reformers.[85] On occasion, then, a remonstrance was deliberately preferred to a petition because of its assertiveness. As John Gale Jones put it to the radical London Hampden Club in 1816, 'It was for courtiers, slaves, and criminals, to petition, but Freemen and Englishmen should remonstrate, resolve and demand those rights which God and nature gave.'[86] The rejection of more than 700 petitions in 1816–17 pressing for reform also caused Henry Hunt to distinguish between a petition

[78] [Defoe], *Two Great Questions Considered*, pp. 5–6. 'Representations' were perhaps less confrontational than he suggested, and echoed parliamentary process, but could still be signed by many; e.g. *An Humble Representation of Many Hundreds of Subscribers ... to the Honourable the House of Commons* (London, 1711).

[79] It was accompanied by a petition.

[80] *A Remonstrance of Many Thousand Citizens* (London, 1646); *The Remonstrance of Many Thousands of the Free-People of England* (London, 1649). The word was also used to satirise the Leveller petitions; e.g. *A Remonstrance of the Shee-Citizens of London* ([London], 1647); *The Remonstrance or, Declaration, of Mr. Henry Martin* ([London], 1648).

[81] *BM Satires*, no. 4386.

[82] *Morning Post*, 16 November 1795: letter from a supporter of Reeves's Association.

[83] J. Jebb, *An Address to the Freeholders of Middlesex, Assembled at Free Masons Tavern, in Great Queen Street, on Monday the 20th of December, 1779*, 4th edn (London, printed for J. Stockdale, 1782), p. 6. For Jebb's beliefs, see A. Page, *John Jebb and the Enlightenment Origins of British Radicalism* (Westport, CT, Greenwood, 2003).

[84] Jebb, *An Address*, pp. 11–12.

[85] Ibid., pp. 14, 21–2.

[86] *A Full Report of the Meeting of the Hampden Club 15 June 1816, upon the Subject of Parliamentary Reform* (London, Wm Hone, 1816), pp. 24–26, quoted by Poole, 'Petitioners and Rebels', p. 571.

and a remonstrance: he called for 'a firm though respectful remonstrance, instead of a creeping, cringing petition', even though it then risked being 'tossed aside' (as another radical, John Kay, put it) as unparliamentary.[87]

Conclusion

Having surveyed cognate subscriptional genres we can see that, unlike a covenant, association, or engagement, the petition did not generally seek to impose an oath or to bind subscribers together in a permanent commitment or seek to be mandatory; unlike an assertive remonstrance, a petition was usually more supplicatory in its language; unlike an address, which was usually loyalist in tone to Crown and government, and bound by certain panegyrical conventions, the petition could be a vehicle of protest and opposition as well as supplication; unlike an instruction, it did not seek to bind a candidate in an election to a cause; and unlike a declaration, which set out a position, a petition was part of a negotiation, even if it was one in which the odds were heavily stacked in favour of those with power. There were also differences in etiquette and legality: petitions, unlike other genres, were the common way to exert pressure on, and trigger debates in, Parliament, but the right to petition Parliament or instruct MPs was contested in a way that the right to address was not.[88]

Institutional bodies and groups of citizens therefore had a series of choices to make when deciding on which subscriptional genre to employ: whether extensive or limited popular mobilisation would add to or detract from their purpose (and whether they had the means or organisation to deliver the former or needed to act quickly);[89] whether they wanted to couch their views in a panegyrical, celebratory way or in a supplicating mode or in an assertive way; whether they sought a temporary or more enduring subscriptional community and how they wanted to bind it together; what performative impact they sought; and increasingly whether the primary objective was the physical meeting that spawned the text, or the text necessitated the meeting.[90] Further decisions related to whether and how to print (and hence also who was the intended audience); whether the intention was to

[87] J. Belchem, *'Orator' Hunt: Henry Hunt and English Working-Class Radicalism* (Oxford, Clarendon Press, 1985), p. 92; Poole, 'Petitioners and Rebels', pp. 565–6, 575; The National Archives, HO 42/184 fol. 329, 9 February 1819, quoted by Poole, 'Petitioners and Rebels', p. 575. For a critique of petitioning as ineffective, see D. Williams, *Letters on Political Liberty*, 3rd edn (London, printed for J. Ridgway, 1789).

[88] Knights, 'The Lowest Degree of Freedom'. For a successful petitioning campaign, see Perry, *Public Opinion*, pp. 54–62

[89] In 1816, when Stockport weavers faced the need for urgent relief from dire economic circumstances, the Revd Prescot, the local magistrate, wanted their petition fast-tracked, since 'much time might be lost by going about for probably fifteen thousand signatures'; quoted by Poole, 'Petitioners and Rebels', p. 555.

[90] Meetings were acknowledged to reach only relatively few, whereas a petition could be made 'easily accessible to the People'; ibid., p. 560.

influence or even challenge the formal representative institutions; and whether the subscriptional text was an end in itself or part of a wider protest that might include more direct action. Contextual factors often played a large part in such choices, and an evolving political culture also shaped responses – oaths fell out of favour, whilst print and then public meetings changed the culture further. But individual and collective agency were also at stake when the choices were made, and, for all their complexity and nuance, these were choices that contemporaries – promoters and subscribers alike – seem to have understood very well.

4

Petitions: Rule-Bound but Malleable

JOANNA INNES

A PETITION IS essentially a request: to put it in modern banal terms, an application; to put it in more archaic and dramatic terms, a supplication. The range of kinds of request covered by this noun or cognate words, or equivalents in other languages, has varied by place and time. In modern English, its standard use is quite narrow: it connotes a collective written request in the form of an expression of opinion followed by a request for action (often some specific action), directed to some authority – especially Parliament or another legislature, though conceivably to some non-public powerful figure, such as an employer or landlord. It also denotes certain kinds of application to law courts, but that is a technical usage which is not generally familiar. In early modern England, its range was wider: requests from individuals often followed a format recognised as a petitionary format and were described as petitions, connoting basically a relatively formal and humble written address to any authority, stating a request, and pleading for action.[1] As discussion in the workshops that gave rise to this book has revealed, in other parts of Europe, the range of documents that historians study under the rubric of 'petitions' is often wider than British historians might anticipate – conditioned as their expectations are by modern British uses of the term. The English word 'petition' (which in the course of the 19th century entered other

[1] For example, F. Dabhoiwala, 'Writing Petitions in Early Modern England', in M. Braddick and J. Innes (eds), *Suffering and Happiness in England 1550–1850: Narratives and Representations. A Collection to Honour Paul Slack* (Oxford, Oxford University Press, 2017), pp. 127–48; and R. A. Houston, *Peasant Petitions: Social Relations and Economic Life on Landed Estates 1600–1850* (Basingstoke, Palgrave Macmillan, 2014). Petitions shade into begging letters, and elements of them can even be found in threatening letters, e.g. *London Gazette*, April 1738, 2, www.thegazette.co.uk/London/issue/7694/page/2 (accessed 27 January 2024). For some websites supplying examples of historical petitions, see the *British History Online* collection 'English Petitions', www.british-history.ac.uk/search/series/petitions (accessed 20 January 2024); and www.civilwarpetitions.ac.uk/ (includes copies of original texts; accessed 27 January 2024).

Proceedings of the British Academy, **262**, 86–103, © The British Academy 2024.

languages as a loan word) may be employed by historians of other places as equivalent to a local word that covers a wide range of banal forms of application: not necessarily (and indeed usually not) collective, and not necessarily either very formal or very humble.[2]

If petitions are conceived as broadly as possible – as requests, oral or written, individual or collective, to people with power, public or private – then they must surely have been and remain a feature of all human societies in which power is concentrated in certain hands. If we insist that to qualify they must be written, then the range of societies in which they have figured will be narrower (though still deep in time and wide in space). There is not necessarily much difference in character between individual and collective petitions. But insofar as collective petitions tilt towards the critical – insofar as they are in effect injunctions to the powerful to discharge responsibilities that they are failing to discharge – then, though they have occasionally been issued in a wide range of places and times in periods of crisis, it seems reasonable to assume that such performances will have been more or less common depending on the cultural setting: upon the kind of tone that is regarded as tolerable (whether or not welcome) between ruler and ruled, between an authority and those subject to authority.

Variations and changes in ways in which the word 'petition' and corresponding terms have been applied, in how public and other power relationships are routinely managed, and in the cultural setting taken, together map out wide parameters for any enquiry into the history of petitioning.

We might respond to this variety by constructing a taxonomy – and mapping different petitioning practices at different times and places on to that taxonomy. In the preceding remarks, I have begun to suggest what some key terms in such an exercise might be. In fact, in what follows, I chiefly want to develop a different line of enquiry. I am going to be concerned especially with fuzzy boundaries within the petitioning form, and with the scope this afforded for creativity and

[2] For range in practice, and various interpretative perspectives, see e.g. D. Feissel and J. Gascou (eds), *La pétition à Byzance* (Paris, Association des Amis du Centre d'Histoire et Civilisation de Byzance, 2004); W. M. Ormrod, G. Dodd, and A. Musson (eds), *Medieval Petitions: Grace and Grievance* (Woodbridge, York Medieval Press, 2009); L. Heerma van Voss (ed.), *Petitions in Social History*, Supplement 9 of *International Review of Social History*, 46 (2001), also in book form (Cambridge, Cambridge University Press, 2002); S. Cerutti and M. Vallerani (eds), 'Suppliques: Lois et cas dans la normativité de l'époque moderne', *L'Atelier du Centre de recherches historiques: Revue électronique du CRH*, 13 (2015); K. Bowie and T. Munck (eds), 'Early Modern Political Petitioning and Public Engagement in Scotland, Britain and Scandinavia, c. 1550–1795', *Parliaments, Estates and Representation*, 38 (2018), 271–8; M. McKinley, 'Petitioning and the Making of the Administrative State', *Yale Law Journal*, 127 (2018), 1538–637; B. Agnès, *L'appel au pouvoir: Les pétitions aux parlements en France et au Royaume-Uni (1814–1848)* (Rennes, Presses universitaires de Rennes, 2018); Y. Ben-Bassat, *Petitioning the Sultan: Protests and Justice in Late Ottoman Palestine 1865–1908* (London, I.B. Tauris, 2013); and R. de Costa, 'Identity, Authority, and the Moral Worlds of Indigenous Petitions', *Comparative Studies in Society and History*, 48 (2006), 669–98.

development in the form, as people employed it as a vehicle for new impulses and new understandings, especially (because this is the time and place that I know best) in later-18th- and early-19th-century Britain.[3]

What is Involved in Petitioning?

Petitions are instrumental, in that they provide ways of doing things, sometimes ordinary and sometimes extraordinary things. They inevitably have a performative dimension, though any given performance may be, on the one hand, routine or, on the other hand, designed for effect. Focusing just on written petitions, significance can be intended or read into the words in which they are couched, the way words are set out on the page, and into their material form; into who delivers them, and the words or movements that accompany their delivery. They may stand alone, or be backed by supporting material, in which the substance of their case may lie. If petitioners want to attract notice, other things may be done around the petition that amplify the performance: they may be advertised or announced or delivered in some dramatic fashion. They may be circulated with paratexts, or made the subject of other forms of event or writing or publication.[4]

There may be rules governing petitioning in any given context, relating to content or form. In modern parliamentary e-petitioning systems, administrators may sift what has been submitted to determine whether petitions raise matters properly dealt with through this channel, and there were surely officials who performed similar functions in the past.[5] The Westminster Parliament used to require that petitions be written on parchment or at least high-quality paper, and until quite recently required

[3] I have previously written about British petitioning in this period in 'Legislation and Public Participation: Aspects of a Changing Relationship 1760–1830', in D. Lemmings (ed.), *The British and Their Laws* (Woodbridge, Boydell Press, 2005), pp. 102–32, and in 'People and Power in British Politics to 1850', in J. Innes and M. Philp (eds), *Re-Imagining Democracy in the Age of Revolutions: America, France, Britain, Ireland 1750–1850* (Oxford, Oxford University Press, 2013), pp. 129–46. This chapter repeats some ideas and illustrations presented there. See also my chapter with Julian Hoppit, 'Introduction' to J. Hoppit (ed.), *Failed Legislation: Compiled from the Commons and Lords Journals 1660–1800* (London, Hambledon Press, 1997), pp. 18–21, and 'Des tisserands au Parlement: La légitimité de la politique du peuple (Angleterre, 1799–1800)', in L. Colantonio, E. Fureix and F. Jarrige (eds), *La souveraineté populaire: Expériences et normalisations en Europe (1800–1848)*, special issue of *Revue d'histoire du XIXe siècle*, 42 (2011), 85–100, for a study of the organisation and effects of a workers' petition to Parliament.

[4] For appropriate bodily postures, in petitioning and other contexts, see J. Walter, 'Gesturing at Authority: Deciphering the Gestural Code of Early Modern England', in M. J. Braddick (ed.), *The Politics of Gesture: Historical Perspectives*, supplement of *Past & Present*, 203 (2009), 96–127. For an English petition with paratexts, see *The Piety and bounty of the Queen of Great Britain: With the charitable benevolence of her loving subjects, toward the support and settlement of the distressed Protestant palatines* (London, Charles Bill [etc.], [1709]). Thanks to Hannah Weiss Muller for this example.

[5] See Dabhoiwala, 'Writing Petitions', p. 130, on channels, and references to accounts of other times and places. Historians seem rarely to discuss sifting explicitly.

that the top sheet be handwritten.[6] Alongside formal rules, powerful conventions may operate. There may be rules as to who can petition, but there may also be conventions as to who can properly petition in a certain kind of case, and how they may proceed. To break the rules or the conventions, inadvertently or on purpose, may determine that a 'petition' is not received or registered as a petition, or gets an unsympathetic hearing.[7] But sometimes rules are stretched or overturned.

Petitions have more than one layer of meaning. They have explicit meanings and implicit meanings. In the course of putting together a petition, a petitioner crafts an identity, representing him- or herself as someone worthy of notice in the given context; this may sometimes have affected how people saw themselves, or realised they could plausibly present themselves. Petitions ask for certain things, but a petitioner or petitioners may know that their request is unlikely to be granted, yet proceed regardless, to make a point. Even if a petition is not intended to fail, especially in the case of collective petitions, organising around it may have its own functions and effects. It may for example provide a means of putting pressure on people who are doing something that others think objectionable to make concessions; it may provide a way of building up or extending networks for future use.[8]

Petitions have functions for recipients as well as for petitioners. Part of the work of government is always generated and fine-tuned by interactions between representatives of authority and applicants or supplicants. Many administrative processes depend upon applications. Moreover, petitions provide authorities with information – including making it possible to identify errant officials and call them to account. Authorities not confident in their own management systems may find complaints very useful in this regard; 'whistle-blowers' perform cognate functions.[9] Implicitly, moreover, petitions acknowledge authority. They provide opportunities for displays of competence, benevolence, mercy, or power – including diverting criticism by casting blame upon subordinates. Even in the worst case – the case of the mass, extraordinary, critical, defiant petition – protestors' adoption of a petitioning form may suggest that there remains space

[6] For stricter rules governing British than French parliamentary petitioning in the 19th century, see Agnès, *L'Appel au pouvoir*. For recent parliamentary practice, see House of Commons Information Office, 'Public Petitions', Factsheet 7, Procedure series (rev. 2010). For current advice, see www.parliament.uk/get-involved/sign-a-petition/paper-petitions/ (accessed 27 January 2024).

[7] See P. Gauci, *The Politics of Trade: The Overseas Merchant in State and Society 1660–1720* (Oxford, Oxford University Press, 2001), pp. 223–6, for parliamentary concern about propriety in mercantile petitioning.

[8] For identity, see esp. Cerutti and Vallerani, 'Suppliques'; and S. King, *Writing the Lives of the English Poor 1750s–1830s* (Montreal, McGill-Queen's University Press, 2019) – which is concerned with applications, if not petitions in the narrow English sense. For petitions to Parliament in the context of ongoing interest-group conflict, see J. Civin, 'Slaves, Sati and Sugar: Constructing Imperial Identity through Liverpool Petition Struggles', in J. Hoppit (ed.), *Parliaments, Nations and Identities in Britain and Ireland 1660–1850* (Manchester, Manchester University Press, 2003), pp. 187–205.

[9] Emphasised in C. Nubola and A. Würgler (eds), *Suppliche e 'gravamina': Politica, amministrazione, giustizia in Europa (secoli XIV–XVIII)* (Bologna, Il Mulino, 2002). See also Ben-Bassat, *Petitioning the Sultan*, esp. pp. 20–43, 135–40, 146–52.

for dialogue. Indeed, authorities may try to push protestors into something like a petitioning approach in order to institute a dialogue: John Bohstedt has suggested that 18th-century English food rioters did not start out with a negotiative 'moral economy' agenda (as E. P. Thompson famously proposed); rather, they were pushed towards that agenda by some of the authorities they dealt with, who saw merit in persuading them to ask what these local officials could see their way to granting. On occasions when local officials responded to protest with brute force, no such programme emerged.[10]

Petitioning often involves intermediaries. These include those from whom petitioners seek advice, who may be lawyers; they may also include scribes or secretaries, whether because petitioners are illiterate or because they need the help of an expert to cast their petition in proper form. In the case of collective petitions, organisers and activists may be needed to arrange meetings, collect signatures, and arrange for the petition's presentation. Receipt of petitions may involve complex bureaucratic processes and layers of officialdom. These players all have their own preoccupations and inclinations, their own stakes and their own agendas, which may play a part in shaping how processes unfold. Those who travelled to present petitions sometimes found that this process opened up a host of new encounters – planned or unplanned.[11]

Choosing to 'petition' in the broadest sense of the term – to apply – sometimes represents just a routine decision to try to get something done. But the choice to petition may be less obvious and accordingly have more significance. It may represent an attempt to formalise a request, to place it on record, or to make it visible. There may be more than one option as to who (or how many) to petition; that choice may be delicate; it may be meaning-laden and strategic.[12] Petitioning, or directing a petition to a particular authority, may reflect other approaches having failed. Petitions may be promoted in parallel with other forms of approach or action – including for example demonstrations, strikes, and threats of violence.[13] Recipients of petitions for their part may impute unexpected meaning to petitions.

[10] E. P. Thompson, 'The Moral Economy of the English Crowd in the Eighteenth Century', *Past & Present*, 50 (1971), 76–136; J. Bohstedt, *Riots and Community Politics in England and Wales, 1790–1810* (Cambridge, MA, Harvard University Press, 1983).

[11] Dabhoiwala, 'Writing Petitions'; Innes, 'Legislation and Public Participation', p. 121. See also my 'Le parlement et la règlementation du travail des enfants dans les fabriques en Grande-Bretagne, 1783–1819', in C. Charle and J. Vincent (eds), *La société civile: Savoirs, enjeux et acteurs en France et en Grande-Bretagne 1780–1914* (Rennes, Presses universitaires de Rennes, 2011), on both brokers and alliance-building.

[12] See Innes, 'People and Power', p. 139, for the striking choice to revive petitioning as an organising mode made by English protestors in the 1760s.

[13] 'Luddite' petitions against changing working practices in British manufacturing in the early 19th century, for example, represented only one among many modes of action pursued – whether the same or different groups of workers pursued different tactics is disputed. J. Dinwiddy, 'Luddism and Politics in the Northern Counties', *Social History*, 4 (1979), 33–63; K. Binfield, *Writings of the Luddites* (Baltimore, Johns Hopkins University Press, 2004). For the general point, with examples from various lines of parliamentary business, see Innes and Hoppit, 'Introduction', pp. 20–1.

They may interpret a petition as so offensive as to merit a punitive response.[14] Or they may (rightly or wrongly) interpret petitioning as a cover for some other activity. Some of those who tried to thrust petitions into the hands of George III in the febrile 1790s were suspected of aiming to assassinate him – but in so confused a manner as to call their sanity into question, justifying their commitment to lunatic asylums.[15]

Petitioners normally act on the basis of beliefs about what normally happens or what ought to happen when one petitions. These beliefs may be based on ideas about what has happened in the relatively distant past – years or generations previously. These beliefs may be well informed, even informed by scholarship, or largely mythical in character. Petitioners may understand their own actions in ways that are strongly coloured by these historical or mythic narratives. Official responses may likewise be shaped by such narratives, which may also be manipulated by any or all parties in a representational struggle.

Taxonomies: Necessary though Not Sufficient

There are good reasons to taxonomise petitions – to try to sort them into categories – because the rules and conventions that govern them vary by time and place, and often also according to who is petitioning whom about what. The practical challenges involved in petitioning, and the meaning and effects of the practice, likewise vary with circumstances. We may want to compare like with like, or like with unlike – to explore the characteristics of petitions of a single kind, or to investigate the significance of difference – but either intention presupposes some taxonomy, and may lead to its refinement.

In a modern context, e-petitioning rules and processes differ significantly from one country to another – even between the Westminster and Scottish Parliaments. In an 18th-century context, Hannah Weiss Muller has demonstrated that French subjects who became British subjects (because their places of residence were conquered and ceded in the course of wars) had to learn new petitioning conventions.[16] In the Westminster Parliament, from the Middle Ages, different rules and conventions governed private petitions – whose function was to activate private bill procedures, or to make claims on behalf of private interested parties – and common or public petitions, which issued general calls for action, or expressed views on legislation in train; the precise character of these distinctions also changed over time. Some public petitions were directed to the king, but the king was also

[14] M. Knights, *Representation and Misrepresentation in Later Stuart Britain* (Oxford, Oxford University Press, 2005), pp. 129–33.

[15] S. Poole, *The Politics of Regicide in England, 1760–1850: Troublesome Subjects* (Manchester, Manchester University Press, 2000).

[16] H. Weiss Muller, 'Bonds of Belonging: Subjecthood in the British Empire', *Journal of British Studies*, 53 (2014), 29–58.

the target of many private and personal petitions.[17] Against the background of constitutional changes in the late 17th century, petitions to the Crown for mercy towards convicted criminals came to be governed by a distinct set of conventions.[18] Specific rules and expectations applied in the case of petitions from the poor to parish officials, and from 'peasants' to landlords (and, as Rab Houston has shown, conventions in the last case also varied, and followed different chronologies, across the different nations of the British Isles).[19]

As these examples illustrate, who was being petitioned about what mattered, especially in terms of formal rules or strong (perhaps invigilated or enforced) conventions. But petitioning practices also varied depending on the petitioners' cultural and organisational resources. The way merchants approached Parliament and government was shaped not just by a framework of rules and conventions, but also by their sense of identity, associational habits, financial resources, cultural know-how, and accumulated experience. Paupers petitioning parish overseers were operating not merely in a different formal context, but with different resources and skills – this is not to imply, though, that they were either clueless or inept; their on-the-face-of-it clumsy presentations were often canny and effective.[20]

Petitions (and related forms of action) gained new meaning and significance when they caught the public eye, especially when they took sides on issues that mapped on to important political fault lines. Jacob Price noted that in the parliamentary session of 1733, Parliament received more petitions complaining about hawkers and pedlars than it did 'instructions' (about which more shortly) concerning the government's Excise Bill; anti-Excise 'instructions', like anti-pedlar petitions, came largely from trading towns.[21] But the campaign against hawkers and pedlars essentially expressed a routine complaint, while the campaign against the Excise Bill jabbed the ministry at a weak spot, at a time when a general election was imminent. Counting does not always offer the best ground for comparison. Or rather, comparison of numbers does not calibrate significance. There are questions one might usefully found on a quantitative comparison: notably, why should a relatively unimportant matter have got more support (as measured by numbers of applications) than a more important matter? Some lines of thought suggest themselves, such as that only major towns felt they had the standing to take a public position on a high-profile political question (as the proposed change to excise policy became), and that, to the extent that the campaign was co-ordinated, the co-ordinators may

[17] Innes, 'Legislation and Public Participation', pp. 114–16; G. Dodd, *Justice and Grace: Private Petitioning and the English Parliament in the Late Middle Ages* (Oxford, Oxford University Press, 2007).

[18] J. M. Beattie, 'The Cabinet and the Management of Death at Tyburn after the Revolution of 1688–1689', in L. Schwoerer (ed.), *The Revolution of 1688–1689: Changing Perspectives* (Cambridge, Cambridge University Press, 1992), pp. 218–33.

[19] King, *Writing the Lives*; Houston, *Peasant Petitions*.

[20] Gauci, *The Politics of Trade*, pp. 209–20; King, *Writing the Lives*.

[21] J. Price, 'The Excise Affair Revisited', in S. B. Baxter (ed.), *England's Rise to Greatness* (Berkeley, University of California Press, 1983), pp. 257–321 (p. 293).

have hoped to maximise impact by demonstrating support from major towns. Yet, among major urban communities, some may have hesitated to take a stance on an issue whereby they risked alienating the ministry, given that political support was routinely repaid in governmental favour. And indeed, as things turned out, Robert Walpole – whose power and policies were in question – survived this challenge (by withdrawing his bill) and retained the premiership for another eight years.[22]

It is important for any student of petitioning to recognise the likelihood that, in any given political culture, more than one set of rules, conventions, and (broadly conceived) sets of circumstances operated in tandem to shape petitioning behaviour. What the main kinds of petition were, and what were the most important shaping circumstances, needs to be worked out, observationally, in each setting. But taxonomies have their limits. One is that they tend not to get us very far in explaining change.

Explaining Change

Why do petitioning forms change, and associated practices develop? Change may be driven from the top down, by changes in rules – but even changes in rules often represent responses to other kinds of change originating elsewhere. A key driver of change is provided by people creatively reacting to changing circumstances, challenging existing rules and conventions, sometimes successfully, sometimes unsuccessfully. The parts played by circumstance, creativity, and official acceptance of, or conversely resistance to, change vary from case to case.

Changes in technology may open the door to changes in petitioning forms: thus, the invention of printing, or of the World Wide Web. Still, at the more formalised, rule-bound end of the spectrum of petitioning practices, approval for the taking up of new opportunities can be slow. Into the 20th century, the British Parliament continued to insist that petitions must be handwritten. Countries' first experiments with e-petitioning have spread out over decades. Changes in manners – in the degree of deference expected in petitioners, or how deference is expressed – may also affect petitioning forms, but again perhaps slowly. In the UK in 2020, those hoping to get their MPs to present a petition are advised that the prefatory material should end with the phrase 'And your petitioner(s) remain(s) etc.'. Conscious that this might strike modern eyes as odd, the instruction sheet advises 'You don't need to change it or add anything.'[23]

Changes in structures of power might be expected to have an effect on who gets petitioned about what, and perhaps how, and how petitions are dealt with. I have already mentioned changes that came about in the 1690s in the handling of petitions

[22] See also P. Langford (to whom Price was critically responding), *The Excise Crisis: Society and Politics in the Age of Walpole* (Oxford, Clarendon Press, 1975).

[23] www.parliament.uk/get-involved/sign-a-petition/paper-petitions/ (accessed 1 September 2020).

to the monarch that asked for mercy for convicted criminals, usually those sentenced to death. These came to be processed in special sittings by the Privy Council. This seems to have been partly because King William III was often absent, making war, so such decisions had to be referred somewhere else – but also the practice may have been welcomed, and have endured, partly because, in the aftermath of the Glorious Revolution, it seemed appropriate in this as in other connections to constrain the monarch's arbitrary will.[24] A more modern example: Richard Huzzey and Henry Miller have noted that in the early 20th century, as petitions to Parliament declined in number, numbers addressed to prime ministers seem to have risen – presumably reflecting petitioners' changing assessment of the locus of decision-making power within British governmental structures.[25]

In all these cases, it seems reasonable to attribute change above all to changing circumstances, though clearly in several cases changing circumstances had their effects in interaction with authorities' greater or lesser willingness to reshape their expectations in the light of other change.

Yet, in other instances, more emphasis needs to be laid on creativity, on petitioners pushing at the boundaries of rules and conventions to initiate new petitioning practices. In so doing, they sometimes exploited fuzziness or ambiguity in petitioning forms: thus, they developed previously marginal kinds of practice, or borrowed those associated with one kind of petitioning for another kind. Sometimes they hybridised petitioning with other practices. Sometimes they drew on history for models, or fashioned new constitutional theories around their own proceedings.[26] In the remainder of this chapter, I will illustrate these processes by sketching and reflecting on some of the changes in petitioning practice that unfolded in late-18th- and early-19th-century Britain.

How Petitioning Burgeoned and Changed: Britain, 1760–1830

Petitioning practices constantly shift, mutate, and develop, and in the long span of British history there have been many periods of notable change. The late 18th and early 19th centuries constitute one such period.[27] During the first two-thirds

[24] Beattie, 'The Cabinet and the Management of Death'.

[25] R. Huzzey and H. Miller, 'Petitions, Parliament and Political Culture: Petitioning the House of Commons, 1780–1918', *Past & Present*, 248 (2020), 123–64 (p. 140). Innes, 'Legislation and Public Participation', p. 112, suggests that long-term declines in numbers of petitions directed to parliaments or other assemblies could be associated with development of governmental infrastructure and clearer demarcations of responsibility.

[26] For a differently conceptualised account of the creativity of popular petitioners in the early stages of the French Revolution, involving 'La politisation de la plainte', see S. Wahnich, *La longue patience du peuple: 1792, naissance de la République* (Paris, Payot, 2008).

[27] Innes, 'Legislation and Public Participation', pp. 112–21; M. Knights, 'Participation and Representation before Democracy: Petitions and Addresses in Pre-Modern Britain', in I. Shapiro, S. Stokes, E. Wood,

of the 18th century, it was rare for public petitions on contentious matters to be proffered to either monarch or Parliament – even though in the previous century they had come to be embraced as important forms of public action. The official view seems to have been that 17th-century petitioning reflected a breakdown, or a series of breakdowns, in relations between government and people.[28] Since the Glorious Revolution of 1688 had led to the constitution being set on a better footing, petitions on public matters had become an unnecessary, disruptive, even unconstitutional form of public action. The House of Commons represented the people; therefore, anyone seeking to challenge it in the name of the people was in effect challenging the legitimacy of the framework of rule. Petitions on public matters were not totally ruled out of court. The 1661 Act against Tumultuous Petitioning (13 Cha. II, s. 1 c. 5.) – passed in the context of a previous attempt to restore political stability, involving the restoration of monarchy – spelled out how non-tumultuous petitioning might proceed in matters involving church or state (petitions should be signed by fewer than 20 people; or they should have been authorised by county magistrates or grand juries, and they must not be presented by more than 10 people). Arguably – it was not clear – the 1689 Bill of Rights's affirmation of the right to petition (the king) was in tension with this act. Still, the imprisonment by Parliament of members of a Kent grand jury for petitioning against the king's foreign policy in 1701 emphasised that this was dangerous ground, to be trodden with caution.[29] And in fact, for more than half a century thereafter, public petitions on such contentious matters were rare – despite the general liveliness and openness of the political culture, by historic standards. People found and exploited other means of representing grievances, especially in print, but also by means that we might think constituted petitioning in all but name: involving the promotion of 'addresses' or issuing of 'instructions' by town or county meetings to local MPs (the instrument employed in 1733 to protest against the government's Excise Bill).[30]

and A. Kirshner (eds), *Political Representation* (Cambridge, Cambridge University Press, 2009), pp. 35–57; P. Fraser, 'Public Petitioning and Parliament before 1832', *History*, 46 (1961), 195–211; C. Leys, 'Petitioning in the Nineteenth and Twentieth Centuries', *Political Studies*, 3 (1955), 45–64. I disagree with Philip Loft, who argues – in his 'Petitioning and Petitioners to the Westminster Parliament, 1660–1788', *Parliamentary History*, 38 (2019), 342–61 (p. 361) – that 'the eighteenth century experienced a "thickening" of petitioning, rather than its fundamental transformation', while agreeing with him that there was more petitioning earlier than is often realised. Still, his case to my mind rests too much on numbers, and de-emphasises the changing character of petitioning.

[28] For the 17th century, see D. Zaret, *Origins of Democratic Culture: Printing, Petitions and the Public Sphere in Early-Modern England* (Princeton, NJ, Princeton University Press, 2001); and M. Knights, *Politics and Opinion in Crisis, 1678–81* (Cambridge, Cambridge University Press, 1994).

[29] Knights, *Representation and Misrepresentation*, pp. 129–33. Lord Somers's informative tracts are reprinted in *Parliamentary History*, V, Apps. xvii–xviii.

[30] Knights, *Representation and Misrepresentation*, is generally inclined to elide the distinction between petitions and addresses, which indeed, perhaps especially in the early 18th century, was not always clear-cut. P. Kelly, 'Constituents' Instructions to Members of Parliament in the Eighteenth Century', in C. Jones (ed.), *Party and Party Management in Parliament 1660–1784* (Leicester, Leicester University Press, 1984), pp. 169–89.

The implication is not that there were no petitions of any kind to monarchs or Parliament during these decades, simply that such petitions as there were mostly had a different character. No historian has studied petitions to monarchs as a general (though heterogeneous) category in this period, but studies of earlier and later periods suggest that there were probably many, from subjects high and low; monarchs were also routinely the recipients of large numbers of addresses, often from counties or towns offering congratulations, on the birth of a royal child, conclusion of a peace, or the like.[31] Parliament was every year the target of many dozens or hundreds of petitions, sometimes on strictly private matters (seeking to initiate legislation relating to individuals, families, companies, or localities), some relating to public matters, but often expressing a mix of principled and interested concern (such-and-such a measure will damage the nation's prosperity and be bad for us).[32] As historians have often noted, from mid-century there was a marked growth both in petitions soliciting enclosures and in petitions seeking permission to effect urban 'improvements'; in the 1790s, Parliament invented a new category to demarcate the kinds of legislation sought by the latter stream of petitions: 'local acts'.[33] Such matters were often locally contentious, debated in local meetings, sometimes the subject of counterpetitions: all in all, providing an education in this form of practical politics.[34]

The last third of the century saw marked shifts in petitioning practice, most obviously but (as is not always emphasised enough) not *only* in relation to petitions on what were most obviously public matters.[35] Changes in the 1760s and 1770s arose, on the one hand, from a shift in the tectonic plates underlying the play of party politics, and, on the other hand, from the crisis in relations between Britain and her American colonies, which in the mid-1770s degenerated into war: the war for American independence. The background political shift followed from the determination of the new king, George III, to break the Whig monopoly on the highest positions in government. The effect was to drive into opposition some Whigs, who saw themselves as defenders of the heritage of 1688, and who in order to defend that heritage now sought to construct new forms of alliance with the people. Meanwhile, disillusioned by politicians' rank opportunism (as some previously

[31] See Poole, *The Politics of Regicide*, for individuals pressing petitions on the monarch. M. Knights, 'The Loyal Address: Prose Panegyric, 1658–1715', in P. Kewes and A. McCrae (eds), *Stuart Succession Literature: Moments and Transformations* (Oxford, Oxford University Press, 2019), pp. 319–35.

[32] Loft, 'Petitioning and Petitioners', is chiefly concerned with petitions of the second kind.

[33] Ibid.; J. Innes, 'The Local Acts of a National Parliament: Parliament's Role in Sanctioning Local Action in Eighteenth-Century Britain', in J. Innes, *Inferior Politics: Social Problems and Social Policies in Britain 1688–1800* (Oxford, Oxford University Press, 2009), pp. 78–105.

[34] M. Knights, 'Regulation and Rival Interests in the 1690s', in P. Gauci (ed.), *Regulating the British Economy, 1660–1850* (Farnham, Ashgate, 2011), pp. 63–81. Various such disputes are mentioned in H. T. Dickinson, *The Politics of the People in Eighteenth-Century Britain* (Basingstoke, Palgrave Macmillan, 1995), pp. 93–124. P. Elliott, *The Derby Philosophers: Science and Culture in British Urban Society, 1700–1850* (Manchester, Manchester University Press, 2009), pp. 115–27.

[35] For overviews see Knights, 'Participation and Representation'; and Fraser, 'Public Petitioning'.

die-hard oppositional 'patriots' rushed into the royal embrace, and old political hacks suddenly began courting the people), some outside Parliament began to try to build on local traditions of 'independency' to constitute a third force in politics, relatively autonomous from magnate direction.[36]

This new shape of things was conducive to bold new initiatives in the ways and means of popular politics, framed by new kinds of constitutional and political imaginary. The Americans' use of petitions to press their complaints on Crown and Parliament directed attention to petitions as political vehicles. In this context, people in a variety of English localities, with some critical encouragement from newly oppositional Whigs, began organising public meetings to promote petitions to the king, asking him to dismiss his ministers.[37] Conscious that, in relation to recent practice, they were doing something new, supporters of this campaign reflected on more distant historical precedents. They cited the Bill of Rights, and recalled (often with indignation, and a measure of bravado) the fate of the Kentish petitioners. (It may have helped that the first volumes in Catherine Macaulay's *History of England*, including accounts of early-17th-century petitioning movements, appeared at this time, though proto-revolutionary precedents of this kind – such as the 'exclusion' petitions, which had attempted to prevent the accession of James II – were rarely cited.)[38]

Bold in some ways, these campaigners respected convention in others, confining their efforts to mobilise opinion to well-defined jurisdictional units, presided over by respectable elites, from whom they drew important support. It seems also that they sought signatures primarily from those with recognised political personalities: freeholders, freemen, and so forth.[39] Their respect for such conventional expectations helped to determine that the absolute number of petitions ultimately sent to the king was quite small – 26 – though, from a different perspective, the 15 county petitions represented over a third of English counties and the 11 borough petitions accounted within their number for over a third of the cities that had county status. Such status considerations probably affected who petitioned (thus, they help to explain why there was a petition from Berwick, and why one was begun in Canterbury, when most smaller towns did not act).[40] However they were assessed, this flow of petitions represented a blow of a kind that the king and his ministers certainly were not happy to incur. (And in fact the king shortly replaced his then

[36] There is useful material on 'independency' in Dickinson, *The Politics of the People*, pp. 13–55. John Brewer characterised it as an 'alternative structure of politics' in *Party, Ideology, and Popular Politics at the Accession of George III* (Cambridge, Cambridge University Press, 1976).

[37] G. Rudé, *Wilkes and Liberty: A Social Study of 1763–74* (Oxford, Oxford University Press, 1962), pp. 105–48.

[38] E.g. *Middlesex Journal*, 13–15 June 1769; and *Gazetteer and New Daily Advertizer*, 27 June 1769. C. Macaulay, *The History of England from the Accession of James I to That of the Brunswick Line*, 8 vols (London, J. Nourse [C. Dilly], 1763–83), Vol. III, pp. 105–14.

[39] J. A. Phillips, 'Popular Politics in Unreformed England', *Journal of Modern History*, 52 (1980), 599–625.

[40] See Rudé, *Wilkes and Liberty*, p. 133, for the list; the interpretation is mine.

prime minister with someone he hoped would do better at getting on top of a difficult situation: the initially successful, later reviled, Lord North).

Petitioning in relation to contentious public issues thus thudded back into the arsenal of possible political devices. Moreover, it reappeared in association with narratives that amplified the challenge latent in the form: narratives that stressed the people's rights, and the potentially disastrous consequences of not listening to the people. Against the background of continuing and worsening imperial crisis – which would not be resolved until 1783/4 – the practice quickly underwent a series of further mutations and developments. Although opposition Whigs had aided and abetted the first petitioning movement, they had also been critical of the tactic of petitioning the king; they thought that it would have been better in constitutional terms to petition Parliament. The next major petitioning campaign, directed towards avoiding war with America, was directed to Parliament, in 1775.[41] (Self-evidently, it failed.) At the low point of the war, 1779–80, a fresh wave of petitions to Parliament, complaining of financial burdens and misgovernment, was initiated in Yorkshire, under the leadership of a sceptical cleric, Christopher Wyvill (again with significant support from opposition Whigs).[42]

At this point petitioning was (as I have put it) hybridised with a widening variety of other forms of activity. Petitions were debated and agreed at county and town meetings (Wyvill's *Political Papers* provide interesting insight into the character of these debates). A web of personal connections combined with press coverage to spread awareness of the campaign.[43] Wyvill then encouraged participating counties (an impressive total of 26 out of 40 English counties petitioned) to join an 'Association'. The immediate object of the Association was to put pressure on candidates in an imminent general election to support a reform platform – a variant on the device of 'instructing' MPs.[44] 'Associations' had traditionally been established to support government in periods of national emergency: during the Spanish Armada, after an assassination attempt on William III, and in the face of the Jacobite rising of 1745. Pro-government Members of Parliament expressed dismay that at this juncture an Association was being instituted to undermine government.[45]

[41] J. Bradley, *Popular Politics and the American Revolution in England: Petitions, the Crown and Public Opinion* (Macon, GA, Mercer, 1986), pp. 12–3, 24–5.

[42] H. Butterfield, *George III, Lord North, and the People* (London, Bell, 1949), stresses the war context but underplays party politics; I. Christie, *Wilkes, Wyvill, and Reform: The Parliamentary Reform Movement in British Politics, 1760–1785* (London, Macmillan, 1962), does the reverse. See also E. C. Black, *The Association: British Extraparliamentary Organization, 1769–1793* (Cambridge, MA, Harvard University Press, 1963).

[43] C. Wyvill, *Political Papers*, 6 vols (York, W. Blanchard, 1794–1804); H. Barker, *Newspapers, Politics, and Public Opinion in Late Eighteenth-Century England* (Oxford, Clarendon Press, 1998).

[44] Wyvill, *Political Papers*, Vol. III, pp. 116–17, cited in Black, *The Association*, p. 38.

[45] For the specific history of 'association' as a political form, see F. O'Gorman, 'Origins and Trajectories of Loyalism in England', in A. Blackstock and F. O'Gorman (eds), *Loyalism and the Formation of the British World, 1775–1914* (Woodbridge, Boydell Press, 2014), pp. 19–42. Black, *The Association*, does not explore the earlier history.

As the war drew to its conclusion (unsuccessful as regards America; successful as regards side-conflicts with other European powers) support for Wyvill's initiatives sagged. In that context, he adopted a new approach, switching the focus to the need to reform Parliament, and sending out letters requesting support in the form of a new round of petitions, not to counties and major towns, but to smaller towns, especially those represented in Parliament by MPs chosen only by their corporate governing bodies.[46] That is, he showed himself willing to trade off the prestige of having the support of the more eminent communities for a broadening of the campaign's base, and an increase in the number of petitions. It is as if he thought it important to keep a petitioning campaign going somehow, and was prepared to experiment with new means to achieve that. In 1783 the political scene became more fluid, when the resignation of the wartime prime minister, Lord North, was followed by a split among opposition Whigs. In that context, the old device of 'addressing' the monarch was adapted to a new purpose. The king was deluged with addresses recommending one or other ministerial team. Unusually, public attention was directed to the numbers of signatures inscribed upon each address.[47]

Innovations thus unfolded in a variety of directions, the only consistent theme being the hope that mobilising some section of the people to express political views might bring about change at the heart of politics. When the king's chosen minister, William Pitt the Younger, managed to stabilise his support base in Parliament during 1784, the flow of political 'applications' (petitions and cognate forms of solicitation) ebbed, though the political atmosphere remained febrile and stagey, as partisan political clubs jousted for pre-eminence in various towns.[48]

A notable feature of the decade inaugurated by these developments was that enthusiasm for petitioning Parliament, and new ideas as to how to petition, spread out from core political and constitutional issues to stimulate striking innovations in the ways that people pursued other concerns. Distinguishing between different kinds of petition helps us to register and characterise this spread – but what is notable is that there was a high degree of cross-fertilisation. An early, shocking instance was the Protestant Association petition of 1780: a petition against recent moves to extend toleration of Catholics, which took the form of a single monster petition, signed by an impressive 40,000 or so apparently mainly middle-class Londoners. To counter insinuations that signatures could easily be forged and did not reliably demonstrate real support, the Protestant Associators decided to present their petition *en masse* (precipitating debate about whether the 1661 Tumultuous Petitioning

[46] Black, *The Association*, pp. 99–101.

[47] J. Cannon, *The Fox–North Coalition: Crisis of the Constitution, 1782–4* (Cambridge, Cambridge University Press, 1969); D. R. McAdam, 'Addresses to the King and the Fox–North Coalition', *Huntingdon Library Quarterly*, 35 (1972), 381–5; Phillips, 'Popular Politics', pp. 610–14.

[48] F. Knights, *The Strange Case of Thomas Walker: Ten Years in the Life of a Manchester Radical* (London, Lawrence & Wishart, 1957); B. Jerrold, introduction to T. Walker, *The Original*, ed. W. B. Jerrold (London, Grant, 1874); A. Goodwin, *The Friends of Liberty: The English Democratic Movement in the Age of the French Revolution* (London, Hutchinson, 1979), pp. 65–98.

Act, whose terms they had plainly breached, was still operative). In fact, it proved impossible to maintain order at the fringes of the mass gathering, and what began as a series of demonstrative attacks on Catholic chapels by way of underlining the campaign's message escalated into a week of riotous disorder, ultimately countered by troops who killed hundreds of people. Some dozens of people were hanged for their part in the riots, and the campaign's leader, Lord George Gordon, was tried for but acquitted of treason.[49]

This did not serve to discredit petitioning as such, however. Wyvill and his supporters continued to strive to organise petitions, and later in the decade several of those who had participated in the political movement launched mass petitioning campaigns to support other objectives, including expanded rights for Protestant Dissenters and the abolition of the slave trade.[50] Both of those causes had previously been promoted by petitions (in relation to Dissenting rights, in the 1730s; in relation to the slave trade, as recently as 1783), but they had not previously been made the subject of mass campaigns: that was the new departure.[51] Moreover, even approaches to more private, interest-group kinds of petitioning were affected. In the middle of the decade, industrialists campaigning against new taxes designed to pay off war debt responded to new ideas as to how to give petitions oomph by asking their workers in their hundreds and thousands to sign their petitions. Workers would later put their newly acquired know-how to ends that the industrialists presumably did not intend: in the 1790s and early 19th century, some of them organised mass petitions to promote 'private' bills designed to enhance the rights of those working in particular lines of production.[52]

In the 1760s, instigating many thousands of people across the country to put their names on petitions to high authorities engaging with contentious public issues had been an innovative, somewhat daring thing to do. In the decades that followed, the approach became familiar, even routine. Expectations changed: small numbers of petitions, or petitions signed by small numbers, ceased to impress. Petitions began to be issued in their hundreds, even thousands, each being signed by large numbers

[49] I. Haywood and J. Seed (eds), *The Gordon Riots: Politics, Culture and Insurrection in Late Eighteenth-Century Britain* (Cambridge, Cambridge University Press, 2012).

[50] G. M. Ditchfield, 'The Parliamentary Struggle over the Repeal of the Test and Corporation Acts, 1787–1790', *English Historical Review*, 89 (1974), 551–77; S. Drescher, *Capitalism and Anti-Slavery: British Mobilization in Comparative Perspective* (New York, Macmillan, 1986); J. R. Oldfield, *Popular Politics and British Anti-Slavery: The Mobilisation of British Public Opinion against the Slave Trade* (Manchester, Manchester University Press, 1995), pp. 96–124.

[51] For Dissenters, see N. C. Hunt, *Two Early Political Associations: The Quakers and the Dissenting Deputies in the Age of Sir Robert Walpole* (Oxford, Oxford University Press, 1961), pp. 113–78; for Quakers' hesitation about launching an anti-slavery campaign in the early 1780s, see C. L. Brown, *Moral Capital: Foundations of British Abolitionism* (Chapel Hill, NC, Omohundro Institute of Early American History and Culture, 2006), pp. 391–450.

[52] Innes, 'Des tisserands', p. 93; and J. Innes, 'Regulating Wages in the Eighteenth and Nineteenth Centuries: Arguments in Context, 1750–1850', in Gauci, *Regulating the British Economy*, pp. 195–215 (p. 209).

of people. By the 1810s, almost every year saw at least one campaign eliciting thousands of petitions: campaigns ranged across a wide gamut, from political and religious through moral, commercial, and industrial, across public and private matters, through a fuzzy middle ground that was beginning to emerge, inhabited by politicised issues.[53] Petitioning had, indeed, played a part in establishing that middle ground, by giving rank-and-file Britons a means of taking a public stance on topics about which they cared but over which they lacked direct leverage. Politicisation of issues such as the slave trade and slavery probably had effects on how people thought about traditional forms of politics. Traditional politics had chiefly been the domain of the adult male voter: that is, of heads of household qualified by property ownership or civic status to play a part in public affairs. By contrast, no such limits were usually set around the right to engage with religious, moral, or economic issues. Women can already be found signing economic and local government petitions earlier in the century.[54] Some signed the Protestant Association petition (in particular sections of the petition, suggesting different approaches by different signature-collectors). Though their role in anti-slavery campaigns did not initially extend to signing petitions, there was a women's petition against slavery in 1825, and many more from 1830.[55]

The story cannot be framed just in terms of 'onward and upward', however. Petitioning remained one element among other campaigning options. It exhibited some rises and falls in favour, as the political climate changed from time to time.[56] In the early 1790s, anti-slavery campaigners had succeeded in eliciting hundreds of petitions. But the abolition of the slave trade in 1807 did not take place against a background of petitioning. Made cautious by the radicalisation of the French Revolution, by the Irish rebellion of 1798, and would-be revolutionary activity within Britain (notably Despard's conspiracy of 1803), campaign leaders thought it safer to employ different tactics, such as writing letters and paying personal visits to MPs.[57] Through most of the first two decades of the 19th century, ministers saw good reason to accept and respond to the swelling tide of petitioning aimed at securing legislation on labour issues. They welcomed the chance to engage with workers' delegates in parliamentary committee rooms, to show them that they were being heard, and to talk through difficult issues with them. But in 1819, a new Act (60 Geo. III & 1 Geo. IV, c. 6) aimed at limiting scope for public meetings

[53] See Innes, 'Legislation and Public Participation', pp. 117–19, for numbers and topics. For a recent discussion of popular petitioning in context, see R. Poole, *Peterloo: The English Uprising* (Oxford, Oxford University Press, 2019), pp. 93–115.

[54] Loft, 'Petitioning and Petitioners', 356–7.

[55] The National Archives, TS 11/389/1124. M. Knights, 'Petitioning Culture and the Gordon Riots', in Haywood and Seed, *The Gordon Riots*, pp. 46–68, notes female signatories (p. 53), but does not linger on them. C. Midgley, *Women against Slavery: The British Campaigns* (London, Routledge, 1992), pp. 62–70.

[56] Leys, 'Petitioning'.

[57] S. Drescher, 'Whose Abolition? Popular Pressure and the Ending of the British Slave Trade', *Past & Present*, 143 (1994), 136–66.

included, alongside predictable constraints on assembling to petition about matters affecting church or state, new constraints on meetings to petition in relation to trade or commerce. And in practice, workers' old 'private petitioning' route to securing a hearing in the House of Commons closed from that date. Thereafter, the legislative initiative passed to MPs. Workers retained the right to petition, but their petitions thereafter could do no more than comment on proposals that they hoped to see originate, or that had originated, in Parliament.[58] Flux and variation thus remained important aspects of the story (and I have been tracing only patterns in parliamentary petitioning; there are other stories to be told about petitioning in other contexts).

Even continuing to confine our attention to parliamentary petitioning, it seems worth noting finally that not all innovations in practice through the early 19th century involved a shift towards the collective. These decades also saw an as-yet-unremarked and uncharted appearance and rise of petitions from individuals commenting on public policies. I have encountered numerous instances of these in relation to welfare issues: poverty, land management and employment on the land, and so forth, and probably further research would show that apparently lone individuals addressed other issues too.[59] I say 'apparently' lone individuals because background research suggests that some lone signatories acted against a background of associational activity. Still, sometimes that collective experience seems to have emboldened individuals to submit petitions offering comment and (sometimes very general) proposals on public-policy matters on their own initiative. The surveyor Matthew Phillips, for example, was active from the 1810s in, and sometimes chaired meetings of, what would later be known as the Labourer's Friend Society (in the period of his involvement, less catchily named the Society for the Encouragement of Industry and the Reduction of Poor Rates). After his involvement with the society had ceased, Phillips repeatedly petitioned Parliament through various intermediaries, latterly his local (Brighton) MP.[60] Another such (repeat) lone petitioner was a James Hantler 'of the parish of Saint Luke, Chelsea', who, for example, in 1830 petitioned the House of Lords, praying their Lordships 'to take into Consideration the Expediency of the Plan for the Payment of Tithes and Employment of the Agricultural Labourer which the Petitioner in his Petition lays before the House'.[61] The rise of petitions of this kind may reflect some relaxation on

[58] These claims draw on my work in progress, but the shift is evidenced by the fall-away in the printed committee reports that had arisen from committee hearings on such petitions. For campaigns around Combination Acts, see I. Prothero, *Artisans and Politics in Early Nineteenth-Century London: John Gast and His Times* (Baton Rouge, Louisiana State University Press, 1979), pp. 172–82.

[59] It's possible to survey petitioners using the *General Index to Reports of Public Petitions 1833–52*, House of Commons Parliamentary Papers (1833), LVI, though the list extends over more than 1,000 pages. I surveyed petitions relating to subjects beginning with 'P' and 'Q'.

[60] Phillips is the subject of my 'Seeing like a Surveyor: Imagining Rural Reform in the Early Nineteenth-Century UK', in B. Kinzer, M. Kraemer, and R. Trainor (eds), *Reform and Its Complexities in Modern Britain: Essays Inspired by Sir Brian Harrison* (Oxford, Oxford University Press, 2021), pp. 57–76.

[61] *Journal of the House of Lords*, 4 May 1830. See also *Journal of the House of Commons*, 7 July 1830.

the part of parliamentary clerks, the gatekeepers of the petitioning system, in terms of what they were prepared to process (there are indications that in the 18th century, representations of this kind were commonly sent to Members of Parliament and government departments, even if they did not reach Parliament as such).[62] But the growth of single-petitioner public petitioning may also reflect something about the changing character of British political culture – for example, developments in associational life, extension in the range of press coverage of public business, changing understandings of 'public opinion' and its role in public life, and associated banalisation of public petitioning as an activity. This plethora of loosely associated changes perhaps operated to embolden quite ordinary middle-class men to think that Parliament might be spurred to take notice of their bright ideas.

Kaleidoscopic and Other Change

In this chapter I have identified some of the contexts that shape changes in petitioning forms and practices, including changes in communication technology, structures of power, and manners. Also, implicitly, changes in political alignments that encourage the sense that a chink in the armour of power has opened, which might possibly be prised open wider, and greater change accomplished. Equally I have identified some of the mechanisms of change that creative human actors have from time to time employed, including playing variations on existing petitioning themes by, for example, borrowing features from other petitioning types; hybridising petitioning with other forms of activity; and constructing new historical or constitutional narratives around the act, in a bid to change its meaning. Resulting patterns of change are often complex and multiform, exhibiting trends but also fluctuations and variations. The basic features of the practice being given by definition, some kaleidoscopic revisiting of practices from other times or places is to be expected. But since the objects in play are many, and are themselves subject to change, the scope for variation continues to intrigue.

[62] Innes, *Inferior Politics*, p. 316 n. 161; J. Innes, 'Parliament and Church Reform: Off and on the Agenda', in M. Davis and G. Pentland (eds), *Liberty, Property, and Popular Politics: England and Scotland, 1688–1815* (Edinburgh, Edinburgh University Press, 2015), pp. 39–57 (p. 49).

5

E-Petitions to Parliaments: Why Processes Matter

CRISTINA LESTON-BANDEIRA

E-PETITIONS ARE A common feature of modern life. Many campaigners use them, while some organisations such as Change.org exist solely to provide a platform for e-petitions. They are an omnipresent element of modern politics and campaigning. Having emerged in the late 1990s, e-petitions were first introduced outside formal political institutions. However, as they became more pervasive, and their advantages more patent in terms of reach and ease of access, legislatures started to introduce their own e-petitions systems from the turn of the century onwards, although the adoption by parliaments overall has been patchy. This is in part because although e-petitions fulfil some of the same functions as traditional paper petitions, but expressed through a different technology, in reality their digital nature introduces significant differences. As this chapter shows, while functionally the same tool, a few characteristics of e-petitions make them a more challenging mechanism for parliaments to adopt. At the same time, while e-petitions are no doubt pervasive, with thousands of them circulated every day, there is considerable scepticism about whether they achieve anything. This chapter argues that in order to evaluate whether e-petitions achieve much, we need to consider the processes that define them and the wider roles that they may perform besides achieving policy change.

This chapter starts by reflecting on the specific challenges that e-petitions bring to parliaments, from the simple but important reality that legislatures as institutions have struggled to implement digital solutions. The chapter then explains why the processes in place are so important. Indeed, it is the process that makes the petition, as the example of the development of the e-petitions system in the UK House of Commons illustrates. This point enables a greater understanding of what e-petitions can achieve. The extent to which e-petitions to Parliament achieve anything is shaped by the formal, institutional processes, procedures, practices, and rules for receiving, considering, and processing them – in short, what politics scholars have

Proceedings of the British Academy, **262**, 104–118, © The British Academy 2024.

described as 'petition systems'.[1] Depending on this context, e-petitions can play a number of different roles in mediating the relationship between parliaments and citizens, through the consequences arising from the submission, dissemination, discussion, and/or consideration of e-petitions. The chapter identifies four possible roles associated with e-petitions: linkage, campaigning, scrutiny, and policy-making. In each case, as the example of the UK House of Commons shows, the ability of e-petitions to perform these roles is determined by the 'petitions system' in place. The reflection developed in this chapter is based on the author's extensive primary research on e-petitions to Parliament, which includes 17 semi-structured interviews with parliamentary officials and MPs of the UK Parliament, as well as petitioners, selected according to a purposive and snowballing sample strategy, supplemented by documentary analysis of official documentation of this and other parliaments.[2]

Why E-Petitions Bring Added Challenges to Parliaments

E-petitions have become popular because they are a simple tool for citizen participation. Having received petitions for centuries, it is perhaps surprising that parliaments did not swiftly adopt online modes of this practice. However, the lag in legislatures establishing e-petitions systems is more understandable when the specific challenges of digital – as opposed to paper – petitions are examined.

The story of the expansion and popularity of e-petitions is in many ways part of a wider story of the expansion of the internet and of digital technologies. It may be tempting to view e-petitions from a historical perspective as a further development of a form that has existed for centuries, but we should also recognise the distinct, unique properties of digital petitions. As the internet emerged in the mid-1990s, so-called *utopians* viewed it as the big breakthrough that would equalise democratic processes and transform democracy more generally into more participatory forms.[3] E-petitions developed very much in this spirit, as a way of using the opportunities offered by web-based forms of communication to strengthen citizens' ability to raise issues from the bottom up to policy-makers, and to galvanise support more easily and quickly.

The first online petition platforms, such as PetitionOnline, emerged in the late 20th century and have expanded exponentially since then. For instance, Change.org boasts over 329 million users (and many more signatories) across the globe, and has local teams established in 18 different countries.[4] After online petitions became

[1] T. Caygill and A.-M. Griffiths, 'Parliament and Petitions', in C. Leston-Bandeira and L. Thompson (eds), *Exploring Parliament* (Oxford, Oxford University Press, 2018), pp. 322–32.

[2] This research was funded by an ESRC Impact Acceleration Account grant, 2016–17.

[3] E.g. H. Rheingold, *The Virtual Community Finding Connection in a Computerized World* (London, Secker & Warburg, 1993); and E. Schwartz, *NetActivism: How Citizens Use the Internet* (Sebastopol, CA, Songline Studios, 1996).

[4] Change.org, *Change.org Impact Report 2019* (2020), https://static.change.org/brand-pages/impact/reports/2020/2020_Impact+Report_Change_EN_final.pdf (accessed 15 August 2023).

increasingly popular at the turn of the 21st century, pressure started building upon parliamentary institutions to follow suit and develop online versions of petitions.

While many legislatures across the world have received paper petitions for centuries, the jump to online petitions has not always been straightforward. One main reason is that because of their institutional characteristics and nature, parliaments and digital media are very awkward bedfellows. Digital means of communication and of working are a very poor fit to the way parliaments operate, which explains why they struggle with implementing and, particularly, keeping up with, digital developments.[5]

One of the defining characteristics of parliaments is their collective nature. Legislatures are collective entities in that they are made up of the different identities and groups that find themselves represented within the institution. The need to take into account different points of view from a wide variety of groups and individuals hinders quick decision-making, even if in some cases the majority voice determines the ultimate decisions taken. This slower pace of decision-making is in marked contrast to the rapid pace at which digital media change, with new technology, apps, and platforms emerging all the time and quickly being superseded in turn. Legislatures also encompass different and often opposing agendas, which further hinders decision-making by making them risk-averse, with a fear of being exposed to criticism. As risk-averse institutions, legislatures struggle with digital adaptation, yet risk and innovation are core drivers of digital change, through trials and experimentation. Their collective nature also means legislatures lack a single voice that speaks for parliament, which results in a lack of leadership to drive change. Leadership is absolutely key to driving and embedding digital change, which often involves risk and considerable disruption to processes and practices. Besides this, legislatures have bicephalous leaderships, which combine political with administrative management structures, with the former temporary (and at the mercy of elections) and the latter permanent. The exact structures vary between legislatures, 'but this combination results in risk averse approaches. Either because the permanent staff act as the guardians of the institution, steering away from risk, and don't have the final say; or because the political leadership may worry about potential drawbacks from ill-fated decisions.'[6] For these reasons, decisions regarding the adoption of online petition systems by parliaments have often been beset by delays.

Finally, legislatures are few and far between. Most countries will only have one – some may have a few more, if we include regional or devolved legislatures. Separated by distance and often by very different political and cultural contexts, parliaments are not always good at learning from each other and sharing lessons

[5] See C. Leston-Bandeira, 'The Impact of the Internet on Parliaments: A Legislative Studies Framework', *Parliamentary Affairs*, 60 (2007), 655–74; C. Leston-Bandeira, 'Seven Reasons why Parliaments Struggle with Digital', Political Studies Association (PSA), *PSA Insight Plus Blog* (2014), www.psa.ac.uk/insight-plus/blog/seven-reasons-why-parliaments-struggle-digital (accessed 19 July 2021).

[6] Leston-Bandeira, 'Seven Reasons'.

or experiences. This again contrasts with the practice of trial and error and learning from others intrinsic to the implementation of new technology; it is also counterintuitive to how digital learning thrives. Overall, the combination of these characteristics explains that, while digital media are a pervasive element of contemporary life, integrating such technologies within and by parliaments is beset with a number of challenges. In particular, legislatures lack the agile, flexible, and risk-friendly structures needed to implement digital processes. This context explains why so many parliaments have resisted the initial implementation or subsequent development of e-petitions. In 2020, only 23 per cent of all national parliaments had introduced an e-petitions system,[7] and most were developed a decade after the first non-official platforms.

A further issue for legislatures with regard to adopting e-petitions is that they do not fit easily with traditional parliamentary processes and procedures. Petitions to parliaments have traditionally been one of the main ways citizens have been able to raise specific issues to policy-makers. If such petitioning existed (and it is important to note that many parliaments do not have processes for receiving petitions, such as examples in Latin America and some of the Nordic legislatures), then this took place within a specific procedural context. Parliamentary processes to consider petitions vary considerably, but regardless of each specific case they are usually framed by procedures that are orientated towards Parliament and legislators rather than petitioners. E-petitions, however, are fundamentally different in that they are petitioner-led. While in principle trying to achieve the same purposes, their nature presupposes a different logic in the way the (e-)petition should be considered. In practice this means that many legislatures, including some early adopters such as the Portuguese Parliament, simply opened an online channel for petitions, but did not adapt their processes to make the most of the potential offered by online means of communication. To put it simply, citizens were able to post a paper petition to Parliament in the traditional way but could now also email their petition or submit it via an online form. In such cases, parliamentary e-petitions systems are not necessarily making the most of the potential offered by the digital mode, which includes some of the reasons why e-petitions became popular in the first place, namely a mechanism for dissemination and galvanising support. Integrating e-petitions, with their essentially petitioner-led focus, with traditional parliamentary procedures can lead to clunky processes. As such, a legislature such as the Scottish Parliament, which introduced its e-petitions system together with its paper petitions systems, is a good example of an institution that developed an integrated, coherent system for e-petitions.

Finally, just as historically petitioners have challenged the legitimacy of parliaments elected under limited suffrage, e-petitions can also question the

[7] Inter-Parliamentary Union, *World E-Parliament Report* (2020), www.ipu.org/resources/publications/reports/2021-07/world-e-parliament-report-2020 (accessed 15 August 2023), p. 66. This value is overestimated, as it includes very diverse types of systems, such as citizens' legislative initiatives.

representative mandate of parliamentarians.[8] A key attribute of e-petitions is their visibility online and the fact that they can be easily disseminated via the internet to raise the profile of the issues being brought forward, as well as that of the petitioners. This context helps to explain why e-petitions can be used to question the representative mandate of parliamentarians, particularly by challenging their responsiveness on particular issues. Although parliamentary e-petitions systems integrate MPs into the process of considering petitions, parliamentarians often dislike e-petitions, as they seem to shift the power away from Members. Combine with this the fact that many legislatures, particularly within the Commonwealth, have had petitions systems that have been mediated by MPs, and the challenge presented by e-petitions is all the more apparent. In these legislatures, such as the Parliament of Ghana,[9] or of Australia until 2008,[10] as well as historically the UK House of Commons, citizens have traditionally presented their petition through the medium of an MP. By introducing the option of citizens submitting a petition online – that is directly onto a parliamentary e-petitions platform – the electronic form of petitioning empowers the citizen further by enabling them to reach out to Parliament, by-passing MPs in the process. One might add that where paper petitions historically played a role in strengthening the link between constituent and MP because petitions had to be presented by legislators,[11] the e-petition mode, while facilitating citizen participation, hinders representation in the traditional way. In practice this has resulted in a few variations. The UK House of Commons introduced a new, separate e-petitions system in 2015, while keeping intact its centuries-old system for paper petitions submitted through MPs. The Canadian House of Commons also introduced e-petitions in 2015 but required them to be sponsored by MPs to be considered, in effect applying the traditional procedure for paper petitions to new digital forms.[12]

Regardless of the actual system in place e-petitions have raised questions regarding their legitimacy and, indeed, their compatibility with representative democracy. E-petitions have often been viewed with suspicion by parliamentarians and/or parliamentary officials, who may perceive them as competing with the parliamentary process and its representative nature.[13] Such suspicions are perhaps

[8] H. Miller, 'Introduction: The Transformation of Petitioning in the Long Nineteenth Century (1780–1914)', *Social Science History*, 43 (2019), 409–29 (p. 415).

[9] E. Azevedo-Hardman, 'Parliaments and Citizens in Sub-Saharan Africa', *Journal of Legislative Studies*, 18 (2012), 419–40 (p. 427).

[10] R. Hough, 'Do Legislative Petitions Enhance the Relationship between Parliament and Citizen?', *The Journal of Legislative Studies*, 18 (2012), 479–95 (p. 484).

[11] H. Miller, *A Nation of Petitioners: Petitions and Petitioning in the United Kingdom, 1780–1918* (Cambridge, Cambridge University Press, 2023), pp. 229–52.

[12] Standing Committee on Procedure and Public Affairs, *Seventy-Fifth Report: Approval and Updating of the House of Commons Electronic Petitions System*, House of Commons of Canada (2017), www.ourcommons.ca/DocumentViewer/en/42-1/PROC/report-75/ (accessed 19 July 2021).

[13] See, for example, F. Matthews, 'The Value of "Between-Election" Political Participation: Do Parliamentary E-Petitions Matter to Political Elites?', *British Journal of Politics and International Relations*, 23 (2020), 410–29.

reinforced when e-petitions are mistakenly labelled as a form of direct democracy that implicitly or explicitly have the potential to challenge the mandate of elected representatives. Such a view is sometimes expressed by petitioners themselves, who may claim a popular mandate from well-supported petitions, as was the case with the e-petition to revoke Article 50, the means by which the UK government triggered the formal process of leaving the European Union, in 2019.[14] However, e-petitions are not a form of direct democracy.[15] Direct democracy implies citizens coming together to make a decision, which is then implemented by decision-makers – as is the case with referendums, where the decision is taken by the participating citizens, with decision-makers then simply implementing it. E-petitions are instead a form of advocacy democracy,[16] whereby citizens bring issues of concern to decision-makers, but it is ultimately up to those decision-makers to take a decision on the issue brought to them; thus, the final decision is made through the representative mandate.

To sum up, parliaments' unsuitability to implement digital tools, the poor fit between citizen-led tools and traditional parliamentary processes, and the potential challenge posed by e-petitions to the mandate of representatives all explain the slow adoption of e-petitions by parliaments. However, the last few years have seen something of a boom in legislatures adopting e-petitions systems, using a wide range of formats and systems. The Scottish Parliament was the first legislature reported to have formally adopted e-petitioning, in 2004,[17] with the German Bundestag following suit the year after,[18] while the Portuguese Parliament was another early adopter.[19] Since 2012 all of the following have also adopted e-petitions: the Irish Oireachtas (2012), the Luxembourgian Chamber of Deputies (2013), the UK House

[14] C. Leston-Bandeira, 'Can the Revoke Article 50 Petition Change the Course of Brexit?, *The Conversation* (2019), https://theconversation.com/can-the-revoke-article-50-petition-change-the-course-of-brexit-114217 (accessed 19 July 2021).

[15] Although we should note the use of petitions as an institutional mechanism to trigger referendums in some polities, such as Switzerland, or the USA in particular states (see Huzzey and Miller's chapter in this volume). Or indeed the use of 'recall petitions' in the UK since 2015, through which voters can trigger a special election to remove an MP; see N. Johnston, 'The First Use of a "Recall Petition" in the UK', *Insight*, House of Commons Library, 10 August 2018, available at https://commonslibrary.parliament.uk/the-first-use-of-a-recall-petition-in-the-uk/ (accessed 27 January 2024).

[16] R. Dalton, S. Scarrow, and B. Cain, 'New Forms of Democracy? Reform and Transformation of Democratic Institutions', in B. Cain, R. Dalton, and S. Scarrow (eds), *Democracy Transformed? Expanding Political Opportunities in Advanced Industrial Democracies* (Oxford, Oxford University Press, 2003), pp. 1–20.

[17] After a pilot from 2000 onwards. J. Seaton, 'The Scottish Parliament and E-Democracy', *Aslib Proceedings*, 57 (2005), 333–7 (p. 336). See also C. Carman, *The Assessment of the Scottish Parliament's Public Petitions System 1999–2006* (Edinburgh, Scottish Parliament Information Centre for the Public Petitions Committee, 2006), available at http://archive.scottish.parliament.uk/business/committees/petitions/reports-06/pur06-PPS-assessment-01.htm (accessed 19 July 2021).

[18] R. Lindner and U. Riehm, 'Broadening Participation through E-Petitions? An Empirical Study of Petitions to the German Parliament', *Policy & Internet*, 3 (2011), 1–23.

[19] C. Leston-Bandeira and T. Tibúrcio, 'Developing Links despite the Parties: Parliament and Citizens in Portugal', *Journal of Legislative Studies*, 18 (2012), 384–402.

of Commons and the Canadian House of Commons (2015), the Australian House of Representatives (2016), the Parliament of New Zealand (2018), and the French National Assembly (2020).[20] But how successful are these systems in realising the potential of digital tools and in enhancing citizens' right to petition?

These petition systems differ very considerably. To state that a parliament has an e-petitions system means little, as there are as many formats as there are systems. And the specific systems in place matter, because it is these distinct processes that shape the potential of e-petitions with regard to the relationship between legislatures and citizens, and which determine the potential roles that parliamentary petitions systems may play.[21] Key to this are the processes through which they are considered by parliaments.

Why Process Matters

No petition or e-petition should be evaluated on its own because they are defined by the process associated with the petition system in question. This applies to any type of petition, but is particularly true with parliamentary petitions, and even more so with e-petitions to parliament, because of the tension between the visibility inherent to its digital presence and institutional processes. An e-petition is simply a piece of text; it usually consists of a title, followed by a short text outlining the action being asked for, often showing how many signatures it has collated. Additional information may include what has happened to the e-petition, such as whether it has been considered by a committee, or whether the petitioner has taken any other action. This second part – *what happens to the e-petition* – is not only the most important stage of the process but is also critical to defining the e-petition.

This applies to all e-petition systems; it is not specific to parliamentary ones. A Change.org e-petition means little just on its own; it is what happens to it that matters, and particularly what the process is for the e-petition other than dissemination and the collection of signatures. This point explains why many e-petitions systems achieve little more than mobilising support (which in itself is important), as they often encompass very basic processes, which tend to focus primarily on the

[20] Respectively: House of Oireachtas Commission, *Annual Report 2012* (2012), https://data.oireachtas.ie/ie/oireachtas/corporate/reports/2013/2013-06-30_houses-of-the-oireachtas-commission-annual-report-2012_en.pdf (accessed 19 July 2021); R. Kies, 'E-pétitions à la Chambre des Deputés: Un succès déstabilisant', in C. Frieseisen, R. Moes, M. Polfer, and R. Wagener (eds), *100 ans de suffrage universel au Luxembourg* (Milan, Silvana Editoriale, 2019); R. Kelly and S. Priddy, *E-Petitions*, House of Commons Library Briefing Paper 06450, 20 October 2015; Standing Committee on Procedure and Public Affairs, *Seventy-Fifth Report*; New Zealand Parliament, *Guide for Petitions* (2018), www.parliament.nz/en/get-involved/have-your-say/guide-for-petitions/ (accessed 19 July 2021); and Assemblée nationale, *Plateforme en ligne des pétitions citoyennes* (2020), www.assemblee-nationale.fr/dyn/actualites-accueil-hub/plateforme-en-ligne-des-petitions-citoyennes (accessed 19 July 2021).

[21] C. Leston-Bandeira, 'Parliamentary Petitions and Public Engagement: An Empirical Analysis of the Role of E-Petitions', *Policy & Politics*, 47 (2019), 415–36.

stage of disseminating the petition to collate signatures, rather than on what happens next. For example, the UK Change.org system has specific sections relating to different institutions and politicians, giving the impression that the petitions listed will be formally considered by the relevant institution. In reality, none of the separate institutional pages corresponds to an actual process of making the respective institution (politician) aware of the petition. That is, there is no consideration process, simply the illusion of one.[22]

The importance of process in defining the e-petition is well illustrated through the case of the UK Parliament. The UK House of Commons e-petitions system was created to redress the problems introduced by preceding government-led systems introduced under the then Prime Minister Tony Blair, in 2006,[23] and followed in 2011 by a revised system introduced by the Coalition Government led by David Cameron.[24] The Coalition Government's e-petitions system, in particular, raised expectations about the potential of petitioning without introducing appropriate processes to deal with incoming e-petitions, which simply led to greater frustration from the public.[25] The system was, to put it simply, a website, rather than an actual 'system': a website to which people submitted petitions. But crucially, there was virtually no formal process to consider those petitions submitted, despite the fact that the site claimed petitions with 100,000 signatures would be debated in Parliament. In reality, no process had formally been introduced or amended to deliver this claim. Unless MPs decided to adopt an e-petition achieving over 100,000 signatures and presented it to the newly created parliamentary Backbench Business Committee, to ask for time to debate it in the main Chamber, there was no procedural follow-up to the petition within Parliament.

This created considerable challenges for Parliament and specifically for the Backbench Business Committee, established in 2010 specifically to provide backbenchers with added time in the chamber to discuss issues selected by them, rather than by the government of the day.[26] There was, therefore, a lack of appropriate processes in place. The heightened expectations (further stoked through the online visibility of the system) that e-petitions with 100,000 signatures would be debated in Parliament, combined with an absence of a process for delivering

[22] See, for example, the Change.org UK Parliament page, www.change.org/decision-makers/uk-parliament (accessed 15 August 2023) – this includes a tab for 'responses', suggesting that the UK Parliament will consider the petition in question and respond to it. In reality, this page and the petitions it entails have no link whatsoever to the UK Parliament. It is simply a category tab.

[23] C. Bochel, 'Petitions Systems: Contributing to Representative Democracy?', *Parliamentary Affairs*, 66 (2013), 798–815.

[24] Hansard Society, *What Next for E-Petitions?* (London, Hansard Society, 2012), https://assets.ctfassets.net/u1rlvvbs33ri/4cT21Ncc6kk8eWAASSA2eu/88137e59f4fa085075beefa6fe96b598/Publication__What-next-for-e-petitions-2012.pdf (accessed 19 July 2021).

[25] Bochel, 'Petitions Systems'; Hansard Society, *What Next for E-Petitions?*; S. Wright, 'Populism and Downing Street Petitions: Connective Action, Hybridity, and the Changing Nature of Organising', *Political Communication*, 32 (2015), 414–33.

[26] Timetabling in the UK House of Commons is determined mostly by the government.

this, predictably led to disappointment among petitioners. As with any petitions system, it was a lack of appropriate processes that led to its ineffectiveness, both in terms of bringing issues to the core of decision-making and in terms of petitioners' expectations.

The new system was introduced in 2015 to remedy the issues that were associated with predecessor government e-petitions initiatives. As such, it was key to providing for formal procedures within Parliament to enable an appropriate consideration of e-petitions submitted. This led to the introduction of a collaborative system between government and Parliament that commits both institutions to a single process for considering e-petitions. This collaborative element is very important to understanding the effectiveness of this new system, as it commits the government to the system and, crucially, ensures that it is responsive to petitions submitted. Many parliamentary petitions systems make provision for the governments of the day to respond to queries raised by petitions, but response rates and timings are often poor.[27] No other parliamentary petitioning system is collaborative in the same way.

The actual e-petitions site is hosted by the Government Digital Service, but the process is managed by a Petitions Committee in Parliament, which was introduced to support the new system. Petitions are submitted online, with signatures collated through the same platform. All e-petitions with 10,000 or more signatures qualify for a response from the government, which is published on the site of the e-petition as well as being emailed to signatories. In the 2015–17 Parliament, the government responded to all petitions with 10,000 signatures or more.[28] As we see below, this integration of the government within the process is key to understanding what this e-petitions system can achieve, a perennial question about petitioning. Besides this, all e-petitions receiving at least 100,000 signatures are considered by Parliament's Petitions Committee for a debate, with the vast majority of these being debated.[29] In the case of those petitions that are not debated, this is typically because Parliament has already debated the issue at stake in the session. More important than these thresholds, the new system established a Petitions Committee to oversee the consideration of e-petitions.

When the Procedure Committee made recommendations (2014) regarding the new e-petitions system, it placed considerable emphasis on the role of the new Petitions Committee, arguing that this was core to the new system's potential. Crucially, the establishment of a committee meant that there would now be a specific group of MPs responsible for considering petitions, supported by a dedicated team of staff to administer the moderation and consideration of e-petitions.[30] When

[27] European Parliament, *The Right to Petition*, Policy Department C: Citizens' Rights and Constitutional Affairs (2015), PE.519.223.

[28] Leston-Bandeira, 'Parliamentary Petitions', p. 424.

[29] Ibid.

[30] European Parliament, *The Right to Petition*; U. Riehm, K. Böhle, and R. Lindner, *Electronic Petitioning and the Modernization of Petitioning Systems in Europe* (Berlin, TAB, Office of Technology Assessment at the German Bundestag, 2014).

the report came to be discussed in February 2015, there was overwhelming support for the proposals brought forward, and the then Leader of the House specifically considered the establishment of a Petitions Committee 'the most significant recommendation' in the new system, representing 'a major change [that] should be the catalyst for a fundamental change in the relationship between parliament and petitioner'.[31]

Strictly speaking, the Petitions Committee is not new, but rather a re-establishment of earlier iterations of parliamentary bodies that administered paper petitions. Although early petitions were listened to by the whole body of Parliament, as the numbers of petitions increased and this became increasingly impracticable, petitions were increasingly referred to committees.[32] Colin Leys notes special committees were set up in the 17th century 'from time to time to review petitions'.[33] In 1832 it was proposed that a sessional committee should be established to keep track of petitions being submitted, and it was established the following year.[34] This was then mainly a move to cope with the increasingly high number of petitions submitted at the time.[35] The Select Committee on Public Petitions, as it was called, was abolished in 1974, following a report by the Procedure Committee the previous year.[36] The Petitions Committee and its chair argued for an expansion of its powers,[37] as these were essentially of an administrative nature to check if petitions were in accordance to regulations and to report on the numbers submitted.[38] Rather than strengthening its powers, and, noting the dwindling number of petitions, the report recommended instead the abolition of the committee. By contrast with the old Petitions Committee, which had done little more than administer the reception and reporting of petitions in the parliamentary records, the 2015 new Petitions Committee has a far more active role and a greater range of powers within the petitions process.

The Petitions Committee has most of the powers of the other existing select committees, namely in terms of undertaking inquiries and holding government ministers to account. These are powers that have been considerably enhanced since the Wright reforms of 2010, when chairs and members of committees started being elected by fellow MPs. This has led to a strengthening of the role played

[31] Hansard, 24 February 2015, Vol. DXCIII, col. 256.

[32] G. Mark, 'The Vestigial Constitution: The History and Significance of the Right to Petition', *Fordham Law Review*, 66 (1998), 2153–231 (p. 2214).

[33] C. Leys, 'Petitioning in the Nineteenth and Twentieth Centuries', *Political Studies*, 3 (1955), 45–64 (p. 49).

[34] Miller, *A Nation of Petitioners*, p. 2.

[35] R. Huzzey and H. Miller, 'Petitions, Parliament, and Political Culture: Petitioning the House of Commons, 1780–1918', *Past & Present*, 248 (2020), 123–64; Miller, *A Nation of Petitioners*, pp. 27–49.

[36] D. Judge, 'Public Petitions and the House of Commons', *Parliamentary Affairs*, 31 (1978), 391–405; House of Commons Information Office, 'Public Petitions: Factsheet' (London, House of Commons, 2010), p. 5.

[37] Judge, 'Public Petitions'.

[38] Ibid.; House of Commons Information Office, 'Public Petitions'.

by committee chairs, which, combined with an enhancement of their core tasks and scrutiny role, has made the House of Commons select committees system the jewel of the crown of its scrutiny.[39] Besides considering whether petitions should be debated, the Petitions Committee has a range of other options available to it to ensure effective scrutiny of the issues raised by e-petitions.

The committee oversees all responses sent by the government, for instance, which means it can chase up any departments that are particularly slow in responding to petitions or, importantly, follow up any government responses deemed to be inadequate. Unlike select committees that shadow government departments, the Petitions Committee has dedicated public engagement officers. These are parliamentary officials whose role is to support and develop the committee's public engagement activity. As we see below, this is critical in enabling the new parliamentary e-petitions system to fulfil its public engagement role. But the main importance of the existence of this committee is in the fact that it formalises a process through which e-petitions are managed and considered, which also means the committee has the discretion to consider each petition on its merits (regardless of the number of signatures or names) and can act accordingly. This explains, for example, why the committee decided in March 2018 to debate an e-petition calling for the inclusion of British Sign Language in the National Curriculum, despite the fact that it had only achieved about 35,000 signatures (rather than the 100,000 threshold).[40] It also explains why the committee decided to carry out an inquiry into the funding of research on brain tumours in October 2015,[41] even though the e-petition had only achieved about 14,000 signatures by this point.

The 2015 transformation of the process of petitioning in the UK House of Commons exemplifies the importance of process in considering the potential of e-petitions. The UK system is now the parliamentary e-petitions system with the highest volume of usage in the world.[42] It has been estimated that around 20 per cent of the UK population have signed an e-petition hosted by the UK Parliament's system.[43] The petitions system has demonstrable outcomes arising from the

[39] L. Maer, 'Select Committee Reform: Shifting the Balance and Pushing the Boundaries', *Parliamentary Affairs*, 72 (2019), 761–78.

[40] 'Make British Sign Language Part of the National Curriculum' (2017), https://petition.parliament.uk/petitions/200000 (accessed 19 July 2021).

[41] 'Fund More Research into Brain Tumours, the Biggest Cancer Killer of Under-40s' (2015), https://petition.parliament.uk/archived/petitions/105560 (accessed 19 July 2021).

[42] Leston-Bandeira, 'Parliamentary Petitions'.

[43] Hansard Society, Audit of Political Engagement 13 (2016), www.hansardsociety.org.uk/projects/research/audit-of-political-engagement (accessed 19 July 2021); Hansard Society, Audit of Political Engagement 14 (2017), www.hansardsociety.org.uk/projects/research/audit-of-political-engagement (accessed 19 July 2021); Hansard Society, Audit of Political Engagement 15 (2018), www.hansardsociety.org.uk/publications/reports/audit-of-political-engagement-15-2018 (accessed 19 July 2021); Hansard Society, Audit of Political Engagement 16 (2019), www.hansardsociety.org.uk/publications/reports/audit-of-political-engagement-16 (accessed 19 July 2021).

e-petitions submitted.[44] But what exactly are these outcomes? Or, put simply, what do e-petitions to parliaments achieve? We turn to this in the following section.

The Potential of E-Petitions to Parliament

The perennial question of whether e-petitions achieve anything is linked to two factors: the ease with which anyone can sign and disseminate an e-petition, and the fact that policy change is opaque and convoluted. This last section demonstrates that judgement on whether e-petitions achieve anything needs to take into account the consequences they have for the relationship between governance structures and citizens over a period of time.

While the accessibility of e-petitions is part of their appeal, they have been criticised for being too easy, requiring minimal effort from those signing them, rather than deeper engagement or more committed, sustained activity. This has led to e-petitioning being referred to as 'clicktivism' or 'slacktivism',[45] whereby citizens participate through a few clicks, rather than committing much time or effort to specific causes. Crucially, this is where e-petitions to Parliament can offer considerable added value in terms of the potential impact of petitioning. Unlike most non-official e-petitioning sites, which do not integrate a process ensuring that e-petitions are considered by a formal decision-making institution, e-petitions to Parliament can place these issues at the heart of policy-making. Depending on the process in place, these can enable e-petitions systems to play a variety of roles.

Petitioning is often evaluated and found wanting on the basis of whether it facilitates opportunities for political participation and/or the extent to which it leads to changes in policy. But these are just two of a range of potential roles that petitioning systems can play. Petitioning systems can perform four different roles: linkage, campaigning, scrutiny, and policy.[46] Each of these four encompasses more specific roles as illustrated in Table 5.1, such as political participation, mobilisation, policy review, and 'fire-alarm', which refers to those instances when citizens identify problems in society of which decision-makers may not be aware – i.e. a bottom-up way of identifying flaws in policy.

So, petitioning systems have the potential to perform a wide range of roles, beyond simply participation or policy-making. However, the extent to which they do so is dependent on the processes in place within those e-petition systems. It is the process that enables e-petitions to fulfil their full potential.

In the UK House of Commons case study, public engagement was the main role for e-petitions in the 2015–17 Parliament, though it also played some part in campaigning, scrutiny, and policy. The new system was introduced to enhance the

[44] Leston-Bandeira, 'Parliamentary Petitions'.

[45] G. Beato, 'From Petitions to Decision', *Stanford Social Innovation Review*, 12 (2014), 20–7.

[46] Leston-Bandeira, 'Parliamentary Petitions'.

Table 5.1 Roles performed by parliamentary petitions systems

Types	Roles
Linkage	• Legitimacy • Safety valve • Grievance resolution • Education • Public engagement • Political participation
Campaigning	• Mobilisation • Group identity strengthening • Dissemination • Recruitment
Scrutiny	• Fire alarm • Agenda-setting • Evidence gathering • Questioning
Policy	• Policy review • Policy improvement • Policy influence • Policy change

Source: C. Leston-Bandeira, 'Parliamentary Petitions and Public Engagement: An Empirical Analysis of the Role of E-Petitions', *Policy & Politics*, 47 (2019), 415–36 (p. 420).

relationship between Parliament and the public, with its new committee including officials specifically dedicated to supporting its public engagement activity, as already mentioned. It is therefore no surprise that this is the main role played by this system, which is reflected in the wide range and volume of activities developed by the committee to engage the public regarding the consideration of specific e-petitions. These have included web forums, one-to-one meetings between petitioners and MPs, and deliberative workshops outside Westminster with groups of people affected by issues raised by specific e-petitions. Often the simplest of methods, such as keeping in regular email contact with signatories to offer updates on how their petition was being considered, were key in giving petitioners a sense that there was someone on the other side paying attention to their petition. The surprise of being contacted by the Petitions Committee often went a long way to restoring people's confidence in the system. The system incorporated several processes that followed up e-petitions with specific public engagement activities.

Likewise, the fact that this system integrates the government into its consideration process was key in strengthening its scrutiny role. This is patent, for instance, in the way ministers have to respond to e-petitions in their debates, which forces the government to have a position on the e-petition in question, articulated in written response as well as debates. Parliamentary e-petitions can also bring new issues to the attention of the government, which it may not otherwise have known about.

This was the case, for instance, with a 2016 petition on workplace dress codes requiring high heels,[47] which led the minister responsible to acknowledge during the debate that the petition was about far more than simply shoes, addressing issues of power and how women are treated in the workplace. By conducting an inquiry into the issues raised by this e-petition, the Petitions Committee raised awareness of an issue that was affecting many women across the country, and particularly those in more precarious or fractional forms of employment. In this specific case, the system performed a fire-alarm role, by identifying a poor implementation of the law (the Equality Act).

The e-petitions system also delivered policy change during the 2015–17 session, thanks to the mechanism whereby MPs on the committee consider each e-petition achieving at least 10,000 signatures on its own merits, such as in relation to the e-petition asking for more funding for research into brain tumours.[48] As the e-petition reached 10,000 signatures, the government offered a technical and dismissive response that prompted the Petitions Committee to initiate its inquiry into the issue.[49] A few months later, the minister acknowledged in debate that the government had got its response wrong, and that funding for research on brain tumours was dismal when compared to other types of cancer.[50] Consequently, the government announced that it would set up a working group on this issue, which included one of the petitioners, and three years later announced a considerable boost in funding for research into brain tumours.[51] Again, what mattered here was the process through which the e-petition was considered. As these examples show, by integrating the evaluation of e-petitions into the core of the parliamentary process, this system is able to perform several roles. Recent research also shows that, because MPs can now access information on how many of their constituents have signed specific e-petitions (which is facilitated by the e-petitions system), they are able to select which debates to participate in to represent their constituents' views.[52]

Processes matter, therefore, in shaping the potential of e-petitions in terms of their consequences for the relationship between the political system and citizens, whether that means mobilising support or influencing the policy-making agenda. While non-official, non-institutional e-petitions sites (such as Change.org, Ipetitions.com, MesOpinions.com, and PetitionOnline.uk) have effective processes in place to disseminate petitions and collate signatures, they are not always as

[47] 'Make It Illegal for a Company to Require Women to Wear High Heels at Work' (2016), https://petition.parliament.uk/archived/petitions/129823 (accessed 19 July 2021).

[48] 'Fund More Research into Brain Tumours'.

[49] M. Lester (2015), 'The Brain Tumour E-Petition', Petitions Launch Event, House of Commons, 2 December 2015.

[50] George Freeman, Hansard, HC Debates, 18 April 2016, Vol. DCVIII, col. 258WH.

[51] *Report of the Task and Finish Working Group on Brain Tumour Research* (2018), https://assets.publishing.service.gov.uk/government/uploads/system/uploads/attachment_data/file/683217/Brain_tumour_research_-_task_and_finish_working_group_report.pdf (accessed 15 August 2023).

[52] J. Blumenau, 'Online Activism and Dyadic Representation: Evidence from the UK E-Petition System', *Legislative Studies Quarterly*, 6 (2021), 889–920.

effective in the follow-up processes of taking the petition to the heart of decision-making. E-petitions to Parliament tend to be more clunky and less effective in disseminating petitions and mobilising support but have more potential to affect decisions if properly linked to the formal decision-making process. They can also strengthen public engagement, as in the case of the UK House of Commons system, which is heavily focused on communicating with petitioners.

Conclusion

This chapter has reflected upon the specificity of e-petitions to parliaments and why process is key in considering their potential to achieve anything. Although petitions to parliaments have in many cases existed for centuries, the adoption of their digital counterpart has raised some new challenges to legislatures. Despite their resemblance to the traditional paper petition, e-petitions have specific characteristics that change the way they operate and their significance. In some ways, because of the internet, e-petitions are far more visible, and are far more citizen-led than the traditional formal petition, which affects their potential to achieve change. The main factor in the effectiveness of e-petitions to parliaments is the processes through which they are considered, and how the digital interface is integrated with the parliamentary processes. Focusing in particular on the 2015 UK House of Commons e-petitions system, the importance of having a committee responsible for overseeing the process, and the commitment of the government, is clear. This combination enables the e-petitions system to perform different roles, including scrutiny. By having a collaborative system between Parliament and government, whereby departments have to respond to petitions with over 10,000 signatures, as well as participating in e-petition debates, ministers are forced to consider the issues raised by e-petitions. We identified four roles – linkage, campaigning, scrutiny, and policy – well beyond the specific roles of participation and policy-making, often the only roles associated with petitions. The extent to which a parliament's e-petitions system is able to perform any of these roles is dependent on the processes in place. In short, more than the actual e-petition to Parliament, what matters is what happens to it thereafter. This is why e-petitions to parliaments, when properly integrated into parliamentary business processes and when making the most of the potential offered by digital technologies in terms of dissemination and ease of access, can be far more effective than non-official e-petitions platforms. E-petitions to Parliament can be directly integrated with the formal decision-making process and therefore facilitate effective channels to achieve change. However, this speaks only of potential: the reality is dependent on the specific processes in place.

Part II

Chronologies, Continuities, and Transformations

6

Transitions and Continuities in Petitioning in Early Modern England

BRODIE WADDELL AND HANNAH WORTHEN

Over the course of the early modern period, England experienced a series of major political changes that had far-reaching consequences for how people engaged with official authority. Both church and state were fundamentally transformed by the events of the Reformation that unfolded between the 1530s and the 1560s. The ground shifted again during the constitutional crisis, Civil Wars, and Interregnum of the 1640s and 1650s. Further changes came in the wake of the Glorious Revolution of 1688–9, including an expanded role for Parliament thanks to regular annual sessions and frequent elections. This chapter is an attempt to explore how the practice of petitioning developed amid the upheavals of this era, attending to transitions but also to long-term continuities.

The focus here is primarily on what we might call 'unrevolutionary' petitioning, rather than the more well-known 'radical' petitioning campaigns that have received the most attention from historians. It has often been noted, most prominently by David Zaret, that partisan petitioning exploded in England in the 1640s thanks to the collapse of royal authority, the expansion of printing, and the increasing accessibility of Parliament.[1] This was undoubtedly a key moment in the history of petitioning and popular politics. However, politically contentious petitions that were printed (or reported in print) were only the tip of the proverbial iceberg. Far more numerous were those that have been called 'traditional' or 'private' petitions that focused on 'bread-and-butter affairs'.[2] This chapter also shows that many of these 'unrevolutionary' petitions had features that overlapped with 'political' petitioning. They could be submitted by large groups and could be semi-public too, even though they were almost never printed. Moreover, as will be seen, apparently

[1] D. Zaret, *Origins of Democratic Culture: Printing, Petitions, and the Public Sphere in Early-Modern England* (Princeton, NJ, Princeton University Press, 2000).

[2] Ibid., Chapter 4; D. Hirst, 'Making Contact: Petitions and the English Republic', *Journal of British Studies*, 45 (2006), 26–50 (p. 28).

'non-political' petitioning could have a mutually influential relationship with the more 'radical' varieties that are already well known.[3] This chapter will highlight the massive expansion in the volume of 'unrevolutionary' manuscript petitioning and consider its 'political' implications.

In the first section, we suggest that a vibrant petitioning culture emerged in England from the late 16th century onwards, especially in the localities, and that it laid the foundation for many of the developments that followed. In the second section, we examine how petitioning practices changed during and after the Civil Wars, beyond the oft-cited rise in printed and mass petitions, which we qualify by highlighting important elements of continuity. In the third section, we sketch out patterns in petitioning from 1660 to the mid-18th century, with special attention to the ambiguous impact of the Restoration and the Glorious Revolution. Finally, in the conclusion, we extend our frame of analysis to survey briefly some of the long-term continuities and changes across the whole period. We find that the prevalence of petitioning at local and national level was rising from the late 16th century if not earlier, and some practical petitions by veterans and war widows adopted sharply partisan vocabulary from the 1640s onwards. Yet, the aims of most petitioners as well as the form and tone of their requests remained remarkably stable across many decades. We should, therefore, seek to understand why petitioning became and remained so popular despite radical shifts in English government and political culture.

Petitioning before 1640

The 16th and early 17th century witnessed the emergence and routinisation of new types of petitioning in England, with growing numbers of people engaging with the state through this process. This broad culture of petitioning was firmly established even before the 1640s, meaning that the spectacular revolutionary petitions that followed were part of a trend that stretched back decades.

Written supplications were hardly a novel phenomenon in early modern England, even if some important changes unfolded in these centuries. In the late medieval period, petitioning by individuals and corporate bodies was already a normal and accepted practice. The Crown and the church received large numbers of these formal appeals from English men and women, mostly relating to local disputes over property or privileges alongside some pleas for mercy from those accused of serious crimes.[4] The National Archives hold over 17,000 petitions

[3] For an examination of this relationship in the Scottish context, see L. Stewart, 'Petitioning in Early Seventeenth-Century Scotland, 1625–41', *Parliaments, Estates and Representation*, 38 (2018), 307–22. This is one of the key themes in B. Waddell and J. Peacey (eds), *The Power of Petitioning in Early Modern Britain* (London, UCL Press, forthcoming).

[4] For a recent survey of this historiography, see T. W. Smith and H. Killick, 'Introduction', in T. W. Smith and H. Killick (eds), *Petitions and Strategies of Persuasion in the Middle Ages: The English Crown and the Church, c. 1200–c. 1500* (Woodbridge, York Medieval Press, 2018), pp. 1–10.

to the Crown dating mostly from the 14th and 15th centuries, the majority of which came from the localities through Parliament.[5] In addition, authorities at the local level undoubtedly received petitions. When compared to those addressed to the Crown or the church, these requests have received relatively little scholarly attention and seem to have survived in much smaller numbers. Still, scattered evidence from chartered cities such as London and York suggests that many medieval townspeople submitted petitions to the urban civic authorities.[6] Written 'bills' and 'plaints', which were petitionary in form, were also used in many judicial contexts, occasionally at very local levels.[7] Existing scholarship nonetheless suggests that submitting written petitions to local justices about most of the sorts of issues discussed below, especially outside the large towns, was not a routine practice before the 16th century. Likewise, sending them to the Crown was in theory a route open to anyone, but in practice the majority of petitioners came from the more affluent sections of society and were men and women with property to defend or to acquire.

During the tumult of the English Reformation in the 1530s and 1540s, the national authorities faced a series of radical petitions from their aggrieved subjects. The tumultuous Pilgrimage of Grace in 1536 was accompanied by petitionary 'articles' that set out a wide range of complaints about the recent 'reforms' to the church.[8] Then, during the major rebellions of 1549, several petitions claiming to speak in the name of 'the Commons' were presented to the king, touching on issues of both landholding and religious policy.[9] Unfortunately, the history of 'unrevolutionary' petitioning during this period has yet to be written. It is clear that, as in the medieval period, civic authorities often received petitions from townspeople about local issues and the Crown received requests on a wide range of topics. In October 1541, for example, the Privy Council dealt with a petition from the town of Hull for

[5] W. M. Ormrod, G. Dodd, and A. Musson (eds), *Medieval Petitions: Grace and Grievance* (Woodbridge, York Medieval Press, 2009); G. Dodd, *Justice and Grace: Private Petitioning and the English Parliament in the Late Middle Ages* (Oxford, Oxford University Press, 2007).

[6] P. Tucker, *Law Courts and Lawyers in the City of London, 1300–1500* (Cambridge, Cambridge University Press, 2007), pp. 142ff.; C. Liddy and J. Haemers, 'Popular Politics in the Late Medieval City: York and Bruges', *English Historical Review*, 128 (2013), 771–805 (pp. 778–9, 781–3). For a 14th-century petition to a manorial lord, see A. Musson, 'Patterns of Supplication', in Smith and Killick, *Petitions*, pp. 88–109 (p. 96).

[7] A. Harding, *Medieval Law and the Foundations of the State* (Oxford, Oxford University Press, 2002), Chapter 6; C. Beattie, 'Your Oratrice: Women's Petitions to the Late Medieval Court of Chancery', in B. Kane and F. Williamson (eds), *Women, Agency and the Law, 1300–1700* (London, Pickering & Chatto, 2015), pp. 17–30; T. Johnson, *Law in Common: Legal Cultures in Late-Medieval England* (Oxford, Oxford University Press, 2019), pp. 202, 213–14, 252–4, 257–60.

[8] R. W. Hoyle, *The Pilgrimage of Grace and the Politics of the 1530s* (Oxford, Oxford University Press, 2001); R. W. Hoyle, 'Petitioning as Popular Politics in Early Sixteenth-Century England', *Historical Research*, 75 (2002), 365–89.

[9] Hoyle, 'Petitioning'; A. Wood, *The 1549 Rebellions and the Making of Early Modern England* (Cambridge, Cambridge University Press, 2007); E. Shagan, *Popular Politics and the English Reformation* (Cambridge, Cambridge University Press, 2002).

various fiscal privileges, and another from Staffordshire men whose grazing cattle were distrained for a debt to the king.[10] One version of the genre that undoubtedly became more common was that of the legal 'petitions' from complainants submitted to royal courts of equity, which expanded substantially under Henry VIII.[11] But without a systematic survey of local records, it is impossible to know whether petitions more generally proliferated in number or changed in focus during this period.

In contrast, the growing prevalence of petitioning from the 1560s to the 1630s is obvious from their ubiquity in the archives of the time. At the national level, innumerable people submitted complaints and supplications to the Crown through high-ranking royal ministers. For example, the personal archive of William Cecil and his son Robert, who served as chief statesmen from 1558 to 1612, includes about 2,500 surviving petitions.[12] To this one must add many more requests preserved in the official state papers of this period, such as the five petitions addressed variously to the queen, the Privy Council, or the Lord High Treasurer in March 1585 alone.[13] However, the strongest evidence comes from the lucky survival of several registers of the Masters of Requests for the early 17th century, because a substantial proportion of petitions to the monarch were handled by these specially appointed officials. Using these registers, Richard Hoyle has estimated that 700–800 petitions per year were dealt with by the Masters of Requests in the first decades of the 17th century, rising to more than 1,000 per year by the mid-1630s.[14] The lack of equivalent sources from the late medieval period means that we cannot prove that petitions to the Crown became significantly more common under the Tudors and early Stuarts, but the evidence does at least show that these monarchs received many hundreds, if not thousands, of written requests from their subjects every year. Most of these petitioners sought similar things to their medieval predecessors: offices, lands, or pardons.

[10] 'Henry VIII: October 1541, 1–10', in James Gairdner and R. H. Brodie (eds), *Letters and Papers, Foreign and Domestic, Henry VIII*, Vol. XVI, *1540–1541* (London, Her Majesty's Stationery Office, 1898), pp. 577–84, *British History Online*, www.british-history.ac.uk/letters-papers-hen8/vol16/pp577-584 (accessed 30 January 2024).

[11] L. Flannigan, 'Litigants in the English "Court of Poor Men's Causes" or Court of Requests, 1515–1525', *Law and History Review*, 38 (2020), 303–37.

[12] 'Introduction', in G. Dyfnallt Owen (ed.), *Calendar of the Cecil Papers in Hatfield House*, Vol. XXIII, *Addenda, 1562–1605* (London, Her Majesty's Stationery Office, 1973), pp. v–xiii, *British History Online*, www.british-history.ac.uk/cal-cecil-papers/vol23/v-xiii (accessed 24 June 2019).

[13] 'Queen Elizabeth – Volume 177: March 1585', in Robert Lemon (ed.), *Calendar of State Papers Domestic: Elizabeth, 1581–90* (London, Her Majesty's Stationery Office, 1865), pp. 229–35, *British History Online*, www.british-history.ac.uk/cal-state-papers/domestic/edw-eliz/1581-90/pp229-235 (accessed 24 June 2024). A systematic survey of the Calendars of State Papers has not been attempted, but it would almost certainly reveal many hundreds if not thousands of similar documents for this period.

[14] R. W. Hoyle, 'The Master of Requests and the Small Change of Jacobean Patronage', *English Historical Review*, 126 (2011), 544–81.

However, as the number of royal offices proliferated and the turnover in Crown lands increased in this period, the number of petitions probably increased too.

Both the Lords and the Commons in Parliament received many petitions, and occasionally the parliamentarians became petitioners themselves when attempting to persuade the monarch. In the Tudor parliaments, however, petitioning does not seem to have been a major part of ordinary business, and the sessions were usually only brief in any case. The *Journals of the House of Commons* for the second half of the 16th century include only a handful of references to petitions, mostly submitted by the House itself on matters of church reformation or royal succession.[15] Evidence of requests about less controversial matters is rare, though the co-ordinated petitions to the House of Lords in 1531 about the hat-making trade show that this sort of formal lobbying was not absent.[16] Under James I and Charles I, Parliament became a much stronger magnet for petitions. As Andrew Thrush has shown:

> the huge growth in the number of petitions directed to the Commons during the early seventeenth century is striking. In 1604 the House considered just two private petitions – one from the puritan minister Bryan Bridger against the bishops and the other from the serjeant-at-mace who had arrested Sir Thomas Shirley – whereas in 1628 it read no less than 65.[17]

In the Lords, there was an equally noticeable increase, especially from 1621 onwards when the peers began to arbitrate on judicial appeals that they had received by petition.[18] Unsurprisingly, as Parliament took on a larger role as a recipient of petitions, it also presented more of its own to the monarch on delicate political issues, including the famous 'Petition of Right' in 1628 against forced loans, arbitrary imprisonment, and billeting soldiers, which was begrudgingly ratified by Charles I.[19] But this constitutionally significant 'petition' was part of a broader wave of parliamentary petitioning that arose during these decades.

Finally, and perhaps most importantly, many thousands of people submitted petitions and supplications to their local magistrates in the late 16th and early 17th

[15] See, for example, 'House of Commons Journal Volume 1: 09 March 1576', in *Journal of the House of Commons*, Vol. I, *1547–1629* (London, His Majesty's Stationery Office, 1802), pp. 112–13, *British History Online*, www.british-history.ac.uk/commons-jrnl/vol1/pp112-113 (accessed 25 June 2019). These are discussed a greater length in E. R. Foster, 'Petitions and the Petition of Right', *Journal of British Studies*, 14 (1974), 21–45 (pp. 27–32).

[16] Parliamentary Archives, HL/PO/JO/10/3/178/1–8. See also D. Dean, *Law-Making and Society in Late Elizabethan England* (Cambridge, Cambridge University Press, 1996), Chapter 5; and I. Archer, 'London Lobbies in the Later Sixteenth Century', *Historical Journal*, 31 (1988), 17–44.

[17] A. Thrush, 'Legislation and Petitions', in A. Thrush and J. P. Ferris (eds), *The History of Parliament: The House of Commons 1604–1629* (Cambridge, Cambridge University Press, 2010), www.historyofparliamentonline.org/volume/1604-1629/survey/xi-legislation-and-petitions (accessed 30 January 2024).

[18] J. S. Hart, *Justice upon Petition: The House of Lords and the Reformation of Justice* (London, HarperCollins, 1991).

[19] Foster, 'Petitions and the Petition of Right'. On the broader sharp rise in petitions from the Commons to the king, see Thrush, 'Legislation'.

century. As noted above, some evidence of this survives for large cities from the late medieval period, but it is only under Queen Elizabeth that the practice can be documented for the rural parishes and small towns where most of the population lived. The papers of the county quarter sessions (a regular meeting of local magistrates that handled judicial and administrative matters) include increasing numbers of petitions about 'bread-and-butter' issues from the 1560s onwards.[20] The exact pattern varies from county to county, with much depending on the vagaries of archival attrition, but they were undoubtedly becoming more common. In the county of Essex, for example, quarter sessions records exist from the mid-1550s, but the first petitions do not appear until 1569. The numbers increased thereafter, with an average of 30 or 40 extant per decade from the 1590s to the 1630s.[21] Moreover, much larger numbers of petitions survive in a few well-documented counties. In Staffordshire and Cheshire, although only a few dozen petitions survive from the late 16th century, each county has well over 1,000 from the period 1600–40.[22] In Lancashire, nearly 700 survive for the 1630s alone.[23] Given that these three counties only had around 1,200 parishes and townships between them, this suggests that at least a few people from almost every rural community would have been involved in petitioning their local magistrates at some point in the early 17th century.

The nature of this local petitioning helps to explain its growth. The vast majority of the petitions were submitted by individuals or by particular parishes, and their aims were usually mundane, with many complaints against neighbours for disorderly behaviour, or appeals for release from prisoners. However, a large and increasing proportion related directly to new national legislation. For example, the 1552 statute requiring every alehouse- and tavern-keeper to hold written approval from the magistrates led to hundreds of petitions from aspiring publicans for licences, and counterpetitions from neighbours seeking to shut them down.[24] Similarly, a statute in 1588 made it mandatory to obtain permission before building a cottage on less than four acres of land, which spurred many written requests from labouring families who could not afford a more substantial farm.[25] Perhaps most importantly, a series of new laws in the late 16th century required

[20] Some analysis that follows is based on a sample of 2,236 petitions to the quarter sessions of 12 English counties, c. 1560–1700, gathered as part of an ongoing project entitled 'The Power of Petitioning' (hereafter 'TPOP data'). Further details can be found on the project website, https://petitioning.history.ac.uk (accessed 30 January 2024).

[21] These estimates are based on catalogue data and archival sampling from Essex Record Office, Q/SR and Q/SBa.

[22] Decadal samples from Staffordshire Record Office, Q/SR; Cheshire Archives and Local History, QJF.

[23] Catalogue data from Lancashire Archives, QSB. Very few sessions records survive for Lancashire before the late 1620s.

[24] M. Hailwood, *Alehouses and Good Fellowship in Early Modern England* (Woodbridge, Boydell & Brewer, 2014), pp. 29–58, 90–4.

[25] D. Tankard, 'The Regulation of Cottage Building in Seventeenth-Century Sussex', *Agricultural History Review*, 59 (2011), 18–35.

every parish in England to support their neediest residents through local rates. As a result, the county magistrates received huge streams of petitions from paupers complaining that their parishes were not relieving them, and from villages seeking to avoid this obligation by sending paupers to their 'home' parishes.[26] Preliminary analysis suggests that about half of all requests submitted to the quarter sessions in this period related directly to new legislation.[27] More generally, the broader intensification of local governance and the spread of literacy among wealthier villagers almost certainly contributed to the rising tide of petitions presented at county courts in the early 17th century.[28] Thus, the massive expansion in local petitioning was directly linked to the wider process of state formation studied by so many scholars in recent decades.[29] As more aspects of life came under the purview of state regulation, so more people used petitioning to deal with the problems they faced in these areas.

At both the national and the local level, then, the practice of petitioning was spreading. The number of petitions received by the Crown was seemingly growing, and the number received by Parliament reached new heights in the 1620s, while at the same time the volume handled by county authorities expanded dramatically. With very few exceptions, the petitions were 'unrevolutionary' in their aims and rhetoric, yet the practice of sending these written requests about ordinary social and economic concerns enabled vast numbers of people to engage with the state in new ways. People with no formal role in governance, including paupers, cottagers, and alehouse-keepers, began to seek out support among their neighbours in order to legitimate their claims and complaints. Although many petitions were unsigned, a substantial minority were supported by subscriptions from 10, 20, or even 50 individuals. In 1615, for example, a Hertfordshire labourer named Robert Portris requested a pension from the county for his military service in the Low Countries and Portugal. His petition was typically deferential, but it was also implicitly justified by the Elizabethan statute ordering publicly funded relief for maimed soldiers and explicitly supported by the 23 signatures and marks of his neighbours in

[26] S. Hindle, *On the Parish? The Micro-Politics of Poor Relief in Rural England, c. 1550–1750* (Oxford, Clarendon Press, 2004), Chapter 6; J. Healey, *The First Century of Welfare: Poverty and Poor Relief in Lancashire, 1620–1730* (Woodbridge, Boydell & Brewer, 2014).

[27] In a multi-county sample covering c. 1560–1640, at least 45 per cent concerned alehouses, cottages, servant and apprenticeship regulation, military pensions, paternal maintenance, or poor relief, and a further 6 per cent related to officeholding or local rates. The remainder were almost entirely for pardon or prosecution of criminal offences; TPOP data. The distribution of petitions across different categories is discussed further in B. Waddell, 'Shaping the State from Below: The Rise of Local Petitioning in Early Modern England', and S. Howard, 'The Local Power of Petitioning: Petitions to Cheshire Quarter Sessions in Context, c. 1570–1800', both in Waddell and Peacey, *The Power of Petitioning*.

[28] In addition, this period also witnessed the emergence of new urban 'corporations' as the monarch granted charters to many towns giving them more formal authority over local matters and creating new targets for ordinary people to send petitions for redress; P. Withington, *Politics of Commonwealth* (Cambridge, Cambridge University Press, 2005), Chapter 2.

[29] Recently summarised in T. Stretton, 'The People and the Law', in K. Wrightson (ed.), *A Social History of England, 1500–1750* (Cambridge, Cambridge University Press, 2017), pp. 199–220.

Flamstead.[30] The growing prevalence of petitioning also encouraged the emergence of 'brokers' such as scribes, agents, and local officeholders who became thoroughly adept at guiding the process and ever more comfortable with facilitating this form of dialogue between ordinary people and the state authorities.[31] Under the early Stuarts, the petition became a widely available tool, one that was perhaps comparable to a petty lawsuit and was much more common than other forms of political engagement such as parliamentary voting or street protests.

By 1640, a substantial proportion of ordinary people had experience as petitioners, whether as instigators or merely as signatories, and practically every community would have had someone familiar with the process and conventions of composing and submitting a formal request. Thanks to this shift, it was easier for activists and ideologues to launch overtly political petitioning campaigns in the decades that followed. However, it also meant that the radical and occasionally revolutionary petitioning of the mid-17th century was only a small part of a much wider petitioning culture.

Petitioning during the Civil Wars and Interregnum (1640–1660)

Research on petitioning in the 1640s and 1650s has tended to focus on the large-scale, public petitioning campaigns of those decades. These petitions, which were intended to intervene in the political process and which brought a new range of people into the political arena, have rightly been highlighted by historians as an important moment in the history of public engagement.[32] The importance of print has also featured in much discussion on the role of petitioning in the Civil Wars.[33] Until very recently, scholars have devoted much less attention to the manuscript petitions of the period: those from soldiers wounded in the fighting, from war

[30] Hertfordshire Archives and Local Studies (hereafter HALS), HAT/SR/27/73.

[31] Though focused primarily on the post-1660 period, the best study of these intermediaries is F. Dabhoiwala, 'Writing Petitions in Early Modern England', in M. J. Braddick and J. Innes (eds), *Suffering and Happiness in England 1550–1850: Narratives and Representations. A Collection to Honour Paul Slack* (Oxford, Oxford University Press, 2017), pp. 127–48. For the role of scribes during and after the 1640s, see L. Bowen, 'Genre, Authorship and Authenticity in the Petitions of Civil War Veterans and Widows from North Wales and the Marches'; and H. Worthen, 'The Process and Practice of Petitioning in Early Modern England', both in Waddell and Peacey, *The Power of Petitioning*.

[32] D. Zaret, 'Petitions and the "Invention" of Public Opinion in the English Revolution', *American Journal of Sociology*, 101 (1996), 1497–555; Zaret, *Origins*; A. M. McIntee, '"The [Un]civill-sisterhood of Oranges and Lemons": Female Petitioners and Demonstrators, 1642–53', *Prose Studies*, 14 (1991), 92–111; P. Higgins, 'The Reactions of Women, with Special Reference to Women Petitioners', in B. S. Manning (ed.), *Politics, Religion and the English Civil War* (London, Edward Arnold, 1973), pp. 179–224; A. J. Whiting, *Women and Petitioning in the Seventeenth-Century English Revolution: Deference, Difference, and Dissent* (Turnhout, Brepols, 2015).

[33] Hirst, 'Making Contact', 45–7; J. Peacey, *Print and Public Politics in the English Revolution* (Cambridge, Cambridge University Press, 2013), Chapter 8.

widows who needed pensions, and from dispossessed royalists seeking the return of their lands. These petitions are important for a full understanding of the role of petitioning during the Civil Wars, as well as for our understanding of petitioning in the early modern period more generally.[34] Therefore, this section will consider how much 'unrevolutionary' petitioning culture changed during this period of revolution.

These wars, which by their nature caused disruption, poverty, death, and disease for military and civilians alike, undoubtedly created more grievances among ordinary people, which may in turn have stimulated more petitions.[35] The death rates during the Civil Wars were higher than during any war in England, Ireland, and Scotland before or since: Ian Gentles estimates that 7 per cent of the population died as a result of battle and disease spread by armies across the three kingdoms.[36] It is notable that the number of petitions of all sorts to the quarter sessions of Kent, Hertfordshire, and Cheshire seems to have peaked in this period, with at least 175 submitted to the Cheshire magistrates in 1648 alone.[37] The significant upturn in petitions for military welfare and pensions during and after the wars from parliamentarian soldiers and widows during the 1640s and 1650s, and then royalists after 1660, certainly suggests that the events of the Civil Wars may have resulted in a greater volume of requests being submitted to local government.[38] In Kent, only one petitioner received a military pension before 1646, but after this date they became a regular feature in the county records and remained so until the mid-1650s (Figure 6.1). Then, after the Restoration in 1660 came an enormous spike in royalist petitions for pensions, all based on hardships due to the wars and their aftermath. Thus, in Kent and elsewhere, it is easy to find petitioners presenting their supplications to the quarter sessions as a direct consequence of the Civil Wars.[39]

[34] This can be seen in the publications emerging from the project 'Conflict, Welfare and Memory during and after the English Civil Wars, 1642–1710', led by Andrew Hopper (www.civilwarpetitions.ac.uk (accessed 30 January 2024)), some of which are cited later.

[35] B. Donagan, *War in England, 1642–1649* (New York, Oxford University Press, 2008), p. 11; M. Bennett, *The Civil Wars Experienced: Britain and Ireland, 1638–1661* (New York, Routledge, 2000); C. Carlton, *Going to the Wars: The Experience of the English Civil Wars* (London, Routledge, 1992).

[36] I. Gentles, *The English Revolution and the Wars in the Three Kingdoms, 1638–1652* (Harlow, Longman, 2007), p. 434.

[37] Howard, 'The Local Power of Petitioning'.

[38] D. Appleby, 'Unnecessary Persons? Maimed Soldiers and War Widows in Essex, 1642–62', *Essex Archaeology and History*, 32 (2001), 209–21; G. L. Hudson, 'Arguing Disability: Ex-Servicemen's Own Stories in Early Modern England, 1590–1790', in R. Bivins and J. V. Pickstone (eds), *Medicine, Madness, and Social History: Essays in Honour of Roy Porter* (Basingstoke, Palgrave Macmillan, 2007), pp. 104–17; H. Worthen, 'The Administration of Military Welfare in Kent, 1642–79', in D. J. Appleby and A. Hopper (eds), *Battle-Scarred: Mortality, Medical Care, and Military Welfare in the British Civil Wars* (Manchester, Manchester University Press, 2018), pp. 174–91; Pells, chapter in this volume.

[39] The proportion seeking military pensions in the multi-county sample increased from around 2 per cent in c. 1570–1640 to around 12 per cent in c. 1640–1700; TPOP data.

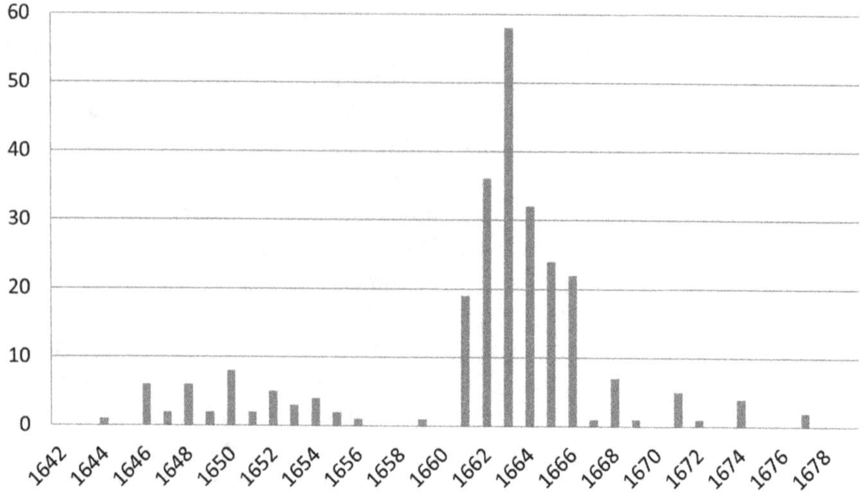

Figure 6.1 Pensions awarded in Kent quarter sessions, 1642–79. Kent History and Library Centre (KHLC), QS Order Books 1642–79 (Q/ SO/ E1–2, W1–3), and QS Sessions Rolls 1642–79 (Q/SB/1–11).

The proliferation of 'unrevolutionary' petitioning, stimulated by the disruption and dislocation of wartime, can also be seen at a national level. There was an explosion of parliamentary petitions in the 1640s and 1650s. For example, over its first two weeks in session in April 1640, the House of Commons dealt with at least eight petitions about elections, seven 'against Grievances', and five about various other matters.[40] The violent constitutional shifts of these decades make tracking petitions to the head of state difficult, but it seems that Oliver Cromwell as Lord Protector 'tried to maintain a high level of responsiveness' to supplicants during England's decade as a republic.[41] Discontented war widows and maimed soldiers, generally of a higher status than those petitioning at the quarter sessions, also submitted their petitions to Parliament before and after the Restoration in the hope of financial relief and recognition of their losses.[42] The Interregnum period, with its explosion of parliamentary committees, provided yet more avenues for the submission of petitions prompted by everyday concerns.[43] For example, the mass of work that the Committee for Compounding undertook, while managing the confiscation of royalist estates, means that hundreds of petitions from former supporters of the king requesting the return of their lands can be found in the

[40] *Journal of the House of Commons*, Vol. II, *1640–1643* (London, His Majesty's Stationery Office 1802), *British History Online*, www.british-history.ac.uk/commons-jrnl/vol2 (accessed 3 July 2019).

[41] Hirst, 'Making Contact', p. 34.

[42] A. Hopper, '"To condole with me on the Commonwealth's loss": The Widows and Orphans of Parliament's Military Commanders', in Appleby and Hopper, *Battle-Scarred*, pp. 192–210.

[43] G. Aylmer, *The State's Servants: The Civil Service of the English Republic, 1649–1660* (London, Routledge and Kegan Paul, 1973).

committee's records.[44] During this period printed pamphlets circulated in London publicising the dates and times of committee meetings so that people would be better able to access Parliament and present their grievances.[45] Thus, the rise of government bodies that validated petitioning as a method of lobbying, and indeed may have used it as a method of confirming their own authority, probably contributed to the rise in the practice of petitioning.

Despite this, the disruptions of war could also prove to be a barrier to any sudden increase in petitioning practices. John Morrill found that 'few quarter sessions were held in any of the counties under [Parliament's] total control'.[46] Even in counties where sessions continued, such as Kent and Sussex, physically travelling to the location of the meeting in order to present a petition could prove impossible in war time. For example, former soldiers John Phillips and John King, from West Sussex and Kent respectively, complained that the cost of travelling to their county's quarter sessions to petition and receive their pensions was as much as the value of the pension itself.[47] Moreover, the multiplying of parliamentary committees did not necessarily mean the act of petitioning became easier. Petitioners could wait outside the committees' doors and still not get a hearing for their grievance.[48] As in the case of Elizabeth, duchess of Hamilton, petitioners might have to submit multiple petitions, or even resort to a printed petition, before their requests could be heard.[49] Like other petitioners, the duchess of Hamilton found herself waiting outside the doors of the committee to present her grievance.[50] Women in particular may have found it especially difficult to access Parliament, with female petitioners to the Commons being barred from entering and told to 'looke after your own businesse, and meddle with your huswifery'.[51] Thus, in some ways the Civil Wars stimulated the production of petitions, and created legitimate avenues for them to be submitted, but this did not necessarily mean a huge change in petitioning culture.

[44] M. A. E. Green (ed.), *Calendar of the Proceedings of the Committee for Compounding with Delinquents, 1643–1660* (London, Her Majesty's Stationery Office, 1889–93).

[45] Peacey, *Print and Public Politics*, pp. 188–90.

[46] J. S. Morrill, *Revolt in the Provinces: The People of England and the Tragedies of War, 1634–1648* (London, Longman, 1999), pp. 116–17.

[47] Petition of John Phillips, October 1650, West Sussex Record Office (WSRO), Q/R/W69, fo. 1r; petition of John King, [1656], Kent History and Library Centre (KHLC), Q/SB/6/67.

[48] D. Dean, 'Public Space, Private Affairs: Committees, Petitions, and Lobbies in the Early Modern English Parliament', in J. Peacey and C. Kyle (eds), *Parliament at Work: Parliamentary Committees, Political Power, and Public Access in Early Modern England* (Rochester, NY, Boydell, 2002), pp. 169–78.

[49] Elizabeth Hamilton, *The Humble Petition of Elizabeth Duchess (Dowager) of Hamilton* ([London], 1651); petition of Elizabeth Hamilton, 21 July 1653, The National Archives (TNA), SP 19/12, p. 399; Peacey, *Print and Public Politics*, p. 282.

[50] J. Peacey, 'Parliament, Printed Petitions, and the Political Imaginary in Seventeenth-Century England', *Parliaments, Estates and Representation*, 38 (2018), 350–63.

[51] R. Ibbitson, *Perfect occurrences of every dayes journall in Parliament ... From Friday April the 20 to Friday April 27 1649* (London, 1649), p. 998. For further discussion of female petitioning and the hostile responses it engendered, see Whiting, *Women and Petitioning*.

Barriers, such as travelling across war-torn countryside to submit a petition, or the closed doors of a committee, continued to exist.

It is also easy to find continuity rather than abrupt change in local records for this period. During the mid-17th century the petitioning practices discussed throughout this chapter, such as petitioning for poor relief, continued. Quarter sessions records often only reflect the effect of the Civil Wars 'incidentally' as the regular concerns of daily life, and the long-established reasons to petition remained unchanged.[52] People presented petitions during these turbulent years in the same ways, and for broadly the same reasons, as they would have done in any other era.[53] Similarly, the language of poverty and humility can be found in petitions submitted during the Civil Wars, just as it can be found in petitions submitted before and after. From aristocratic royalist widows to poor parliamentarian soldiers, describing oneself as starving and in desperate need of aid was a useful tactic, and one that drew on pre-existing petitioning culture.[54] Furthermore, despite the remarkable uptake in the use of printed petitions, the form remained rooted in its scribal origins, with even some of the most radical petitions retaining standard forms of address and exhortation.[55]

Nevertheless, aside from the well-documented rise in radical printed petitioning, there was something else that the Civil War contributed to the language of more ordinary 'unrevolutionary' petitioning: the language of allegiance. Ann Hughes has found that the parliamentary committees' 'whole rationale' was 'to make it necessary for petitioners (and where possible defendants) to present themselves as loyal servants of a parliamentarian "public interest"'.[56] As a result, 'particular individual and local experiences were framed by more general, national constructions'.[57] We can see this in the petitions submitted by those accused of royalism to Parliament's Committee for Compounding.[58] For example, Lucy Pope, countess of Downe's petition claimed that she had 'never as yet given any aid or Assistance to the

[52] B. C. Redwood, 'Introduction', in B. C. Redwood (ed.), *Quarter Sessions Order Book, 1642–1649* (Lewes, Sussex Record Society, 1954), p. xxi.

[53] See, for example, petition to erect a house on the waste, April 1654, East Sussex Record Office (ESRO), QR/103; petition for an ale house licence, January 1650, ESRO, QR/86.

[54] On the language of poverty in petitions, see P. Sharpe, 'Survival Strategies and Stories: Poor Widows and Widowers in Early Industrial England', in S. Cavallo and L. Warner (eds), *Widowhood in Medieval and Early Modern Europe* (New York, Longman, 1999), pp. 220–39; Hindle, *On the Parish?*, Chapter 6; Healey, *The First Century of Welfare*; G. Dodd, 'Writing Wrongs: The Drafting of Supplications to the Crown in Later Fourteenth-Century England', *Medium Ævum*, 80 (2011), 217–46; and Flannigan, 'Litigants'.

[55] Peacey, *Print and Public Politics*, Chapter 8.

[56] A. Hughes, 'Parliamentary Tyranny? Indemnity Proceedings and the Impact of the Civil War: A Case Study from Warwickshire', *Midland History*, 11 (1986), 49–78 (p. 69).

[57] A. Hughes, '"The Accounts of the Kingdom": Memory, Community, and the English Civil War', *Past & Present*, 233 (2016), 311–29 (p. 328).

[58] R. Weil, 'Thinking about Allegiance in the English Civil War', *History Workshop Journal*, 61 (2006), 183–91; H. Worthen, 'Supplicants and Guardians: The Petitions of Royalist Widows during the Civil Wars and Interregnum, 1642–1660', *Women's History Review*, 26 (2017), 528–40.

forces raised against the Parlyament' but also that she had not in 'any waies in her desires or Affecions adheared thereunto'.[59] The many royalist maimed soldiers who received pensions at the Restoration frequently presented petitions laced with the language of loyalty and faithfulness to the king. William Pledger, a Kentish former royalist soldier, was described as having carried out 'true and faithful service' to the king in his petition.[60] 'Faithful' was a word used frequently in these petitions and probably reflected the authorities' own preferred choice of language. When the Kent justices of the peace (JPs) handed out pensions, their order book formulaically named recipients as those who had been 'active and faithful in the service of the Kings Majestie and of his Royall father'.[61] Furthermore, the Civil Wars, and the political divisions of the country, could appear in petitions that were not directly related to the wars. In 1646 the residents of the parish of Buckstead in parliamentarian-controlled Sussex petitioned the JPs at quarter sessions, claiming that a poor man named Thomas Puxtie, who had recently erected a cottage on the waste, was not only 'idle lewd wicked and vngodly' but was also 'liveing for the most part by dishonest and vnlawfull Courses', having deserted his colours after enlisting as a soldier.[62]

Thus, whilst the practice of petitioning may have remained relatively consistent, the language of petitioning at a local and national level changed to reflect the political discourse of the mid-17th century. But, in many ways, this shift also demonstrates an essential continuity with the rest of the period: petitioning required the legitimacy of the state to be effective, and thus the language that supplicants used was necessarily shaped by national discourse. We see this during the Civil War period in a particularly dramatic fashion, when the language of allegiance and loyalty pervaded even the most mundane of petitions. Yet this change faithfully reflected the nature of petitioning in general in early modern England, for while petitions were documents that were submitted from below, their language was often shaped from above.

Looking more closely at the strategies and challenges of one well-documented petitioner shows how this period saw change, as well as a measure of continuity, in the ways in which people presented their grievances to the state. Dame Margaret Rudstone was the wife of Sir Walter Rudstone, an East Yorkshire landowner with estates in Hayton. Sir Walter signed the Yorkshire Engagement, an agreement to stand security for a loan for the king, and all the Rudstone estates were subsequently confiscated by Parliament. He died early in 1651 whilst the case was still in progress with Parliament's sequestration committees in London, and his wife immediately took the reins in attempting to regain the lands on behalf of their son Thomas. A rich collection of records at East Yorkshire Record Office reveals not

[59] Petition of Lucy Pope, 3 September 1645, TNA, SP 20/11/23, fo. 105r.
[60] Certificate on behalf of William Pledger, April 1662, WSRO, Q/R/W103, fo. 66r.
[61] For example West Kent Quarter Sessions Order Book, September 1662, KHLC, Q/SO/W2, fo. 83r.
[62] East Sussex Quarter Sessions Order Book, January 1646, ESRO, QR/70, fo. 10r.

just that Margaret Rudstone submitted numerous petitions, but also that she relied upon networks of local powerful men to draft them and lobby Parliament on her behalf. She corresponded directly with her lawyer, John Hall, to direct him about the manner in which he should pursue her case.[63] Hall's accounts reveal payments for the obtaining of witnesses, for transcribing their depositions, and for entering her petitions to the Committee for Compounding.[64] Rudstone also corresponded with prominent local royalist men who formed an advice network, wrote to Hall on her behalf, and even drafted petitions for her.[65] For example, Lawrence Squibb filed petitions with the Compounding Committee for her and passed on his own advice about the content of the petitions in doing so.[66] Her petitions show the ways in which the language of allegiance pervaded petitions. In one draft petition, for example, Rudstone stated that she 'Confesseth that her deceased husband was a delinquent or assisting the late Kings p[ar]ty in the first warr'.[67] However, a second draft (possibly altered on Squibb's advice) removed the phrase 'was a delinquent', thus making Rudstone's declaration of her husband's guilt slightly less forthright, and perhaps more politically prudent.[68]

The case of Dame Margaret Rudstone illustrates some of the ways in which the events of the Civil Wars created even more reasons to supplicate the state, but also reveals that these wars did not necessarily fundamentally change the nature of, or the barriers to, petitioning. To protect her son's inheritance and her own jointure from Parliament, Rudstone used the medium of the petition to engage directly with the political sphere in Westminster. Her frequent letters, sent across the country between London and Yorkshire, demonstrate that she was an active participant in the petitioning process. The methods that she used to lobby Parliament were by no means novel: she engaged the services of lawyers and powerful friends to advise her on strategy, as well as to write out and physically present her petitions in the same way that people did throughout the 17th century. The events of the Civil Wars may have created the stimulus for Rudstone's engagement with petitioning culture, but the means and method of her petitioning remained consistent. Furthermore, the Civil Wars had not removed all the barriers to petitioning. Petitioners, particularly women, still had to rely upon powerful friends, and a great deal of persistence, to have their cases heard.

[63] Letter from Margaret Rudstone to John Hall, 27 January 1651, East Riding of Yorkshire Record Office (ERYRO), DDCR/5/1/46.

[64] Notes of John Hall, 1651, ERYRO, DDCR/5/1/82; pocket book of John Hall, 1651–3, ERYRO, DDCR/5/1/83.

[65] For example, letter from William Bernard, 7 January 1651, ERYRO, DDCR/5/1/42; letter from Marmaduke Prickett, 25 January 1651, ERYRO, DDCR/5/1/44.

[66] Letters from Lawrence Squibb, 1651, ERYRO, DDCR/5/1/75, 76; Lawrence Squibb was the royalist brother to the parliamentarian Arthur Squibb who sat on the Committee for Compounding; Aylmer, *The State's Servants*, p. 217.

[67] Petition of Dame Margaret Rudstone, [1651], EYRO, DDCR/5/1/54.

[68] Petition of Dame Margaret Rudstone, [1651], EYRO, DDCR/5/1/56.

It is impossible to separate petitioning culture from national events, the rise and fall of government bodies, and the changing nature of political ideas. Thus, the practice of petitioning in the Civil Wars should not be seen in isolation. It is useful to examine petitioning culture during the turbulent years of the mid-17th century because here changes are visible in the most dramatic ways. But we should not allow this to blind us to the fact that the culture of petitioning, as well as its power to link ordinary people with the state, remained remarkably consistent with the rest of the century.

Petitioning from 1660 to c. 1750

The immediate impact of the Restoration of the monarchy in 1660 on the practice and culture of petitioning was substantial, but, much like the collapse of royal authority in the early 1640s, its effects should not be exaggerated. New laws only affected a small minority of complaints, while institutional and ideological shifts more gradually changed patterns of 'unrevolutionary' petitioning.

In 1661, the newly elected royalist Parliament passed 'An Act against Tumults and Disorders upon pretence of preparing or presenting publick Peticions or other Addresses to His Majesty or the Parliament', which forbade gathering 20 or more signatures without official authorisation, and physically presenting petitions in groups of 10 or more people.[69] This statute focused on campaigns 'for alteracion of matters established by Law in Church or State' and targeted the sort of mass oppositional petitioning that had flourished in the 1640s and 1650s. However, the 1661 law was not a complete novelty, as a Declaration issued by Parliament in 1648 had imposed similar restrictions, and enforcement of the new Act was inconsistent, especially from 1679 onwards.[70] Moreover, the vast bulk of petitioning on less controversial matters was untouched by the law, meaning that such petitions continued to be submitted on the same legal basis that had been in place for decades.

At the national level, the Restoration spurred a surge in personal petitions seeking the favour of the new king and Parliament. Many of these came from royalists who claimed to have been loyal during the Interregnum and who sought

[69] 'Charles II, 1661: An Act against Tumults and Disorders upon p[re]tence of p[re]paring or p[re] senting publick Petic[i]ons or other Addresses to His Majesty or the Parliament', in John Raithby (ed.), *Statutes of the Realm*, Vol. V, *1628–80* (n.p., 1819), p. 308, *British History Online*, www.british-history.ac.uk/statutes-realm/vol5/p308 (accessed 14 October 2019). For the occasional use of this law, and the Riot Act of 1715, to regulate the presentation of petitions, see P. M. Loft, 'Peers, Parliament, and Power under the Revolution Constitution, 1685–1720', PhD thesis (University College London, 2015), pp. 271–8.

[70] 'May 1648: Declaration against tumultuous Assemblies, under Pretence of preparing Petitions', in C. H. Firth and R. S. Rait (eds), *Acts and Ordinances of the Interregnum, 1642–1660* (London, His Majesty's Stationery Office, 1911), p. 1139, *British History Online*, www.british-history.ac.uk/no-series/acts-ordinances-interregnum/p1139 (accessed 14 October 2019). For the return of mass petitioning from 1679, see M. Knights, 'London's "Monster" Petition of 1680', *Historical Journal*, 36 (1993), 39–67.

revenge against their 'oppressors' or material compensation for their suffering.[71] This was, however, just part of a broader wave of petitioning, similar to the waves that had been seen in the wake of previous royal accessions. Overall, according to an estimate by Brian Weiser, the new king probably received about 10,000 petitions from individuals in the 1660s, with only a fraction coming from steadfast royalists.[72] Meanwhile, Parliament continued to receive petitions at a high rate, even if its role was less prominent under Charles II and James II than it had been in the 1640s or 1650s. In fact, after the Revolution of 1688, Parliament began to meet for regular annual sessions, and it again became powerful magnet for a diverse range of 'interest groups'. Lobbying about potential legislation relating to trade, transport, and taxation became especially prevalent.[73] By the end of the 17th century, it was common for 100 or more collective petitions to be submitted during each parliamentary session, peaking at close to 500 in the session of 1719–20.[74] The monarch received fewer direct petitions as Parliament took on more powers, though over 30 thick volumes of royal 'petition entry books' survive from 1688 to 1784.[75] Moreover, the proliferation of government departments, such as the Navy Office and Council of Trade, meant that the central authorities as a whole continued to receive innumerable supplications throughout this later period. Estimating the overall level of national petitioning in the late 17th and early 18th centuries would require much more methodical primary research, but it seems that a decline in some jurisdictions may have been more than offset by a rise in others.

A similar pattern can be found at the local level. Here too there was a rush of petitioning in the wake of the Restoration, especially from royalists attempting to secure places or pensions from the county magistrates. As we have seen, this included huge numbers of royalist veterans and war widows who had been ignored by the previous regime, but who received a sympathetic hearing from benches of magistrates that had been purged of their most zealously parliamentarian justices.[76] Over subsequent decades, the number of petitions handled at county quarter sessions declined in some places, perhaps because of the rise of poorly documented

[71] A. Button, 'Royalist Women Petitioners in South-West England, 1655–62', *The Seventeenth Century*, 15 (2000), 53–66; S. Beale, 'War Widows and Revenge in Restoration England', *The Seventeenth Century*, 33 (2018), 195–217; S. Beale, '"Unpittyed by Any"? Royalist Widows and the Crown, 1660–70', *Historical Research*, 92 (2019), 737–53.

[72] B. Weiser, 'Access and Petitioning during the Reign of Charles II', in E. Cruickshanks (ed.), *The Stuart Courts* (Stroud, Sutton, 2000), pp. 203–13 (p. 207).

[73] P. Gauci, *Politics of Trade: The Overseas Merchant in State and Society, 1660–1720* (Oxford, Oxford University Press, 2001); J. Hoppit, *Britain's Political Economies: Parliament and Economic Life, 1660–1800* (Cambridge, Cambridge University Press, 2017), p. 153.

[74] P. Loft, 'Petitioning and Petitioners to the Westminster Parliament, 1660–1788', *Parliamentary History*, 38 (2019), 342–61 (p. 346). See also J. Innes, 'Legislation and Public Participation, 1760–1830', in D. Lemmings (ed.), *The British and Their Laws in the Eighteenth Century* (Woodbridge, Boydell & Brewer, 2006), pp. 102–32 (p. 118).

[75] TNA, SP 44/235–266A.

[76] See figures for Kent, p. 130. See also Worthen, 'The Administration of Military Welfare', p. 178.

'petty sessions' that dealt with many matters that had previously come under the purview of the whole county bench.[77] However, this was not a universal trend: the magistrates of Lancashire received hundreds of petitions about poor relief in every decade of the late 17th century.[78] Likewise, about 10,000 petitions to the London magistracy relating to poverty, taxation, and petty crime survive from the 18th century.[79] In fact, several new pieces of legislation led directly to new petitions. The many acts passed from 1701 onwards 'for the relief of insolvent debtors' gave imprisoned debtors the right to petition the quarter sessions for release.[80] Similarly, the Toleration Act of 1689 encouraged protestant dissenters to apply to the county magistrates for a licence designating a particular building as a legitimate place of worship.[81] The 18th century also witnessed the emergence of so-called 'pauper letters'; these were less formal requests for aid that were submitted to parish authorities rather than to county magistrates.[82] So it would be premature to suggest that ordinary people became less likely to submit written requests and complaints to their local authorities towards the end of the early modern period.

The rhetoric used in later Stuart petitions mixed old and new elements. Most requests from individuals, especially the thousands submitted to local officials, continued to emphasise the petitioner's deference and powerlessness. Some even offered explicit prayers for the health and salvation of the recipients, maintaining a religious component that might seem more suited to the 15th than the 17th century.[83] At the other end of the spectrum, some highly politicised petitions also circulated, despite the attempted restrictions imposed by the 1661 Act. For example, almost 16,000 Londoners signed an oppositional petition to Charles II to recall Parliament during the Exclusion Crisis of 1678–81.[84] Nine years later, during the Glorious Revolution, the Convention Parliament received a printed petition from 'the Widdows and Fatherless Children in the West of England' demanding vengeance against Judge Jeffreys, who had presided over the execution of scores of men involved in the Duke of Monmouth's Rebellion.[85] However, such politically

[77] The declining number of surviving petitions in some county records is discussed in more detail in Waddell, 'Shaping the State'; and Howard, 'The Local Power of Petitioning'.

[78] Healey, *The First Century of Welfare*, p. 214.

[79] S. Howard, 'The London Lives Petitions Project', https://london.sharonhoward.org/llpp/ (accessed 30 January 2024).

[80] See, for example, 'Staffordshire Quarter Sessions: 1729', in B. Waddell (ed.), *Petitions to the Staffordshire Quarter Sessions, 1589–1799*; *British History Online*, www.british-history.ac.uk/petitions/staffordshire/1729 (accessed 4 November 2019).

[81] For example, 'Staffordshire Quarter Sessions: 1769', in Waddell, *Petitions to the Staffordshire Quarter Sessions*; *British History Online*, www.british-history.ac.uk/petitions/staffordshire/1769 (accessed 4 November 2019).

[82] T. Sokoll, *Essex Pauper Letters, 1731–1837* (Oxford, Oxford University Press, 2001); S. King, *Writing the Lives of the English Poor* (Montreal, McGill-Queen's University Press, 2019).

[83] B. Waddell, *God, Duty and Community in English Economic Life* (Woodbridge, Boydell & Brewer, 2012), pp. 68–9.

[84] Knights, 'London's "Monster" Petition'.

[85] L. G. Schwoerer, 'Women and the Glorious Revolution', *Albion*, 18 (1986), 195–218 (pp. 200–1).

contentious mass petitions remained relatively rare in this period. Instead, most followed the conventions that had been established decades earlier, while occasionally drawing on new rhetorical tropes in order to make their cases. In particular, patriotic appeals to Englishness and denunciations of foreignness seem to feature more often in the many petitions about trade and manufacturing submitted in the later Stuart period.[86]

Institutional shifts in this period such as the rising importance of Parliament from 1689 and the growing use of petty sessions at the local level led to changing patterns of petitioning across the late 17th and early 18th centuries. Yet, despite the prominence of the Restoration and the Glorious Revolution in political histories of this period, their impact on the culture of petitioning was less dramatic. A remarkable range of people continued to use petitioning to engage with the state in ways that developed only slowly amid these revolutionary events.

Long-Term Trends and Continuities

Over the course of the 16th, 17th, and 18th centuries, petitioning practices were far from stable. The most well-known change was the outpouring of politically contentious mass petitioning in the mid-17th century, but this 'revolutionary' shift should not be seen in isolation. It was only one of several important changes in the period, and its visibility in print also obscures a strong element of stability in the wider culture of petitioning. There were genuine continuities in concept, form, rhetoric, and often motive, even during the crisis of the mid-17th century and its aftermath.

Some trends in the prevalence of local petitioning are unmistakable, despite jurisdictional shifts and archival gaps. As noted above, petitions to Parliament and to local magistrates became increasingly common by the early 17th century, and petitions to the Crown also probably grew more frequent. In the 1640s, the numbers rose still further, accompanying a wider wave of popular political engagement and a proliferation of new political bodies to which one could appeal. The Restoration in 1660 spurred an immediate wave of royalist petitioning at national and local levels, while the Glorious Revolution led to the normalisation of petitions to Parliament on a wide variety of subjects.

Changes in quantity were accompanied by changes in quality. The most well-known aspect was the increasing 'politicisation' of petitioning in the early modern period, a trend that has received much scholarly attention. Medieval petitions could be sharply political on occasion, and the Tudor authorities certainly regarded some as deeply subversive.[87] Nonetheless, many scholars have rightly argued that the number and scale of petitions that explicitly addressed questions of church and state grew exponentially in the 1640s and recurred frequently thereafter, such as

[86] Waddell, *God, Duty and Community*, pp. 163–78.

[87] See Dodd's chapter in this volume; and Hoyle, 'Petitioning'.

during the Exclusion Crisis of 1678–81.[88] Such petitions were much more likely to use contentious, partisan rhetoric, in sharp contrast to their Tudor and early Stuart precursors. As shown earlier, this language sometimes infused local 'bread-and-butter' petitions too, especially those of veterans and war widows whose appeals drew on increasingly contested vocabularies of allegiance. In many cases, however, this shift towards the use of more overtly partisan language seems to have been less about the ideological motives of the petitioners and more of an attempt to match the shifting expectations of the authorities.

Mass petitions to national authorities also became more common. Subscription lists numbering in the hundreds were almost unknown before the 1640s, but thereafter they became a recurrent feature of petitions and addresses. This meant that many more people were able to participate directly in the process of engaging with Crown or Parliament, even if that often only entailed adding their mark to an already long list of names. The simultaneous shift to the printing of petitions was another major change, though one that was perhaps less abrupt than is sometimes implied.[89] In a large corpus of more than 60,000 printed texts, the use of the word 'petition' was relatively uncommon before 1640. There were, however, a few years when it appears to have been used significantly more often, most noticeably in 1537–8, 1570, 1588, and 1626 (Figure 6.2). As we might expect, there was an extraordinary peak in the use of this term in print in the 1640s and 1650s, with smaller peaks around the time of the Exclusion Crisis of 1678–81. So, just as some petitions began attracting extremely long lists of subscribers, so too did some petitions reach much wider audiences with the help of the printing press.

These many changes in the culture of petitioning – both gradual trends and sudden shifts – unfolded alongside very evident long-term continuities. For example, while requests about new issues such as statutory poor relief or national ecclesiastical policy became common, huge numbers of petitions continued to pursue very 'traditional' aims, such as redress for victims of unpunished misbehaviour, mercy for those facing punishment, or favour for aspiring officeholders. Similarly, although some new authorities received growing numbers of requests, England's monarchs remained one of the pre-eminent targets for petitioners thanks to their wide jurisdiction and unmatched visibility. Many of George I's subjects supplicated for royal favour in the 18th century just as their predecessors had done for centuries before them.

Another notable continuity in petitioning is its typical form and tone. Many variants can be found in every era and occasionally scribal conventions shifted significantly, and yet a degree of standardisation ensured that many later petitions

[88] Summarised in M. Knights, 'Participation and Representation before Democracy: Petitions and Addresses in Pre-Modern Britain', in I. Shapiro, S. C. Stokes, E. J. Wood, and A. Kirshner (eds), *Political Representation* (Cambridge, Cambridge University Press, 2009), pp. 35–58.

[89] For the ambiguities of printed parliamentary petitions, see Peacey, *Print and Public Politics*, Chapter 8. For pre-1640 examples, see D. Coast, 'Speaking for the People in Early Modern England', *Past & Present*, 244 (2019), 51–88.

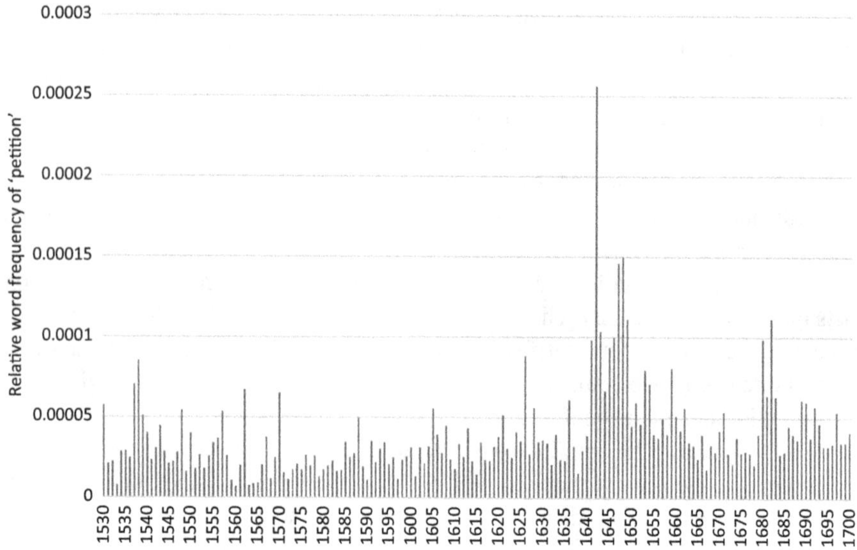

Figure 6.2 Relative word frequency of 'petition' in the Early English Books Online TCP Corpus. Extracted from the Early Print Lab N-Gram Browser, created by Anupam Basu and Stephen Pentecost, http://earlyprint.wustl.edu/url/1674041122 (accessed 1 February 2024).

followed almost precisely the same structure as their much earlier counterparts. In the papers of the Hertfordshire magistrates, for instance, one finds documents from both the 1590s and the 1790s that use nearly matching phrases to introduce 'the humble petition', to address it to 'the right worshipful justices of the peace', to 'humbly sheweth' the grievance, and to conclude with an offer to 'daily pray' for the health and prosperity of the recipients.[90] Similarly, a highly deferential tone, though never quite universal, was also almost always used throughout this period, even in the turbulent decades of the mid-17th century. A typical petitioner was one who was 'humble' and who 'beseeched' his or her superiors for redress, but who ultimately deferred to their 'grave wisdom' for judgement. Even after the breakdown of censorship and the rise of radical public protest in the 1640s, the vast majority of petitions followed rules that had been established long before.

The expanding scale and deepening social reach of petitioning in early modern England left a strong imprint on the historical record. This is not entirely surprising given the other historical trends in this period and the fact that, as historians, we are always alert to signs of change, especially when those changes seem to be tending in the direction of 'modern' outlooks and behaviours. Thus, it is crucial to note that

[90] HALS, HAT/SR/4/97; HALS, QSR 47/1796/122.

the overwhelming bulk of these growing waves of petitions were 'unrevolutionary' in purpose and tone.

There is still much work to be done in exploring the complex and reciprocal relationship between local and national, manuscript and print, ordinary and 'political' petitioning. We also need to know more about the actual process of composition, including the involvement of clerks, lawyers, and other advisors. This preliminary survey of the culture and practice of petitioning in early modern England thus poses questions for further research as well as offering some possible answers. Nevertheless, we have highlighted some of the diverse ways that changing state structures could influence the quantity, form, and language of petitioning. At the very least, this chapter has demonstrated that if we want to understand the well-known moments of spectacular political crisis and popular mobilisation during these years, we cannot ignore the vast ocean of 'unrevolutionary' petitioning.

7

Strategies of Collectiveness: Representative Claims in Dutch Petitionary Practices, c. 1600–1940

MAARTJE JANSE, JORIS ODDENS, ANNE PETTERSON, JORIS VAN DEN TOL, EDURNE DE WILDE, AND ELSA MIEDEMA

WHOEVER INTENDS TO petition an authority needs to make a choice: will they petition alone, possibly with the help of a professional, or petition together with others? There are cases where it may seem obvious that petitioning collectively is the better option: individuals who suffer from the same wrong or who see the same business opportunity, or individuals who share ideas about a change of legislation or political reform, stand stronger when they petition together. When a person requires an individual favour, such as a job, a licence, or an act of grace, an individual petition seems most appropriate, although in such cases as well it can be advantageous to petition together. A person who does petition alone may still choose to make clear to the recipient of the petition that there are others who share his or her grievance or desire.

It is possible to think about these choices in terms of 'representative claim-making', following the work of the political theorist Michael Saward. According to Saward, political representation can be studied as a process of claim-making that takes place not only in formal representative institutions such as parliaments but everywhere in society. He suggests that every representative claim involves a 'maker' (the actor producing a claim), a subject (the actor who represents), and an object (the actor or interest that is represented).[1] This scheme can fruitfully be applied to petitions, which Mark Knights has rightfully identified as a 'very important informal representative institution'.[2] Below we identify three

[1] M. Saward, *The Representative Claim* (Oxford, Oxford University Press, 2010). What we present here is a simplified version of Saward's scheme.

[2] M. Knights, 'Participation and Representation before Democracy: Petitions and Addresses in Premodern Britain', in I. Shapiro, S. Stokes, E. Wood, and A. Kirshner (eds), *Political Representation* (Cambridge, Cambridge University Press, 2009), pp. 35–57 (p. 39).

Proceedings of the British Academy, **262**, 142–159, © The British Academy 2024.

strategies that petitioners might deploy to suggest 'collectiveness'. Each of these strategies makes use of a different type of representative claim. It should be noted that these three forms of collectiveness are ideal types; in reality combinations are possible.

(1) One or more petitioners claim to represent (the interests of) others, but these others have not signed the petition, nor actively consented to being represented (representation without consent).

> *Example (a)* A professional scribe (maker), petitioning on behalf of a war widow for a law change that would grant this widow a pension, claims that this widow (subject) represents her own interests as well as the interests of other war widows who would also benefit from this law (object);
>
> *Example (b)* The author of a petition to ban tobacco (maker) claims that the 100,000 subscribers to this petition (subject) represent the interests of themselves and all other inhabitants of the country (object).

(2) One or more petitioners claim to represent others who have actively consented to being represented (representation with consent).

> *Example (a)* The secretary of a voluntary association petitioning for royal patronage (maker) claims that s/he and the president of the association, the only signatories of the petition (subject), represent themselves and all the other members of this association (object);
>
> *Example (b)* A notary, the author and only signatory of a petition for pardon (maker and subject), claims to represent 20 prisoners requesting to be pardoned (object).

(3) A petition is signed or presented by more than one petitioner (self-representation).

> *Example (a)* A woman petitioning for poor relief (maker) claims that she and her two sisters, all signatories of the petition (subject), represent themselves (object);
>
> *Example (b)* An inhabitant of a street petitioning against odour nuisance (maker) claims that s/he and the other 30 inhabitants of said street, all signatories of the petition (subject), represent themselves (object).

Thinking about petitions in this way invites us to go beyond the dichotomy between individual (private) and collective (public) petitions that is common among historians.[3] For instance, examples 1(a) and 1(b) would normally be considered an

[3] On this dichotomy, see for instance A. Würgler, 'Voices from among the "Silent Masses": Humble Petitions and Social Conflicts in Early Modern Central Europe', in L. Heerma van Voss (ed.), *Petitions in Social History*, Supplement 9 of *International Review of Social History*, 46 (2001), 11–34; G. Vermeesch, 'Professional Lobbying in Eighteenth-Century Brussels: The Role of Agents in Petitioning the Central Government Institutions in the Habsburg Netherlands', *Journal of Early Modern History*, 16 (2012), 95–119 (p. 101); and L. Stewart, 'Petitioning in Early Seventeenth-Century Scotland, 1625–51', *Parliaments, Estates and Representation*, 38 (2018), 307–22 (p. 308).

individual and a mass petition respectively and thus on opposite sides of the petitionary spectrum. However, they both make use of the strategy of representation without consent, which sets them apart from the other examples.

Michael Saward argues that for a representative claim to be considered democratically legitimate, there should be evidence that those who are claimed to be represented accept this claim, or that they are at least aware of it, so that they can protest if they feel that they are being misrepresented.[4] This is perhaps the case in present-day democratic societies, but we may expect views on what type of claim-making is considered legitimate to have evolved through time. In this chapter we therefore aim to historicise the practice of representative claim-making in petitioning. Did petitioners in the past believe that authorities would find it acceptable if they resorted to representation without consent, did they strive to acquire and demonstrate consent, or did they feel that they had a stronger case if they gathered as many signatures as possible?

In this chapter we will study the occurrence of the above-mentioned types of representative claims in petitioning from a long-term perspective. We will be concerned with key moments in the history of the Netherlands between the early 17th and the mid-20th century. The focus is on petitions addressed to authorities at the level of the (nation) state. We will try to account for changes in the types of claims that were considered legitimate, by linking them to the evolution of norms in other representative institutions at various levels, such as corporations, voluntary associations, and the national Parliament. Our most important conclusion will be that during this period, there is no simple linear development towards an ever-growing perception of the need to demonstrate that all those that are claimed to be represented by a petition have in fact actively consented to this petition – as might perhaps have been expected during the centuries that saw the rise of the system of representative democracy – but that we are presented with a more complex picture.

The 17th-Century Dutch Republic

After the Act of Abjuration and subsequent establishment of the Dutch Republic in the 1580s, the provinces in the northern Low Countries governed themselves. The sovereignty formally belonged to the people of the provinces, but de facto the highest authority in each province was exercised by a collegiate board of representatives: the provincial states.[5] Delegates of the provincial states met several times a week in The Hague during meetings of the States General. This was an

[4] Saward, *The Representative Claim*, Chapter 6.

[5] S. Groenveld, *Unie-Bestand-Vrede: Drie fundamentele wetten van de Republiek der Verenigde Nederlanden* (Hilversum, Verloren, 2009), pp. 16–18.

intergovernmental body of deliberation rather than a centralised government. The seven provinces of the Dutch Republic each had one vote.[6]

Petitions could thus be submitted to at least three different political levels: the local level (cities and seigneurial lords), the provinces, or the States General. Within cities, collectives could be organised in different corporations such as guilds, civic guards, or religious organisations. With 20 to 30 per cent of the urban households involved in some sort of corporation, it has been argued that the role of these corporations in presenting petitions became increasingly important during the early modern period.[7] It should be noted, however, that inhabitants (*ingezetenen*) who were not citizens (*poorters*) of a city could not be guild members, but did have the possibility of petitioning urban governments. Moreover, any increasing importance of corporations for petitioning should be considered concomitant to the growing accessibility of city citizenship from the second half of the 17th century onwards: more access to citizenship meant more access to guilds, meant more petitions through corporations.

The most important innovation for petitioning in the beginning of the 17th century was the introduction of signature drives before submitting the petition. Groups of urban citizens and members of church congregations were among the first to organise such drives.[8] Initially signatures seem to have served to demonstrate the support of those petitioners who could not be physically present when the petition was submitted. The signatures were not always written on the petitions themselves. Petitioners could also carry a letter of credence on behalf of others whose interest they represented.[9] Keeping the signatures on a separate letter of credence allowed the delegated petitioners to use them for multiple petitions. An important benefit of collecting signatures instead of relying on corporations or associations to represent collective interests was that signature drives allowed inclusion beyond the adherent

[6] T. Thomassen, 'Instrumenten van de macht: De Staten-Generaal en hun archieven 1576–1796', PhD thesis (University of Amsterdam, 2009).

[7] M. R. Prak, 'The Dutch Republic as a Bourgeois Society', *BMGN: Low Countries Historical Review*, 125 (2010), 107–39; M. R. Prak, 'Corporate Politics in the Low Countries: Guilds as Institutions, 14th to 18th Centuries', in C. Lis, H. Soly, and M. Prak (eds), *Craft Guilds in the Early Modern Low Countries: Work, Power and Representation* (Aldershot, Ashgate, 2006), pp. 74–106.

[8] The earliest example of more than 10 signatures on a petition dates from Amsterdam in 1608; see J. G. van Dillen (ed.), *Bronnen tot de geschiedenis der wisselbanken (Amsterdam, Middelburg, Delft, Rotterdam)*, 3 vols (The Hague, Nijhoff, 1925), Vol. I, 14–17. For an example of a religious group, see Stadsarchief Amsterdam, 612, 'Archief van de Remonstrantse Gemeente', inv. no. 290, 'Stuk bevattende handtekeningen van remonstrantsgezinden ter adhesie aan het voornemen om enigen ter hunner een adres tot "exercitie van religie, inkomen ende relaxatie van predikanten" te laten richten aan burgermeesters en regeerders van Amsterdam. (1628)'.

[9] This can be seen, for example, in a petition from 1637 presented to the States General, where 56 main investors from Zeeland signed a letter of credence: The Hague, National Archives (NA), 1.01.02, Staten-Generaal, inv. no. 5754, 4 February 1637, letter of credence by the Zeeland main investors. The Zeelanders did this in response to petitioners from Amsterdam who showed numerical support in physical presence.

group; it created interest alliances that transcended traditional borders of ethnicity, religion, language, gender, or the city or province.[10]

Petitions with no signature whatsoever continued to be submitted as well. By 1623, the States General introduced legislation that required all petitions presented to them to have at least one signature. Clearly this did not have the desired effect, because resolutions confirming this requirement had to be passed in 1628 and 1646.[11] As late as August 1650, the States of Zeeland refused to resolve on a particular petition until the petitioners signed their request.[12] Resolutions mandating signatures not only served to make the bureaucratic process more uniform, but also had the important consequence that someone could be held accountable for the contents of each petition by authorities.

Most petitions submitted to the States General in the 17th century were presented by individuals. In 1670, for instance, individuals were responsible for 71 per cent of all petitions submitted in that year (mainly regarding individual problems), against 22 per cent from corporations. These corporations included local religious and urban corporations, as well as national corporations such as the Dutch East India Company. The remaining petitions submitted in 1670 were mainly presented by two or three individuals, or by groups that were not corporations.[13] Petitions of that last category came both with and without signatures. For instance, one petition by 'several merchants from the city of Amsterdam having a commission from their friends in England' contained no signatures, whereas another petition by 'merchants from the city of Amsterdam trading to Spain' was signed by 32 individuals.[14] With regard to this category, there had been little development since the early 17th century, because in 1601 as well, one petition was submitted on behalf of 'the common merchants of Amsterdam, and some other in the province of Holland, that are trading to Königsberg', while another petition by 'common merchants of Amsterdam was signed by one individual 'in the name, and on behalf, of the supplicants'.[15]

In those instances where merchants claimed to represent others who had not signed, we can in most cases only assume that those whose interests were claimed to be represented had been consulted. The same is true for petitions signed only by representatives of corporations, such as the governing boards of local guilds or parishes. These signatories claimed to represent the corporation as a whole.

[10] J. van den Tol, 'Lobbying in Company: Mechanisms of Political Decision-Making and Economic Interests in the History of Dutch Brazil, 1621–1656', PhD thesis (Leiden University, 2018), Chapter 4.

[11] Thomassen, 'Instrumenten van de macht', p. 276.

[12] *Notulen van de ed. mog. heeren Staten van Zeeland d'Anno 1650* (n.p., 1650), p. 123.

[13] There were 135 petitions submitted in this year. These can be found in NA, 1.01.02, inv. no. 7492, Liassen Rekesten 1670.

[14] Petition of several merchants from the city of Amsterdam to the States General, [1670]; petition of merchants from the city of Amsterdam trading to Spain to the States General, [1670]: NA, 1.01.02, inv. no. 7492.

[15] Petition of common merchants of Amsterdam and other places to the States General, [1601]; petition of common merchants of Amsterdam to the States General, [1601]: NA, 1.01.02, inv. no. 7474.

They derived their authority to do so from an understanding of representation as a form of corporate identity (*repraesentatio identitatis*) that dictated that a corporation could be represented (embodied) by its most distinguished members.[16] That these governing boards did not always consult with the ordinary members of their corporations became painfully clear when such members of the corporation started presenting dissenting petitions.[17] Throughout the 17th century, petitioners who could not claim to have a wider constituency often claimed in their petitions that their request served the interest of 'the common wealth' (*gemeene best*) in an attempt to avoid the suspicion that they were petitioning to advance their private interests. Even individuals petitioning for, say, a monopoly to print a book on the general history of churches in the valleys of Piedmont, could claim to do this 'in the interest of the common wealth'.[18]

It is important to realise that different strategies of collectiveness were by no means mutually exclusive in the Dutch Republic. This becomes clear, for instance, in a petition requesting assistance in maintaining the Dutch West India Company (WIC), submitted in 1669 to the States General by its main shareholders (*hooftparticipanten*). The petitioners started by acknowledging that the directors (*bewindhebbers*) of the WIC had the best interest of this corporation at heart. They reminded their addressee how the corporation had been 'in the service of the state' during the Eighty Years War with Spain, and claimed that its investors were the 'most distinguished patriots'. The logical conclusion of this was that the corporation's 'lawful and reasonable request would certainly be to the benefit of the state'. The petition ends with a list of 66 signatures. Most signatories signed for themselves, but some also signed for others. In the case of 'Philippe and David d'Orville' it is clear that one of these signatories signed on the other's behalf, while the names of Antoni Wilmerdonx and Cornelis Wilmerdonx were also almost certainly written in the same hand. The name of Giacomo Bessels was not put down by himself but by someone else because he was still a minor (*onmondige zoon*), while Johan van de Poele signed 'both for himself and with the power of attorney for the main shareholders in the Chamber Zeeland in Middelburg'.[19] The petition thus combined several strategies of representative claim-making, which suggests that the petitioners perceived the sum of representation with consent, representation without consent, and self-representation as adding to its persuasive power.

[16] On this understanding of representation, see Hasso Hofmann, *Repräsentation: Studien zur Wort- und Begriffsgeschichte von der Antike bis ins 19. Jahrhundert* (Berlin, Duncker & Humblot, 1974), p. 216; and T. Weller, 'Political Representation and Symbolic Communication in the Early Modern Period: The Imperial Free Cities of the Holy Roman Empire', in J. Albareda and M. Herrero Sánchez (eds), *Political Representation in the Ancien Régime* (Abingdon, Routledge, 2018), pp. 105–20.

[17] Van den Tol, 'Lobbying in Company', Chapter 3.

[18] Petition of Johannes le Carpentier to the States General, [1670]: NA, 1.01.02, inv. no. 7492.

[19] Petitions of the main shareholders of the WIC to the States General: NA, 1.01.02, inv. no. 5768, [1669].

The Revolutionary Era

In the 1780s, authorities in the Netherlands started to receive political petitions with unprecedented numbers of signatures. Between 1780 and 1787, the stadtholder William V of Orange and the oligarchic system of the Dutch Republic were challenged by the 'Patriot movement'. Citizens calling themselves 'Patriots' demanded a great number of constitutional reforms, the most radical of which was the introduction of 'true' representative government at the local level.[20] Patriot petitions often exceeded 1,000, and sometimes even several thousand, signatures.[21]

The organisers of political petitions in the Dutch Republic before the 1780s had believed that it was not so much the quantity but the quality of the petitioners that mattered. In order for a petition to have a chance of being granted by the authorities, it would have to be signed by some of the most distinguished members of a local community.[22] The organisers of the large-scale collective petitions of the Patriot movement still belonged to an urban elite, but they believed in strength in numbers. Their attitude in favour of a more inclusive type of political petitioning was directly connected to their view of representative government. The Patriots rejected the legitimacy of *repraesentatio identitatis* and advocated a new system of electoral representative democracy. However, as long as this demand had not been met, they considered the practice of petitioning to be the best alternative form of representation.[23]

This meant that they deemed it appropriate for all citizens, who would in their ideal political system be eligible to vote, to participate in political petitioning. Opinions differed among the Patriots about the likely electorate. It would certainly include urban male citizens (*poorters*), mostly members of the guilds and merchants operating outside the guild structure. Some of the earlier large Patriot petitions had been produced with the approval and collaboration of the powerful guild boards. In collecting signatures for these petitions, the organisers had depended on the corporate structure of the local guilds.[24] Later, when the Patriot Revolt further radicalised, large petitions were increasingly signed by town dwellers without urban citizenship (*ingezetenen*).

At the core of the large-scale Patriot petitions were alternative representative institutions. The first of these associations, the Citizen Committee of Deventer, was

[20] On the Patriot movement, see S. R. E. Klein, *Patriots republikanisme: Politieke cultuur in Nederland (1766–1787)* (Amsterdam, Amsterdam University Press, 1995); and W. R. E. Velema, *Republicans: Essays on Eighteenth-Century Dutch Political Thought* (Leiden, Brill, 2007).

[21] See e.g. W. te Brake, *Regents and Rebels: The Revolutionary World of an Eighteenth-Century Dutch City* (Cambridge, MA, Basil Blackwell, 1989); and E. H. de Jong, *Weldenkende burgers en Oranjeliefhebbers: Patriotten en Prinsgezinden in Leiden, 1775–1795* (Hilversum, Verloren, 2014).

[22] J. Oddens, '"The Greatest Right of Them All": The Debate on the Right to Petition in the Netherlands from the Dutch Republic to the Kingdom (c. 1750–1850)', *European History Quarterly*, 47 (2019), 634–56 (p. 641).

[23] Ibid., p. 651.

[24] See for instance M. de Jong, *Johan Derk van der Capellen: Staatkundig levensbeeld uit de wordingstijd van de moderne demokratie in Nederland* (Groningen, Wolters, 1922), p. 492.

constituted in 1782 by a formal act of appointment signed by many of the town's inhabitants. The citizen committee consisted of 12 citizens, among whom were senior officers of the guilds and of the civic guard, the other traditional pillar of the urban corporative structure.[25] The signatories of the act of appointment authorised the committee to draft petitions, which would be read to them and which, upon approval, they would then sign.[26] Local Patriots in other towns went a step further and created so-called colleges of delegates (*colleges van geconstitueerden*). Here the model was provided by the Patriot movement in Utrecht, where 1,215 inhabitants authorised, in the presence of a notary, 24 delegates to present petitions in their name. From that moment on, petitions that were signed by the delegates were to be understood as if they bore 1,215 signatures. The Patriots also created supra-local citizen assemblies, such as the Provincial Assembly of Civic Militias, which was made up of local civic militias in the province of Holland. During a meeting of delegates from these local militias in 1786, this political association drew up a loyal address to the Provincial States of that province. The only signature under this address was that of the leading Patriot Pieter Vreede, who signed in the name of the assembly that was gathered in Leiden.[27]

The Patriot movement was suppressed in 1787, but re-emerged in 1795, when Patriots ended the oligarchic system of government of the Seven United Provinces and founded the Batavian Republic with the support of a French revolutionary army. Radical Patriots now strived to institute representative democracy at all levels of government, but they met with resistance from moderates who wanted to maintain more of the existing confederative structure of the Dutch Republic.[28] Radical citizen assemblies challenged the political deadlock caused by these positions. They petitioned in much the same way as their predecessors from the Patriot era: in September 1795, a national political association that called itself 'Central Assembly' presented an address to the provincial assembly of Holland. This address was only signed by the chairman and the secretary of this association, but they claimed to represent all of its members: 'We confidently dare to demand, in the name of as many thousands of brave citizens as we have constituents ... that there will be as soon as possible a national parliament.'[29]

[25] Te Brake, *Regents and Rebels*, p. 80.

[26] *Egte stukken betreffende het voorgevallene te Deventer, in den jaare 1782, en vervolgens* (Deventer, G. Brouwer, 1783), pp. 24–30.

[27] Petition of the Provincial Assembly of Civic Militias to the States of Holland, 6 September 1786, in *Verzameling van placaaten, resolutien en andere authentyke Stukken enz....*, 50 vols (Kampen, n.p., 1788–95), Vol. XVII, pp. 86–91.

[28] On the Batavian Republic, see J. Oddens, *Pioniers in schaduwbeeld: Het eerste parlement van Nederland 1796–1798* (Nijmegen, Vantilt, 2012); M. Rutjes, *Door gelijkheid gegrepen: Democratie, burgerschap en staat in Nederland 1795–1801* (Nijmegen, Vantilt, 2012); and F. Grijzenhout, N. van Sas, and W. Velema (eds), *Het Bataafse experiment: Politiek en cultuur rond 1800* (Nijmegen, Vantilt, 2013).

[29] Address of the General Central Assembly to the Representatives of the People of Holland, 4 September 1795, in *Dagblad van het verhandelde, ter vergadering van de provisioneele repraesentanten van het Volk van Holland*, 2 vols (The Hague, J. van Cleef, 1795–6), Vol. III, pp. 9–10. The address was signed by F. W. M. Ruysch (president) and C. Arnold (secretary).

In 1796, a democratically elected National Assembly was indeed established. Most of its members considered the pressure exerted by the citizen assemblies a dangerous precedent. They particularly disapproved of the fact that the members of a national political association such as the Central Assembly allowed their board members to sign petitions on their behalf. Especially now that a national representative institution had been founded in the Netherlands, its representatives believed that this type of representative claim-making would amount to some sort of dual representative power if it were to continue. The National Assembly therefore issued a decree in its first week of existence. This decree was the first positive law ever to confirm the right to petition in the Netherlands, but its primary aim was to limit this right. The decree granted the right to petition to individual citizens, but not to associations: if groups of citizens wanted to petition together, every single one of them would have to sign, and citizens could no longer authorise others to sign in their name.[30] This decree also reflected a notion dominant in late-18th-century revolutionary politics, that consent was the sole source of legitimate authority, and that representation should always be based on consent.[31]

The decree issued by the National Assembly in 1796 was to have a long-lasting impact. In 1798 and 1801 respectively, the ban on petitioning in the name of others was included in the article on the right to petition in the first and second written constitutions of the Netherlands, where they applied to all political authorities and not just the Parliament. The Batavian Republic was ended by Napoleon, but after the Napoleonic era, the 1815 constitution of the United Kingdom of the Netherlands reaffirmed the article on the right to petition from the 1801 constitution.[32]

The 1796 decree that banned the signing of petitions in the name of others did not in any way stop the Dutch people from petitioning; on the contrary, authorities never received more petitions than during the first years of the Batavian Republic. The political clubs that were targeted by the decree turned to printing petitions for the purpose of collecting signatures. Whereas petition drives had until that moment most often been organised locally and sometimes provincially, the printing of petitions contributed to the nationalisation and professionalisation of petitioning. Packs of preprinted petitions could be easily sent to even the most remote parts of the country, leaving blank only the space where the name of a village or town could be added. This strategy was used not only by Patriots, but also by those opposing the ideals of the Batavian revolution. By far the largest petition drive was organised by the formerly privileged Dutch Reformed Church, opposing the implications of the separation of church and state that had been

[30] *Publicatie van de Nationale Vergadering, representeerende het volk van Nederland: Over het recht van voordracht, petitie of verzoek* (The Hague, Lands Drukkery, 1796). This ban on corporate petitioning reflected a broader trend in revolutionary Europe; see H. Miller, 'Introduction: The Transformation of Petitioning in the Long Nineteenth Century (1780–1914)', *Social Science History*, 43 (2019), 409–29 (p. 415).

[31] B. Manin, *The Principles of Representative Government* (Cambridge, Cambridge University Press, 1997), pp. 83–93.

[32] Oddens, 'The Greatest Right', pp. 639–40.

decreed by the National Assembly. It has been estimated to have gathered 200,000 signatures: 10 per cent of the Dutch population.[33] No other petition comes even close to this, but between 1796 and the end of the democratic phase of the Batavian Republic in 1801, the national Parliament received around 400 petitions with between 100 and 4,000 signatures.[34]

The 1796 decree and the subsequent constitutional clauses based on this decree also affected collective petitioning by corporations. As we have seen, it had been common practice for the governing boards of corporations to petition on behalf of their members, but this had now become problematic. For the members to be understood as supporting a petition, their signatures would now have to be collected. Moreover, corporations could no longer petition as corporations but just as groups of individuals, and they were no longer privileged ahead of any other groups.

The ban on corporate petitioning caused petitioners to be more self-reflective about claiming to represent the interests of others without their consent, but this did not mean that this strategy suddenly disappeared. For one, an exception was made for (the members of) established authorities such as local governments, who continued to be allowed to sign petitions to higher authorities on behalf of their constituency. In practice, moreover, while the new standard practice became that petitions were submitted and signed by 32 individual shoemakers instead of the deacons of the shoemakers' guild, not all corporations respected the ban (probably out of ignorance as much as out of intent). As long as petitions were not overly political and came for example from a local church council or a local branch of the Maatschappij tot nut van 't Algemeen (Society for Public Welfare), authorities continued to accept them nonetheless.[35]

More importantly, even if legally petitioners could no longer petition on behalf of others, this did not prevent (groups of) individuals from *discursively* claiming to represent the interests of others without their consent in the text of the petition. In 1797, for instance, over 500 inhabitants of Middelburg petitioned the National Assembly with the request to make this city the capital of the new department of the Scheldt and the Maas, which was to replace the province of Zeeland. The petitioners argued that the choice for Middelburg would be in the interest of most of the inhabitants of the department, as a majority of the population lived closer to Middelburg than to Zierikzee, the other candidate city. In addition, they pointed out that making Middelburg the capital would be cheaper for everyone in the Batavian

[33] J. H. Kompagnie, 'Tekenend de kleine luiden: Een protestactie van 215.000 ingezetenen anno 1797', *Gens nostra*, 40 (1985), 291–4.

[34] See the dataset 'Petitions to the parliament of the Batavian Republic, 1796–1801', created by Joris Oddens and others in collaboration with the Dutch National Archives: https://www.nationaalarchief.nl/onderzoeken/zoekhulpen/verzoekschriften-aan-het-parlement-van-de-bataafse-republiek-1796–1801 (accessed 1 February 2024).

[35] E.g. Petition of the Department of the Society for Public Welfare in Bergen op Zoom to the Constituerende Vergadering: NA, access no. 2.01.01.01, Wetgevende Colleges, inv. no. 314 (2 February 1798); petition of the church board of the Dutch Reformed congregation in Lekkerkerk to the Vertegenwoordigend Lichaam: NA, 2.01.01.01, inv. no. 382 (17 February 1801).

Republic, because Middelburg, which had also been the provincial capital, already had a government building that could be used, but Zierikzee did not.[36] So while the old-regime understanding of representation was rejected by the revolutionary generation on the level of political institutions, clear traces of it survived in the practice of petitioning.

The Age of Representative Democracy

The memory of the revolutionary era shaped political practices for decades: political mass petitions were strongly associated with radicalism, as it seemed to challenge the existing representative bodies.[37] The enlightened absolutism of King William I reinforced this notion.[38] This does not mean, however, that collective petitioning in general was avoided or frowned upon during his reign (1814–40). Requests by groups of individuals who for instance shared a profession, place of residence, or religious belief, continued to be common. In 1822, for example, 23 shopkeepers from Arnhem signed a petition to the Second Chamber asking them to take measures against the many hawkers in their city, whose business practices were considered unfair.[39]

Even though the concept of popular sovereignty was almost universally rejected in the Netherlands of the 19th century, the notion of representative government, in the sense that the people should have a voice in politics, was broadly accepted. After the reintroduction of a more democratic representative system under the liberal constitution of 1848, the argument of quantity, for instance in the form of thousands of signatures attached to a petition, became increasingly important in parliamentary debates.[40] The paradox here is that the half century in which mass politics was introduced saw only a limited number of large-scale petition campaigns in which citizens represented themselves through a signature. There was the 'April Movement' of 1853: a national petition campaign against the re-establishment of

[36] Petition of citizens and inhabitants of Middelburg to the Nationale Vergadering: NA, access no. 20.01.01.01, inv. no. 294 [January 1797].

[37] J. Talsma, *Vijf historische en rechtshistorische studies over het recht van petitie, verzoekschriften aan de Tweede Kamer en het ombudsmanvraagstuk: Nederland, 1795–1983* (Arnhem, Gouda Quint, 1989); M. Janse, '"What Value Should We Attach to All These Petitions?": Petition Campaigns and the Problem of Legitimacy in the Nineteenth-Century Netherlands', *Social Science History*, 43 (2019), 509–30.

[38] J. van Zanten, *Schielijk, Winzucht, Zwaarhoofd en Bedaard: Politieke discussie en oppositievorming, 1813–1940* (Amsterdam, Wereldbibliotheek, 2004).

[39] NA, access no. 2.02.22, Tweede Kamer der Staten-Generaal, inv. no. 979, no. 22 (8 February 1822). This section is the outcome of the research project 'Languages of Citizenship: Conceptions of Politics and Discursive Strategies in Petitions to Dutch Parliamentary Assemblies, 1796–1940' carried out in the framework of the Leiden University Research Traineeship Programme (2018), in which five of the authors of this chapter were involved. They would like to thank Ton van Haeften for his role as co-supervisor on this project.

[40] Janse, 'What Value Should We Attach to All These Petitions?'.

the episcopal hierarchy that followed from the liberal constitution. About 200,000 men and women, many from an orthodox Protestant background, signed. In 1878 Calvinist hardliners organised a 'People's *Petitionnement*' against a liberal education law that acquired more than 460,000 signatures from all over the country.[41] Both campaigns were highly contested and this type of political mass petitioning was the exception rather than the rule at this time.

Especially in the decades after 1848 fear of revolution and the mobilisation of the working classes stimulated a new-found attachment to representative forms in politics. Mass petitions with thousands of subscribers, known as *petitionnementen*, reminded people of direct democracy. The form of collective petitioning whereby a collective was represented through one or two signatories was an alternative that regained popularity fast, as it invoked the notion of representative democracy. This practice was tolerated by authorities despite the constitutional ban on corporate petitioning, which was lifted only in 1983.

The smaller-scale, traditional petitions to the national Parliament signed by 23 shopkeepers, 15 candlemakers, or seven butchers saw a steep decline in the second half of the 19th century.[42] These groups of individuals seem to have found new ways to have their interests represented, partly through the early trade unions that gained strength towards the end of the century. For example, in 1897 bakers united in local cooperative baking associations supported an earlier request to prevent working overtime in the baking industry with declarations of support (*adhesiebetuigingen*) from all over the country.[43] Each petition was only signed by the president, secretary, or treasurer of the local association.

The revival of associational life could be an important explanation for the changing character of petitioning in this period. As we have seen, corporate bodies such as guilds, corporations, and voluntary associations had played a crucial role in the development and sustenance of petitioning practices before. In the second half of the 19th century associational life developed in new ways. Compared to the revolutionary era, we see that voluntary associations scaled up, often turning into full-fledged national organisations that fostered ambitions to speak for their members nationwide. Participation in associational life had been a touchstone of good citizenship from the 18th century.[44] Now civil society was becoming more inclusive,

[41] A. Houkes, 'Het succes van 1848: Politiek in de Aprilbeweging', in J. Vis and W. Janse (eds), *Staf en storm: Het herstel van de bisschoppelijke hiërarchie in Nederland in 1853* (Hilversum, Verloren, 2002), pp. 87–104; A. Houkes, *Christelijke vaderlanders: Godsdienst, burgerschap en de Nederlandse natie, 1850–1900* (Amsterdam, Wereldbibliotheek, 2009), pp. 218–29.

[42] It is important to note that there is no clear break: petitions by formal groups already appeared before the second half of the 19th century, and even though the number of petitions by groups of individuals decreased, these petitions continued to appear throughout the 19th century.

[43] Tweede Kamer der Staten-Generaal, 'Register verzoekschriften 1896–1897 Tweede Kamer', pp. 49–50, available at https://zoek.officielebekendmakingen.nl/sgd:18961897:0001836 (accessed 1 February 2024).

[44] W. W. Mijnhardt, *Tot heil van 't menschdom: Culturele genootschappen in Nederland, 1750–1815* (Amsterdam, Rodopi, 1987).

and after a few relatively depoliticised postrevolutionary decades it politicised once more.[45] At the same time, organisational forms institutionalised and voluntary associations professionalised in the course of the century, which meant in practice that parliamentary rules and bureaucratic procedures started to dominate instead of the loosely institutionalised personal networks of earlier generations.

This burgeoning associational life and the new practices of collective petitioning were mutually reinforcing. Voluntary associations submitted an increasing number of petitions. Claiming to represent others was attractive for three reasons. First, it was more practical and much less time-consuming than organising a nationwide petition campaign. Second, organisation could have a symbolic value. Voluntary associations, like petitions, could function as important informal representative institutions. Both claimed to represent the people's voice during a time when universal suffrage still had a radical ring to it and mass petitions with hundreds of thousands of signatures were associated with mobilising the masses in a revolutionary sense. Creating distance from contested modes of mass petitioning was therefore the third, and perhaps most important, attraction of collective petitioning through representation by an association.

The democratic governance structure of voluntary associations ensured that they legitimately represented their members through petitions signed by their board members. Through their election, the president and secretary were formally given a mandate to represent their members following procedures that very much resembled parliamentary practices. These mandates signified trust and consensus within a community that shared moral values and/or socio-economic interests. Sometimes petitioners offered additional proof of the number of members and on the process of deliberation that had preceded the petition. In 1939, for example, the Dutch Association of Gravel Dealers submitted a petition to the Second Chamber in response to a Transport Bill, signed only by its president and secretary: 'The [Association], comprising 90 per cent of the trade in gravel within the Netherlands, indicates … that on 17 November 1938, the Association has held a general meeting in Utrecht, that at the meeting a motion was passed, reading as follows …'.[46]

Those who wanted to make a legitimate public claim did so by following the rules of civil society: after public deliberation, in a respectful tone, with the consent of those they claimed to represent. The appeal of the civil society discourse proved so great that petitioners adopted it for individual cases as well. They could do so by pointing out that there were others in the same position (who might not have sent a petition) or, for example, by putting emphasis on their citizenship (and therefore placing themselves within the collectivity of Dutch citizens). For instance, in 1857 a day labourer addressed Parliament as the 'representatives of the entire Dutch

[45] R. Aerts, 'Civil Society or Democracy? A Dutch Paradox', *BMGN: Low Countries Historical Review*, 125 (2010), 209–36; M. Janse, 'Towards a History of Civil Society', *De negentiende eeuw*, 32 (2008), 104–21. See also S.-L. Hoffmann, *Civil Society, 1750–1914* (Basingstoke, Palgrave, 2006).

[46] Petition of the National Association of Gravel Dealers to the Second Chamber: NA, 2.02.22, inv. no. 1348, no. 213 (6 January 1939).

nation' in a request to exempt himself and 'all the needy ones' from paying taxes.[47] In 1859 a distiller, who was the only signatory of his petition, explained that he had not bothered to ask his fellow distillers to sign. Still, he claimed to represent their interests as well as his own. Instead of collecting signatures to legitimise his claims, he explicitly placed his trust in the Members of Parliament as 'representatives of every tax paying subject'.[48]

This points to a popularisation of the notion of Parliament as a trustworthy national representative body. By reading petitions in this light, we can also better understand seemingly irrational requests. For instance, in 1919 the retired postman Van Wijk asked Parliament to help him to find a golden necklace that had been lost in the mail.[49] This request seems naïve at first: busy Members of Parliament had better things to do than play detective. But a more sensitive reading of Van Wijk's request could interpret it as a sign of trust in the near-unlimited power of Parliament. What is more, citizens expected Parliament to lend their ears benevolently to their requests, a trust that previously had been mostly reserved for monarchical figures.[50] And even in this case of a highly individual and idiosyncratic request, Van Wijk employed discursive strategies that involved representative claim-making, such as when he claimed that the public at large should be able to trust the National Post Office and that its non-responsiveness was an indication of class-based discrimination: '[H]ad I been a baron or an earl I would probably have received an answer … Is it surprising then that the common man stands up against this behaviour?'.[51] Petitions therefore could convey the general dissatisfaction of ordinary citizens, which politicians became increasingly eager to learn about as the 20th century progressed.

One would perhaps expect that, after the introduction of general suffrage for men and women in 1917–19, the meaning of petitioning changed, but more research is needed to test such intuitions. It has been argued that after the Second World War citizen letters addressed to individual politicians partly took over the role of petitions to political institutions.[52] However, during the second half of the 20th century, large numbers of petitions continued to be addressed to the national

[47] Petition of H. Kleyn to the Second Chamber: NA, 2.02.22, inv. no. 1073, no. 400 (17 February 1857).

[48] Petition of H. Therkatz to the Second Chamber: NA, 2.02.22, inv. no. 1080, no. 335 (22 January 1859).

[49] Petition of M. U. van Wijk to the Second Chamber, NA, 2.02.22, inv. no. 1270, no. 203 (13 January 1919).

[50] See for instance M. Van Ginderachter, 'Public Transcripts of Royalism: Pauper Letters to the Belgian Royal Family (1880–1940)', in J. Deploige and G. Denecker (eds), *Mystifying the Monarch: Studies on Discourse, Power, and History* (Amsterdam, Amsterdam University Press, 2006), pp. 223–34; and J. Judge and J. Oddens, 'Father Figures and Faction Leaders: Identification Strategies and Monarchical Imagery among Ordinary Citizens of the Northern and Southern Low Countries (c. 1780–1820)', *BMGN: Low Countries Historical Review*, 133 (2018), 72–97.

[51] Petition of M. U. van Wijk to the Second Chamber.

[52] H. Kaal, 'The Voice of the People: Communicative Practices of Popular Political Engagement in the Netherlands, 1950s–1960s', *Archiv für Sozialgeschichte*, 58 (2018), 183–200. Cf., on postwar citizen letters, M. Fenske, *Demokratie erschreiben: Bürgerbriefe und Petitionen als Medien Politischer Kultur, 1950–1974* (Frankfurt, Campus, 2013).

Parliament as well. This fact alone at the very least suggests that enfranchised citizens in the postwar period did not consider electoral democracy and petitioning to be mutually exclusive representative practices.

Conclusion

In this chapter we have diachronically studied the existence of three types of representative claims in Dutch petitionary practices. It has become clear that all three types, albeit in different guises, continued to be present from the early 17th to the mid-20th century. However, when we look at why people chose one strategy of representative claim-making over another, it appears that their reasons for doing so have changed over time.

The first type of representative claim-making that we have considered is self-representation. In the practice of petitioning individuals can represent themselves directly by being physically present when a petition is presented to an authority, but also indirectly, by signing a petition. Physical presence added to the performative power of a petition, but can also indicate that the idea that a signature could serve as a stand-in for a person was not yet fully established. The advent of subscriptional practices made it easier for more people, or for people living further away, to participate in petitioning.

While the notion of strength in numbers with respect to signatures increased over the course of the early modern period and only became commonplace in the revolutionary era, it was never fully absent in the Dutch Republic. This shows in the example of the most famous petition in the history of the Netherlands before its independence: in 1566, several hundred nobles presented a petition against the Spanish Inquisition to Governess Margaret of Parma in Brussels. The original petition did not contain any signatures, but the nobles had signed the covenant (*eedverbond*) that preceded it.[53] From a premodern perspective, these nobles automatically represented all the inhabitants of their counties and duchies through *repraesentatio identitatis*, regardless of their consent. Nonetheless, *after* the petition had been presented, signatures were collected across the provinces to add to its legitimacy; it was claimed that in Brabant alone 40,000 people were willing to sign the petition.[54]

At the beginning of the 17th century, authorities started to demand that petitions be signed by at least one person, in order to be able to hold someone accountable for the contents of the petition. During the late-18th-century revolutionary era, they decreed that each person that wanted to be understood to support a petition had to sign this petition personally; the principal reason for this was that, if petitioners

[53] NA, 1.11.01.01, inv. no. 1925, Smeekschrift der edelen, copy.

[54] F. Deen, *Publiek debat en propaganda in Amsterdam tijdens de Nederlandse Opstand: Amsterdam 'Moorddam', 1566–1578* (Amsterdam, Amsterdam University Press, 2015), p. 69.

claimed to represent others without these others having signed the petition, it was impossible to know whether they had truly consented to it. While this limitation of the right to petition was introduced with the intention to prevent alternative representative claims that challenged formal representative institutions, it triggered a belief in the strength of numbers and resulted in large mass petitions for which thousands of signatures were canvassed. In the long 19th century, the instrument of mass petitioning was mainly used for religious issues, by religious organisations and churches.

Within the second type of representative claim-making – representation with consent – two subtypes can be distinguished. First, people could authorise one or more individuals to draw up and submit one or more petitions on their own initiative. Second, people could express explicit consent to the content of a petition, often during an assembly. The two forms of representative claim-making that follow from these two types of consent are analogous to political representation with free and binding mandate respectively. In the early modern Dutch Republic, representation with consent was the customary strategy in corporations such as guilds. It is difficult to say which of the two subtypes was resorted to, but the fact that guild members sometimes petitioned to protest against previous petitions submitted on their behalf by their board members suggests that their explicit consent was not always sought. In collectives with a less hierarchical structure, such as groups of merchants, the obtaining of explicit consent seems to have been standard practice.

In the Patriot era this type of political representation came under attack. Now explicit consent was needed also for political petitions from groups of citizens who were not united in corporations. Because it was difficult to obtain this explicit consent time and time again in practice, the Patriots devised the system of one-time authorisation for multiple petitions. The sort of free mandate they thus created diverged from the system of binding mandate that was customary in the Republic at all supra-local political levels. It anticipated the rupture with this system that was brought about during the Batavian Revolution. However, when Batavian revolutionaries introduced a representative system with free mandate, they restricted the practice of petitioning on behalf of others, because no alternative representative institutions were tolerated.

In the course of the 19th century associational life developed and it became customary for the president and secretary of an association to petition on behalf of its members. As a rule, petitions were preceded by an associational meeting during which (the exact formulation of) the request was discussed. Such consent mechanisms were sometimes referred to in the petitions. This shows that there was an awareness that it was important to demonstrate consent. While the modern custom of associations' boards signing petitions on behalf of their members was outwardly similar to the boards of corporations doing the same in the early modern period, the underlying concept of representation that legitimised this practice was very different.

Finally, we considered the practice of representation without consent. In the early modern era, the idea existed that a local community could be represented by its most distinguished members. Urban governments complemented themselves; there were no elections, but local rulers nevertheless felt that they represented the local community. This was paralleled in the practice of petitioning, where a small group of citizens submitted political petitions to the authorities and claimed to represent the community at large, but did not consider it necessary for the members of that community to give their individual consent. The latter practice was abolished by law in 1796, but a remnant of this type of thinking still existed, because local governments continued to be allowed to petition higher authorities on behalf of their local community.

Representation without consent could and can also take place at a discursive level. Both individual petitioners and petitioning collectives claimed that they are not only petitioning for themselves, but also for all others who find themselves in the same situation with regard to the subject matter of the petition (sometimes this is deemed to apply to all members of a community: in that case it is an appeal to the general interest). Such a claim suggests that those others will support the petition – even if they do not know of its existence – because it is also in their interest. The strategy of claiming to represent others without their consent has continued to exist throughout the centuries. We have seen it being used in 1669, when the shareholders of the WIC claimed to be concerned with the interest of the state; in 1797, when inhabitants of Middelburg claimed that most of the inhabitants of the department of the Scheldt and the Maas would benefit if their request was granted; and in 1857, when a day labourer claimed to represent the interests of 'all the needy ones'. It is not difficult to think of examples also in present-day petitionary practices.

When considering the practice of representative claim-making in petitioning, we see developments over time that are directly or indirectly influenced by changing standards of representative governance. The long-term trend up to 1940 moves towards collective petitions that are submitted by the few on behalf of the many, but have a mechanism in place through which consent is obtained (which may or may not be explicitly stated in the petition), comparable to the practice of citizens being represented by their representatives in an electoral democracy. The instances of mass-petitioning that occurred in the Netherlands as well demonstrate that there was an increasing demand for citizen participation in politics, but their insistence on self-representation was as controversial as it was exceptional within the Dutch context. The persistence of discursive representation without consent (which finds a parallel in the populist reflex in formal representative politics – i.e. politicians and parties who claim to express the voice of the people regardless of the number of votes cast for them) shows, however, that the increase of a perceived need to demonstrate consent in the age of representative democracy is only relative. In democratic as well as non-democratic periods, people continued to believe that speaking for others without a mandate was a legitimate strategy. By invoking an 'intended constituency' in this way, individuals as well as groups hoped that they could convince the recipients of their petitions, as well as other audiences.[55]

[55] On 'intended constituencies', see Saward, *The Representative Claim*, p. 148. An important aspect of Saward's theory is the idea that representative claims could have multiple audiences (pp. 62–6). While we have not elaborated on this point, this certainly applies as well to petitions, which can also appeal to the wider public, the media, and potential signatories, for example.

8

Power, Policy, and Petitions in Jamaica, 1664–1834

AARON GRAHAM

IN 1817 THE magistrates and parish vestry of the parish of St James' in the north-western part of Jamaica found themselves in a minor spat with the trustees of the free school of the town of Montego Bay. Growing out of a disagreement about whether the vestry had the right to preside at meetings of the trustees, the real reasons came into the open in October when the trustees petitioned the vestry to call a meeting of the freeholders of the parish to consider 'extend[ing] the benefit of education generally to the youth of the parish at the expence of the inhabitants thereof'. What this meant in practice was accepting free children of colour as well as white children as pupils, part of a wider debate about the position of this group within Jamaican society as the island reluctantly moved towards the emancipation of slaves and the removal of racial legislation favouring white privilege.[1] The vestry refused this request, and instead agreed with the suggestion of their Member in the House of Assembly at Spanish Town, Richard Barrett, to present a petition to the House for a new school act '[to] new-model the same, with the view of diminishing the expenses and enlarging the scale of that institution'.[2] The clear intention was to remove the control of the school from the trustees and thus scotch their proposals, and when the petition failed to get action the vestry decided instead

[1] Jamaica Archives, Spanish Town, Jamaica (JA), 2/3/1, St James' Vestry Minutes, 1807–25, fos 83v–84r, 85r. This coincided with other efforts to open up schools in Jamaica to Jewish and free children of colour. See P. E. Bryan, *The Legacy of a Goldsmith: A History of Wolmer's Schools, 1729–2003* (Kingston, Jamaica, Arawak Publications, 2004), pp. 8–21, 33–6; M. K. Bacchus, *Utilization, Misuse, and Development of Human Resources in the Early West Indian Colonies* (Waterloo, ON, Wilfrid Laurier University Press, 1990), pp. 100–8, 119–23; and K. Brathwaite, *The Development of Creole Society in Jamaica, 1770–1820* (Oxford, Clarendon Press, 1971), pp. 268–77. For the social reforms of the early 19th century, see G. Heuman, *Between Black and White: Race, Politics, and the Free Coloreds in Jamaica, 1792–1865* (Westport, CT, Greenwood Press, 1981), pp. 25–31.
[2] JA, 2/3/1, fos 87v, 95r, 99v.

to place pressure on the trustees by cutting off their funding, which was enough to bring them into line. The episode probably passed largely unnoticed at the time; however, it offers a useful example of the importance of petitioning in early-19th-century Jamaica, first in raising a matter with the local government, and then in escalating it to the colonial Assembly, but also its limitations. This chapter will suggest what the history of similar petitions in Jamaica before 1840 can contribute to the wider history of the petition as a form of political action for marginal social groups across the 'long' 18th century.

Preliminaries

Petitions were clearly important within Jamaican politics and society. When the Assembly was debating in May 1748 a bill promoted by the governor and the Board of Trade in London to loosen some of the restrictions on free people of colour, the opposition of wide segments of the population was displayed not only through their petitions to the Assembly but also by a satirical petition circulated widely at a public meeting held in Kingston.[3] Claiming to be written by a free person of colour called 'Cudjoe' on behalf of his community, it is 'a rare example of the popular political discourse of mid-eighteenth century free white Jamaica'.[4] Since satire often proves most effective when it subverts familiar and established forms, the decision to use the petition shows the importance of petitions within Jamaican popular political culture. By the same token, in 1792 a genuine petition was circulated within the community of free people of colour in Jamaica that complained about continued restrictions on their civil rights.[5] Although it was not formally presented to the House, manuscript copies were deliberately circulated among members, and created such alarm, particularly in light of the recent slave revolt in nearby Saint Domingue in 1791, that copies were forwarded to the governor and the island's agent in London.

Petitions were therefore a significant part of Jamaican political culture, as in the colonies of British North America before 1775. A brief statistical overview by Alison Olson, discussed in more detail on pp. 168–9, found that the numbers of petitions received by American colonial legislatures rose steadily in the 18th century, especially during moments of political crisis or as other institutions proved unable to respond to local grievances.[6] More detailed studies of Pennsylvania,

[3] J. Robertson, 'A 1748 "Petition of Negro Slaves" and the Local Politics of Slavery in Jamaica', *William and Mary Quarterly*, 67 (2010), 319–46.

[4] Ibid.

[5] Heuman, *Between Black and White*, pp. 23–4; D. Livesay, *Children of Uncertain Fortune: Mixed-Race Jamaicans in Britain and the Atlantic Family, 1733–1833* (Chapel Hill, University of North Carolina Press, 2018), pp. 232–44; C. Petley, *Slaveholders in Jamaica: Colonial Society and Culture during the Era of Abolition* (London, Pickering & Chatto, 2009), p. 71.

[6] A. Olson, 'Eighteenth-Century Colonial Legislatures and Their Constituents', *Journal of American History*, 79 (1992), 543–67 (pp. 556–9).

New Jersey, and Virginia have shown that colonial legislatures actively solicited petitions, offering inhabitants important opportunities for political participation.[7] 'Even disenfranchised individuals – women, free blacks, the very poor, even an occasional slave – sent petitions to the legislature' in Virginia, notes Raymond Bailey, '[and] as a result, petitioning served as the most important channel of communication between local citizens and the assembly'.[8] Indeed, that petitions allowed disempowered persons to obtain redress and assert agency, and historians to recover records of that assertion, has been one of the most important findings of this work, and Daniel Carpenter and Nicole Topich have shown that the situation persisted into the Early Republic.[9] A study of petitioning in Jamaica can develop this further by examining the opportunities open to marginal groups in a society built to an even greater extent on enslaved labour, and with even larger numbers of marginal groups, who turned to the petition as one of the very few avenues open to them to obtain agency.[10]

At the heart of this chapter therefore lies a quantitative survey of petitioning to the Jamaican House of Assembly between 1709, when reliable and relatively accurate records begin, and 1834, when slavery was abolished in Jamaica, leading to a major shift in the social and political culture of the island over subsequent decades. My earlier work has applied a similar approach to legislative output in Jamaica and the British Atlantic during this period, and has successfully demonstrated both the great importance of legislation in the island and its broad overlap with very similar trends in other parts of the British Atlantic.[11] In both cases the key sources are the printed

[7] T. L. Purvis, *Proprietors, Patronage, and Paper Money: Legislative Politics in New Jersey, 1703–1776* (New Brunswick, NJ, Rutgers University Press, 1986), pp. 176–99; A. Tully, *William Penn's Legacy: Politics and Social Structure in Provincial Pennsylvania, 1726–1755* (Baltimore, MD, Johns Hopkins University Press, 1977), pp. 188–9.

[8] R. C. Bailey, *Popular Influence upon Public Policy: Petitioning in Eighteenth-Century Virginia* (Westport, CT, Greenwood Press, 1979), p. 6. For a more focused study, see also P. K. Longmore, 'From Supplicants to Constituents: Petitioning by Virginia Parishioners, 1701–1775', *Virginia Magazine of History and Biography*, 103 (1995), 407–42.

[9] D. Carpenter and C. D. Moore, 'When Canvassers Became Activists: Antislavery Petitioning and the Political Mobilization of American Women', *American Political Science Review*, 108 (2014), 479–98; D. Carpenter and N. Topich, 'Contested Boundaries of Representation: Patterns of Transformation in Black Petitioning in Massachusetts, 1770–1850', in E. Avril and J. N. Neem (eds), *Democracy, Participation, and Contestation: Civil Society, Governance, and the Future of Liberal Democracy* (New York, Routledge, 2015), pp. 201–22.

[10] For the social and economic situation of Jamaica between 1660 and 1834, see T. G. Burnard, *Planters, Merchants, and Slaves: Plantation Societies in British America, 1650–1820* (Chicago, IL, University of Chicago Press, 2015), pp. 157–210; R. S. Dunn, *Sugar and Slaves: The Rise of the Planter Class in the English West Indies, 1624–1713* (Chapel Hill, University of North Carolina Press, 1972), pp. 149–87; R. B. Sheridan, *Sugar and Slavery: An Economic History of the British West Indies, 1623–1775* (Barbados, Caribbean University Press, 1974), pp. 208–33; Petley, *Slaveholders in Jamaica*, pp. 15–52; Brathwaite, *The Development of Creole Society*, pp. 135–211; and W. A. Green, *British Slave Emancipation: The Sugar Colonies and the Great Experiment, 1830–1865* (Oxford, Clarendon Press, 1976), pp. 1–64.

[11] A. Graham, 'Jamaican Legislation and the Transatlantic Constitution, 1664–1839', *Historical Journal*, 61 (2018), 327–55; A. Graham, 'Legislatures, Legislation, and Legislating in the British Atlantic, 1692–1800', *Parliamentary History*, 37 (2018), 369–88.

journals of the colonial legislature, collected into 14 volumes as the *Journals of the House of Assembly of Jamaica* in 1826 and continued by successive *Votes of the House of Assembly* thereafter, and the indices created to accompany them.[12] These indices make it possible to collate basic data about the numbers, dates, and overall topics of petitions. Unfortunately the arrangement of these indices was altered in 1828, making it difficult to categorise individual petitions after this date, and while the petitions themselves were all printed in the *Journals* and *Votes*, generally verbatim, the signatories were not recorded and almost all of the additional materials appended to the petitions were left out. As a result, it is impossible to recover more details except where the respective petitions survive elsewhere.

Furthermore, although the Assembly was probably the largest single recipient of petitions in this period, a focus on those petitions ignores the very large numbers received by other political and administrative bodies in the island, who acted both to filter petitions that might otherwise have reached the Assembly but could also petition the Assembly in their own right. The example of parishes such as St James' has already been noted. The council of the island, which acted as a privy council for administrative purposes and an upper house for legislative ones, received a large number of petitions on both matters.[13] The governor of the island likewise received petitions, both from colonial groups and from imperial officials and troops resident in the island, which were sometimes then forwarded on to the Assembly.[14] Other petitions were heard by the standing executive committees of the Assembly, such as the Commissioners of Public Accounts and the Commissioners of Forts, Fortifications, and Public Works, and individuals might therefore be forced to petition several of these bodies in succession in order to achieve their purposes.[15] The patchy survival of records from these bodies, however, means that it is almost impossible to obtain the continuous sample of petitions offered by the journals of the House of Assembly.

For those petitions that did come before the Assembly, the process very closely resembled that of the Westminster Parliament. They would be presented by a Member of the House, and if the Assembly agreed to hear the petition it would be

[12] For the nature and powers of the Jamaican legislature, see H. Taft Manning, *British Colonial Government after the American Revolution, 1782–1820* (Hamden, CT, Archon Books, 1966), pp. 127–49; N. A. T. Hall, 'Constitutional and Political Developments in Barbados and Jamaica, 1783–1815', PhD thesis (London, 1965), pp. 26–52; F. G. Spurdle, *Early West Indian Government: Showing the Progress of Government in Barbados, Jamaica and the Leeward Islands, 1660–1783* (Palmerston North, NZ, published by the author, 1962), pp. 28–32; and G. Metcalf, *Royal Government and Political Conflict in Jamaica, 1729–1783* (London, Longmans, 1965), pp. 27–32.

[13] For the council, see Spurdle, *Early West Indian Government*, pp. 32–47; Graham, 'Jamaican Legislation', 333–4, 341–4; and Metcalf, *Royal Government*, pp. 23–5.

[14] See, for example, the petition of A. Wrange; *Journals of the House of Assembly of Jamaica* (*JHA*), 14 vols (Kingston, Jamaica, 1808–26), Vol. X, pp. 614–15, 620.

[15] Spurdle, *Early West Indian Government*, pp. 120–2, 129–34. See, for example, the petition of John Parker in 1772: JA, 1B/5/15/1, Commissioners of Forts and Fortifications, Minute Book, 1768–75, fo. 70r; and JA, 1B/5/15/2, Commissioners of Forts and Fortifications, Minute Book, 1775–83, 16/5/1775, 1/3/1776, 29/5/1776.

read and referred to a committee or specific individual for action, or left on the table for Members to read and take action later, or rejected. Petitioners therefore had to find a Member willing to present the petition for them, and in a suitable form.[16] The petition itself could also cover a wide range of issues, though the indices for the *Journals* suggest that by the early 19th century a basic set of categories had become commonplace. One group were the administrative petitions, consisting mainly of invoices by officials and contractors for payment. In essence the continuation of an early modern use of the petition as a 'venerated instrument of state', to use David Zaret's term, these were essentially routine requests for payments that had generally already been approved and rarely caused much debate.[17] The other main group were political petitions, containing representations for and against legislation or other aspects of imperial and colonial policy, as well as a wide range of miscellaneous requests that could not be dealt with routinely but required the consideration of the House. Both groups contained petitions from otherwise disenfranchised people, as contractors and public creditors on the one hand and as aggrieved individuals or parties on the other, and combining a brief statistical overview with a series of case studies makes it possible to draw broader conclusions about the wider patterns and purposes of petitioning in Jamaica.

Patterns

Between 1700 and 1834, around 7,000 petitions were submitted to the Assembly of Jamaica. As Figure 8.1 shows, the overall level rose gradually until the 1780s, but then exploded, with only a brief dip in the second decade of the 19th century. This was not merely an artefact of the rising population of the island, since petitions per 10,000 people grew from 1.5 per year to 4.8 per year by the 1800s, but then fell to 2.4 per year between 1810 and 1834. The balance also shifted, with the 'political' petitions predominating until the 1770s, when the 'administrative' petitions began to predominate – during the 1790s and 1800s they accounted for 90 per cent of all petitions heard by the Assembly – before they moved back towards a rough equilibrium in the late 1820s. Studies of petitioning in North America have rarely broken down petitions into specific categories, but Alan Tully's study of Pennsylvania between 1717 and 1775 divided them into 'legislative' and 'financial' categories, and found that 57 per cent of the 1,922 petitions received were legislative.[18] During the same period in Jamaica, 721 petitions, or 65 per cent, were 'political' or legislative, which suggests a high degree of overlap in petitioning strategies in the two colonies up to 1775, when the balance in Jamaica began the radical shift just noted.

[16] JA, 2/3/1, fo. 144v.

[17] D. Zaret, 'Petition-and-Response and Liminal Petitioning in Comparative/Historical Perspective', *Social Science History*, 43 (2019), 431–51.

[18] Tully, *William Penn's Legacy*, p. 141n.

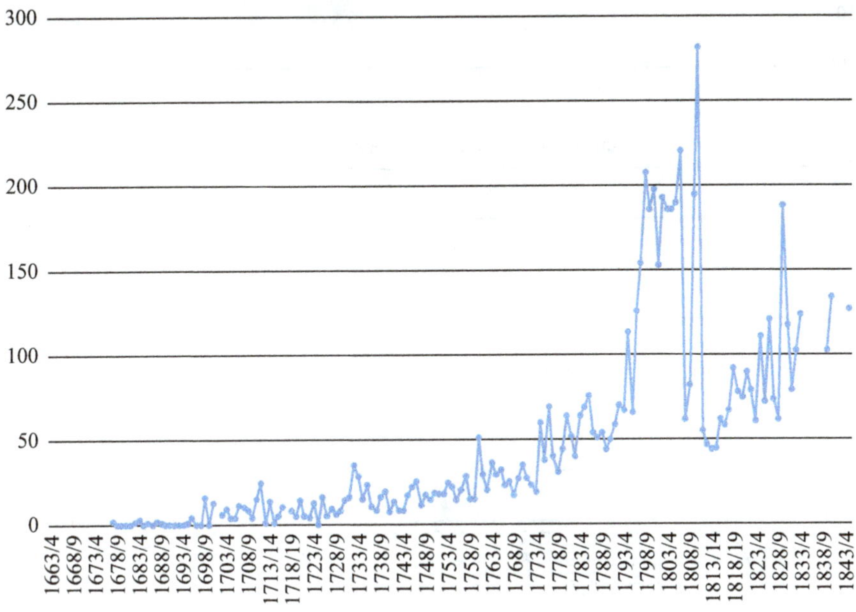

Figure 8.1 Petitions to the Jamaica Assembly, 1663–1834. A. Olson, 'Eighteenth-Century Colonial Legislatures and Their Constituents', *Journal of American History*, 79 (1992), 543–67 (pp. 556–9); *Journals of the House of Assembly of Jamaica*, 14 vols (Kingston, Jamaica, 1808–26).

Petitioning therefore remained an aspect of the political process in Jamaica across this period, but both its intensity and nature fluctuated in complex ways related to the two key outputs of the Assembly, namely legislation and spending. As I have shown elsewhere, legislative initiatives rose steadily in Jamaica throughout this period, stabilising around the turn of the 19th century but then rising rapidly in the 1830s.[19] I argued that this pattern reflected in large part a growing demand within Jamaica for legislation, and since many 'political' petitions were concerned with initiating, amending, or opposing legislation, it is not surprising that the general pattern of political petitioning matched that of legislative output. As Figure 8.2 shows, both rose sharply during the 1820s and 1830s, for example, which reflected growing conflicts within the House over the introduction of legislation to ameliorate and eventually entirely abolish slavery.[20] At least one aspect also reflected a growing number of petitions received for privileges. As described in more detail on pp. 170–2 the Assembly passed a number of private acts giving limited civil rights to individual free people of colour. It received over 100 such petitions between 1825 and 1830, which in turn accounted for nearly a third of the privilege bills passed by the House across the entire period since 1664 before a general grant of civil rights was made in 1830.

[19] Graham, 'Jamaican Legislation', pp. 327–55, esp. pp. 347–55.

[20] Ibid., pp. 327–55, esp. pp. 347–55.

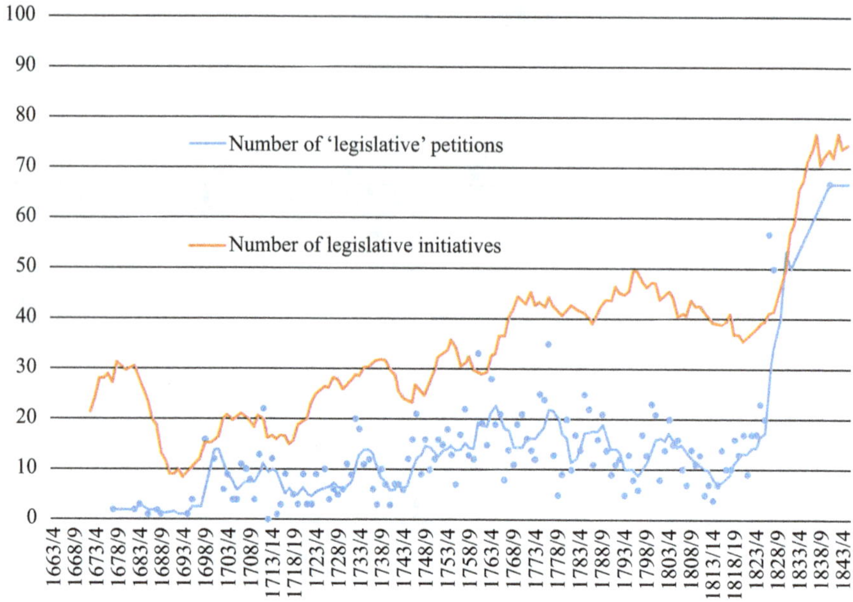

Figure 8.2 'Political' petitions and legislative initiatives in Jamaica, 1663–1834. A. Olson, 'Eighteenth-Century Colonial Legislatures and Their Constituents', *Journal of American History*, 79 (1992), 543–67 (pp. 556–9); *Journals of the House of Assembly of Jamaica*, 14 vols (Kingston, Jamaica, 1808–26); A. Graham, 'The Colonial Sinews of Imperial Power: The Political Economy of Jamaican Taxation, 1768–1838', *Journal of Imperial and Commonwealth History*, 45 (2017), 188–209.

By the same token, 'administrative' petitions related almost exclusively to financial matters, and rose largely in step with the increasing expenditures of the Jamaican Assembly. These rarely exceeded J£50,000 before the mid-18th century, but after 1775 the Assembly voted increasing sums, mainly to subsidise an expanded imperial garrison and maintain its own defences, and Figure 8.3 shows how numbers of 'administrative' petitions rose steeply as growing numbers of contractors came to the House with rapidly increasing demands for payment.[21] From 1795 the house also began to allocate an increasing amount of money – around J£15,000 per annum by 1800 – for improving roads and bridges on the island, and solicited petitions from the parish vestries and individuals suggesting which roads to upgrade.[22] The result was a tidal wave of petitions. In the 1800/1 session, some 94 of the 177 'administrative' petitions related to roads and bridges, and by the 1810/11 session this had increased to 189 of the 269 'administrative' petitions: about 70 per cent.[23] As a result the Assembly resolved the following year

[21] A. Graham, 'The Colonial Sinews of Imperial Power: The Political Economy of Jamaican Taxation, 1768–1838', *Journal of Imperial and Commonwealth History*, 45 (2017), 188–209.

[22] *JHA*, Vol. IX, pp. 450, 538, 539; Spurdle, *Early West Indian Government*, pp. 140–3.

[23] *JHA*, Vol. X, pp. 488–527, *passim*; Vol. XII, pp. 254–306, *passim*. They were referred for examination to the Roads Committee, which had been established (or revived) in 1784 to assess petitions for road bills; *JHA*, Vol. VIII, pp. 20, 35, 62, 75. Spurdle notes an earlier Roads Committee in 1768; Spurdle, *Early West Indian Government*, p. 141.

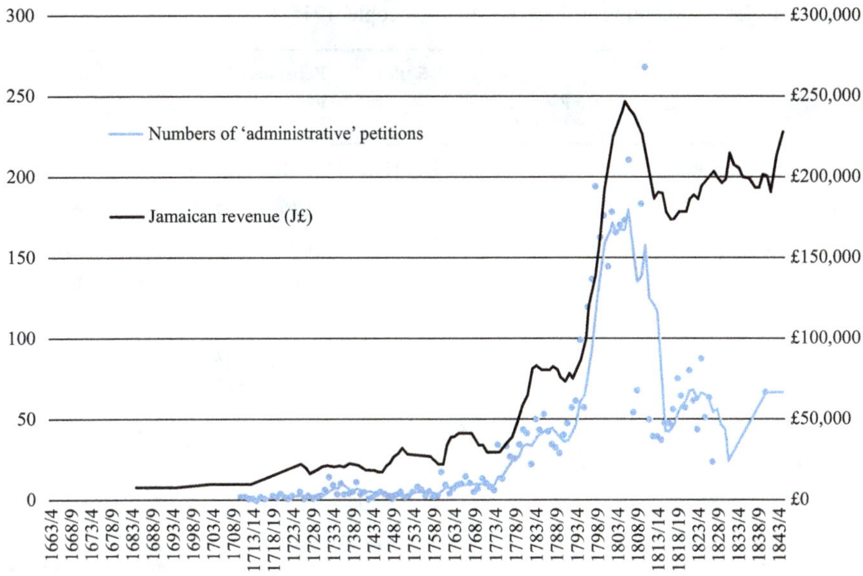

Figure 8.3 'Administrative' petitions and public expenditure in Jamaica, 1663–1834. A. Olson, 'Eighteenth-Century Colonial Legislatures and Their Constituents', *Journal of American History*, 79 (1992), 543–67 (pp. 556–9); *Journals of the House of Assembly of Jamaica*, 14 vols (Kingston, Jamaica, 1808–26); A. Graham, 'Jamaican Legislation and the Transatlantic Constitution, 1664–1839', *Historical Journal*, 61 (2018), 327–55.

to appoint a committee that would sift these petitions on behalf of the Assembly and make recommendations, and the number of administrative petitions consequently fell to 50 in the 1811/12 session, none of them relating to roads.[24] This created a new, stable equilibrium by 1815, though 'administrative' petitioning then began to drift upwards again as spending slowly increased in the 1820s and 1830s. The rise and fall of 'administrative' petitions in the Assembly was therefore largely a product of its spending patterns.

The relative importance of petitioning within Jamaica compared to other colonies in this period can be seen by comparing the numbers presented here with the incidence of petitioning in British North America before 1775 as calculated by Olson. As Table 8.1 shows, there was a great diversity, with the very high rates of petitioning within the New England colonies of Massachusetts, New Hampshire, Connecticut, and Rhode Island arguably reflecting the more 'democratic' and egalitarian political culture of these regions.[25] Although the level of petitioning in Jamaica was very low even by colonial standards in the 1710s, 50 years later it was broadly comparable with other plantation colonies such as South Carolina

[24] *JHA*, Vol. XII, pp. 458, 468, 523, 530, 568, 607, 724.

[25] This is based primarily on R. R. Beeman, *The Varieties of Political Experience in Eighteenth-Century America* (Philadelphia, University of Pennsylvania Press, 2004). For an alternative view stressing convergence and similarity, see H. James Henderson, 'Taxation and Political Culture: Massachusetts and Virginia, 1760–1800', *William and Mary Quarterly*, 47 (1990), 90–114.

Table 8.1 British Atlantic petitions, per 10,000 people, 1715–65

	1715–20	Pop.	Petitions per 10,000	1750–5	Pop.	Petitions per 10,000	1760–5	Pop.	Petitions per 10,000
Connecticut	**39.0**	39,450	9.89	**90.3**	111,280	8.11	**130.3**	142,470	9.15
Maryland	**17.8**	42,741	4.16	**16.3**	141,073	1.16	**28.0**	162,267	1.73
Massachusetts	**95.2**	62,390	15.26	**212.0**	188,000	11.28	**257.0**	222,600	11.55
New Hampshire	—	5,681	—	**47.0**	27,505	17.09	**62.0**	39,093	15.86
New Jersey	**13.6**	19,872	6.84	**18.5**	71,393	2.59	**43.1**	93,813	4.59
New York	**13.8**	21,625	6.38	**13.8**	76,696	1.80	**12.2**	117,138	1.04
Pennsylvania	**18.0**	24,450	7.36	**26.6**	119,666	2.22	**25.5**	183,703	1.39
Rhode Island	**2.2**	7,573	2.91	**58.1**	33,226	17.49	**100.3**	45,471	22.06
South Carolina	**10.8**	26,003	4.15	**17.6**	64,000	2.75	**9.6**	94,704	1.01
Virginia	**28.5**	78,281	3.64	**60.0**	231,033	2.60	**88.8**	339,726	2.61
Average	**26.5**	**32,807**	**8.09**	**56.0**	**106,387**	**5.27**	**75.7**	**144,099**	**5.25**
Jamaica	**5.8**	65,000	0.89	**20.0**	131,000	1.53	**33.0**	182,900	1.80

Sources: For North America petitions, A. Olson, 'Eighteenth-Century Colonial Legislatures and Their Constituents', *Journal of American History*, 79 (1992), 543–67 (pp. 556–9); for Jamaica, *Journals of the House of Assembly of Jamaica*, 14 vols (Kingston, Jamaica, 1808–26).

and Virginia, and even the mid-Atlantic colonies of Pennsylvania, Maryland, and New York. Indeed, examining rates of petitioning amongst the much smaller white populations in Virginia, South Carolina, and Jamaica, as shown in Table 8.2, indicates that the island had rates of petitioning that were actually closer to those of New England, reflecting the minuscule size of the white community in Jamaica and its total control of island politics.[26] Petitioning in Jamaica was therefore at least as important a part of the political culture as it was in South Carolina and Virginia before 1775, and potentially at least as important to the *free* population as it was in Massachusetts.

Finally, to return to the issues raised at the start of this section, can a quantitative analysis suggest something not just about who was petitioning and why, but also about how successful they were, and how far petitioning offered a means of access and agency to the disenfranchised in colonial society? Bailey has estimated that

[26] T. G. Burnard, *Mastery, Tyranny, and Desire: Thomas Thistlewood and His Slaves in the Anglo-Jamaican World* (Jamaica, University of the West Indies Press, 2004), pp. 70–100, 151–2; Brathwaite, *The Development of Creole Society*, pp. 20–3, 135–50, 266–305; D. Lambert, *White Creole Culture, Politics, and Identity during the Age of Abolition* (Cambridge, Cambridge University Press, 2005), pp. 73–104; Petley, *Slaveholders in Jamaica*, pp. 53–60, 62–3.

Table 8.2 British Atlantic petitions, per 10,000 whites, 1715–65

	1715–20	Pop.	Petitions per 10,000	1750–55	Pop.	Petitions per 10,000	1760–65	Pop.	Petitions per 10,000
Jamaica	**5.8**	7,000	8.29	**20.0**	15,000	13.33	**33.0**	20,000	16.50
Virginia	**28.5**	55,000	5.18	**60.0**	130,000	4.62	**88.8**	200,000	4.44
South Carolina	**10.8**	5,115	21.11	**17.6**	25,000	7.04	**9.6**	36,740	2.61

Sources: A. Olson, 'Eighteenth-Century Colonial Legislatures and Their Constituents', *Journal of American History*, 79 (1992), 543–67 (pp. 556–9); for Jamaica, *Journals of the House of Assembly of Jamaica*, 14 vols (Kingston, Jamaica, 1808–26).

about 44 per cent of the legislation passed by the House of Burgesses in Virginia between 1710 and 1730 was the result of a petition, rising to 50 per cent between 1752 and 1770.[27] He has argued on this basis that the petition was an accessible and surprisingly effective means for a variety of interest groups in Virginia to advance their interests or have grievances redressed. Tully likewise concluded that about 52 per cent of the statutes passed in Pennsylvania between 1717 and 1775 were the result of such a petition, and Purvis found that the percentage in New Jersey rose from about 14 per cent between 1702 and 1721 to 21 per cent between 1722 and 1749, and then 43 per cent between 1750 and 1764.[28] Across British North America, the petition was therefore the stimulus for around half the colonial legislation passed before 1775, and the close parallels that existed in legislative matters between Jamaica and the mainland colonies suggest that the same was true for Jamaica, especially because both legislative petitions and legislation, as noted above, rose largely in step during this period. Success was not guaranteed, but petitions did at least have a chance of success, and were more accessible than some of the other ways of raising issues in the Assembly, such as the election or the issuing of 'instruction' to representatives.[29]

Access

Across this period petitioning was therefore a common form of gaining access to the power of the Jamaican legislature. Yet statistical overviews can only go so far in suggesting how and why inhabitants used petitioning; how and why they were

[27] Bailey, *Popular Influence*, p. 62.

[28] Tully, *William Penn's Legacy*, pp. 188–9; Purvis, *Proprietors*, pp. 176–7.

[29] Brathwaite, *The Development of Creole Society*, pp. 47–9; Petley, *Slaveholders in Jamaica*, pp. 62–4; Hall, 'Constitutional and Political Developments', pp. 99–121; A. Graham, 'The Principle of Representation in Jamaica and the British Atlantic in the Age of Revolutions, 1768–1807', *Parliaments, Estates, and Representation*, 40 (2020), 1–20.

successful; and, in particular, whether petitioning offered otherwise disempowered groups a form of political action, whether this changed across the period in question, and, if so, why. This section therefore adopts a more focused approach, examining how two important but disenfranchised groups in Jamaica – free people of colour and Jews – used petitions. It argues that they could be used both communally and individually to press for, and in some cases to secure, general and specific aims from the Assembly, particularly during the campaigns for civil rights that peaked in 1830. These episodes reveal, however, that the mere act of petitioning was also rarely sufficient. Equally important was the wider context, with Jewish petitions failing in the early 18th century because they clashed with the wider political and economic priorities of the white elite, but succeeding in 1830 because they happened to coincide with the self-interested aims of that elite. The format and structure of the petition and petitioning process had remained relatively constant throughout this time, so it was the wider balance of political forces that helped to make them effective, though equally some skill and strategy was still required by petitioners if they were to use their petition effectively and exploit the situation.

Petitions were one of the main instruments used by the Jamaican community of free people of colour for redress, especially because all but a few were banned from testifying in court against whites.[30] From the early 18th century the Assembly began to pass private 'privilege' bills granting a range of civil rights to free people of colour upon their petition to the Assembly.[31] About 300 bills were introduced up to 1830 for about 700 people in total, and Daniel Livesay has shown that these records are an extremely rich source for understanding the lives and circumstances of this group.[32] Other petitions, not by but for free people of colour, can likewise provide evidence of how petitioning could benefit them. Legislation in 1761 limited the amount of property that could be devised or willed to free people of colour to J£2,000, in order to maintain their economic subordination.[33] At least 20 petitions were introduced into the Assembly, however, by planters asking for private bills enabling them to set aside the terms of this Act. Thomas Wynter and William Wright both secured portmanteau Acts in 1783, for instance, that authorised and enabled them to settle the entirety of their estates on their free children of colour and to grant them the necessary rights and privileges.[34] All of these concessions were effected through the Assembly, but were brought to their attention through the petition, which became an instrument of social ascent for a select few free persons of colour.

[30] Brathwaite, *The Development of Creole Society*, pp. 168–72.

[31] S. Hurwitz and E. Hurwitz, 'A Token of Freedom: Private Bill Legislation for Free Negroes in Eighteenth-Century Jamaica', *William and Mary Quarterly*, 24 (1967), 423–31; Livesay, *Children of Uncertain Fortune*, pp. 20–41, 193–232, 307–23; B. N. Newman, 'Contesting "Black" Liberty and Subjecthood in the Anglophone Caribbean, 1730s–1780s', *Slavery & Abolition*, 32 (2011), 169–83; Graham, 'Jamaican Legislation', p. 354.

[32] Livesay, *Children of Uncertain Fortune*, pp. 14–18, 41–52.

[33] Ibid.

[34] *JHA*, Vol. VII, pp. 536, 544, 586.

Alongside these substantial requests were smaller petitions brought by free people of colour for more mundane or prosaic measures that nevertheless helped them to survive in a society overwhelmingly hostile to them. About 30 or 40 petitions were received before 1834 by or on behalf of free and enslaved people of colour asking for rewards for loyal service during conspiracies or revolutions. John Perkins, a free person of colour from Jamaica and one of the first black naval officers in the Royal Navy, petitioned the house in 1790 to ask them to recommend him to the Lords of the Admiralty for promotion, which they agreed to, 'signifying at the same time to Their Lordships that the promotion of so deserving an officer will be highly gratifying to this community, and be considered as a very obliging mark of attention by Their Lordships to the wishes and representations of the house'.[35]

The petition also enabled collective appeals from groups. Free and enslaved people of colour were a significant presence, for example, among the pilots who guided ships around the harbours of the island, a niche that often afforded them considerable autonomy and status.[36] Two Acts of 1736 and 1737 permitted black pilots to be employed if sufficient white pilots were not available, leading to a series of petitions in the 1740s from white pilots who wanted this loophole closed, and several counterpetitions from several slave-owners on behalf of their black pilots.[37] The petition therefore proved a highly flexible instrument that enabled a wide range of matters to be brought to the attention of the Assembly, even if the success of these petitions depended on wider political circumstances.

However, while free and enslaved people of colour could use the petition to make requests for specific concessions or actions, often with some success, any grant of collective privileges ultimately depended on the wider political situation. Building on the unsuccessful petition of 1792 noted above, two petitions were presented to the assembly in 1813 with over 2,400 signatures from the community of free people of colour, successfully pressing for the removal of some of the most egregious limits on their civil rights.[38] Further petitions on the same basis followed in 1816 and 1823, the latter organised by a committee that methodically circulated the petition around the island for signature and hired their own agent in London to correspond directly with the Colonial Office and the new Anti-Slavery Society, which had launched its own petitioning campaign.[39] The petitions were therefore

[35] Ibid., Vol. VIII, pp. 581, 593, 620.

[36] N. Rogers, *The Press Gang: Naval Impressment and Its Opponents in Georgian Britain* (London, Continuum, 2007), pp. 91–3; K. Dawson, 'The Cultural Geography of Enslaved Ship Pilots', in J. Cañizares-Esguerra, M. Childs, and J. Sidbury (eds), *The Black Urban Atlantic in the Age of the Slave Trade* (Philadelphia, University of Pennsylvania Press, 2013), pp. 163–84; K. Dawson, 'Enslaved Ship Pilots in the Age of Revolutions: Challenging Notions of Race and Slavery between the Boundaries of Land and Sea', *Journal of Social History*, 47 (2013), 71–100.

[37] See 9 Geo. II, c. 11, and 10 Geo. II, c. 4, in *The Laws of Jamaica*, 7 vols (St Jago de la Vega, Jamaica, 1802–24), Vol. I, pp. 243–5, 246–7; *JHA*, Vol. IV, pp. 83, 87, 88, 119, 123, 130, 132, 140, 237, 248, 253, 254, 263, 269–75.

[38] Heuman, *Between Black and White*, pp. 27–31; Livesay, *Children of Uncertain Fortune*, pp. 323–46.

[39] Heuman, *Between Black and White*, pp. 33–6, 44–7; R. Huzzey, 'A Microhistory of British Antislavery Petitioning', *Social Science History*, 43 (2019), 599–623.

part of a wider political campaign in Britain that successfully pressured the imperial government to adopt policies after 1823 for 'ameliorating' the conditions of both free and enslaved people of colour, and persuaded some planters in Jamaica that strategic concessions might delay or deter outright emancipation.[40] It was therefore neither the huge rise in petitions for privileges and the corresponding increase in privilege bills in the late 1820s noted earlier, nor the grant of general privilege bills in February and November 1830, that reflected any change in the nature of petitions and petitioning, but rather the fact that the community of free people of colour was pushing at a door that, even if it was still not wholly open, was now for various reasons at last partially ajar.

The complexity of the petitioning process in Jamaica across this period, dependent upon the shifting configurations of political power and policy and often overlapping with petitions to other bodies in Jamaica and Britain, can be seen even more clearly in the experiences of another minority group in the island, the Jewish community. Whereas free people of colour only arose as a coherent interest group in the late 18th century, Jews had been settled in the island as merchants, retailers, and even planters since the late 17th, forming a cohesive grouping with religious and communal structures that allowed them to organise petitioning campaigns from the outset.[41] Although, as naturalised subjects, Jews resident in Jamaica supposedly had the same civil and legal rights as other white subjects there, from the late 17th century the Assembly refused to make these available, passing an Act in 1711 that banned Jews from voting or holding public office.[42] Though it was disallowed by the Board of Trade in 1717, in practice it remained in force, and was upheld in 1750 despite the petition of Abraham Sanches to the Assembly to receive his legal rights.[43] This in turn meant that they were unable to resist directly various discriminatory policies enacted by the legislature, especially a series of additional taxes levied on the community between the 1680s and 1730s. Individual Jews were still able to petition the Assembly for private business, and several did successfully, as did the community, but the mixed record of its failures and successes demonstrates the limits of the petition as an instrument of agency.[44]

[40] Petley, *Slaveholders in Jamaica*, pp. 86–102; Heuman, *Between Black and White*, pp. 44–51; Livesay, *Children of Uncertain Fortune*, pp. 375–97.

[41] F. W. Pitman, *The Development of the British West Indies, 1700–1764* (New Haven, CT, Yale University Press, 2017), pp. 28–30; J. S. Gerber (ed.), *The Jews in the Caribbean* (Portland, OR, Littman Library, 2013).

[42] H. Snyder, 'Rules, Rights, and Redemption: The Negotiation of Jewish Status in British Atlantic Port Towns, 1740–1831', *Jewish History*, 20 (2006), 147–70; S. Hurwitz and E. Hurwitz, 'The New World Sets an Example for the Old: The Jews of Jamaica and Political Rights, 1661–1831', *American Jewish Historical Quarterly*, 55 (1965), 37–56. For similar clashes elsewhere, see N. Zacek, *Settler Society in the English Leeward Islands, 1670–1776* (New York, Cambridge University Press, 2010), pp. 133–49.

[43] *JHA*, Vol. IV, pp. 238, 243, 246, 247, 249, 250.

[44] These included Joseph Ydana in 1744 (ibid., Vol. III, p. 611; Eli Faber, *Jews, Slaves, and the Slave Trade: Setting the Record Straight* (New York and London, New York University Press, 1998), p. 282n), Judith Silvera in 1799 (*JHA*, Vol. X, p. 349), Abraham Mendes Belisario in 1800 (*JHA*, Vol. X, p. 520),

The efforts to remove the additional taxation, for example, were largely a failure. In 1693 the Assembly passed an Act imposing a communal tax of £750 for the defence of the island, a measure repeated several times up to 1739.[45] The taxes had the active support of many of the planters and non-Jewish merchants in the island, on the supposed basis that the community was unfairly exploiting its position on the island to make vast profits without discharging any of the corresponding civic duties that Christian merchants had to undertake. The Jewish community made numerous petitions to the Assembly for relief – at least a dozen before 1729 – and several others to the Board of Trade in London, as well as also mobilising the Jewish community in London to lobby the Board on their behalf. However, the petitions ultimately failed to effect any change. The Board sent numerous orders to governors to refuse their assent to such bills, but had limited power over the Assembly, and Mirvis argues that the issue of Jewish taxation became caught up in wider contests between imperial and colonial interests over their respective powers of taxation.[46] Petitions were therefore submitted to the Assembly as part of a wider campaign for relief by the Jewish community, but were ultimately unsuccessful because of wider conditions.

By contrast, a renewed push by the Jewish community in the 1820s for civil rights was successful largely owing to wider circumstances. An attempt by Levy Hyman to cast a vote in the elections at Kingston in 1820 was rejected by the House of Assembly, but as abolitionist pressures increased, the white elite began to look to Jewish as well as free-coloured planters and slave-owners as bulwarks against the abolition of slavery.[47] In 1826 a bill therefore passed through the House granting Jews the same rights as white Christian subjects in Jamaica, notwithstanding the strong objections of merchants and other freeholders in Kingston, and further bills in 1828 and 1829. Indeed, this time the key opposition actually came from the imperial government and the governor, who held the bills hostage in order to insist that the Assembly likewise enfranchise free people of colour. Once this had passed

Abraham David Mendes Henriques in 1802 (*JHA*, Vol. XI, p. 15), and Abraham and Esther Moreno in 1826 (*JHA*, Vol. XIV, p. 639). Other communal petitions included a request in 1732 to be deemed white for the purpose of the 'deficiency' laws (*JHA*, Vol. III, pp. 55, 126; for the laws, see N. A. T. Hall, 'Some Aspects of the "Deficiency" Question in Jamaica in the Eighteenth Century', *Caribbean Studies*, 15 (1975), 5–19); in 1734 to be allowed to purchase white indentured servants (*JHA*, Vol. III, pp. 261, 265); and in 1808 for poor relief (*JHA*, Vol. XII, pp. 30, 46, 47, 67, 82). All were unsuccessful.

[45] S. Mirvis, 'Between Assembly and Crown: The Debate over Jewish Taxation in Jamaica (1692–1740)', *Journal of Early American History*, 6 (2016), 196–219. For Jewish merchants, see A. D. Meyers, 'Ethnic Distinctions and Wealth among Colonial Jamaican Merchants, 1685–1716', *Social Science History*, 22 (1998), 47–81 (pp. 54–60, 66–75); and Faber, *Jews, Slaves*, pp. 49–53, 57–90, 105–29.

[46] Mirvis, 'Between Assembly and Crown', pp. 208, 216–17. For the constitutional clashes, see A. M. Whitson, *The Constitutional Development of Jamaica, 1660 to 1729* (Manchester, Manchester University Press, 1929), pp. 33–8; and Metcalf, *Royal Government*, pp. 128–57.

[47] Snyder, 'Rules, Rights, and Redemption', pp. 147–70; Hurwitz and Hurwitz, 'The New World', pp. 37–56; Heuman, *Between Black and White*, pp. 47–50. For a parallel experience of petitioning and enfranchisement in the Jewish community of Barbados, see L. Arnold Leibman and S. May, 'Making Jews: Race, Gender and Identity in Barbados in the Age of Emancipation', *American Jewish History*, 99 (2015), 1–26.

in February 1830, the bill for Jewish enfranchisement was finally approved. Wider political circumstances therefore determined its success, though the community recognised that skill and judgement had been required to petition the Assembly and manoeuvre the necessary legislation through the house. They duly voted an expensive gift of silver plate to Moses Delgado, who had organised the extramural campaign and petitions, and Augustus Hardin Beaumont, a gentile and Jamaican radical who had supported the cause from principle rather than calculation.[48]

Conclusion

A study of petitioning in Jamaica therefore confirms its importance to the politics and society of the island during the 18th century. As in Virginia and other parts of the British Atlantic, including the British Isles itself, petitioning served as a means of communication between authority and society, enabling the legislature in this case to hear and respond to the needs of that society.[49] Denied a direct role in colonial politics by discriminatory legislation, petitions nevertheless enabled marginalised groups such as women, free people of colour, Jews, and others to put their case before the Assembly for redress, and to insist on participation even if they were denied direct representation. These petitions were sometimes part of wider public campaigns that gave them additional rhetorical force, and many of the petitions for civil rights heard by the Assembly in the 1820s and 1830s can therefore be understood as contributions to a broader debate taking place within the public spheres of Jamaica, the West Indies, and Britain about the potential transition from slavery into a free society. Ranging from these openly political petitions down to the more mundane one examined at the start of this chapter, such petitions were often embedded in wider sets of local and imperial politics that cannot always be fully recovered from the Assembly *Journals*, but can be appreciated in those cases where the necessary sources survive. Petitions were therefore a key part of the continuum of political and social practices, ranging from private intercession to outright violence, used by parties and individuals in slave societies such as Jamaica to overcome restrictions on formal political participation. Had they not been effective, it is doubtful whether any of these groups would have continued to employ them.

Petitions can also help to identify some of the issues within societies such as Jamaica, and even to recover the voices of marginal peoples and groups that might survive nowhere else. The reconstruction of the lives and identities of free people of colour from their petitions to the House for privileges by Daniel Livesay is an

[48] W. H. Maehl, 'Augustus Hardin Beaumont: Anglo-American Radical (1798–1838)', *International Review of Social History*, 14 (1969), 237–50 (p. 241).

[49] For Britain, see M. Knights, 'Participation and Representation before Democracy: Petitions and Addresses in Premodern Britain', in I. Shapiro, S. C. Stokes, E. J. Wood, and A. S. Kirshner (eds), *Political Representation* (Cambridge, Cambridge University Press, 2009), pp. 35–58.

example in this respect. Yet caution is also required in drawing broader conclusions about the power of petitions or their nature as weapons of the weak. As this chapter has shown, petitions could make very little headway when political circumstances were unfavourable, and the rise of petitioning was driven by a corresponding rise in the legislative and financial business of the Assembly, much of it concentrated on the maintenance of state structures intended to preserve the slave society. The act of petitioning also stated – as several petitioners recognised – an acceptance of, and even submission to, the legitimacy and power of the authority being petitioned. In this respect it was an inherently conservative act, at least compared to the more open and direct forms of resistance seen in slave rebellions such as the Haitian Revolution in nearby Saint Domingue between 1791 and 1804. The petition was therefore a complex tool, whose effectiveness was often tied to wider circumstances that had little to do with the petition itself, but which was sometimes as much a manifestation of underlying change as a force or instrument for it.

9

Petitioning in Transition: Switzerland, 1481–1891

ANDREAS WÜRGLER

PETITIONING SEEMS TO be a universal phenomenon. In all known societies and periods of history, people have addressed oral and/or written requests to more powerful persons, authorities, or institutions. But despite their ubiquitous appearance, the procedures of petitioning, as well as the form and content of petitions, have undergone changes in specific historical contexts.[1] In what follows, the Swiss example shall be analysed by focusing on the 18th and 19th centuries, a period in which the Confederacy, a late medieval and early modern construction, was transformed through several revolutions and restorations. These transitions not only affected the practices of petitioning and the right to petition but were partly triggered and shaped by petitionary movements and activities. The Swiss case deserves special attention because in spite of all these transitions, the Swiss Confederacy, uniquely in the European context, was and remained republican, federal, and comparatively democratic during the 18th and 19th centuries. At the same time, Switzerland provides an excellent vantage point to survey the changes and continuities in petitions and petitioning during the 'age of revolutions' from the late 18th century onwards.

[1] B. Kümin and A. Würgler, 'Petitions, 'Gravamina' and the Early Modern State: Local Influence on Central Legislation in England and Germany (Hesse)', *Parliaments, Estates and Representation*, 17 (1997), 39–60; A. Würgler, 'Voices from among the "Silent Masses": Humble Petitions and Social Conflicts in Early Modern Central Europe', in L. Heerma van Voss (ed.), *Petitions in Social History*, Supplement 9 of *International Review of Social History*, 46 (2001), 11–34; A. Würgler, 'Bitten und Begehren: Suppliken und Gravamina in der deutschsprachigen Frühneuzeitforschung', in C. Nubola and A. Würgler (eds), *Bittschriften und Gravamina: Politik, Verwaltung und Justiz in Europa (14.-18. Jahrhundert)* (Berlin, Duncker & Humblot, 2005), pp. 17–52; D. Zaret, 'Petition-and-Response and Liminal Petitioning in Comparative/Historical Perspective', *Social Science History*, 43 (2019), 431–51.

Proceedings of the British Academy, **262**, 176–193,

To speak of Switzerland is a simplification, because during this period there were many 'Switzerlands'. The fundamental revolutions and restorations that occurred between 1798 and 1848 produced many different political systems on the cantonal (or regional) as well as on the federal level. In place of a very loose confederacy, constructed in the late Middle Ages and named *Corpus helveticum* in the *ancien régime*, a centralised sister of the French Republic, called the Helvetic Republic, was founded in 1798. But after only five years of existence, this new system underwent two restorations, one introduced by Napoleon in 1803 that was called Mediation; the other prepared by Swiss conservatives, imposed by the European powers in 1814/15, and called Restoration. Both reintroduced greater federalism and weakened the elements of modern representative democracy. Nonetheless, Switzerland remained 'Napoleon's only republic' until 1815 – and Europe's only republic until 1870. After some 15 years of relative calm, two new waves of cantonal revolutions re-established liberal representative democracies in some, but not all, cantons in 1830/1 and 1845/6. In 1848 liberal representative democracy was established at the national (or federal) level. But even this constitution, introducing a federal representative democracy, was substantially modified with regard to the instruments of popular participation in politics in 1866, 1874, and 1891.[2] The one constant in all these changes, and in contrast to most European polities, was that for domestic issues the Swiss petitioned only councils or parliaments and the republics' governments, but never princes or kings.

The transformations in petitioning during these periods will be discussed in chronological order, as well as the possible contributions of petitions and petitioning to these transitions by focusing on actors, reactions, and forms of actions in the context of petitioning.

The Tradition of Petitioning until 1798

Addressing oral or written requests, supplications, or grievances to the state or other authorities as well as to powerful individuals was very common in old-regime Switzerland. Even if petitioning was not an official right granted by law, it was a ubiquitous practice. The very term 'petition' was rare in German and French Swiss sources from the time. Typically, petitionary documents were described in terms that were equivalents of 'supplication', such as *Bittschrift*, *Beschwerde*, *Ansuchen*, *Begehren*, *Eingabe* or *supplique*, *supplication*, *requête*, *revendication*, *grief*, *doléance*.[3] Early modern petitioning mostly took the form that the servile subject obsequiously asked for a favour that was granted (or not) by the grace of the

[2] G. Kreis (ed.), *Die Geschichte der Schweiz* (Basel, Schwabe, 2014); Gerold Steinmann, 'Petitionsrecht', in *Historisches Lexikon der Schweiz* (*HLS*), version of 27 September 2010, https://hls-dhs-dss.ch/de/articles/010370/2010-09-27/ (accessed 3 July 2019).

[3] For which see the contribution of Joris Oddens in this volume.

sovereign or his authorities. Typically, the content of these petitions addressed economic issues, tax relief, and assistance in emergency situations as well as claims for granting privileges, favours, or patronage. Everyone, regardless of age, sex, social and legal status, origin, or 'nationality' could address a supplication to anyone holding power. For example, condemned criminals could ask for pardon, beggars for support, and foreigners or refugees for protection.[4]

In some domains, supplicating became a routine part of bureaucratic procedure. For instance, the poor relief system in the canton of Bern, at least during the 18th century, was structured by a sequence of supplications. The request was first addressed to local officials who had to approve and attest the authenticity of the author and the petition's content. Local officials then forwarded the supplication to the central administration to decide whether or not to grant relief. Interestingly, the number of petitions by the poor was growing quicker than the population during the 18th century. The number of poor people receiving state support grew from below 1 per cent to about 5 per cent of the population. For two districts analysed by Erika Flückiger Strebel the number of supported poor persons increased tenfold and thirtyfold respectively, whereas the amount of support per person decreased at about 20 per cent.[5] This impoverishment of a part of the population stood in clear contrast to the general economic prosperity during the 18th century.[6]

There were also numerous collective supplications launched either by organised groups such as craftsmen's corporations, parishes, and communities, or by informal collectives such as neighbourhoods, groups of soldiers, or victims of catastrophes. In general, the poor, as well as the victims of famine, flood, and fire, had a good chance of being heard and getting positive answers. Even collective economic demands were often fulfilled.

However, collective petitions concerning political claims were much less successful. In these cases, the authorities tended to react sharply. They rejected the subjects' wishes for more participation in political decision-making, for more transparency regarding public finances, and for better access to public jobs and political functions.[7] Governments tried to criminalise such petitioning on the grounds that the grievances had been drafted on the occasion of assemblies. While petitioning was accepted, autonomous assemblies were not. Such gatherings had been prohibited

[4] Würgler, 'Voices', pp. 12, 14–15; A. Würgler, 'Asymmetrie und Reziprozität: Herrschaft und Protektion in Suppliken der Frühen Neuzeit', in T. Haug, N. Weber, and C. Windler (eds), *Protegierte und Protektoren: Ungleiche politische Beziehungen zwischen Partnerschaft und Dominanz (16. bis frühes 20. Jahrhundert)* (Vienna, Böhlau, 2016), pp. 279–94.

[5] E. Flückiger Strebel, *Zwischen Wohlfahrt und Staatsökonomie: Armenfürsorge auf der bernischen Landschaft im 18. Jahrhundert* (Zurich, Chronos, 2002), pp. 59–60, 142–6.

[6] S. Altorfer-Ong, *Staatsbildung ohne Steuern: Politische Ökonomie und Staatsfinanzen im Bern des 18. Jahrhunderts* (Baden, Hier und Jetzt, 2010), pp. 173–5, 282–8.

[7] A. Würgler, *Unruhen und Öffentlichkeit: Städtische und ländliche Protestbewegungen im 18. Jahrhundert* (Tübingen, Bibliotheca Academica Verlag, 1995), pp. 116–32.

already in 1481 to prevent these meetings from collecting grievances, drafting petitions, and turning into revolts.[8]

Collective supplications or petitions often proposed different and sometimes new solutions to grinding problems, or sought greater political participation. This was especially the case when protest movements established long lists of grievances demanding greater involvement in politics or even sketching alternative political structures. Not surprisingly, authorities regarded such petitions as politically subversive. As this survey demonstrates, supplications, petitions, and related forms were varied and numerous. They constituted one of the most important channels of political communication between rulers and ruled in the era before the age of revolutions.

The Right to Petition and Petitioning in the Helvetic Republic (1798–1803)

The Helvetic Constitution, drafted by the Basel merchant and politician Peter Ochs on the model of the French Constitution of Year III (1795) and then 'corrected' by the French government, was imposed by the French invasion army in April 1798, and was Switzerland's first modern constitution. The constitution contained a bill of rights, separation of powers, representative democracy, and state centralisation. It did not explicitly grant a right to petition, but by outlining what the administration had to do with the petitions it received, the constitution implicitly conferred such a right. This inference is confirmed by the fact that petitioning was referred to as a 'sacred right' in many laws and parliamentary debates.[9] Furthermore, the authorities actively encouraged the citizens to hand in petitions. For instance, the Helvetic Directorate, the Republic's central government, emphasised that the 'right to petition is one of the most holy citizenship rights. Every citizen should not only find open access and impartial audition; but he has also the right and sometimes the duty to frankly communicate his opinion about the state affairs concerning the common public weal to those authorities who could profit from it.'[10]

[8] P. Blickle, *Unruhen in der ständischen Gesellschaft, 1300–1800* (Munich, Oldenbourg, 1988); E. Walder, *Das Stanser Verkommnis: Ein Kapitel eidgenössischer Geschichte* (Stans, Historischer Verein Nidwalden, 1994); M. König and A. Würgler, 'Soziale Konflikte', in *HLS*, version of 8 January 2013, https://hls-dhs-dss.ch/de/articles/025757/2013-01-08/ (accessed 2 July 2019).

[9] J. Strickler (ed.), *Amtliche Sammlung der Acten aus der Zeit der Helvetischen Republik (1798–1803)* (*ASHR*), 9 vols (Bern: Stämpflische Buchdruckerei, 1887–1902), Vol. II, p. 529 (Lüthi from Solothurn in the Senate, 13 July 1798).

[10] 'Das Petitions-Recht ist eines der heiligsten Rechte des Staats-Bürgers. Nicht nur soll ein jedweder mit seinem eignen Anliegen immerdar freyen Zugang und ein unbefangenes Gehör finden; sondern er hat auch das Recht und zuweilen die Pflicht auf sich, seine Meynung über allgemeine und das öffentliche Wohl ansehende Staats-Angelegenheiten denjenigen Behörden, welche davon Gebrauch machen können, mit Freymüthigkeit vorzutragen.' Schweizerisches Bundesarchiv (Swiss Federal Archives) (BAr), Bern, BO 1000/1483, Vol. B535, p. 26 (Vollziehungs-Direktorium [Executive Directorate] to the Grossen Rat [Great Chamber of Parliament], 17 December 1798).

Under the short-lived Helvetic Republic, petitionary rhetoric was transformed. Instead of grovelling before authority as in the *ancien régime*, petitioners now performed their newly acquired political equality and freedom by addressing the authorities as 'Citizen Legislators!' or 'Citizen Governor!' and by adding the final formula 'with republican greetings!' instead of the old obsequious phrases that addressed 'our high-born, very honoured, venerable and graceful Lords', and closed with 'for ever ready to serve, your humblest subject'.[11]

Such new formulas were not just spontaneous expressions of revolutionary boldness. They also became legal requirements, although interestingly the use of these phrases preceded the laws in which they were imposed by several weeks. Some months before the end of the Helvetic Republic, the old form of the address reappeared without any modifications in the law.[12] It seems, then, that petitions may be read as seismographs announcing socio-political 'earthquakes' by atmospherically perceiving and sensitively reacting to slightly shifting power relations, and even anticipating major ruptures in those power relations. Petitioners skilfully adapted to regime changes through their faithful performance of the rhetorical formulas that successive authorities wanted to hear.

In the content of petitions there was continuity as well as change. A sample of petitions sent to the city authorities of Bern during April for the years 1798–1802 reveals that 300 of the 1,890 petitions (16 per cent) comprised requests for financial relief or support in emergency situations (famine, fire, and flood), which had also been common under the *ancien régime*. At the local level, such as in the city of Bern, new motives for petitioning included the quartering of troops, with which 800 petitions in the sample (42 per cent) were concerned; with a few local exceptions, there had been no military occupation in Switzerland during the previous 300 years. Requests concerning applications for or registration of citizenship, which was connected to the new right to vote, made up 11 per cent of the Bern local administration's workload (200 petitions of the sample). Women's share of the petitions made up 15 per cent of the general total and and 23 per cent of the total regarding quartering issues, that is about the same range as in the early modern period.[13] On the national level, hundreds of petitions protested against the Helvetic Republic's reorganisation of traditional cantons into entities of approximately the same size, or proposed alternative boundaries for these new cantons.[14] Finally, when

[11] A. Würgler, 'Kontinuität und Diskontinuität zwischen Ancien Régime und Helvetischer Republik am Beispiel der Bittschriften', in D. Schläppi (ed.), *Umbruch und Beständigkeit: Kontinuitäten in der Helvetischen Revolution von 1798* (Basel, Schwabe, 2009), pp. 49–64.

[12] A. Würgler, 'Existenzielle Not oder Menschenrecht? Argumente in Bittschriften während der Helvetischen Republik (1798–1803)', in S. Arlettaz, R. Pahud de Mortanges, D. Tröhler, A. Würgler, and S. Zurbuchen (eds), *Droits de l'homme et constitution moderne: La Suisse au tournant des XVIIIe et XIXe siècles* (Geneva, Slatkine, 2012), pp. 297–314 (p. 302).

[13] A. Würgler, 'Grenzen des Zumutbaren? Revolution und Okkupation als Erfahrung und Erinnerung', in A. Würgler (ed.), *Grenzen des Zumutbaren: Erfahrungen mit der französischen Okkupation und der Helvetischen Republik (1798–1803)* (Basel, Schwabe, 2011), pp. 9–27 (p. 20).

[14] F. Walter, 'Échec de la départementalisation: Les découpages administratifs de la République helvétique (1798–1803)', *Revue suisse d'histoire*, 40 (1990), 67–85; A. Würgler, 'Expérimenter

the Helvetic government invited – during the summer of 1800 and again in the spring of 1801 – the people to make proposals for a better, revised constitution, the central authorities were overwhelmed with petitions.[15]

Did the new constitutional guarantee of petitioning fundamentally change the way that petitioners addressed authority through political argument? Did the petitioners refer to fundamental constitutional values as 'liberty', 'equality', or 'human rights' in order to achieve their goals?[16] Although many petitioners, even on the local level, cited the slogan '*liberté – égalité*' in their letterheads, only 5 per cent used 'liberty' or 'natural freedom' as an argument for their purpose. And some of them did it in a surprising way. The pedlar Marx Schmid, for instance, complained about all the new grocers who placed their market stalls exactly in the same spot that he had been using during the previous 30 years. The new competitors, Schmid said, were legitimising their behaviour through 'pretended liberty and equality'.[17]

The allusion to 'equality' and 'justice', however, was very frequent. The petitions did not usually complain about quartering as such (which would have been useless), but they complained about the fact that a rich neighbour had a bigger house and no children yet had to accommodate fewer soldiers.[18] This reveals the continuity with the older tradition of petitioners seeking fairness or equity rather than equality. Overall, about 50 per cent of a sample of 100 local petitions used traditional arguments already present in old regime supplications: about 20 per cent argued on the basis of existential need, heavy poverty, or urgent problems; some other 20 per cent demanded justice and equity (fairness); and the remaining 10 per cent cited tradition and custom. Only 11 of the 100 texts referred to new

l'occupation de l'espace: La population suisse face à l'invasion française et à la formation de la République helvétique (1798–1803)', in J.-F. Chanet, A. Crépin, and C. Windler (eds), *Le temps des hommes doubles: Les arrangements face à l'occupation, de la Révolution française à la guerre de 1870* (Rennes, Presses universitaires de Rennes, 2013), pp. 195–212 (pp. 197–200).

15 There is no in-depth study of these petitions, but see *ASHR*, Vol. V, no. 401, pp. 995–1036 (petitions to the legislature, April–July 1800); *ASHR*, Vol. VI, no. 3, pp. 7–23 (petitions concerning the constitution, August–September 1800), no. 235, pp. 737–51 (addresses, petitions, propositions from officials, individuals, and communities concerning the constitution, February–March 1801), and no. 236, pp. 752–62 (various individual and collective petitions concerning the constitution, March–April 1801); *ASHR*, Vol. VII, no. 103, pp. 453–92 (letters and petitions from groups, village communities, and their local authorities concerning the constitution, August–October 1801); H. Böning, *Der Traum von Freiheit und Gleichheit: Helvetische Revolution und Republik (1798–1803). Die Schweiz auf dem Weg zur bürgerlichen Demokratie* (Zürich, Orell Füssli, 1998), pp. 232–3; and Würgler, 'Kontinuität und Diskontinuität', pp. 60–2.

16 The usual terms in German are *Freiheit*, *Gleichheit*, and *Menschenrecht(e)*; Würgler, 'Existenzielle Not oder Menschenrecht?', pp. 312–13. The term *Rechte des Staatsbürgers* (citizenship rights) was also used sometimes; cf. n. 10.

17 'Unter dem Vorwand, die nun anerkante Freyheit und Gleichheit erlaube ihnen, ihre Stände, wo sie gut finden, aufzurichten', Stadtarchiv Bern (SAB), A244, V-80 (12 April 1799). See also Würgler, 'Existenzielle Not oder Menschenrecht?', pp. 301–3.

18 Würgler, 'Grenzen des Zumutbaren?', pp. 21–2.

constitutional values; six to the constitution or laws; and five to human rights, especially liberty, equality, and property.[19]

These findings may be somewhat surprising, as every citizen had sworn an oath on the constitution and every petition had to be written on stamped paper that was decorated with the official slogan 'Liberty, equality, trust [*Zutrauen*]'.[20] We may, however, find more allusions to the constitution if we turn to the national level and consider collective petitions addressed to the central authorities, government, or Parliament. The Bernese 'Cercle social', a club of 'Friends of the People', blamed the newly elected government (*Direktorium*) for not respecting the new constitution: indeed, the Helvetic government helped the king of Sardinia-Piedmont to crush the republican movement in Piedmont with Swiss mercenaries. Parliament (*Gesetzgebender Rat*) commented on this petition with a '*mention honorable*'[21] – but it did not recall the troops, because the kingdom of Sardinia-Piedmont was under the protection of France as well. Regarding economic grievances, the same club accused the government of violating the constitution by still accepting the bakers' and butchers' privileges that amounted to monopoly rights for producing and selling bread and meat respectively at the expense of the poor. The club also attacked some officials of the Helvetic Republic for acting against the constitution, because 'their hearts are still devoted to the old system', and for taking decisions that went against the constitution.[22] This time, the authorities reacted promptly by banning the club and confiscating its archive. This case shows that petitioning remained risky even under the Helvetic Republic, where, as in other European states in the early modern period and the long 19th century, authorities had a low tolerance for clubs or associations that petitioned in the name of the people.[23]

The new constitution could also be used to defend old privileges. About three dozen innkeepers of the canton of Bern cited the constitutional guarantee of property rights and argued that their traditional economic monopolies – each tavern was granted a monopoly in a locality – were a form of property (as they had paid for them). The innkeepers complained that the policy of promoting economic liberty, permitting the establishment of numerous inns and taverns out of the authorities' control, would necessarily promote alcoholism and counter-revolution, as well as infringing their property rights. Actually, the period of

[19] Würgler, 'Existenzielle Not oder Menschenrecht?', p. 301.

[20] Ibid., pp. 301–2; Würgler, 'Kontinuität und Diskontinuität', pp. 53, 60–1.

[21] BAr, Bern, BO 1000/1483, Vol. B222, p. 208 (protocol of the Society of the People of Bern, 13 May 1798: report of the Legislative Council's decision).

[22] BAr, Bern, BO 1000/1483, Vol. B222, pp. 79–81 (petition of the Society of the People of Bern to the Legislative Council, 7 June 1798).

[23] See H. Miller, 'Introduction: The Transformation of Petitioning in the Long Nineteenth Century (1780–1914)', *Social Science History*, 43 (2019), 409–29. For the early modern period, see Würgler, *Unruhen und Öffentlichkeit*, pp. 54, 93; and R. Fuhrmann, B. Kümin, and A. Würgler, 'Supplizierende Gemeinden: Aspekte einer vergleichenden Quellenbetrachtung', *Historische Zeitschrift*, Beihefte N.F. 25 (1997), 267–323, 304–19.

commercial freedom was short-lived. From 1799, the inns and taverns needed a licence, and in 1800 new taverns were required to prove that there was really a need for them.[24] So in the end, the traditional claims of property seem to have been upheld against liberty.[25]

From a diachronic perspective, we can see that the references to human rights were most frequent just in the months before and the first year after establishing the Helvetic Republic. The enthusiasm for human rights, liberty, and freedom seems to have disappeared towards the end of the Helvetic Republic – or perhaps it was just an expression for the petitioners' realistic analysis of the changing political atmosphere.

If the form and content of petitions were marked by continuities with the *ancien régime*, there were also key changes during the Helvetic Republic. Petitions signed by large numbers of individuals that were not institutionally organised became much more frequent. Dozens, hundreds, and even thousands of men (and occasionally women) confirmed their requests with their signatures. Mass subscription petitions were, if not unknown, very rare in the old Confederacy when collective supplications and petitions were typically signed by a few persons representing their communes, parishes, and corporations.[26]

There is another, related, phenomenon that deserves our attention. Petitioning became an issue of public debate as it had never been before, particularly through the medium of the periodical press. Whereas the contents of petitions were only occasionally reported on or even reprinted in newspapers before 1798, thereafter they were regularly discussed in the context of the parliamentary treatment of petitions. One of the most important newspapers, called *Der Republikaner* (*The Republican*) has an index for the year 1799. About 15 per cent of all entries were relating to petitions.[27] This high interest referred to specific contents as well as to political discussions about the functions of petitioning. Some petitioners managed to publish their requests in a newspaper in order to serve as a template for other groups or communities, such as the newspaper *Ami de la liberté* or *Régénérateur*, published in Lausanne by Louis Reymond (1772–1821). which usually printed the petitions of the Lausanne-based *Société des Amis du peuple*.[28]

[24] Würgler, 'Existenzielle Not oder Menschenrecht?', pp. 305–10.

[25] A. Holenstein, 'Aporien der Gleichheit: Probleme der Armenfürsorge beim Übergang zum Einheitsstaat der Helvetik', in A. Holenstein, B. Kapossy, D. Tosato-Rigo, and S. Zurbuchen (eds), *Reichtum und Armut in den schweizerischen Republiken des 18. Jahrhunderts* (Geneva, Slatkine, 2010), pp. 227–36; D. Schläppi, 'Grenzen der Gleichheit: Wie und warum die helvetischen Regenten vor dem Gemeinbesitz von Korporationen kapitulierten', in Würgler, *Grenzen des Zumutbaren*, pp. 46–65.

[26] Würgler, 'Kontinuität und Diskontinuität', p. 63.

[27] A. Würgler, 'Censorship and Public Opinion: Press and Politics in the Helvetic Republic (1798–1803)', in J. Oddens, M. Rutjes, and E. Jacobs (eds), *The Political Culture of the Sister Republics: France, the Netherlands, Switzerland, and Italy* (Amsterdam, Amsterdam University Press, 2015), pp. 159–70, 297–301 (p. 168).

[28] A. Cabanis, *La presse politique vaudoise sous la République helvétique: Contribution à l'étude de l'opinion publique* (Lausanne, BHV, 1979), pp. 42, 49, 106, 110. For the 1830s, see pp. 186–9.

Another stage where petitioning was debated was the Parliament itself. Here the relation between mass petitions and parliamentary representation, or, more generally, the status of petitioning within a representative democracy, was the subject of lively debate – as later on in the 19th century in almost all European countries.[29] Petitions organised by revolutionary clubs and societies urging the government to implement the constitution more rigorously caused some problems for Parliament. Already in June 1798, the Legislative Chamber (*Grosser Rat*) decided to forbid these clubs to file collective petitions with the following arguments: 'the Helvetic people cannot be represented lawfully but by their representatives elected according to the Constitution', but 'against this fundamental rule, some clubs called "people's societies" usurped the right to represent the people, although this is the exclusive right of the constitutional organs', and 'in general, it seemed necessary to limit those clubs to the lawfully established limits of liberty'.[30] Collective petitions of radical clubs focusing on general political issues were thus prohibited, but corporate (and individual) petitions on specific issues continued to be received and accepted by the authorities. The authorities of the Helvetic Republic used the same type of arguments against a third stage of discussion: the pamphlets. So the Minister of Justice argued that pamphleteers claimed to speak in the name of the people, whereas they were just pronouncing their particular interests.[31]

The constitutional status of petitioning and the high value placed on popular participation in revolutionary ideology doubtless favoured the drafting and filing of a great number of demands and proposals concerning both traditional everyday problems of individuals and groups and more general political debates about liberty, equality, and justice in politics, law, and the constitution.[32] But, as in new revolutionary regimes in the period, the more the authorities were confronted by high numbers and also increasingly critical petitions, the more they started to restrain petitioning by prescribing formal requirements and prohibiting certain types of collective petitions that challenged their authority.

[29] J. Oddens, '"The Greatest Right of Them All": The Debate on the Right to Petition in the Netherlands from the Dutch Republic to the Kingdom (c. 1750–1830)', *European History Quarterly*, 47 (2017), 634–56 (p. 650); B. Agnès, *L'appel au pouvoir: Les pétitions aux parlements en France et au Royaume-Uni (1814–1848)* (Rennes, Presses universitaires de Rennes, 2018); Miller, 'Introduction', pp. 414–15 .

[30] *ASHR*, Vol. II, p. 86, no. 6, 16c: 'Beschluss des Grossen Rates, 16. Juni 1798', and contribution to the discussion, pp. 84–6. See also Würgler, 'Kontinuität und Diskontinuität', pp. 62–3. For similar discussions in Vaud in 1845, see M. H. Lerner, *A Laboratory of Liberty: The Transformation of Political Culture in Republican Switzerland, 1750–1848* (Leiden, Brill, 2012), pp. 278–82.

[31] *ASHR*, Vol. V, pp. 1036–7, no. 401, 62: 'Schreiben des Justizministers an den Regierungsstatthalter, 17 April 1800'.

[32] The Bundesarchiv (Federal Archives) hosts some 80 volumes containing petitions mostly addressed to the central authorities; see G. Hunziker, A. Fankhauser, and N. Bartolome (eds), *Das Zentralarchiv der Helvetischen Republik 1798–1803*, 2 vols (Bern, Schweizerisches Bundesarchiv, 1990). For the cantonal and communal level, the respective archives store many more volumes with petitions. All these petitions have been barely explored; see Würgler, 'Kontinuität und Diskontinuität'.

Backlash: Mediation (1803–1813) and Restoration (1814/15–1830)

For the following era of the two restorations historiography is quite poor in general, and particularly so concerning petitioning.[33] Restoration in Switzerland started with Napoleon's Act of Mediation in 1803. This was a constitution imposed by France, but partially based on Swiss proposals. It replaced the centralised Helvetic Republic and reintroduced sovereign cantons and federalism, while maintaining some revolutionary innovations such as legal equality, the freedom of settlement, and territorial subdivisions. This system perished with Napoleon in 1813. Swiss conservative forces sought a strengthened restoration, and this renewed old order – fixed in the Confederal Contract – was accepted in a modified version by the great powers during the Congress of Vienna in 1815. Its essential features were greater federalism and a shift away from the political equality that had defined the revolutionary regimes: cities and urban citizens were again privileged compared to the countryside and rural population; the old penitentiary law (in some cantons the Carolina from 1532) was reintroduced, including torture and the death penalty.[34]

The right to petition was also weakened. The Act of Mediation did not mention the right to petition on the national or confederate level – just as it omitted the freedom of press, settlement, and religion as well.[35] Consequently, the *Landammann*, a sort of weak president of the loose confederation, soon refused to accept petitions and to present them to the federal assembly. On the cantonal level, only one of the 19 cantons (Uri) explicitly mentioned the right of each citizen as well as that of the communes to present petitions to the legislative body. All other cantonal constitutions lacked a positive right to file petitions. They indirectly accepted petitions by stating that all demands to be treated by the government or Parliament must strictly follow the rules specified in the restrictive law of 1801: requests had to be written on stamped paper and collective petitions were illegal.[36] Under the restoration regimes after 1803 and 1815, petitioning was not mentioned in any cantonal constitutions except in those of Aargau and Schaffhausen.

Despite these restrictions, it seems that individual and economically or socially motivated petitions continued as under the old regime. As political assemblies were forbidden and the authors of some political collective petitions had been severely prosecuted, there seems to be a remarkable decrease in petitioning activities – except perhaps for the two years of 'anarchy' after the breakdown of

[33] But see V. Monnier (ed.), *Bonaparte et les Suisses: L'Acte de Médiation de 1803* (Geneva, Bibliothèque publique et universitaire, 2003); and I. Herrmann, *12 septembre 1814. La Restauration: La Confédération réinventée* (Lausanne, Presses Polytechniques et Universitaires Romandes, 2016).

[34] Herrmann, *12 septembre 1814*, pp. 65–72.

[35] A. Kölz, *Neuere schweizerische Verfassungsgeschichte*, Vol. I (Bern, Stämpfli, 1992), p. 149.

[36] W. Gisiger, *Das Petitionsrecht in der Schweiz: Historische Entwicklung und rechtliche Bedeutung* (Zurich, R. Kretz, 1935), pp. 41–7.

Mediation in 1813 and the establishing of the Vienna order in 1815.[37] During these years of turmoil, petitions were even encouraged by governments. In 1814 the provisional government of the former prince-bishopric of Basel, which had been annexed by the French in 1792 and held by them until 1813, launched a petition demanding the allied European powers as well as the Swiss Federal Diet to attach the principality as an independent canton to Switzerland rather than to France. This request was signed by 77 per cent of all heads of families (mostly by men).[38] In the same year, a similar petition was organised by the provisional government of the former republic of Geneva to promote its 'turning Swiss' and to avoid its becoming French again (as it had been from 1798 to 1813). By also collecting the signatures of some women, aliens, and even children, this petition obtained 6,500 signatures from the city of Geneva, which had a population of fewer than 22,000 inhabitants.[39] As this demonstrates, popular or 'democratic' petitions could become a useful weapon in the authorities' hands when they furthered the territorial aims of the state.

The Power of Petitioning (1830–1874/1891)

In contrast to the failure of bourgeois revolutions in Europe in 1830, the liberal movements in 1830/1 and again the radical movements in the 1840s were very successful in some of the Swiss cantons. And in 1848, the new constitution of the Swiss Confederation was almost the only permanent liberal and democratic outcome of Europe's revolutionary year.[40]

The heyday of Swiss petitioning came in 1830 and 1831. Under the conservative restoration regimes that had provided a calm context for early industrialisation, a liberal movement slowly developed during the 1820s. Since some cantons were less repressive, a sort of public opinion and free press developed in some parts of Switzerland, especially Appenzell, Zurich, Aargau, and Vaud.[41]

[37] Gisiger, *Das Petitionsrecht in der Schweiz*, pp. 48–50; Kölz, *Neuere schweizerische Verfassungsgeschichte*, p. 336; Lerner, *A Laboratory of Liberty*, pp. 151–2; Herrmann, *12 septembre 1814*, pp. 66–8; Rolf Graber, *Demokratie und Revolten: Die Entstehung der direkten Demokratie in der Schweiz* (Zurich, Chronos, 2017), pp. 65–70, 181–3. Cf. SAB, A208, 'Bernische Handwerkerbittschriften 1816'.

[38] V. Jeanneret and J.-C. Rebetez, 'Les "consultations populaires" de 1814 sur le sort de la principauté', in J.-C. Rebetez and D. Bregnard (eds), *De la crosse à la croix: L'ancien Évêché de Bâle devient suisse (Congrès de Vienne – 1815)* (Neuchâtel, Éditions Alphil, 2018), pp. 169–96.

[39] I. Herrmann, 'Comment le "Centre du monde" peut-il devenir le dernier Canton?', in I. Herrmann (ed.), *Quand le monde a changé ... L'entrée de Genève dans la Confédération suisse* (Geneva, Georg, 2016), pp. 253–82 (p. 268).

[40] M. Schaffner, 'Direkte Demokratie: "Alles für das Volk – alles durch das Volk"', in M. Hettling, M. Schaffner, and M. König (eds), *Eine kleine Geschichte der Schweiz: Der Bundesstaat und seine Traditionen* (Frankfurt am Main, Suhrkamp, 1998), pp. 189–226 (pp. 212–21); A. Tanner, 'Radikalismus', in *HLS*, version of 29 January 2013, https://hls-dhs-dss.ch/de/articles/027156/2013-01-29/ (accessed 3 July 2019).

[41] Kölz, *Neuere schweizerische Verfassungsgeschichte*, pp. 210–11.

The liberal takeover in 11 of the 22 cantons, namely Ticino (1829), Thurgau, Aargau, Lucerne, Zurich, St Gall, Fribourg (1830), Vaud, Solothurn, Bern, and Schaffhausen (1831), affected two-thirds of the Swiss population. The first liberal Constitution, that of the Italian-speaking canton Ticino, voted by Parliament on 23 June 1830, contained the right to petition alongside other elements of representative democracy, such as a separation of powers and freedom of the press.[42] The general pattern of the liberal takeovers was more or less the same in all cantons and built on traditions of popular protest,[43] press coverage of the events, and a rich pamphlet literature diffused by liberal networks. Small groups of liberals, led by a few urban intellectuals and many progressive members of the rural elite – mostly lawyers, physicians, and the *nouveau riches* in industrialised regions – organised popular, outdoor 'people's assemblies' (*Volksversammlungen*), usually near small towns in the countryside rather than in the cantons' respective capitals.[44] In the case of the canton of Bern, the power of almost 600 petitions – 80 per cent of them written by communes and parishes – presented at the popular assembly near Münsingen, a village about 15 km outside Bern, urged the government to abdicate in 1831.[45] During these mostly peaceful assemblies,[46] the political programme – including the election of a representative convention to establish a new, liberal constitution containing fundamental political rights – was promoted in the form of mass petitions to be passed to the cantonal parliaments. The petitions had mostly been precirculated in printed pamphlets and newspapers and were discussed and signed during the assemblies. They included more popular social and economic demands such as maintaining corporate privileges in partial contradiction to liberal ideology. This points at social differences within the petition movement. Whereas the liberal elite of lawyers, physicians, or industrial entrepreneurs opted for the free market, artisans tried to preserve their corporatist privileges, and workers supported elements of the moral economy like just prices.[47]

Once again petitioning was a tool to legitimate a new regime. In seven cantons the liberal movement immediately installed a constituent or constitutive assembly

[42] Schaffner, 'Direkte Demokratie', pp. 193, 201–2; M. Marcacci and N. Valsangiacomo, 'Tessin', Chapter 4.1.2, in *HLS*, version of 30 May 2017, https://hls-dhs-dss.ch/de/articles/007394/2017-05-30/#HPolitischeGeschichteundVerfassungsentwicklung (accessed 3 July 2019).

[43] Würgler, *Unruhen und Öffentlichkeit*, pp. 295–301, 314–28; J. Eibach and M. Cottier, 'Popular Protest in Switzerland during the 1830s: Opposing Models of Political Participation and Citation of Traditional Ritual', *European Review of History*, 6 (2013), 1011–30; Graber, *Demokratie und Revolten*, pp. 71–3, 77–9.

[44] Listed in Kölz, *Neuere schweizerische Verfassungsgeschichte*, pp. 219–20; Schaffner, 'Direkte Demokratie', 193.

[45] Kölz, *Neuere schweizerische Verfassungsgeschichte*, pp. 459–64, 469–77, 503.

[46] Exceptions in ibid., pp. 220, 194–5; Schaffner, 'Direkte Demokratie', 194–5; and Graber, *Demokratie und Revolten*, p. 77.

[47] Kölz, *Neuere schweizerische Verfassungsgeschichte*, p. 306 (Bern); B. Weinmann, *Eine andere Bürgergesellschaft: Klassischer Republikanismus und Kommunalismus im Kanton Zürich im späten 18. und 19. Jahrhundert* (Göttingen, Vandenhoeck & Ruprecht, 1998), pp. 181–2, 208, 241–62; Graber, *Demokratie und Revolten*, pp. 73–90.

with liberal majorities, or charged the newly elected Parliament, as in Zurich and Thurgau, or the old council, as in Basel and Solothurn, with drafting the new constitution.[48] Even if these events violated the Confederal Contract of 1815, the confederal Diet – the assembly of the cantons' deputies – did not interfere, because it respected the cantons' sovereignty. Most of the constitutional assemblies, being aware that they had been appointed by a revolutionary movement rather than lawfully by general and fair elections, compensated for their lack of legitimacy by encouraging the people to file petitions with their proposals for the new constitution.[49]

All these new, liberal cantonal constitutions were inspired by petitions and then submitted to universal male suffrage (except in Fribourg). They were accepted by great majorities in the cantons of Zurich, Bern, Thurgau, Solothurn, Aargau, and Vaud; by just a small majority in Lucerne; and only after a second vote in Schaffhausen. In the canton of St Gall the constitution was accepted by 9,190 voters and rejected by 11,091. But as the Constitutional Assembly counted the 12,000 men who did not vote 'yes' (assuming that they were not against the new constitution), the constitution was introduced in St Gall as well. Placed in a European context, the Swiss revolutions in the 1830s were triggered by petitions, and were thus peaceful and successful, as well as in the vanguard of these trends. For example, although the French July Revolution of 1830 stimulated the Swiss regeneration movement, the latter had already started in the 1820s. The first liberal constitution was adopted by the regional assemblies in the canton of Ticino on 4 July 1830 – more than three weeks before the *trois glorieuses* of the Paris revolution. While the European powers were preoccupied with Paris and the other revolutionary hot spots, the Swiss were able to carry out their programme quickly: a constellation of factors that occurred in 1830/1 as well as in 1848.[50]

All liberal constitutions on the cantonal level guaranteed the right to petition. However, there were some important differences: whereas individual petitions were undisputed, some cantons prohibited collective political petitions (Zurich, Solothurn) while some allowed them explicitly (Aargau, Thurgau), and it was unclear whether petitioning by 'women and foreigners' was permitted.[51]

The instrument of petitioning, once guaranteed by the constitution, was also used by conservative movements, as was already the case during the Helvetic Republic. The example of Zurich is paradigmatic. In 1839, conservative forces profited from and encouraged the popular disapproval of the appointment of a new professor of theology at the University of Zurich, which had just been founded six years previously by the liberal government. The theologian David Friedrich Strauss (1808–74), from Germany, was known for his historical and critical approach to

[48] Kölz, *Neuere schweizerische Verfassungsgeschichte*, pp. 220, 305–7; Schaffner, 'Direkte Demokratie', 201–3.

[49] Kölz, *Neuere schweizerische Verfassungsgeschichte*, p. 221; Weinmann, *Eine andere Bürgergesellschaft*, pp. 180–3 (Zurich); Graber, *Demokratie und Revolten*, pp. 77–90 (St Gall and Basel-Landschaft).

[50] Schaffner, 'Direkte Demokratie', p. 192.

[51] Kölz, *Neuere schweizerische Verfassungsgeschichte*, p. 336.

the life of Jesus. The conservatives organised popular open-air assemblies with 10,000 participants and triggered a petitioning movement mingling the grievances of those discontented with the liberal, centralising, and plutocratic regime. This petition cocktail gathered more than 39,000 signatures. To compare, in 1831, the constitution was accepted with 40,503 to 1,721 votes. Even if we consider demographic growth, the figure remains impressive, as it represents about two-thirds of the canton's male adult population.[52] It is interesting to see that this movement, labelled conservative by the dominant liberal historiography because of its religious focus, had clearly democratic political goals: it asked for direct elections, limited terms of office, and an optional popular *Referendum* against parliamentary legislation (called *Veto* in the sources). These goals were opposing elitist liberal politics with democratic arguments. So, in Switzerland, conservatism could also be democratic and republican, and was not necessarily reactionary and monarchical as elsewhere in Europe.[53] Needless to say, the conservatives proposed – in this case – to legalise collective political petitioning, which had been prohibited by the Zurich constitution of 1831: a restriction they had openly disregarded.[54] In September 1839, about 4,000 armed men from the countryside entered the city. After some short skirmishes between the rebels and the military forces, the liberal government resigned. This event became famous as the 'Zurich Putsch'.[55] One week later, new parliamentary elections resulted in a massive triumph for the conservatives, with the consequence that the new government was able to enforce its ecclesiastical politics.[56] But by 1844 the liberals were winning the elections and they remained in power until the 1860s.

In the 1860s, the new democratic movement, led by the rural elites, organised petitioning campaigns and mass assemblies against the allegedly corrupt liberal government. This democratic movement of the 1860s was a particularly Swiss phenomenon without any European parallel.[57] As in Zurich in 1869, it made use of

[52] Lerner, *A Laboratory of Liberty*, p. 233; Graber, *Demokratie und Revolten*, p. 94–101. In 1850, population of the canton of Zurich was 250,000. If we assume about 125,000 males of whom about 60,000 were adults, we may say that 40,000 signatures represent roughly two-thirds of the adult male population; Mario König, 'Zürich (Kanton)', Chapter 5.1, in *HLS*, version of 24 August 2017, https://hls-dhs-dss.ch/de/articles/007381/2017-08-24/#HBevF6lkerungundSiedlung-1 (accessed 26 May 2020).

[53] A. Würgler, 'Eidgenossenschaft', in *HLS*, version of 8 February 2012, https://hls-dhs-dss.ch/de/articles/026413/2012-02-08/ (accessed 26 May 2020); Kölz, *Neuere schweizerische Verfassungsgeschichte*, pp. 409–49.

[54] Weinmann, *Eine andere Bürgergesellschaft*, pp. 269–76; Graber, *Demokratie und Revolten*, pp. 91–117.

[55] Weinmann, *Eine andere Bürgergesellschaft*, pp. 154, 274–80.

[56] Kölz, *Neuere schweizerische Verfassungsgeschichte*, p. 412. For the use of petitioning by conservative movements, see M. Janse, '"What Value Should We Attach to All These Petitions?": Petition Campaigns and the Problem of Legitimacy in the Nineteenth-Century Netherlands', *Social Science History*, 43 (2019), 509–30 (pp. 509, 526–7).

[57] P. Hersche, 'Demokratische Bewegungen in der Schweiz', *Aufklärung – Vormärz – Revolution*, 1 (1981), 37–45; Schaffner, 'Direkte Demokratie', pp. 222–3. For Zurich, see M. Illi, 'Zürich', Chapters 4.1.2 and 4.1.3, in *HLS*, version of 24 August 2017, https://hls-dhs-dss.ch/de/articles/007381/2017-08-24/#HVerfassungsentwicklungundpolitischeGeschichteseit1798 (3 July 2019).

the right to petition in order to change the constitutions in some other cantons as well by introducing the *Referendum*, the people's right to initiate a vote about a new law passed by Parliament and possibly reject the law by vote. The democrats also demanded salaries for MPs (allowing 'poorer' people to be elected) and they introduced the right of *Initiative* to enable popular votes on some newly proposed articles or even the whole constitution. *Referendum* and *Initiative* had to be signed by a certain quorum of citizens. Actually, it was a similar procedure to those used for collective mass petitions, but henceforth these practices became institutionalised as legal, constitutional instruments of direct democracy in some cantons and, from 1874 and 1891 respectively, also at the federal (or national) level. As a result, the respective governments had to organise a general vote on an issue as soon as the signatures were handed in; they could not just put aside the requests.[58] In this sense, the democratic movement, by introducing the *Referendum* and the *Initiative*, put an end to the important function of collective political petitioning in shaping politics and constitutions during the old regime and the period from 1798 to 1874/91. Petitioning, however, did not disappear, but it had become the instrument of relatively small or powerless groups. Women, for example, remained dependent on petitioning, although they had raised the criticism in 1868 that 'It would be sad and shameful if each of the men of the people only claimed the fullest freedom for themselves, but not for others and least of all for us women.'[59] But Swiss men did not grant women the right to sign for *Referendum* or *Initiative* or to vote until 1971. More important and powerful political actors preferred to invest their energy and their resources into *Referendum* and *Initiative* rather than petitioning campaigns.

In the end, petitioning in Switzerland underwent similar transitions to other European countries – from corporate and specific grievances to individually signed mass petitions on general issues.[60] What was perhaps different was the way that petitions successfully transformed constitutions on the cantonal and national levels and subsequently mutated into powerful constitutional instruments of direct democracy.

Conclusion

Studying petitioning in 18th- and 19th-century Switzerland reveals a picture of both continuity and significant change. Petitioning continued to be a device through which anyone could raise any topic by writing to the authorities, although the share

[58] Kölz, *Neuere schweizerische Verfassungsgeschichte*; W. Linder, *Schweizerische Demokratie: Institutionen – Prozesse – Perspektiven* (Bern, Stuttgart, and Vienna, Paul Haupt, 1999), p. 235; M. Bürgi, 'Demokratische Bewegung', in *HLS*, version of 30 June 2014, https://hls-dhs-dss.ch/de/articles/017382/2014-06-30/ (accessed 3 July 2019). Some success also in Lucerne, 1863; Bern, 1869; and Aargau 1870; see Weinmann, *Eine andere Bürgergesellschaft*, pp. 303–29; and Graber, *Demokratie und Revolten*, pp. 135–73.

[59] Anonymous petition of 'several women', Zurich, 25 May 1868, quoted in Graber, *Demokratie und Revolten*, pp. 141–2.

[60] For Europe, see Miller, 'Introduction', p. 417.

of female petitioners remained much greater in everyday individual than in collective political petitions.[61] Even if the right to petition was only constitutionally granted on the national level from 1798 to 1803 and again after 1848 (although in some cantons the right was entrenched from the 1830s), the everyday practice of filing individual petitions was little changed under the Swiss Confederacy before 1798, as well as during the restorative periods (1803 to 1830). Furthermore, as much as all these consecutive political systems were different they were all republics and were not superseded by the emergence of new forms of authority, as in the installation of a parliament in Denmark (1848) or the inauguration of a monarch in the Netherlands (1806/15).[62]

But petitioning in Switzerland also changed significantly in several respects, especially in terms of the shifting constitutional framework that defined the context for petitioning. The changes affected not only the requests' rhetoric and style, but especially the status of political collective petitions. They were in principle prohibited in most early modern contexts as well as during the restoration periods, but they became legal in 1798 for a time, and again in most of the regenerated cantons following 1830, as well as by the federal constitution of 1848. Collective political petitioning became a crucial, if suspected, instrument of political debate and change in the context of 18th-century revolts and helped to shape the second Helvetic Constitution (1802) as well as the liberal (Regeneration, 1830–1), radical (1845–6), conservative (1839–41), and democratic (1861–9) transformations in many cantons. One of the key elements to explain this remarkable success of petitioning movements in Switzerland is the absence of a professional standing army. Because of the militia system, petitioners were soldiers and soldiers were petitioners. Thus, the ruling government had little physical power to use against citizens.

Other important changes in collective petitioning concerned the petitioners' social structure and the communicative context. Whereas collective petitions under the old regime were mostly filed by corporations or communes (parishes) who were by definition local and thus limited in the number of their members, the petitioners after the end of the 18th century, and especially during the Helvetic Republic and the Regeneration period, were organised differently. Thanks to elite networks, pamphlet campaigns, and press coverage, petitioning became better linked to more and more areas. During the *ancien régime*, collective petitions in general voiced corporate communal interests; during the 19th century petitioning campaigns increasingly united individuals who lived in different villages and towns through shared common interests, and were sometimes organised in ideologically focused associations or clubs.[63]

[61] Würgler, 'Grenzen des Zumutbaren?', p. 20.

[62] See the chapter by Janse et al. in this volume.

[63] A. Würgler, 'Factions and Parties in Early Modern Swiss Conflicts', in M. Caesar (ed.), *Factional Struggles: Divided Elites in European Cities and Courts (1400–1750)* (Leiden and Boston, MA, Brill, 2017), pp. 196–215.

In Swiss historiography, petitioning is not as prominent a topic as in Britain – perhaps because national state-building in Switzerland in 1848 was managed by negotiations between states (liberal versus conservative cantons) after the Civil War of 1847,[64] rather than by social movements' petition campaigns from below versus the central state (which did not really exist before 1848). Therefore, the national Swiss master narrative – which changed towards the end of the 19th century from celebrating 'Swiss liberty' to praising 'Swiss democracy' – was obviously focused on the 'heroes' of *Referendum* and *Initiative* rather than on petitioning – although these two instruments of direct democracy had been triggered by petitions.[65]

Transformations in petitioning during the past 3,000 years in Europe and Asia have been generalised by the dichotomous model of the premodern 'petition-and-response' model in the form of deferential individual (private) petitions and 'modern petitioning' referring to defiant collective political (public) mass petitions signed by individuals. In this view, expressed by David Zaret, among others, the 18th century serves as the crucial period of transition called 'liminal petitioning'. Zaret has argued that the premodern model is one where petitioning was primarily an 'instrument of state', because it occurs in virtually all states in Eurasia since we have written records. By contrast, modern petitioning is closely associated with insurgent social movements.[66] But even if there was such a shift in general, examples of 'premodern' humble petitioning can be found in the 19th and 20th centuries, while defiant examples of petitioners, mostly linked to revolts, can be found in the 18th century and earlier, such as the Swiss Peasants' War of 1653, the English Revolution of the 1640s, the Frankfurt urban revolt between 1612 and 1616, or the German Peasants' War of 1525.[67] Many early modern petitions were delivered through symbolic actions transforming the simple administrative act of handing in a letter into a public demonstration of power. And obviously, (oral) petitioning is not only older than 'the state', but coexisted with written petitioning even in modern bureaucracy.[68] In short, petitions as media are used by all kinds of actors: collective

[64] J. Remak, *A Very Civil War: The Swiss Sonderbund War of 1847* (Boulder, CO, Westview Press, 1993); Schaffner, 'Direkte Demokratie', pp. 210–12.

[65] I. Herrmann, 'Woe of Tale? The Emergence, Vicissitudes, and (Over-) Efficiency of the Swiss Narrative of Democracy', *Journal of Modern European History*, 2 (2019), 135–46. For Britain, see H. Miller, *A Nation of Petitioners: Petitions and Petitioning in the United Kingdom, 1780–1918* (Cambridge, Cambridge University Press, 2023).

[66] Zaret, 'Petition-and-Response', p. 433.

[67] Würgler, *Unruhen und Öffentlichkeit* (for urban and rural revolts in German-speaking 18th-century Europe); A. Würgler, 'Rebellion or Revolution? European Newspapers Reporting the Swiss Peasants' War 1653', in B. Dooley and P. Molino (eds), *Years of News* (Turnhout, Brepols, forthcoming); D. Zaret, 'Petitions and the "Invention" of Public Opinion in the English Revolution', *American Journal of Sociology*, 101 (1996) 1497–555; A. Würgler, 'Revolts in Print: Media and Communication in Early Modern Urban Conflicts', in R. Schlögl (ed.), *Urban Elections and Decision-Making in Early Modern Europe, 1500–1800* (Newcastle, Cambridge Scholars, 2009), pp. 257–75 (for Frankfurt am Main, 1612–16); P. Blickle, *The Revolution of 1525: The German Peasants' War from a New Perspective* (Baltimore and London, Johns Hopkins University Press, 1981 [German original 1975]).

[68] Würgler, 'Voices', pp. 16–17, 32–4.

political petitioning in Switzerland has been, in general, a weapon of the underprivileged and mostly rural elites – with the support of many ordinary people – against the privileged and mostly urban governing elites.[69] According to the changing historical contexts, collective petitioning was successfully used by subjects against lords and by rebel movements against aristocratic governments before 1798, by revolutionaries against traditional forces in 1798, by federalists against Unitarians and vice versa from 1798 to 1803, by state authorities against foreign powers in 1814, by liberals against conservatives from 1803 to 1831, by conservatives against liberals from 1839 to 1841, and by democrats against liberals from 1861 to 1869. What is called petitioning today remains, however, a tool of individual and even collective political activity, but its importance has become relatively weak in Switzerland since the introduction of *Referendum* and *Initiative*. Because, by these two procedures, petitioners can not only ask the authorities for a favour, but lawfully impose a general vote about their proposal – be it the rejection of a law (*Referendum*) or the addition of a new article to the constitution (*Initiative*) – these are constitutional instruments of power. They are, however, limited to citizens. But as, during the 19th century, citizenship and political rights at the communal, cantonal, and federal level were tied to several restricting criteria such as the Christian religion (until 1866), sex (exclusively male until 1959/71), age (a minimum age of 25, 21, and 20 years respectively), the amount of tax paid (census until 1915), permanent residence in the same commune, and service in the militia (five years at least), there were, even apart from immigrating foreigners, still many people who had no other legal means to voice their interests than by petitioning.[70]

Acknowledgements

I would very much like to thank my colleague Irène Herrmann in Geneva for helpful comments, as well as Henry Miller, Joris Oddens, and Brodie Waddell for remarks and linguistic support.

[69] Würgler, *Unruhen und Öffentlichkeit*, pp. 270–5, 314–28; A. Würgler, 'Vormoderne Revolten und moderne Demokratie? Protestbewegungen im Ancien Régime und liberale Prinzipien im 19. Jahrhundert', in R. Roca and A. Auer (eds), *Wege zur direkten Demokratie in den schweizerischen Kantonen* (Zurich, Basel, and Genf, Schulthess, 2011), pp. 107–21; Graber, *Demokratie und Revolten*, pp. 181–9.

[70] A. Tanner, *Arbeitsame Patrioten – wohlanständige Damen: Bürgertum und Bürgerlichkeit in der Schweiz 1830–1914* (Zurich, Orell Füssli Verlag, 1995), pp. 587–622; Graber, *Demokratie und Revolten*, pp. 197–202; T. Poledna, 'Stimm- und Wahlrecht', in *HLS*, version of 2 December 2022, https://hls-dhs-dss.ch/de/articles/026453/2014-08-06/#HVonderHelvetikbiszurRegeneration (accessed 16 January 2023).

10

The Evolution of Petitioning in Europe and North America, 1850–2000

RICHARD HUZZEY AND HENRY MILLER

BY THE 20TH century petitioning was a ubiquitous practice in many polities across North America and Europe, but that very ubiquity has ensured its invisibility to many scholars at the time and since. Petitions and petitioning are certainly mentioned in passing in many studies of politics, institutions, political movements, and political culture, whether by historians or social scientists. However, petitioning as a phenomenon has not received sustained, detailed treatment comparable to earlier periods. Gabriel Almond and Sidney Verba's classic 1963 study of political culture in Mexico, the USA, Italy, West Germany, and the UK mentioned petitions just a handful of times. And yet, in a passage discussing how citizens cooperate informally with each other, it is striking that quotations from a Mexican housewife, an American salesman, and an English gardener list petitions as the first thing they would do if they had a concern.[1] This example provides a tantalising glimpse of mid-20th-century citizens' awareness of petitioning, and is suggestive of its use as an everyday political practice. More typical of scholarly treatment of petitioning was an 1955 article that remained the standard work on petitions in modern Britain until recently, which began by asking 'is petitioning a sufficiently important phenomenon to merit attention from students of politics?'.[2] Social scientists have sometimes treated political participation as a synonym for voter turnout, marginalising non-electoral forms of participation such as petitioning.[3] To give another example, petitioning was

[1] G. Almond and S. Verba, *The Civic Culture: Political Attitudes and Democracy in Five Nations* (Princeton, NJ, Princeton University Press, 1963), p. 152.

[2] C. Leys, 'Petitioning in the Nineteenth and Twentieth Centuries', *Political Studies*, 3 (1955), 45–64 (p. 45).

[3] M. Rolfe, *Voter Turnout: A Social Theory of Political Participation* (Cambridge, Cambridge University Press, 2012); A. Gallego, *Unequal Political Participation Worldwide* (Cambridge, Cambridge University Press, 2015).

Proceedings of the British Academy, **262**, 194–215, © The British Academy 2024.

conspicuous by its absence in a historical survey of political participation in postwar Europe.[4]

The perception that petitioning was a widespread activity within political culture implied by Almond and Verba's study is confirmed by studying late-20th-century surveys of political participation across democracies (Table 10.1). Although

Table 10.1 Percentage of respondents who had signed or would sign a petition from selected countries, 1981–1999

Country	Year	Have signed petition	Might sign	Would never sign	Source
Australia	1981	68.60	24.90	5.10	WVS
	1995	78.00	16.10	5.40	WVS
Canada	1981	60.60	25.60	11.20	WVS
	1990	75.90	14.70	8.20	WVS
	2000	72.70	18.50	8.00	WVS
Finland	1981	29.00	40.00	28.40	WVS
	1990	40.70	45.50	13.80	EVS
	1999	49.60	36.80	13.60	EVS
France	1981	44.60	31.50	23.90	EVS
	1990	53.70	29.00	17.30	EVS
	1999	68.30	22.40	9.30	EVS
West Germany	1981	45.70	36.80	17.50	EVS
Germany	1990	58.80	30.30	11.00	EVS
	1999	50.60	35.20	14.20	EVS
Great Britain	1981	63.20	27.00	9.80	EVS
	1990	75.40	16.90	7.70	EVS
	1999	79.30	15.10	5.50	EVS
Ireland	1981	28.90	46.80	24.30	EVS
	1990	42.00	39.80	18.20	EVS
	1999	58.60	26.70	14.70	EVS
Italy	1981	40.90	32.00	27.10	EVS
	1990	46.40	34.60	18.90	EVS
	1999	54.60	30.40	15.00	EVS

(*Continued*)

[4] B. Davis, 'What's Left? Popular Political Participation in Postwar Europe', *American Historical Review*, 113 (2008), 363–90.

Table 10.1 (*Continued*)

Country	Year	Have signed petition	Might sign	Would never sign	Source
Japan	1981	42.40	28.50	13.40	WVS
	1990	52.00	21.40	11.20	WVS
	1999	56.80	26.60	6.50	WVS
New Zealand	1998	88.10	7.70	1.50	WVS
Norway	1981	54.60	26.90	18.60	EVS
	1990	61.10	27.80	11.10	EVS
	1996	64.50	25.90	9.30	WVS
Spain	1981	23.70	43.90	32.40	EVS
	1990	22.00	39.80	38.20	EVS
	1999	28.60	38.70	32.70	EVS
Sweden	1981	54.20	37.40	8.50	EVS
	1990	71.70	23.80	4.50	EVS
	1999	87.40	10.20	2.50	EVS
Switzerland	1989	61.20	16.30	19.30	WVS
	1996	62.30	17.40	18.30	WVS
USA	1982	65.50	20.90	10.00	WVS
	1989	69.60	19.20	8.20	WVS
	1999	80.70	15.80	3.00	WVS

Sources: World Values Survey (WVS); European Values Survey (EVS). R. Inglehart, C. Haerpfer, A. Moreno et al. (eds), *World Values Survey. All Rounds: Country-Pooled Datafile Version* (Madrid, JD Systems Institute, 2014).

the surveys only provide snapshots, they indicate that a large percentage of respondents, in many cases a majority, had signed petitions. For example, the data suggest that 60 per cent of Canadians in the early 1980s had signed petitions, and this probably increased, with growing numbers sent to the House of Commons from the middle of the decade.[5] The proportion of signers was particularly marked in English-speaking countries and Scandinavia. An increasing percentage signed petitions in other countries, such as Japan, France, Italy, and Ireland.[6] It might be

[5] R. Marleau and C. Montpetit (eds), *House of Commons Procedure and Practice* (2000), Chapter 22, Table 22.1, www.ourcommons.ca/MarleauMontpetit/DocumentViewer.aspx?DocId=1001&Sec=Ch22&Seq=1&Language=E (accessed 18 November 2020).

[6] For the increase in Italy, see also M. Quaranta, 'The Rise of Unconventional Political Participation in Italy: Measurement Equivalence and Trends, 1976–2009', *Bulletin of Italian Politics*, 4 (2012), 251–76 (pp. 261–2).

tempting to interpret such data as evidence of a late-20th-century emergence of critical citizens, as argued by some politics scholars.[7] However, given the absence of comparable surveys before the 1970s, such a view would be mistaken. This chapter will reveal a longer history of petitioning by drawing on evidence of its ubiquity and explaining why this has largely gone unnoticed by scholars. In doing so, it provides a missing chapter in the long history of petitioning; charts the adaptation of petitioning traditions in mass democracies in North America and Europe, as well as international and global developments; and suggests how the study of petitions offers new perspectives on modern political culture.

A growing body of scholarship has emphasised the late 18th and early 19th century as the critical period for the emergence of collective, mass petitioning on public issues on an unprecedented scale, directed at representative institutions, linked to ideas of popular sovereignty, and grounded in the constitutional right to petition.[8] This shift was registered by the coining of terms derived from the English word 'petition' to differentiate this new form of petitioning from older traditions of supplication.[9] The key period for this shift in western Europe and North America was the Atlantic 'age of revolutions' (c. 1789–1848). Yet the later experiences of early Meiji Japan, the late Ottoman empire, and tsarist Russia confirm a wider association between the emergence of the new type of petitioning and the establishment of representative institutions.[10]

[7] P. Norris (ed.), *Critical Citizens: Global Support for Democratic Government* (Oxford, Oxford University Press, 1999).

[8] D. Carpenter, *The Democracy of Petitions: Popular Politics in Transformation, 1790–1870* (Cambridge, MA, Harvard University Press, 2021); H. Miller, *A Nation of Petitioners: Petitions and Petitioning in the United Kingdom, 1780–1918* (Cambridge, Cambridge University Press, 2023); H. Miller, 'Introduction: The Transformation of Petitioning in the Long Nineteenth Century (1780–1914)', *Social Science History*, 43 (2019), 409–29; D. Palacios Cerezales, 'Embodying Public Opinion: From Petitions to Mass Meetings in Nineteenth-Century Portugal', *E-Journal of Portuguese History*, 9 (2011), 1–19, D. Palacios Cerezales, 'Re-Imagining Petitioning in Spain (1808–1823)', *Social Science History*, 43 (2019), 487–508; J. Oddens, '"The Greatest Right of Them All": The Debate on the Right to Petition from the Dutch Republic to the Kingdom (c. 1750–1830)', *European History Quarterly*, 47 (2017), 634–56; C. Wilton, *Popular Politics and Political Culture in Upper Canada, 1800–1850* (Montreal, McGill-Queen's University Press, 2000); D. Carpenter and D. Brossard, '*L'éruption patriote*: The Revolt against Dalhousie and the Petitioning Explosion in Nineteenth-Century French Canada', *Social Science History*, 43 (2019), 453–86; B. Agnès, *L'appel au pouvoir: Les pétitions aux parlements en France et au Royaume-Uni (1814–1848)* (Rennes, Presses universitaires de Rennes, 2018); C. Lipp and L. Krempel, 'Petitions and the Social Context of Political Mobilization in the Revolution of 1848/49: A Microhistorical Actor-Centred Network Analysis', in L. Heerma van Voss (ed.), *Petitions in Social History*, Supplement 9 of *International Review of Social History*, 46 (2001), 151–69; J. Oddens, *Op veler verzoek: Inclusieve politiek in Nederland (1780–1860)* (Amsterdam, Boom, 2023); J. Harvard, 'En helig allmännelig opinion: Föreställningar om offentlighet och legitimitet i svensk riksdagsdebatt 1848–1919', PhD thesis (Umeå, 2006), pp. 105–6, 237. We are grateful to Jonas Harvard for sharing his thesis with us.

[9] See Oddens, chapter in this volume.

[10] K. H. Kim, *The Age of Visions and Arguments: Parliamentarianism and the National Public Sphere in Early Meiji Japan* (Cambridge, MA, Harvard University Press, 2007); Y. Ben-Bassat, 'The Ottoman Institution of Petitioning when the Sultan No Longer Reigned: A View from Post-1908 Ottoman Palestine', *New Perspectives on Turkey*, 56 (2017), 87–101; A. Verner, 'Discursive Strategies in the 1905 Revolution: Peasant Petitions from Vladimir Province', *Russian Review*, 54 (1995), 65–90 (pp. 66, 68, 73).

However, from the late 19th and early 20th century, in many representative polities, there was a shift away from national parliaments as the primary loci for the reception of petitions. As we will show in the first part of our chapter, petitioning remained a widespread, popular political activity in many nation states, even authoritarian ones, but it increasingly operated outside legislative petition systems. Petitioning was thus ubiquitous but also often unrecorded, which goes a long way to explaining its neglect. Reinforcing these trends was the establishment of international institutions that offered new arenas for petitioners, and the growth of petitioning aimed at mobilising global public opinion and civil society, both of which are explored in the second part of this chapter. Finally, the chapter reflects on the implications of rediscovering petitioning for the study of 20th-century history and politics.

Petitioning within the Nation State

From the late 19th century, petitioners in many countries decentred national parliaments as the primary recipients for their petitions. This altered the place of petitioning in many political cultures, reflecting changes in state and society, but obscured the continuing use of subscriptional appeals in alternative settings. To put it another way, petitioning did not decline but was displaced, and still remained widespread, if diluted, among a broader range of participatory activities.

Many countries formally recorded a decline in the number of petitions to legislatures. In the UK, the numbers of petitions to the House of Commons collapsed during the First World War and thereafter never recovered to their previous peaks; indeed, the Select Committee on Public Petitions was abolished in 1974.[11] There was a similar decline of petitions to the US Congress and the French National Assembly during the first half of the 20th century.[12] It might be tempting to conclude that such trends reflected the replacement of petitioning by elections under an extended franchise, or by the growth of the mass-media- and opinion-polling that provided more modern technologies for the construction of public opinion.[13] Yet

[11] R. Huzzey and H. Miller, 'Petitions, Parliament and Political Culture: Petitioning the House of Commons, 1780–1918', *Past & Present*, 248 (2020), 123–64 (p. 139); D. Judge, 'Public Petitions and the House of Commons', *Parliamentary Affairs*, 31 (1978), 391–405.

[12] M. McKinley, 'Petitioning and the Making of the Administrative State', *Yale Law Journal*, 127 (2018), 1538–637 (p. 1572); J.-G. Contamin, 'Contribution à une sociologie des usages pluriels des formes de mobilisation: L'exemple de la pétition en France', PhD thesis (Université Paris 1, 2001), pp. 13–14; M. Illaire and R. Salmon, 'Les pétitions aux assemblées de la Révolution à 1958: Constitution des sources et méthodologie d'approche', *La revue adminstrative* (2008), special issue, *L'individu face au pouvoir: Les pétitions aux assemblées parlementaires*, 9–32 (p. 17). We are grateful to Jean-Gabriel Contamin for the reference to his PhD thesis.

[13] R. J. Krotoszynski Jr, *Reclaiming the Petition Clause: Seditious Libel, 'Offensive Protest', and the Right to Petition Government for a Redress of Grievances* (New Haven, CT, Yale University Press, 2012), p. 103; S. Igo, *The Averaged American: Surveys, Citizens, and the Making of a Mass Public* (Cambridge, MA, Harvard University Press, 2007); J. Thompson, *British Political Culture and the Idea of 'Public Opinion', 1867–1914* (Cambridge, Cambridge University Press, 2013).

when studied in detail a more complicated picture emerges than that implied by a decline-and-fall narrative.

The apparent waning of petitions was partly a product of procedural changes that obscured the number sent to legislatures or legislators. From the mid-19th century, the clerk's office of the lower house of the Dutch Parliament counted petitions with standardised texts as one rather than multiple petitions, thus undercounting the total numbers received.[14] In Restoration Spain (1874–1923) there was a shift away from petitions that were formally registered to *exposiciones*, which were petitions and addresses that were not formally recorded, even if they continued to be circulated and cited in legislative debates and committees.[15] At the same time, innovative methods for petitioning individual legislators, often using novel communications technologies, escaped the formal systems for recording petitions. In the UK, from the final decades of the 19th century, individual MPs received petitions addressed to them, often called memorials, and campaigners sometimes sent petition postcards or telegrams; these were never formally presented or recorded as part of parliamentary business.[16] The adoption of postcards for petitioning campaigns was also evident in the USA, where, for example, the dairy industry distributed preprinted cards for citizens to demand regulatory changes from their representatives in the 1880s.[17] In these ways, legislative petitioning might evade record-keeping systems and overstate absolute decline.

However, the expansion and reconfiguration of state bureaucracies did redirect petitioning away from legislatures and to the executive in many specific cases. Maggie Blackhawk has shown how the growth of the US government and new administrative agencies made them the focus of certain types of petitions previously directed to Congress.[18] In the UK there was a similar transfer of specific types of petitions (such as those regarding naturalisation, divorce, or elections) to specialised judicial or executive processes. More generally, the transfer of powers to local government and self-governing colonies meant that petitions on certain policy areas were no longer the responsibility of Parliament.[19] In France and the UK, petitioners increasingly aimed their petitions at the executive rather

[14] J. Talsma, *Vijf historische en rechtshistorische studies over het recht van petitie: Verzoekschriften aan de Tweede Kamer en het ombudsmanvraagstuk. Nederland, 1795–1983* (Arnhem, Gouda Quint, 1989), pp. 303–6. We are indebted to Joris Oddens for this reference.

[15] We are grateful to Diego Palacios Cerezales for this point.

[16] Miller, *A Nation of Petitioners*, pp. 259, 261.

[17] 'Postcard Petitions to Label Oleomargarine Sent to W. E. Fuller from Citizens from Iowa, 1886', Petitions and Memorials, Resolutions of State Legislatures, and Related Documents which Were Referred to the Committee on Ways and Means during the 49th Congress, 1885–1887, US National Archives, https://catalog.archives.gov/id/5716618 (accessed 26 November 2020).

[18] M. McKinley, 'Petitioning', pp. 1548–9, 1574–1600.

[19] R. Huzzey and H. Miller, 'The Politics of Petitioning: Parliament, Government and Subscriptional Cultures in the United Kingdom, 1780–1918', *History*, 106 (2021), 221–43 (pp. 227, 238–40); R. Huzzey and H. Miller, 'Colonial Petitions, Colonial Petitioners, and the Imperial Parliament, c. 1780–1918', *Journal of British Studies*, 61 (2022), 261–89 (pp. 268–9).

than the legislature.[20] In the USA, too, some petitioners only addressed Congress alongside the president. [21]

The place of petitioning within political culture was reshaped by the growth of alternative forms of participation that themselves grew out of existing cultures of subscription. Scholars of politics have become increasingly interested in referendums as part of a wider interest in direct democracy.[22] Yet as historical studies of the USA and Switzerland have made clear, the emergence of referendums and initiatives in the early 20th century and late 19th century respectively developed from petitioning.[23] To give another example, in the Republic of Ireland, the constitutions of 1922 and 1937 institutionalised petitions as a mechanism for triggering referendums.[24] In 1990s Austria, both the women's movement and Jörg Haider's anti-immigration campaign garnered thousands of signatures for *Volksbegehren* to draw attention to issues they felt legislators had ignored.[25] Even in the UK, where there is a long-running debate about whether referendums are compatible with parliamentary traditions, an older generation of scholars noted the genealogical connection between referendums and 19th-century mass petitioning.[26]

Petitioning was partially displaced by the growth of mass letter writing to political leaders as well as to elected representatives and countless other sources of authority.[27]

[20] Huzzey and Miller, 'Petitions, Parliament and Political Culture', pp. 123–64 (pp. 161–2); H. Miller, 'The British Women's Suffrage Movement and the Practice of Petitioning, 1890–1914', *Historical Journal*, 64 (2021), 332–56 (p. 341, 352–3); Contamin, 'Contribution', pp. 13–14.

[21] 'Petition to the Senate from the National Businessmen's League', Petitions and Memorials, 1817–2000, US Senate Committee on Foreign Relations, US National Archives, https://catalog.archives.gov/id/595414 (accessed 30 March 2021).

[22] D. Altman, *Citizenship and Contemporary Direct Democracy* (Cambridge, Cambridge University Press, 2019); M. Qvortrup, *Government by Referendum* (Manchester, Manchester University Press, 2018); M. Qvortrup (ed.), *Referendums around the World: The Continued Growth of Direct Democracy* (Basingstoke, Palgrave, 2014); D. Butler and A. Ranney (eds), *Referendums around the World: The Growing Use of Direct Democracy* (Washington, DC, AEI Press, 1994); L. Atkinson, A. Blick, and M. Qvortrup, *The Referendum in Britain: A History* (Oxford, Oxford University Press, 2020).

[23] Krotoszynski, *Reclaiming the Petition Clause*, pp. 128–33; Würgler, chapter in this volume.

[24] R. Sinnott, 'Cleavages, Parties, and Referendums: Relationships between Representative and Direct Democracy in the Republic of Ireland', *European Journal of Political Research*, 41 (2002), 811–26.

[25] E. M. Appelt, 'Women in the Austrian Economy', in G. Bischof, A. Pelinka, and E. Thurner (eds), *Women in Austria* (New Brunswick, NJ, Transaction, 1998), pp. 83–103 (p. 95); T. Fillitz, 'Neo-Nationalism, the Freedom Party and Jörg Haider', in A. Gingrich and M. Banks (eds), *Neo-Nationalism in Europe and Beyond* (New York, Berghahn, 2006), pp. 139–61 (pp. 144–5); A. Holmes Cooper, 'Party-Sponsored Protest and the Movement Society: The CDU/CSU Mobilises against Citizenship Law Reform', *German Politics*, 11 (2002), 88–104 (p. 91).

[26] R. J. Williams and J. R. Greenaway, 'The Referendum in British Politics: A Dissenting View', *Parliamentary Affairs*, 28 (1975), 250–60 (p. 253).

[27] L. A. Sussman, *Dear FDR: A Study of Political Letter-Writing* (New York, Bedminster Press, 1963); H. Kaal and V. van de Griend, 'Postwar Popular Politics: Integrating the Voice of the People in Post-War Political History', in H. Kaal and D. Slootjes (eds), *New Perspectives on Power and Political Representation from Ancient History to the Present Day* (Leiden, Brill, 2019), pp. 124–43 (pp. 132–8); M. Fenske, *Demokratie erschreiben: Bürgerbriefe und Petitionen als Medien politischer Kultur, 1950–1974* (Frankfurt am Main, Campus Verlag, 2013); S. Hazareesingh, *In the Shadow of the General: Modern France and the Myth of De Gaulle* (Oxford, Oxford University Press, 2012), p. 8.

Scholars suggest that, adjusting for literacy and population growth, American presidents from the 1930s to the 1950s received letters at more than twice the rate of their predecessors; in subsequent decades, major crises led to further surges in correspondence.[28] According to one study, British MPs received 10,000 letters a week in 1964; this had risen to 40,000 by 1997.[29] Universal literacy meant that 'writing upwards', as Martin Lyons has called it, became an accessible form of political expression for citizens, who now had less need for scribes or brokers.[30] In some cases, mass letter writing – the coordinated direction of individual missives – was a partial mutation of petitioning, given that campaigns could circulate suitable prayers and specify a time for maximum impact on the target. In other cases, group letter-signing, the collective subscription as senders of a single letter, merely adopted an epistolary form to fulfil the collective representative function of mass petitioning. Whether these were classified as correspondence or a 'petition' or any other term is largely a matter of bureaucratic or archival caprice.[31]

While the trends just outlined reshaped the context for petitioning from the late 19th century, it remained ubiquitous as part of a broadening array of campaigning tactics. The emergence of new social movements in North American and Europe in the second half of the 20th century is often studied in terms of expanding or novel repertoires of protest and direct action. The use of petitioning has often been appreciated only in the context of 19th-century origins, or misidentified as a 'conventional' alternative to more dramatic 'extrainstitutional actions'.[32] Despite its conceptualisation as a low-risk means of protest within democratic societies, historic disenfranchisement and active intimidation could make petitioning

[28] L. Sussman, 'Mass Political Writing in America: The Growth of an Institution', *Public Opinion Quarterly*, 23 (1959), 203–12; B. Rottinghaus, 'What Predicts Trends in the White House Mail? The Macro Causes of Mass Political Writing to the Chief Executive', *American Political Research*, 40 (2012), 205–31.

[29] O. Gay, 'MPs Go Back to Their Constituencies', *Political Quarterly*, 76 (2005), 57–66 (p. 58).

[30] M. Lyons, 'Writing Upwards: How the Weak Wrote to the Powerful', *Social History*, 49 (2015), 317–30.

[31] 'Petition from Baltimore City to Senator Millard Tydings Opposing Stock Exchange Regulation', 29 March 1934, SEN 73A-J8, US National Archives, https://catalog.archives.gov/id/5557817 (accessed 23 February 2021); M. Jolly, '"We are the Web": Letter Writing and the 1980s Women's Peace Movement', in C. A. Huff (ed.), *Women's Life Writing and Imagined Communities* (Abingdon, Routledge, 2005), pp. 196–218; L. Heerten, *The Biafran War and Postcolonial Humanitarianism: Spectacles of Suffering* (Cambridge, Cambridge University Press, 2017), pp. 130, 135, 221; D. G. Loconto, *Social Movements and the Collective Identity of the Star Trek Fandom: Boldly Going where No Fans Have Gone Before* (London, Lexington, 2020), pp. 51–3.

[32] S. Tarrow, *Power in Movement: Social Movements and Contentious Politics*, 2nd edn (Cambridge, Cambridge University Press, 1998), pp. 38–9; W.A . Samson and D. S. Meyer, 'Framing Political Opportunity', in D. McAdam, J. D. McCarthy, and M. N. Zald (eds), *Comparative Perspectives on Social Movements: Political Opportunities, Mobilizing Structures, and Cultural Framings* (Cambridge, Cambridge University Press, 1996), pp. 275–90 (pp. 293–4; see also pp. 374–5 n. 7); R. Dalton, A. Van Sickle, and S. Weldon, 'The Individual–Institutional Nexus of Protest Behaviour', *British Journal of Political Science*, 40 (2010), 51–73 (pp. 61–2 and n. 41); J. Markoff, *Waves of Democracy: Social Movements and Political Change* (Thousand Oaks, CA, Pine Forge Press, 1996), p. 112.

less attractive and just as dangerous compared to marches and sit-ins for some campaigners. For example, when the National Association for the Advancement of Colored People (NAACP) organised school desegregation petitions in Yazoo City, Mississippi, in 1955, the White Citizens' Council published the names of all 53 signatories, and used economic and physical threats to coerce all but six into renouncing their support.[33]

The precise role of petitions, in relation to other forms of activism, has therefore varied between causes and social groups in representative polities. Marco Giugni's comparison of forms of protest in the peace, anti-nuclear, and environmental movements suggests that preferences varied according to national political cultures, as well as among the three causes.[34] Opponents of reformist social movements quickly adapted their techniques, including petitions, to conjure a conservative 'silent majority' of greater numbers.[35] Moreover, political parties have increasingly placed themselves at the head, rather than as the target, of petitioning campaigns, as in the German Christian Democratic Union's 1999 *Unterschriftenaktion* against dual citizenship, which garnered 5 million signatures and gave the party an electoral bounce in state elections.[36]

Still, a remarkable range of campaigns incorporated petitioning as a means of recruiting supporters, enthusing activists, and attracting publicity, regardless of the receptivity of authorities and formal petition systems. Petitioning remained a way to identify sympathisers and transform them into active supporters. In the United States, the Revd Raymond T. Ritchie encouraged fellow practitioners of faith-healing to post their signed petition slips back to him, rather than directly to President Truman, giving him a mailing list of those who shared his fears of an 'UN-AMERICAN' law regulating the practice.[37] Mairead Corrigan and Betty Williams of Northern Ireland won the 1976 Nobel Peace Prize for their cross-community 'Peace People' movement, which built a series of rallies after gathering

[33] N. Caren, R. A. Ghoshal, and V. Ribas, 'A Social Movement Generation: Cohort and Period Trends in Protest Attendance and Petition Signing', *American Sociological Review*, 76 (2011), 125–51; J. M. Bloom, *Class, Race, and the Civil Rights Movement*, 2nd edn (Bloomington, Indiana University Press, 2019 [1987]), pp. 128–9, 195.

[34] M. Giugni, *Social Protest and Policy Change: Ecology, Antinuclear, and Peace Movements in Comparative Perspective* (Lanham, MD, Rowman & Littlefield, 2004), pp. 43, 131–2.

[35] M. Derks, 'Modern Crusaders: The Conservative Catholic Politics of Resistance in Post-Conciliar Netherlands', pp. 227–50 (p. 240), and L. Black, '1968 and All That(cher): Cultures of Conservatism and the New Right in Britain', pp. 356–76 (p. 372), both in A. von der Goltz and B. Waldschmidt-Nelson (eds), *Inventing the Silent Majority in Western Europe and the United States* (Cambridge, Cambridge University Press, 2019).

[36] S. Green, *The Politics of Exclusion: Institutions and Immigration Policy in Contemporary Germany* (Manchester, Manchester University Press, 2004), pp. 95–102; Holmes Cooper, 'Party-Sponsored Protest'.

[37] Petition from O. Bradshaw to President Harry S. Truman, 1949, OF 286a, Official Files, Harry S. Truman Presidential Library, https://catalog.archives.gov/id/169049773 (accessed 27 November 2020); D. E. Harrell, *All Things Are Possible: The Healing and Charismatic Revivals in Modern America* (Bloomington, Indiana University Press, 1975), p. 16.

6,000 signatures from women in their neighbourhood within a day of sectarian violence that killed three children.[38] The 1985 Dutch 'People's Petition' against cruise missile deployment attracted support from friendship groups and 'self-applications', even if activist networks remained vital for converting sympathisers into signatories in many cases.[39]

Petitioning could supplement and encourage, rather than divert from, direct action. Hence, the US movement against the Vietnam War deployed petitions from intellectuals and celebrities as both a demonstrative act of support and a pledge by them to support the conscientious objections of young draftees.[40] Social movements continued a tradition of long marches that displayed their physical commitment to delivering a petition – from Jacob Coxey's 1894 'petition in boots', to the US Capitol to the 1936 Jarrow March to the UK Parliament.[41] In 1972, anti-nuclear activists and rural communities in the Rhine Valley complemented a slow-motion tractor procession to the proposed site of a new reactor with separate village petitions, winning 889 signatures from Burkheim's 891 eligible voters, for example.[42] While the 1963 March on Washington was metaphorically described by organisers and the press as a 'living petition', overseas supporters (both citizens and sympathetic locals) were encouraged to demonstrate solidarity by delivering petitions, in a form distributed through European newspapers, to their nearest US embassy.[43] Indeed,

[38] L. A. Smithey, 'The Peace People: Principled and Revolutionary Non-Violence in Northern Ireland', in L. Bosi and G. De Fazio (eds), *The Troubles in Northern Ireland and Theories of Social Movements* (Amsterdam, Amsterdam University Press, 2017), pp. 203–22 (pp. 206–12).

[39] D. Oegema and B. Klandermans, 'Why Social Movement Sympathizers Don't Participate: Erosion and Nonconversion of Support', *American Sociological Review*, 59 (1994), 703–22; H. Kriesi, 'Local Mobilization for the People's Social Petition of the Dutch Peace Movement', in Bert Klandermans, Hanspeter Kriesi, and Sidney Tarrow (eds), *From Structure to Action* (Greenwich, CT, JAI Press, 1988), pp. 41–83; D. Della Porta and M. Diani, *Social Movements: An Introduction*, 2nd edn (Oxford, Blackwell, 2006), p. 123.

[40] Anti-Draft Petition, 1/14/1968, Precedent case files, Record Group 118, Records of US Attorneys, 1821–1994, National Archives at Boston, https://catalog.archives.gov/id/7419599 (accessed 8 February 2024).

[41] B. F. Alexander, *Coxey's Army: Popular Protest in the Gilded Age* (Baltimore, MD, Johns Hopkins University Press, 2015), Chapter 3; E. S. Clemens, 'Organizational Form as Frame: Collective Identity and Political Strategy in the American Labor Movement, 1880–1920', in McAdam et al., *Comparative Perspectives*, pp. 205–26 (pp. 218–19); L. Beers, *Red Ellen: The Life of Ellen Wilkinson, Socialist, Feminist, Internationalist* (Cambridge, MA, Harvard University Press, 2016), pp. 338–42; F. Ennis, 'The March of 1936: The Symbolic Expression of Protest', PhD thesis (Durham University, 1982), pp. 122–7, 145–6.

[42] S. Milder, 'The "Example of Whyl": How Grassroots Protest in the Rhine Valley Shaped West Germany's Antinuclear Movement', in E. Conze, M. Klimke, and J. Varon (eds), *Nuclear Threats: Nuclear Fear and the Cold War of the 1980s* (Cambridge, Cambridge University Press, 2016), pp. 167–85 (p. 172).

[43] *The Crisis*, 70:8 (October 1963), p. 464; *Ebony*, 19:1 (November 1963), p. 35; M. L. Dudziak, 'The 1963 March on Washington: At Home and Abroad', *Revue française d'études américaines*, 107:1 (March 2006), 61–76; K. Hammond Perry, '"U.S. Negroes, Your Fight Is Our Fight": Black Britons and the 1963 March on Washington', in R. D. G. Kelley and S. Tuck (eds), *The Other Special Relationship: Race, Rights, and Riots in Britain and the United States* (New York, Palgrave, 2015), pp. 7–24.

petitions remained attractive as a way to secure media coverage through visual demonstrations of numerical support, even where the right to petition remained conventional and familiar.[44] The performative and dramatic moment of presentation when petitioners publicly handed over a petition to an authority – for instance at No. 10 Downing Street, or a US embassy – was particularly useful in creating photo opportunities and media-friendly images to be reproduced or broadcast in the mass media.

Perhaps the best way to highlight the ubiquity and adaptability of petitioning is to point to its persistence in periods of time or systems of government without representative electoral norms, such as in wartime crises or in authoritarian dictatorships. While other forms of political activity were often suspended during wartime, petitioning gained added importance as a mechanism for the expression of grievances. As has been well documented, petitions from soviets, soldiers, and peasants were crucial in catalysing the February revolution in Russia.[45] Petitions were used by mutinous French soldiers in 1917, and later by American troops questioning why they were being kept in Europe after the First World War's end.[46] On the home front, petitions were utilised by citizens and subjects, and particularly women, to raise everyday concerns about food, housing, and other matters to authorities. For example, petitions and letters from Viennese citizens to the emperor of Austria-Hungary increased during the First World War as conditions in the city deteriorated.[47] In the Ottoman empire, soldiers' wives and widows petitioned the state on behalf of their husbands or to claim pensions.[48] Petitioning the war minister in May 1916, the 'peasant women of the Russian soil' thundered 'Act on our demands now and do not delay. Give us bread. Down with the war. Down with the treacherous, treasonous ministers, and the entire government.'[49]

A survey of British newspapers during the Second World War confirms the widespread use of petitions to raise concerns at a time when there was a party political truce and the country was governed by a broad coalition. In November 1943,

[44] R. Koopmans, 'The Dynamics of Protest Waves: West Germany, 1965 to 1989', *American Sociological Review*, 58 (1993), 637–58 (p. 654); L. S. Wittner, *Toward Nuclear Abolition: A History of the World Nuclear Disarmament Movement, 1973 to Present* (Stanford, CA, Stanford University Press, 1993), p. 160; L. S. Wittner, 'The Forgotten Years of the World Nuclear Disarmament Movement, 1975–1978', *Journal of Peace Research*, 40 (2003), 435–56 (p. 437).

[45] D. Stevenson, *1917: War, Peace, and Revolution* (Oxford, Oxford University Press, 2017), p. 113.

[46] L. Smith, 'Remobilizing the Citizen-Soldier through the French Army Mutinies of 1917', in J. Horne (ed.), *State, Society and Mobilization in Europe during the First World War* (Cambridge, Cambridge University Press, 1997), pp. 144–59 (p. 157); J. Keene, *The United States and the First World War* (London, Routledge, 2000), p. 68.

[47] M. Healy, 'Vienna Falling: Total War and Everyday Life, 1914–1918', PhD thesis (University of Chicago, 2000), p. 343; M. Healy, *Vienna and the Fall of the Habsburg Empire: Total War and Everyday Life in World War I* (Cambridge, Cambridge University Press, 2004), p. 24.

[48] E. Mahir Metinsoy, *Ottoman Women during World War I: Everyday Experiences, Politics, and Conflicts* (Cambridge, Cambridge University Press, 2017), pp. 75–84.

[49] Reprinted in M. Hickey (ed.), *Competing Voices from the Russian Revolution* (Santa Barbara, CA, Greenwood, 2011), p. 56.

for instance, a 'procession of taxi cabs' delivered a petition to Parliament containing over 4 million signatures from electors protesting against the government's pensions bill and asking for an immediate increase in the pension without a means test.[50] Even in wartime, then, petitioning could provide a focal point for mass political participation. At the same time, petitions provided a mechanism for citizens to complain to central and local government about grievances occasioned by the war, such as rationing, or the provision of bomb shelters.[51] Key workers within the war economy also used petitions to make high-profile demands to the state. In 1942, London munitions workers delivered a petition to Winston Churchill at Downing Street to agitate for the immediate opening of a second front in Europe to hasten Germany's defeat.[52] The exigencies of total war required the suspension of normal politics, and, in this context, petitions provided a mechanism for political activity and the raising of grievances occasioned by wartime by key groups, including women, soldiers, and munitions workers.

A second example of the ubiquity of petitions is in their persistence within modern authoritarian regimes. In the European context, even as authoritarians extinguished or marginalised representative legislatures in the first half of the 20th century, they preserved traditions of petitioning. While the use of petitioning as a means for independent, collective representation and participation was curtailed in such contexts, for the state, as a study of modern China has suggested, petitions were valued as 'useful complaints', providing advance warning of popular grievances and a means of checking abuses by local officials.[53] In some cases, such as the Soviet Union, new regimes drew on a paternalistic tradition of petitioning the monarch, even as they sought to revolutionise national political structures.[54] In East Germany, Paul Betts has written, individual petitions were the 'main form of personal contact with the state', and the right of citizens to petition was guaranteed by the 1949 constitution. Indeed, by the time the Berlin Wall fell in 1989, the German Democratic Republic's citizens were 'writing over a million complaint letters a year, making this at once a mass produced yet highly individualized mode of communication between citizen and state'.[55]

[50] *Nottingham Journal*, 30 October 1943, p. 1; Hansard, HC Debates, 2 November 1943, Vol. CCCXCIII, col. 493.

[51] *Yorkshire Post*, 8 December 1939, p. 14; *Worthing Gazette*, 10 January 1940, p. 5.

[52] *Hartlepool Northern Daily Mail*, 25 July 1942, p. 5.

[53] J. Chen, *Useful Complaints: How Petitions Assist Decentralized Authoritarianism in China* (Lanham, MD, Rowman & Littlefield, 2016). See also P. Betts, *Within Walls: Private Life in the German Democratic Republic* (Oxford, Oxford University Press, 2010), p. 180.

[54] L. Douds, 'Lenin's "Living Link"? The Soviet Government Reception, 1917–1921', in L. Douds, J. Harris, and P. Whitewood (eds), *The Fate of the Bolshevik Revolution: Illiberal Liberation, 1917–41* (London, Bloomsbury, 2020), pp. 63–76; S. Fitzpatrick, 'Editor's Introduction: Petitions and Denunciations in Russia and Soviet History', *Russian History*, 24 (1997), 1–9 (pp. 2–3).

[55] Betts, *Within Walls*, p. 174. See also S. Fitzpatrick, 'Supplicants and Citizens: Public Letter-Writing in Soviet Russia in the 1930s', *Slavic Review*, 55 (1996), 78–105; and H. Luenders, 'Electoral Responsiveness in Closed Autocracies: Evidence from Petitions in the Former German Democratic Republic', *American Political Science Review*, 116 (2022), 827–42.

Letters or petitions to leaders, especially those with dictatorial powers, assumed even greater importance within authoritarian states as a means to advance patronage requests, resolve disputes, or rectify complaints.[56] Throughout his long rule (1932–68), the dictator António de Oliveira Salazar 'patiently scrutinised' the thousands of petitions, letters, and other communications he received every month from Portuguese citizens.[57] In some polities, such as the Soviet Union in the Stalinist era or Nazi Germany, 'denunciations' – written complaints, allegations, and malicious gossip made by citizens to authority about other citizens – evolved as a distinct genre.[58] As Robert Gellately has observed, 'denunciations from the population were the key link in the three-way interaction between the police, people, and policy in Nazi Germany'.[59] While the possibilities of petitioning as mechanisms of mass, collective political expression and contestation were circumscribed within modern authoritarian regimes, a rich historical literature has shown how petitions, letters, and other related genres were a key form of interaction through which the relationships between citizens and state were negotiated. These techniques also meant that, when repression eased after 1987, dissidents could quickly adopt petitions, as a means to connect pro-democracy sympathisers in Czechoslovakia; to oppose a hydro-electric dam in Hungary; or to mobilise Orthodox worshippers in pressing for the consecrated reburial of Nicholas II, the last tsar, in Russia.[60]

Petitioning beyond the Nation-State: International Institutions

If the history of petitioning is the history of addressing power, then the establishment of new international institutions in the 20th century provided a novel outlet for petitioners of all kinds. While studies of modern petitioning have often focused on interactions between citizens or 'proto-citizens' and the state,[61] new international

[56] H. Eberle and V. Harris (eds), *Letters to Hitler* (Cambridge, Polity, 2012), pp. 110–21; R. Gow, 'Citizenship and Self-Representation in the Public Letters Sent to General Primo de Rivera in Spain, 1923–1930', PhD thesis (Trinity College Dublin, 2018).

[57] T. Gallagher, *Salazar: The Dictator who Refused to Die* (Oxford, Oxford University Press, 2020), pp. 5, 56, 98.

[58] S. Fitzpatrick and R. Gellately, 'Introduction to the Practices of Denunciation in Modern European History', *Journal of Modern History*, 68 (1996), 747–67.

[59] R. Gellately, *The Gestapo and German Society: Enforcing Racial Policy, 1933–1945* (Oxford, Oxford University Press, 1991), pp. 132–58 (p. 136).

[60] A. Oberschall, 'Opportunities and Framing in the Eastern European Revolts of 1989', in McAdam et al., *Comparative Perspectives*, pp. 93–121 (p. 117); B. Morton and J. Landy, 'East European Activists Test Glasnost', *Bulletin of Atomic Scientists* (May 1988), 18–31 (p. 24); N. N. Petro, *The Rebirth of Russian Democracy: An Interpretation of Political Culture* (Cambridge, MA, Harvard University Press, 1995), pp. 86–7.

[61] A critique expressed by A. Irfan, 'Petitioning for Palestine: Refugee Appeals to International Authorities', *Contemporary Levant*, 5 (2020), 79–96 (p. 82).

bodies provided a forum for petitioners who were stateless, such as displaced persons or refugees.[62] Other petitioners, such as anti-colonial movements or European secessionists, claimed statehood by asserting their right of self-determination in such arenas.[63]

While scholars have documented the growth of internationalist ideals, networks, and activism from the late 19th century onwards,[64] the focus in this chapter is on the establishment of formal mechanisms to petition international authority. Although the analysis here largely focuses on the League of Nations and the United Nations, there was a wider universe of international bodies created during the 20th century. For example, a study of 'international parliamentarism', has noted the proliferation of bodies with parliamentary representatives from more than one state set up after 1945, with a second wave in the post-Cold War era of globalisation.[65]

While there had been various attempts to organise petitions across borders or direct appeals to foreign governments from the 19th century onwards, such as British appeals to the tsar regarding the treatment of Jews in Russia,[66] a key moment for the establishment of formalised mechanisms for receiving petitions by international authority were the rules for the 1919 Paris Peace Conference. These 'provided that the secretariat would compile a list of petitions from private groups and individuals and distribute it to the government delegations', a critical departure from the usual practices of conferences comprising the Great Powers.[67] Many of the petitions received by the Paris peacemakers in this 'Wilsonian moment' concerned claims of national self-determination using the new language of internationalism, for instance from Irish soldiers for Irish home rule, to be referred to conference.[68] Other claims included those of women. The Allied Women's Suffrage Congress,

[62] K. Nowak, '"To Reach the Lands of Freedom": Petitions of Polish Displaced Persons to American Poles, Moral Screening, and the Role of Diaspora in Refugee Resettlement', *Cultural and Social History*, 16 (2019), 621–42; P. Gatrell, A. Ghosal, K. Nowak, and A. Dowdall, 'Reckoning with Refugeedom: Refugee Voices in Modern History', *Social History*, 46 (2021), 70–95.

[63] A. B. Lorca, 'Petitioning the International: A "Pre-History" of Self-Determination', *European Journal of International Law*, 25 (2014), 497–523.

[64] D. Laqua, W. Van Acker, and C. Verbruggen (eds), *International Organizations and Global Civil Society: Histories of the Union of International Associations* (London, Bloomsbury, 2019); D. Laqua, *The Age of Internationalism and Belgium, 1880–1930: Peace, Progress, and Prestige* (Manchester, Manchester University Press, 2013); D. Laqua (ed.), *Internationalism Reconfigured: Transnational Ideas and Movements between the World Wars* (London, Bloomsbury, 2011); G. Sluga and P. Clavin (eds), *Internationalisms: A Twentieth-Century History* (Cambridge, Cambridge University Press, 2017).

[65] L. M. De Puig, 'International Parliamentarism: An Introduction to Its History', *Parliaments, Estates, and Representation*, 24 (2010), 13–62.

[66] *Manchester Guardian*, 29 June 1903, p. 5. See also A. R. Higgins, 'Writing for Peace: Reconsidering the British Public Peace Petitioning Movement's Historical Legacies after 1898', in M. Abbenhuis, C. E. Barber, and A. R. Higgins (eds), *War, Peace, and International Order? The Legacies of the Hague Conferences of 1899 and 1907* (Abingdon, Routledge, 2017), pp. 138–54.

[67] S. Charnovitz, 'The Emergence of Democratic Participation in Global Governance (Paris, 1919)', *Indiana Journal of Global Legal Studies*, 10 (2003), 45–77 (pp. 62, 75).

[68] *Daily Mail*, 10 March 1919, p. 5; E. Manela, *The Wilsonian Moment: Self-Determination and the International Origins of Anticolonial Nationalism* (Oxford, Oxford University Press, 2007).

meeting in Paris, petitioned the French Prime Minister Georges Clemenceau that women be represented at the conference.[69]

The League of Nations, founded in 1920, instituted a formalised petition process in two areas. First, minorities within European states covered by the peace treaties were able to petition the League's council to allege violations; those that were deemed 'receivable' were passed on to *ad hoc* committees. The committees usually settled cases through bilateral negotiations with the specific government rather than discussing cases in the League council.[70] Second, people in territories that were ruled on behalf of the League by a mandatory government (such as Britain over Palestine, or France over Lebanon) could petition the Permanent Mandates Commission indirectly through their mandatory government.[71] Colonised peoples in South-West Africa (later Namibia) petitioned the League to critique the mandatory rule of South Africa.[72] As Natasha Wheatley has written in her study of Palestine, in this way 'petitions enacted a jurisdictional hierarchy with the League at its apex'.[73] This explains why the League became a magnet for petitions even outside its formal institutional systems, and a forum for expressing complaints about imperial rule from colonised peoples.[74] As Susan Pedersen has reflected, 'there are revealing glimpses of … local inhabitants using the petition process to garner international support, and of opinion-sensitive governments forestalling criticism by adjusting course'.[75] Minorities not covered by treaties also petitioned the League. Petitions for racial equality from the USA, Canada, France, South Africa, and India were directed at the League, but as this risked provoking powerful member states such as Britain and France, these were often not received, despite the sympathy of officials.[76] Finally, the League, like the Paris peacemakers, continued to be addressed by groups and peoples claiming the right to national self-determination. In 1922 the Universal Negro Improvement Association (UNIA), led by Marcus Garvey, petitioned the League assembly for the transfer of the mandate for the

[69] *Manchester Guardian*, 13 February 1919, p. 9.

[70] S. Pedersen, 'Back to the League of Nations', *American Historical Review*, 112 (2007), 1091–117 (pp. 1110–11); A. W. Simpson, *Human Rights and the End of Empire: Britain and the Genesis of the European Convention* (Oxford, Oxford University Press, 2004), pp. 131–2.

[71] Simpson, *Human Rights*, pp. 147–8.

[72] T. Dedering, 'Petitioning Geneva: Transnational Aspects of Protest and Resistance in South West Africa/Namibia after the First World War', *Journal of Southern African Studies*, 35 (2009), 785–801.

[73] N. Wheatley, 'Mandatory Interpretation: Legal Hermeneutics and the New International Order in Arab and Jewish Petitions to the League of Nations', *Past & Present*, 227 (2015), 205–48 (p. 211).

[74] J. McQuade, 'Beyond an Imperial Foreign Policy? India at the League of Nations, 1919–46', *Journal of Imperial and Commonwealth History*, 48 (2020), 263–95; E. Vezzadini, *Lost Nationalism: Revolution, Memory, and Anti-Colonial Resistance in Sudan* (Woodbridge, Boydell & Brewer, 2015), p. 46; A. Burra, 'Petitioning the Mandates: Anti-Colonial and Anti-Racist Publics in International Law', PhD thesis (Universitiy of Michigan, 2017).

[75] Pedersen, 'Back to the League of Nations', p. 1107. See also S. Pedersen, *The Guardians: The League of Nations and the Crisis of Empire* (Oxford, Oxford University Press, 2015), pp. 66–93.

[76] P. G. Lauren, *The Evolution of International Human Rights: Visions Seen*, 3rd edn (Philadelphia, University of Pennsylvania Press, 2011), p. 127.

ex-German colonies in South-West Africa from South Africa to UNIA to govern in the name of the 'Negro peoples of the world'.[77]

On its establishment in 1946, 'almost immediately the UN was deluged by a huge wave of individual petitions complaining about a range of official crimes and misdemeanours'. One of the most famous was from W. E. B. Du Bois on behalf of NAACP highlighting 'the history of racial discrimination in the USA'.[78] This episode was part of a broader debate over the meaning of the right to petition in the early years of the UN that has been reconstructed by scholars of human rights. British officials fought a rearguard action against including a right to petition in the UN Declaration on Human Rights, largely owing to the fear of the likelihood of this being used by colonised peoples to protest about British rule. The Colonial Office privately stated 'our overriding object must be to remove so far as possible all teeth from the petition procedure and make it as innocuous as we can'.[79] Given that colonised peoples' petitions to imperial governments often met with a combination of indifference and arbitrariness, it is hardly surprising that they increasingly addressed their grievances to international bodies in the 20th century.[80] The influence of powerful states such as France, the USA, Britain, and the Soviet Union meant the upshot of these debates was that the Commission on Human Rights agreed to receive petitions, but in 1947 denied itself the authority to consider or take action upon them, despite pressure from Arab, Asian, and Latin American delegates to do so.[81]

However, despite these setbacks petition procedures remained fluid in the early postwar era. The UN secretariat received many petitions regarding human

[77] Universal Negro Improvement Association, 'Petition to the League of Nations, 1922', in *The Marcus Garvey and Universal Negro Improvement Association Papers*, ed. R. A. Hill et al., 13 vols (Berkeley, CA and Durham, NC, University of California Press and Duke University Press, 1983–2016), Vol IV, pp. 735–40; D. Jones, '"The League Will Not Ignore the Cry of the Negro Race for Justice": Marcus Garvey, the League of Nations, and South-West Africa', *Journal of Southern African Studies*, 48 (2022), 103–17.

[78] M. Mazower, 'The Strange Triumph of Human Rights, 1933–1950', *Historical Journal*, 47 (2004), 379–98 (p. 395). For a detailed study of the episode, see C. Anderson, *Eyes off the Prize: The United Nations and the African American Struggle for Human Rights, 1944–1955* (Cambridge, Cambridge University Press, 2003), pp. 81–97.

[79] Simpson, *Human Rights*, p. 497; see also pp. 493–8. For similar French anxieties, see M. Duranti, 'Decolonizing the United Nations: Anti-Colonialism and Human Rights in the French Empire', in A. D. Moses, M. Duranti, and R. Burke (eds), *Decolonization, Self-Determination, and the Rise of Global Human Rights Politics* (Cambridge, Cambridge University Press, 2020), pp. 54–78 (pp. 61–2); and, for more general anxieties from powerful states, N. Kurz, *Jewish Internationalism and Human Rights after the Holocaust* (Cambridge, Cambridge University Press, 2020), p. 69.

[80] R. de Costa, 'Identity, Authority, and the Moral Worlds of Indigenous Petitions', *Comparative Studies in Society and History*, 48 (2006), 669–98 (p. 671); S. Pedersen, 'Samoa at Geneva: Petitions and Peoples before the Mandates Commission of the League of Nations', *Journal of Imperial and Commonwealth History*, 40 (2012), 231–61. For the treatment of petitions from colonised peoples within the British empire for the preceding period, see Huzzey and Miller, 'Colonial Petitions', pp. 276–87.

[81] R. Burke, *Decolonization and the Evolution of International Human Rights* (Philadelphia, University of Pennsylvania Press, 2010), pp. 60, 63.

rights violations in French colonies, especially from Algeria, between 1950 and 1962.[82] The UN Trusteeship Council, akin to the League's Mandate Commission, was another key authority for petitioners in the era of decolonisation: the council received 45,000 petitions from Cameroonian territories under its supervision in 1956.[83] The UN Relief and Rehabilitation Administration; the International Refugee Organization; and, from 1951, the UN High Commissioner for Refugees received petitions and letters from displaced persons.[84]

As newly independent African countries joined the UN in the late 1950s and 1960s, they pressed for an expanded petition process for the special committees on decolonisation and apartheid, including hearing petitioners.[85] At the same time, the position of western powers became more favourable to deploying human rights in the context of Cold War diplomacy, leading to the eventual establishment of a procedure for considering individual petitions regarding human rights abuses in 1967.[86] Beyond the creation of formal petition procedures in the case of human rights and other matters, the UN also became the target for global campaigns expressed through petitions, as the final section will show.

Petitioning beyond the Nation State: Global Campaigns

In his classic essay, Lex Heerma van Voss observed that 'petitions seem to be a global phenomenon'.[87] From the late 19th century, petitions also became a mechanism to give global public opinion cohesion and represent it in material form. These global petitions were part of transnational campaigns designed to gain maximum publicity for their cause by directing their appeals to international bodies or leading states. The petitions aimed to speak for, but also speak to, wider international opinion. Crucially, this form of petitioning often rested its representative claims only partially on individual signatures, but also on 'attested' signatures – that is organisations, charities, associations, and other voluntary bodies signing on behalf of their members. For this reason, global petitions were not simply an output of cooperation between civil society actors in different countries but facilitated transnational coalitions and networks between non-governmental organisations.[88]

[82] Duranti, 'Decolonizing the United Nations', pp. 68–78.
[83] M. Terretta, *Petitioning for Our Rights, Fighting for Our Nation: The History of the Democratic Union of Cameroonian Women, 1949–1960* (Bamenda, Cameroon, Langaa RPCIG, 2013), pp. 1, 10–11.
[84] Gatrell et al., 'Reckoning with Refugeedom'.
[85] Burke, *Decolonization*, pp. 69–70; T. J. M. Zuijdwijk, *Petitioning the United Nations: A Study in Human Rights* (New York, Gower, 1982), pp. xiii–xiv.
[86] Burke, *Decolonization*, pp. 78–84.
[87] L. Heerma van Voss, 'Introduction', in Heerma van Voss, *Petitions in Social History*, pp. 1–10 (p. 2).
[88] M. Keck and K. Sikkink, *Activists beyond Borders: Advocacy Networks in International Politics* (Ithaca, NY, Cornell University Press, 1998). See also P. Goldman, 'From Margin to Mainstream: The Jubilee 2000 Campaign and the Rising Profile of Global Poverty Issues in the United Kingdom and the United States', PhD thesis (Harvard University, 2010), p. 84.

Since the 1990s scholars have debated the existence and conceptual coherence of 'global civil society'.[89] Adding a new perspective on this discussion, a focus on petitioning emphasises some of the ways in which civil society actors and publics have been organised and mobilised on the global stage.

Perhaps the first modern example of a global petitioning campaign in the style that would become familiar to late-20th-century campaigners was the 'polyglot petition', organised by the Women's Christian Temperance Union (WCTU) in the 1880s.[90] Conceived by the WCTU's leader, Frances Willard, the petition aimed to showcase the breadth and diversity of support from women across religious, linguistic, and national divides for action against alcohol and opium.[91] As the WCTU's second convention of 1893 proudly commented: 'there has never been a petition to which so large a number have given their influence and names … Catholic and Protestant; Gentile and Jew, Christian, Hindoo and Mohammedan have found in the Polyglot Petition a common ground of faith and works'. [92] Addressing themselves to 'honoured rulers, representatives and brothers', the organisers wished to present the final petition 'in its completeness to all the Governments of the civilized world by delegations of representative women appointed for that purpose'.[93] Prior to its presentation to US President Benjamin Harrison in February 1891, the petition went on a 'world-wide journey' designed to promote the cause across different countries. For instance, the chief British organiser, Lady Isabella Somerset, carried 250,000 signatures across the Atlantic to the first WCTU convention held in Boston in 1891.[94] The final petition, over 6 miles long, claimed to represent 7.5 million people across 50 countries, 1.5 million of whom had signed as individuals, the remainder consisting of signature endorsements by men and attested signatures from organisations.[95]

Significant global petitions in the early and mid-20th century included the 1932 Disarmament Petition organised by the Women's International League for Peace and Freedom, which garnered 8 million signatures from 56 countries, while the Communist-inspired Stockholm Peace Appeal of 1950 claimed 450 million signatures from 75 countries, including 200 million from China and 100 million

[89] J. Keane, *Global Civil Society?* (Cambridge, Cambridge University Press, 2003); J. Dryzek, 'Global Civil Society: The Progress of Post-Westphalian Politics', *Annual Review of Political Science*, 15 (2012), 101–19; L. Amoore and P. Langley, 'Ambiguities of Global Civil Society', *Review of International Studies*, 30 (2004), 89–110.

[90] I. Tyrrell, *Women's World/Women's Empire: The World Temperance Union in International Perspective, 1880–1930* (Chapel Hill, University of North Carolina Press, 1991), pp. 39–42.

[91] S. Rimner, *Opium's Long Shadow: From Asian Revolt to Global Drug Control* (Cambridge, MA, Harvard University Press, 2018), p. 122.

[92] *Minutes of the Second Biennial Convention and Executive of the World's Woman's Christian Temperance Union* (Chicago, 1893), p. 178.

[93] Lady Henry Somerset, 'The Polyglot Petition', in *Life and Light for Woman*, Vol. XXIV (Boston, 1894), p. 256.

[94] Ibid.

[95] Tyrrell, *Women's World*, pp. 46–7.

from the USSR.[96] Another example of a major global petition relying on 'attested' signatures would be the campaign launched by the British Anti-Apartheid Movement in 1964 following the Rivonia trial, at which Nelson Mandela and other ANC activists were convicted.[97] The final petition, presented to the UN secretary-general U Thant in support of a resolution to release all South African political prisoners, contained 194,387 individual signatures; but more importantly, campaigners claimed that through attested signatures the petition represented 259 million people.[98] In particular, organisers highlighted the endorsement of civil society bodies associated with organised labour, youth and student associations, and anti-colonial and anti-racist movements.[99] Activists claimed that support for the petition truly spanned the globe, pointing to signatures and endorsements from across North America and western Europe, but also the Eastern Bloc, India, and South America.[100] The utility of the petition was that, like the petitions addressed within the nation state discussed in the first half of this chapter, it served as a linchpin for a broader programme of activity at a national and local level. For example, British supporters were urged to write letters to the South African minister of justice; demonstrate outside the South African embassy in London; lobby councillors, MPs, and government to make representations to the Apartheid regime; and, as members of organisations, pass resolutions condemning the trial that could be transmitted to the South African authorities.[101]

Late-20th-century examples confirm the importance of global petition campaigns in agenda-setting, forging transnational networks and coalitions, mobilising popular support, and garnering media coverage for a cause to exert pressure on policy-makers on the international stage, while exhibiting a shift away from attested signatures. Women activists and women's groups targeted the 1993 World Conference on Human Rights in Vienna with a view to making women's rights central to the discussions and outcomes of the summit. A key part of their campaign was a petition two years in the making, which was translated into 26 languages, and was signed by 500,000 people from 128 countries.[102]

Petitions allowed organisers and campaigners to make a representative claim on behalf of publics across different countries, and not simply a coalition of

[96] T. R. Davies, *The Possibilities of Transnational Activism: The Campaign for Disarmament between the Two World Wars* (Leiden, Brill, 2006), pp. 115, 235; H. Harrison, 'Popular Responses to the Atomic Bomb in China, 1945–1955', *Past & Present*, 218 (2013), 98–116 (p. 106); G. Roberts, 'Averting Armageddon: The Communist Peace Movement, 1948–1956', in S. Smith (ed.), *The Oxford Handbook of the History of Communism* (Oxford, Oxford University Press, 2013), pp. 322–38 (p. 327).

[97] Anti-Apartheid Movement, *Annual Report*, October 1964, p. 5, Anti-Apartheid Movement (AAM) Archives, Bodleian Library, Oxford.

[98] *World Campaign for the Release of South African Political Prisoners* (*WCRSAPP*), 3 (June 1964), [p. 2], AAM Archives, Bodleian Library, Oxford.

[99] Ibid., [pp. 2, 7–8].

[100] Ibid., [pp. 3, 7–8]; *WCRSAPP*, 4 (September 1964), [p. 1], AAM Archives, Bodleian Library, Oxford.

[101] *WCRSAPP*, 2 (May 1964), [p. 1], AAM Archives, Bodleian Library, Oxford.

[102] C. E. Lockwood, *The International Human Rights of Women: Instruments of Change* (Washington, DC, American Bar Association, 1998), p. 26; E. Reichert, 'Women's Rights are Human Rights: Platform for Action', *International Social Work*, 41 (1998), 371–84 (p. 384).

NGOs.[103] As one UN watcher was quoted as saying regarding the women's rights issue: 'This is somehow taking on a greater importance than most other issues, because there's pressure from the grassroots.'[104] One of the architects of the campaign, Dorothy Thomas of Human Rights Watch, singled out the particular contribution of the petition in a CNN interview when she declared that 'It took over 240,000 people from 124 countries just to get women's rights on the agenda of the World Conference on Human Rights.'[105]

A final example of the significance of global petition is the Jubilee 2000 campaign of the late 1990s: a campaign for debt relief for developing nations.[106] As part of the campaign, Jubilee coalitions and campaigns were formed in 69 countries.[107] The petition was signed by 24 million people across 166 countries, for which it secured a place in the *Guinness Book of Records*, thus achieving an aim of the organisers.[108] Again the petition was subsumed into a general campaign, including lobbying of political leaders, protests at world summits, and promotional activity. Particularly innovative was the prominence of celebrity endorsements, such as that of Bono, the lead singer of U2, to promote signing among a broad public beyond politicised sympathisers.[109] The petition was a key element of the public-facing dimension of the campaign, which aimed to educate the public and the media on the debt issue.[110] The petition was handed over to world leaders at the UN General Assembly in 2000.[111] While not all global campaigns have been as effective in achieving policy changes as Jubilee 2000, which prompted the USA, the UK, and other western states to agree to debt cancellation or relief, the use of petitions has been an important element in catalysing coalitions of activists and NGOs across borders and mobilising popular support behind such causes.

Conclusion

This chapter has roamed a wide territory to show that petitioning remained a ubiquitous practice across modern democracies in the 20th century, with petitions directed to myriad authorities, domestic and international, and used by a diverse

103 See M. Saward, *The Representative Claim* (Oxford, Oxford University Press, 2010).

104 L. Hossie, 'Women Want Concerns Raised at UN Rights Conference', *The Globe and Mail* (Canada), 7 November 1992.

105 'Women Succeed in Pressing for Rights Hearing at Vienna', CNN News, 22 June 1993, CNN Transcripts, lexis.com (accessed 9 March 2021).

106 M. Mayo, '"The World Will Never Be the Same Again"? Reflecting on the Experiences of Jubilee 2000', *Social Movement Studies*, 4 (2005), 139–54.

107 A. Pettifor, 'The Jubilee 2000 Campaign: A Brief Overview', in C. Jochnick and F. Preston (eds), *Sovereign Debt at the Crossroads: Challenges and Proposals for Resolving the Third World Debt Crisis* (Oxford, Oxford University Press, 2006), pp. 297–318 (p. 300).

108 Goldman, 'From Margin to Mainstream', p. 164.

109 Ibid., p. 120.

110 Pettifor, 'The Jubilee 2000 Campaign', pp. 313–16.

111 Ibid., p. 305.

range of political actors from global campaigning NGOs, political parties, interest groups, protestors, and social movement activists, as well as ordinary citizens complaining of everyday concerns. In connecting these developments in the history of petitioning over the *longue durée* there are three significant implications of the foregoing analysis that we wish to emphasise.

First, contemporary political scientists have debated the role of e-petitions in fostering public participation and engagement in the early 21st century.[112] Considering the 20th-century transformations we have outlined here, e-petitions systems have been most distinctive in reasserting the centrality of legislatures to the petitioning cultures of different states to a degree not seen since the 19th-century heyday of petitions. The uses of e-petitions for legislatures are explored elsewhere in this book.[113] For campaigners, e-petitions provide a conveniently centralised form of signature collection as opposed to the dispersed or serial presentation of petition sheets that was a product of the local signature-gathering process for paper petitions.

Second, surveying 'mature' democracies in the late 20th and early 21st centuries, politics scholars have pointed to the emergence of 'critical citizens' and the growth of direct democracy and 'advocacy democracy' alongside the traditional mechanisms of representative democracy, such as elections and mass membership of parties and trades unions.[114] However, we can trace 'an emerging political system that is pluralized, multi-venued and de-centred' long before the turn of the new millennium.[115] Within this literature, petitions have often been grouped with 'new' forms of citizen engagement and participation.[116] Yet as we have shown, petitioning was a ubiquitous and often lively form of political participation evident in many 20th-century democracies, which should lead us to question older assumptions

[112] C. Bochel, 'Petitions Systems: Contributing to Representative Democracy?', *Parliamentary Affairs*, 66 (2013), 798–815; C. Bochel, 'Petition Systems: Outcomes, "Success" and "Failure"', *Parliamentary Affairs*, 73 (2020), 233–52; S. Wright, '"Success" and Online Political Participation: The Case of the Downing Street E-Petitions', *Information, Communication, & Society*, 19 (2016), 843–57; C. Leston-Bandeira, 'Parliamentary Petitions and Public Engagement: An Empirical Analysis of the Role of E-Petitions', *Policy & Politics*, 47 (2019), 415–36; U. Riehm, K. Böhle, and R. Lindner, *Electronic Petitioning and Modernization of Petitions Systems in Europe* (Berlin, TAB, 2013); L. Reid, 'Are E-Petitions a Viable Tool for Increasing Citizen Participation in Our Parliamentary Institutions?', *Canadian Parliamentary Review*, 37 (2014), 3–9; S. Rosenberger, B. Seisl, J. Stadlmair, and E. Dalpra, 'What Are Petitions Good For? Institutional Design and Democratic Functions', *Parliamentary Affairs*, 75 (2022), 217–37.

[113] See Leston-Bandeira, chapter in this volume.

[114] Norris, *Critical Citizens*; P. Norris, *Democratic Deficit: Critical Citizens Revisited* (Cambridge, Cambridge University Press, 2012); R. J. Dalton, B. E. Cain, and S. E. Scarrow, 'Democratic Publics and Democratic Institutions', in B. E. Cain, R. J. Dalton, and S. E. Scarrow, *Democracy Transformed? Expanding Political Opportunities in Advanced Industrial Democracies* (Oxford, Oxford University Press, 2003), pp. 250–75.

[115] M. Warren, 'A Second Transformation of Democracy?', in Cain et al., *Democracy Transformed?*, pp. 223–49 (p. 227).

[116] E.g. K. Newton and J. Van Deth, *Foundations of Comparative Politics: Democracies of the Modern World*, 4th edn (Cambridge, Cambridge University Press, 2021), Chapter 9.

about a 'golden age' of representative democracy based on elections and parties, but also the supposed novelty of recent changes.

Finally, this chapter has shown how the framing of topics of historical research, as well as practices of record-keeping and archiving, can obscure new patterns and uses of political practices, such as petitioning. Although petitions usually formed part of the wider repertoire for any particular cause or group, it remained a refrain common to citizens, if less popular as a subject of research. A shift away from institutions that welcomed and recorded petitions, especially legislatures, has also overstated the extent to which voting or alternative forms of protest diluted the recourse to petitioning. Indeed, while executive branches of government or new international bodies might receive petitions instead, the striking feature of 20th-century petitioning is that it largely escaped institutional systems, with the functions of recruitment and publicity predominating beyond the reception and acceptance of a petition by one particular authority. In this sense, the chapter draws attention to the significant reinvention of familiar, 'traditional' modes of protest, which predated and prefigured digital technology or millennial globalisation. While it is impossible for this chapter to do justice to various national and transnational developments in petitioning across a century-and-a-half, it is possible to discern the endurance and versatility in different cultures and polities across North America and Europe, increasingly intertwined with campaigns in other parts of the globe.

Part III

Petitions and Petitioning in Context

11

Unanimity, Anonymity, and Immunity: Thomas Haxey and the Form of the Common Petition in 14th-Century England

GWILYM DODD

THE PLACE OF late medieval English common petitions in broader narratives of petitionary development has been somewhat neglected. A common assumption is that in England, as in other contexts in the premodern era, petitioning exclusively took the form of individual supplicants seeking redress – or favour – for matters relating to their own particular circumstances, and that more sophisticated forms of representative petitioning, which reflected broad interests, public opinion, and shared political goals, were an innovation of later periods.[1] However, in the early-14th-century English Parliament, common petitions emerged alongside the more justice-oriented category of individual complaints (known as 'private petitions') to form a key component of the political dialogue between the Crown and the elected representatives of the shires and towns – the Commons.[2] Common petitions are very far removed from the phenomenon of mass petitioning that emerged in England in the 17th century, fundamentally because they articulated political opinions that emanated from within, rather than outside, the political elite, and also because they did not involve large-scale public mobilisation.[3] Yet

[1] D. Zaret, 'Petition-and-Response and Liminal Petitioning in Comparative/Historical Perspective', *Social Science History*, 43 (2019), 431–51.

[2] I outline the development and nature of the two types of petition in G. Dodd, *Justice and Grace: Private Petitioning and the English Parliament in the Late Middle Ages* (Oxford, Oxford University Press, 2007), pp. 1–2, and Chapters 5, 7, and 8. Common petitions were routinely enrolled on the parliament rolls from the 1340s, for which consult C. Given-Wilson et al. (eds), *The Parliament Rolls of Medieval England*, CD-ROM (Leicester, Scholarly Digital Editions, 2005), CD-ROM (*PROME*). See also W. M. Ormrod, H. Killick, and P. Bradford (eds), *Early Common Petitions in the English Parliament c. 1290–c.1420*, Camden Fifth Series, 52 (2017).

[3] D. Zaret, *Origins of Democratic Culture: Printing, Petitions, and the Public Sphere in Early Modern England* (Princeton, Princeton University Press, 2000); P. Loft, 'Involving the Public: Parliament,

Proceedings of the British Academy, **262**, 219–238,

they are a category of petition that defies a recent characterisation of premodern petitions as 'venerated instrument[s] of the state' serving the needs and interests of rulers by facilitating conflict resolution and the projection of centralised authority and control.[4]

Common petitions purported to represent the common concerns of the king's subjects and so *were* a method of expressing a quasi-form of public opinion, albeit the more limited public opinion of the landed gentry and urban oligarchy on whose behalf Members of Parliament (MPs) attended Parliament. Furthermore, while many common petitions raised relatively uncontentious concerns about various aspects of general governance, occasionally, at times of heightened political tension, they might also be used more aggressively, as a means of exerting real political pressure on the king and his officials. In these circumstances, they were far more than merely a reputable means of gaining assistance: they became the tool of acerbic *complaint*. Yet, while common petitions had undoubted strengths as a mode of political agitation, they also had weaknesses, for like other forms of petitioning, their chances of making a difference greatly depended on the willingness of the king to yield to their demands. The intensely politicised nature of common petitions, however, meant that what determined the receptivity of the king to these demands was not at all straightforward, since it involved a complex interplay of negotiation, persuasion, and hard-bargaining with the broader political community.

In this discussion, I explore more fully the factors that determined the strengths and weaknesses of this type of petition. Crucially, in discussing the demands articulated by the representatives elected to Parliament, I extend my consideration to include *all* requests or complaints made by the parliamentary Commons, including those made orally in the course of discussion, dialogue, and negotiation with the Crown. It is possible to incorporate requests of this nature because the record of Parliament – the parliament roll – often noted the matters that MPs raised in discussion with the king, separate from their more formal written petitions, as part of the general reportage of Parliament's business. This evidence provides a rare opportunity to extend the scope of our consideration of petitions beyond the limitations set by the survival of the petitions themselves, and to acknowledge that 'petitioning', the act of articulating a request or complaint, was not necessarily confined to written text. For the present purposes, I want to suggest that the distinction between formal written petitions (i.e. common petitions) presented by MPs and petitions *voiced* by MPs is an important one because in the negotiations between the Crown and the political community the question of how

Petitioning, and the Language of Interest, 1688–1720', *Journal of British Studies*, 55 (2016), 1–23; H. Miller, 'Introduction: The Transformation of Petitioning in the Long Nineteenth Century (1780–1914)', *Social Science History*, 41 (2019), 409–29.

[4] Zaret, 'Petition-and-Response', p. 431 (quotation), pp. 434, 436, 439–40.

requests came to be presented to the king (either in writing or orally) could often shape what these requests demanded and how effective they were in securing their goals. The relationship between orality and the written word, in the context of the petitioning activities of late medieval English MPs, is not a subject that has been directly considered in scholarship, yet it is an approach that offers interesting ways of assessing how and why petitions mattered.[5] This is a discussion, then, that underlines how petitionary processes could be as important as petitionary content in determining reception and outcome. My discussion focuses on three key parliamentary episodes that took place in the 14th century and which are especially helpful in illustrating how petitions were formulated by the Commons and how they were received by the Crown: we begin with detailed focus on the assembly of January 1397, before considering the assemblies that met in January and March 1340 and 1376. But the questions I consider are pertinent to the petitionary form in general, and especially to petitions from, or in the name of, collective entities, for they speak to the much wider theme of how power and authority came to be negotiated between parties of unequal political standing: that is, between subjects and citizens, on the one hand, and those who ruled over them, on the other.

Thomas Haxey's Petition of January 1397

My starting point is an episode that took place in a parliament that met in January 1397. At this point, Richard II had been on the throne of England for almost 20 years. He was 30 years old and on the cusp of a dramatic reassertion of royal authority after an incredibly difficult earlier part to his reign.[6] As a result of these experiences, and as the events in this parliament were to show, Richard had become hypersensitive to anything that suggested criticism of his person, or the encroachment of his authority. On 1 February, almost midway through the parliament, and presumably at some point in the evening (because we are informed that it was after Richard had eaten), the king summoned the Lords into his presence, where he told them that he had heard that they had been in discussions with the Commons, during which various matters had been touched on that 'it seemed to the king were contrary to his regality and estate and his royal liberty'.[7] Upon further enquiry the

[5] Though, on the significance of orality in parliamentary proceedings, see G. Dodd, '"Nother by Addicions, nother by Diminucions": The Parliament of April 1414 and the Drafting of Late Medieval English Legislation', in G. Dodd and C. Taylor (eds), *Monarchy, State, and Political Culture in Late Medieval England: Essays in Honour of W. Mark Ormrod* (Woodbridge, York Medieval Press, 2020), pp. 117–43 (pp. 131–4).

[6] The standard work on the reign remains N. Saul, *Richard II* (New Haven, CT, Yale University Press, 1997).

[7] For this and the following quotations, see *PROME*, parliament of January 1397, items 13–17.

king had learnt (he said) that the Commons had raised four concerns, or requests, these being:

(i) that sheriffs should not be in office for more than one year, in accordance with a statute enacted in 1371;[8]

(ii) that the Scots had committed great outrages in the border regions, for which a remedy was urgently needed;

(iii) that liveries[9] should not be distributed to valets or yeomen unless they were the servants of lords, in accordance with a statute made in 1393;[10] and

(iv) that the great and excessive charge of the king's household should be amended and reduced.

It was almost certainly the fourth request that prompted an extreme reaction by the king. The complaint specifically targeted 'the multitude of bishops who had lordships and were promoted by the king, and their followers; and also ... the ladies and their attendants who dwelt in the king's household and at his expense'. The parliament roll notes that 'the king took great offence and affront in that the commons, who were his lieges, should wrongly take upon themselves or presume any ordinance or governance of the king's person, or his household, or other persons of standing whom it should please him to have in his company'. The king then let it be known that he knew that the request for household reform that had emanated from the Commons had itself been prompted by a 'bill' delivered by an individual,[11] and he charged the Speaker of the Commons, Sir John Bussy (a royal knight and loyal servant of the king),[12] 'to recount and tell him the name of whomsoever [had] submitted the said bill to the said commons'. The bill was duly handed over with the name of its author indicated. The Commons then submitted themselves to the grace of the king, declaring, with suitable humility, that 'it had never been their intent nor will to speak, show nor do anything which would give offence or displeasure to the king's royal majesty'. The author of the bill, a certain

[8] *PROME*, parliament of 1371, item 39. No statute was made in this parliament relating to sheriffs, and the Crown's response to the issue was, at this point, ambivalent; but this date does mark the point when the majority of sheriffs were changed on an annual basis. N. Saul, *Knights and Esquires: The Gloucestershire Gentry in the Fourteenth Century* (Oxford, Oxford University Press, 1981), pp. 110–11.

[9] Livery badges were usually worn by retainers and household servants to indicate their allegiance to a particular lord. From the late 14th century they became the subject of intense debate, since some contemporaries equated their distribution with increased lawlessness and unrest. N. Saul, 'The Commons and the Abolition of Badges', *Parliamentary History*, 9 (1990), 302–15.

[10] *Statutes of the Realm* (*Stats Realm*), 11 vols (London, 1810–28), Vol. II, p. 84 (iv).

[11] The term 'bill' was often used interchangeably with the term 'petition', both signifying written supplications. In this context, the term 'bill' may have been selected to signal the more private origins of the supplication.

[12] J. S. Roskell, L. Clark, and C. Rawcliffe (eds), *The House of Commons 1386–1421*, 4 vols (Stroud, History of Parliament, 1992), Vol. II, pp. 449–54, esp. p. 452.

Thomas Haxey, a long-serving king's clerk,[13] was initially sentenced to a traitor's death, but this sentence was remitted after the intercession in Parliament of the archbishop of Canterbury and prelates.[14] Later, in May 1397, Haxey received a full pardon.[15] It was within the text of this pardon that the full contents of Haxey's bill come to light, and we learn that in addition to the cost of the royal household, he also complained about papal taxation.[16] Haxey's bill is set out in full in the Appendix to this chapter. With the identity of the bill's author now known, Richard took the opportunity to make a more general pronouncement of policy, declaring, through the mouths of the Lords, that henceforth if anyone should incite ('moverit vel excitaverit') the Commons to criticise the king's person, his rule ('nostrum regimen') or regality ('regalitatem nostram'), that person should be held to be a traitor.[17] What the Commons were henceforth to be permitted to petition about had thus been dramatically and drastically curtailed.

The episode has understandably been regarded by historians as a striking, even disturbing, display of the absolute power that Richard II was able to exercise over Parliament.[18] At every turn the king appears to have been in control of the parliamentary agenda: at his command, the Lords were sent to the Commons to tell them that he was most displeased with the reports that he had heard of their discussions;

[13] A. K. McHardy, 'Haxey's Case, 1397: The Petition and Its Presenter Reconsidered', in J. L. Gillespie (ed), *The Age of Richard II* (Stroud, Sutton, 1997), pp. 93–114. 'King's clerk' is a fairly elastic term that includes people, like Haxey, who appear to have operated on the periphery of the Crown's service.

[14] *PROME*, parliament of January 1397, item 23.

[15] For the full text of the pardon, see J. Strachey et al. (eds), *Rotuli parliamentorum* (*Rot. Parl.*), 6 vols (London, Record Commission, 1783), Vol. III, pp. 407–8 (calendared in *Calendar of the Patent Rolls: Richard II* (*CPR*), Vol VI, *1396–1399* (London, HMSO, 1909), p. 141. Ratification of Haxey's estates was recorded by letters patent on 25 February 1397; *CPR, 1396–1399*, pp. 88, 123. For detailed discussion of the case, see Roskell, *et al.*, *House of Commons*, Vol. I, pp. 80–2; and G. Dodd, 'Richard II and the Transformation of Parliament', in G. Dodd (ed.), *The Reign of Richard II* (Stroud, Tempus, 2000), pp. 71–84. McHardy, 'Haxey's Case', p. 108, discusses the identity of the alleged parasitical bishops of the court, though it is possible that John Fordham, bishop of Ely, a close ally of the king and bitter enemy of one of Haxey's benefactors, Ramsey Abbey, may have been especially in his sights, *CPR, 1396–1399*, p. 57.

[16] The existence of the text of the bill disproves beyond question earlier theories that Haxey was responsible for all four of the concerns raised by the Commons and recorded on the parliament roll; of these matters, it was only the fourth, concerning the royal household, that Haxey had articulated. His complaint about papal taxation has for the most part escaped scholarly attention, probably because it is not mentioned in the recorded parliamentary proceedings. The tax was requested by Boniface IX in 1394, and was considered by the convocation of Canterbury in 1394 and 1395; W. E. Lunt, *Financial Relations of the Papacy with England 1327–1534*, 3 vols (Cambridge, MA, Medieval Academy of America, 1962), Vol. II, p. 120. Lunt concluded that the tax was not in the end granted: Haxey's bill clearly casts doubt on this conclusion.

[17] This important pronouncement was not recorded in the parliament roll, but in the letter patent dating to 27 May 1397; *Rot. Parl.*, Vol. III, pp. 407–8.

[18] A. Tuck, *Richard II and the English Nobility* (London, Edward Arnold, 1973), pp. 181–3; Saul, *Richard II*, pp. 369–70; M. Bennett, *Richard II and the Revolution of 1399* (Stroud, Sutton, 1999), pp. 85–8; G. L. Harriss, *Shaping the Nation: England 1360–1461* (Oxford, Oxford University Press, 2005), p. 478.

at his insistence, the Commons dutifully gave up the name of the original sponsor of the offending bill about the royal household; as a result of considerable pressure brought to bear, the Commons then, crucially, acknowledged that such matters 'did not pertain to them, but only to the king himself and to his ordinance'; and without due process the king sentenced the original sponsor of the petition to death. The king had successfully imposed his authority on Parliament and had made clear that petitions that went against his 'regality and royal estate and liberty' were no longer to be tolerated.

But if we probe more deeply into the petitionary form and procedural conventions of this time, a more nuanced picture emerges. For, while Richard's dominion over Parliament is plain to see on a superficial level, the severity of his reaction nevertheless suggests a king who felt threatened not only by the criticism implied in the bill composed by Haxey, but by the petitionary form itself.[19] It is natural to measure the impact and effect of petitions solely in terms of the changes that they brought about; but the Haxey episode indicates that even the simple expediency of *asking* for change could be the cause of considerable consternation for the king. The power of suggestion, set out authoritatively in writing, could be immense. It is even possible that some petitions were formulated and presented not with any great expectation that they would achieve success, but simply because the petitionary form was powerful enough in its own right to influence or shape political agendas.[20] Fundamentally, the king had the right to refuse a petition, but refusal did not equate to disproving the truth of the claims that a petition made. Richard II's clear intention was to shut down the process before such claims gained momentum: that is, before they attracted wider support and became an overwhelming and irresistible political 'truth' that he would find even more difficult to counteract. It is this imperative that explains his extreme reaction to the bill. While it is highly unlikely that the affair was initially orchestrated by the Crown to serve the king's needs,[21] nevertheless, it probably is the case that Haxey's actions, once they came to the king's attention, gave him a welcome opportunity to reset the accepted parameters of petitionary content. The meticulous way in which the episode was noted in the parliament roll, and then subsequently in the patent letter issued four months

[19] Richard II's sensitivity to criticism was not a new development in 1397: in 1387 a proclamation issued to Londoners warned the king's subjects not to 'speak or publish anything, in private or openly, that was evil or dishonest, about the king, the queen, or any of the lords dwelling with the king, now or in the future' (R. R. Sharpe (ed.), *Calendar of Letter-Books of the City of London (H)* (London, Corp. of the City of London, 1907), p. 321; L. C. Hector and B. F. Harvey (eds and trans) *The Westminster Chronicle 1381–1394* (Oxford, Clarendon Press, 1982), pp. 214–16). In the Cambridge Parliament of 1388 the law known as *scandalum magnatum* was reissued, which forbade the telling of 'false [fake?] news, lies or such other false things' of the nobility and the king's ministers; *Stats. Realm*, Vol. II, 59 (xi).
[20] The conundrum of why petitioners petitioned even though the chances of achieving success might have been small is considered in detail for a later period by Miller, 'Introduction', pp. 421–6.
[21] As suggested by R. H. Jones, *The Royal Policy of Richard II: Absolutism in the Later Middle Ages* (Oxford, Basil Blackwell, 1968), p. 73. This is not a view that has commanded widespread support.

later recording Haxey's pardon,[22] suggests that Haxey's fate was to serve as a warning to all future would-be critics of the king and his household. This was a drastic action, but it should be noted that the episode attracted no comment, let alone criticism, in contemporary chronicles.[23] Significantly, when the 'Haxey incident' was recalled in the first parliament of Henry IV's reign, in 1399, it was not as part of the formal, 'official' charges levelled against the former king by the new Lancastrian regime,[24] but was initially part of a personal campaign by Haxey himself to be exonerated from the stain of his treason conviction. Only then was it taken up and turned into a point of constitutional principle by the Commons in an attempt to reaffirm the accepted norms of the petitionary process.[25]

What in particular were the characteristics of the supplicatory form that pushed Richard II into such a defensive mode? Richard's discomfort stemmed in the first place from the fact that he had been entirely separated from key behind-the-scenes discussions going on in Parliament, between the Lords and Commons. Their reformist agenda had evidently been taking shape for some time before the king got wind of what was happening. Procedurally, this had placed him at a disadvantage. But the thing that made these discussions such a serious threat to the king was his fear of where they might lead, and the possibility that the Commons, with the support of the Lords, might stand their ground and insist, as a unified body, on the legitimacy of their appeals for reform. This brings us to a key point about the nature of petitions and the petitionary form in late medieval England. It is easy to assume that, within a supplicatory system in which the grace and benevolence of rulers was solicited by the humble requests of their lower-status subjects, rulers were free to discard calls on their favour that did not meet with their approval; but in some contexts, and particularly in some political contexts, the asymmetrical distribution of power that the supplicant–recipient relationship suggested often masked a more evenly distributed power-sharing – or competing – political dynamic. In other words, between a humble petition, on the one hand, and an uncompromising and forceful demand, on the other, there was often only a very thin dividing line, even though the latter might still be couched in conventionally deferential and supplicatory tones.

[22] *Rot. Parl.*, Vol. III, pp. 407–8. The pardon was authorised by warrant of the privy seal. It does seem, on the face of it, strange that Haxey's bill should have been reproduced, word for word, within the overall text of the pardon recorded in May 1397; this may be a sign of the highly politicised nature of the episode and the unshakable belief in the justification of his actions by the king. An alternative, and perhaps more far-fetched, explanation is that the case was recorded with such meticulous care by chancery clerks eager to assert, albeit obliquely, the validity of Haxey's complaints, and the soundness of the subsequent decision to pardon him. My thanks to Alison McHardy and Helen Lacey for discussions around this particular point.

[23] See discussion of this point in *PROME*, parliament of January 1397, introduction.

[24] In particular, the 33 charges of misgovernance levelled against the king in the so-called 'Record and Process': C. Given-Wilson (ed. and trans.), *Chronicles of the Revolution, 1397–1400: The Reign of Richard II* (Manchester, Manchester University Press, 1993), pp. 168–89.

[25] See pp. 235–6.

Refusing to respond to such 'directives' might have dangerous political consequences. In the 1380s Richard II had been forced to concede to similar requests of the Commons, in part because he faced the concerted opposition of the Commons and Lords, and in part also because agreeing to reform, and placing his household under public scrutiny, was the price the king had been forced to pay in return for grants of taxation.[26] In 1397 Richard was determined to avoid replaying the difficult early years of his reign. He tried to do this in the first instance by neutralising the financial leverage that the Commons might otherwise have been able to bring to bear to force him to agree to their demands. By the time the Haxey incident blew up in Parliament, the possibility that the king might secure a grant of direct taxation had already been removed from the negotiating table: the king had been at pains to reassure MPs that he would not be expecting them to pay for his proposed expedition to Milan.[27] But this still left open the question of indirect taxation – the wool subsidy, which the king did need. It is possible that Richard's reaction to Haxey's bill lay in his fears that the reforms discussed amongst the Lords and Commons might be proposed as preconditions of their agreeing to provide the king with the proceeds of the wool subsidy. If such 'linkage' was afoot, it makes better sense of the king's extreme reaction, for the wool subsidy had by this point become a permanent form of taxation in all but name, and it would have been pushing the established conventions of the medieval constitution for the Commons to have used it as a bargaining chip for political concessions.[28] The great procedural difficulty that confronted the king, therefore, was that criticism of his household was being fomented before the Commons had shown their fiscal hand. By nipping the criticism in the bud, the king was ensuring that questions over reforms to his household were entirely disconnected from questions over finance. Timing, as we shall see, was the critical factor in this process.

For King Richard the most effective way of nullifying this developing situation proved to be unmasking the original sponsor of the demand for reform. Again, this decision requires careful unpacking. The Haxey incident holds particular interest because it reveals how the petitionary agenda of MPs could be influenced by individual lobbyists. Ordinarily, in these circumstances, the identity of such individuals or groups remains hidden, because once the Commons had agreed to make a request of the king, these were almost always presented in the name of the Commons as a whole. It is worth recalling that the originators of the first three requests (relating

[26] J. J. N. Palmer, 'The Parliament of 1385 and the Constitutional Crisis of 1386', *Speculum*, 46 (1971), 477–90; C. Given-Wilson, *The Royal Household and the King's Affinity: Service, Politics and Finance in England 1360–1413* (New Haven, CT, Yale University Press, 1986), pp. 104–6, 113–17, 121–8; C. Fletcher, *Richard II: Manhood, Youth, and Politics, 1377–99* (Oxford, Oxford University Press, 2008), pp. 88–90, 107–8, 114.

[27] *PROME*, parliament of January 1397, items 10 and 17.

[28] The wool subsidy had been collected almost continuously since 1342. There were, however, three brief interruptions during the 1380s. Richard was granted the wool subsidy for life in early 1398. For an overview, see W. M. Ormrod, 'Finance and Trade under Richard II', in A. Goodman and J. L. Gillespie (eds), *Richard II: The Art of Kingship* (Oxford, Oxford University Press, 1999), pp. 155–86.

to sheriffs, the incursions of the Scots, and liveries) remained undisclosed, and so their presentation and projection as the ostensible fabrications of the Commons persisted. The term 'the Commons' – or *les communes*, as it appeared in the French of the contemporary written record[29] – carried huge political weight. It suggested unity of purpose and broad-based support. Because the term was inherently (and deliberately) ambiguous – it could signify both the Commons in Parliament *and* the wider body of the common people throughout the realm – it also carried immense moral force.[30] The Commons, simply by virtue of this descriptor, could claim to speak with some authority for the overall common good, or 'common profit', of the realm.[31] Thus, petitions in the name of the Commons theoretically articulated the aspirations of *all* the king's subjects, and the king – as principal defender of the common interests of the realm[32] – had an almost irresistible moral, as well as political, obligation to respond to these requests. This is the second factor, alongside fiscal pressure, that could transform a petition or supplication into a super-charged political ultimatum. In January 1397 Richard II understood the danger and neutralised it by having the identity of Haxey revealed. In doing so he turned an issue that purported to articulate a matter of general concern into the narrow 'private' grievance of a single individual. In this new (or original) form, the issue could be (and was) dismissed out of hand, as the misguided insolence of an impudent and subversive maverick. Fearful of the king's wrath, the Commons appeared happy to accept this new state of affairs, for they cast Thomas Haxey adrift by disassociating themselves from his request, and pretended that the whole thing had been a terrible mistake. The king, for his part, was happy to make an example of Thomas Haxey and leave the matter there.[33]

[29] *Les communes* (i.e plural) was a term used for the most part in the parliament record from the later 14th century; before the 1370s, MPs were typically described as *le commun* or *la commune*: *PROME*, word search.

[30] J. Watts, 'Public or Plebs: The Changing Meaning of "The Commons", 1381–1549', in H. Pryce and J. Watts (eds), *Power and Identity in the Middle Ages: Essays in Memory of Rees Davies* (Oxford, Oxford University Press, 2007), pp. 242–60, esp. pp. 248–50; G. Dodd, 'A Parliament Full of Rats? *Piers Plowman* and the Good Parliament of 1376', *Historical Research*, 79 (2006), 21–49 (pp. 44–5); D. Rollison, *A Commonwealth of the People: Popular Politics and England's Long Social Revolution, 1066–1649* (Cambridge, Cambridge University Press, 2010), esp. pp. 91–5, 138–43, 241–7; W. M. Ormrod, 'The Good Parliament of 1376: Commons, *Communes*, and "Common Profit" in Fourteenth-Century English Politics', in D. Nicholas, B. S. Bachrach, and J. M. Murray (eds), *Comparative Perspectives on History and Historians: Essays in Memory of Bryce Lyon (1920–2007)* (Kalamazoo, MI, Medieval Institute Publications, 2012), pp. 169–88; J. Watts, 'The Commons in Medieval England', in . J.-P. Genet (ed.), *La légitimité implicite* (Paris, Éditions de la Sorbonne, 2015), available at https://books.openedition.org/psorbonne/6618 (accessed 9 January 2020).

[31] W. M. Ormrod, '"Common Profit" and "The Profit of the King and Kingdom": Parliament and the Development of Political Language in England, 1250–1450', *Viator*, 46 (2015), 219–52, esp. pp. 237–9.

[32] The best general description of the late medieval king's obligation to uphold the common good remains J. Watts, *Henry VI and the Politics of Kingship* (Cambridge, Cambridge University Press, 1996), pp. 16–39.

[33] Haxey's full rehabilitation within three months has also caused puzzlement; for useful discussion of this point, see T. Jones, 'Was Richard II a Tyrant? Richard's Use of the Books of Rules for Princes', in N. Saul (ed.), *Fourteenth Century England V* (Woodbridge, Boydell, 2008), pp. 130–60 (p. 153).

It was almost certainly the impersonal and anonymous nature of the appellation 'the Commons' that emboldened MPs into making what at times were very hard-hitting and intrusive demands of the Crown, safe in the knowledge that whoever amongst their number had been responsible for first airing such criticism now had the full support, backing, and even protection of all the MPs. Anonymity ensured immunity. It says much about the strength of this principle of collective responsibility that, with the exception of 1397, there is no evidence of MPs breaking ranks and splintering into opposing factions when especially contentious petitions or requests were presented. Even in 1397 it is worth noting that Thomas Haxey was not himself an MP, but a royal clerk, standing in for the abbot of Selby as his proctor, and therefore, strictly speaking, a member of the Lords.[34] This may have made the willingness of the Commons to reveal his identity (that is, in effect, to betray him) all the easier to contemplate. It was virtually the only occasion when a late medieval English king had forced the Commons into revealing the source of one of their demands.[35] This says much about the tense political atmosphere of the parliament of January 1397, as well as the particular temperament of Richard II; but it may also have something to tell us about the petitionary process, and the strengths and weaknesses of the Commons' organisation, political resolve, and collective identity. The Haxey 'incident' highlighted the importance for the parliamentary Commons of pressing for reform with conviction and unity of purpose. But it should also be clear how vital it was to those individuals who initiated such reforms – whether they were members of the Commons or not – to maintain the fiction that these suggestions had sprung from the spontaneous and unanimous collective thinking of the whole body of MPs: the immunity that anonymity provided facilitated a supplicatory culture that permitted investigation into even the most sensitive areas of the workings of royal governance. Once MPs broke ranks and turned on each other, or on those who sought to influence their actions, as happened in 1397, the case for reform was doomed.

The Strengths and Weaknesses of Oral and Written Petitions

It is now time to consider how these preliminary observations might be applied to a more general investigation into the ways the Commons pushed for change across the 14th century. This is a task that continues to place importance on the notion that the processes that governed how such requests were managed within Parliament could be as important as the content of the requests in determining how they were received. This procedural approach again underscores the importance of

[34] McHardy, 'Haxey's Case', p. 100; P. Bradford and A. K. McHardy (eds), *Proctors for Parliament: Clergy, Community and Politics, c. 1248–1539 (The National Archives, Series SC 10), c. 1248–1377*, Canterbury and York Society 107, 2 vols (Woodbridge, Boydell Press, 2017 and 2018), Vol. I, index (the introductions to both volumes provide excellent general context).

[35] For one exception see pp. 229–30.

the timing of petitions within the political process, and it explores in more detail the distinction to be drawn between petitions presented in written form and those communicated to the Crown orally. It must be stressed, however, that the purpose of this discussion is not to suggest that the Commons and the king were locked in a constitutional struggle to achieve political hegemony: the ways and means by which petitioning in Parliament developed over the course of the 14th century were driven for the most part by a shared desire to maintain a workable and reasonable *modus operandi*, such that the king would never be forced into making concessions that damaged his prerogative, and the Commons would never be denied an opportunity to request reform where these reforms were needed. In other words, it was not the intention that one party deny the other manoeuvrability in the petitionary process, but instead to ensure that the process worked in a fair and balanced manner.

As noted already, for much of the 14th century, the essential vehicle of the Commons' political voice, and the basic tool of reform in Parliament, was the common petition. Common petitions had emerged in the course of Edward II's reign when the elected MPs took over from the barons the right to articulate matters that were presented in the name of the generality of the king's subjects.[36] All the evidence suggests that at this time, in the early 14th century, petitions really were 'petitions of the parliamentary Commons' – that is to say, Commons' petitions ('s' apostrophe): requests devised and written up at Parliament on behalf of the community of the realm by the MPs returned to each assembly. Their tight control of these petitions meant that MPs exercised equally close control over reform agendas, and in relatively short time the representatives in Parliament had formulated a deeply rooted political programme of reform that transcended the changes in regime in 1327 and 1330, as well as the regular turnover of the personnel of the Commons that occurred from one parliament to the next.[37] These consolidated schedules of common petitions gave the requests political clout and a measure of constitutional protection. Indeed, it is significant that the only occasion in the 14th century, besides 1397, when the Crown took action against a petition presented in the name of the commons, occurred in the early 1300s before such complaints or requests came to be presented by MPs as part of a co-ordinated programme of reform. On this earlier occasion Henry of Keighley, one of the representatives for Lancashire, produced a bill in the Lincoln parliament of 1301 that demanded the king's observance of Magna Carta and the Charter of the Forest, as well as the completion of the perambulations of the Forest.[38] Although Keighley's bill was said

[36] M. Prestwich, 'Parliament and the Community of the Realm in Fourteenth-Century England', in A. Cosgrove and J. I. McGuire (eds), *Parliament and Community* (Belfast, Appletree Press, 1983), pp. 5–24; J. R. Maddicott, *The Origins of the English Parliament, 924–1327* (Oxford, Oxford University Press, 2010), pp. 331–75.

[37] W. M. Ormrod, 'Agenda for Legislation, 1322–*c*. 1340', *English Historical Review* (*EHR*), 105 (1990), 1–33; Dodd, *Justice and Grace*, pp. 133–41.

[38] H. Rothwell (ed.), *English Historical Documents III: 1189–1327* (*EHD*) (London, Routledge, 1975), pp. 510–12 (no. 88); M. Prestwich, *Edward I* (New Haven, CT, Yale University Press, 1988), pp. 525–6; Maddicott, *The Origins*, p. 304.

to be in the name of the 'people of the community of this land', it was presented not by the representatives in Parliament but by 'the prelates and leading men of the kingdom ... on behalf of the whole community in ... parliament'.[39] Without the moral and political force of the collective body of representatives behind the demands, Edward I, much like Richard II and Thomas Haxey, was able to identify and isolate Keighley and have him imprisoned for having 'pressed us outrageously at the Lincoln parliament'.[40] No such course of action was open to Edward II or Edward III: by the 1320s MPs were sufficiently co-ordinated and politically mature to avoid such a scenario. Although evidence for the mechanics of creating these later schedules of common petitions is lacking, it seems likely that they were the product of collective discussion, common resolve, and shared responsibility. This created an altogether more unfettered petitionary environment than had previously been the case, and one that the Crown now found extremely difficult to challenge or undermine.

One of the high points of the petitionary form in a late medieval English political context occurred in 1340, when Edward III's military ambitions on the continent generated a financial and political crisis of the first magnitude.[41] It was at this time that the full political force of common petitions came to be realised when MPs presented a series of requests as the price for their agreement to provide the king with a generous grant of taxation. It was the exploitation of this close relationship between redress and supply that effectively transformed supplications into powerful instruments of far-reaching political reform. What enabled the Commons to force through these demands was the procedural advantage they enjoyed, by insisting that the king show his hand and accede to their demands *before* they, in turn, decided what tax to grant him. This particular dynamic played out over the course of two parliaments, the first assembly in January 1340, the second in March 1340. In January 1340, in response to the king's desperate need for funds, the Commons provisionally offered a grant of 30,000 sacks of wool, but did so only 'under certain conditions':[42] that is to say, providing that the king addressed the petitions that had been presented to him. It was even noted in the parliament roll that if the conditions were not accepted, the Commons 'would not be required to make the aid'.[43] The 'conditions', though still couched in suitably deferential terms, were of a radical nature and included: demands for an investigation into the administration of recent taxes, the reservation of all royal revenues for the upkeep of the war, the resumption of royal lands alienated since the death of Edward I, the redress of grievances through the council and Parliament, and parliamentary

[39] *EHD*, no. 88.

[40] Ibid., no. 94.

[41] The definitive discussion of this episode is G. L. Harriss, 'The Commons' Petitions of 1340', *EHR*, 78 (1963), 625–54. I follow Harriss's argument that the petitions presented in March 1340 had initially been aired in January 1340.

[42] *PROME*, parliament of January 1340, item 7.

[43] Ibid.

authority to prosecute and punish the king's ministers.[44] Because these terms 'so closely touched the estate of our lord the king' (who was at this time leading his army on the continent),[45] Parliament was dissolved without anything apart from a tokenistic tax grant being made. It reconvened a month later, in March, when the king had returned to England. In this assembly Edward III had no choice but to agree to the MPs' petitions (demands), in return for a grant of a ninth part of total goods assessed.

The political crisis of 1340 highlighted the strength of the petitionary form when the political and procedural stars were closely aligned. That is to say: when the subject matter of the petitions found common cause with influential members of the Upper House; when the king's pressing need for taxation necessarily made him more receptive to the matters raised in the petitions; when the Commons were united behind their own reform agenda and exercised total control over the content of their petitions; and when they were able to insist on the redress of their petitions before they, in turn, supplied taxation. In the course of Edward III's reign, however, two developments occurred that had the effect of undermining the potency of the common petition form. First, by the end of the 1340s Edward III had established the principle that common petitions would not be answered until *after* MPs had made their grant of taxation.[46] Thus, in the assembly of 1346 the Commons granted the king direct taxation on Thursday 14 September, just three days after Parliament had begun, and only then were they invited to submit their petitions. The MPs learned the outcome to their requests after the council had considered them between 16 and 18 September; Parliament ended on 20 September.[47] The decoupling of common petitions from questions about taxation, so skilfully managed by Edward III, did not prevent MPs from presenting petitions on 'political' matters, but it did reduce the chances of such petitions directly affecting the course and agenda of a parliamentary session. In effect, it reversed the political dynamic: redress came to be dependent upon supply, rather than the other way round. Occasionally, such as in 1371, the delay that the king imposed on the consideration of petitions could mean that Parliament ended before all such requests were considered.[48] Common petitions continued to be presented and considered by the Crown in large numbers and often with tangible effects, as is testified by the voluminous legislation of this period; but the control that the Crown now exerted over *when* they were presented in Parliament to some extent blunted them as instruments of hard-hitting political reform.

Second, over the course of Edward III's reign, there are signs that the Commons' exclusive management over the content of common petitions also began to weaken.

[44] A. W. Goodman (ed.), *The Chartulary of Winchester Cathedral* (Winchester, Warren and Son, 1927), pp. 131–3; *PROME*, parliament of March 1340, Appendix, item 1.

[45] *PROME*, parliament of January 1340, item 7.

[46] For discussion, see G. L. Harriss, *King, Parliament, and Public Finance in Medieval England to 1369* (Oxford, Clarendon Press, 1975), pp. 358–70.

[47] *PROME*, parliament of 1346, item 11. And see also *PROME*, parliament of March 1348, item 4.

[48] *PROME*, parliament of 1371, item 8.

The turning point once again came shortly after the crisis of 1340–1, when common petitions began to be enrolled for the first time on the parliament roll as a 'neat' record of the matters that had been brought to the king's attention.[49] In having these petitions enrolled the Commons gave up a crucial element of control over what was – or what was not – presented to the Crown as a common petition. Whereas the earlier schedules of common petitions could truly be said to have been Commons' petitions (i.e. products of the Lower House), now they came to be, more straightforwardly, just common petitions – that is to say, petitions that related to matters of general or common concern, only a proportion of which may actually have been compiled by MPs themselves.[50] With enrolment now came the question of who arbitrated over which petitions came before the king and his council: MPs or the clerks who drew up the formal parliamentary record? If the latter, to what extent was subject matter vetted or even omitted entirely from the record? In his analysis of the parliament rolls of Edward III's reign, Mark Ormrod has suggested that there were three stages to writing up common petitions: first, *ad hoc* memoranda were produced; second, the memoranda were collected together into a single working document; and third, the working document was written up into a final, polished 'fair copy', to form part of the parliament roll.[51] According to Ormrod, the third stage was only reached after 'a set of decisions [had been] taken by the clerk of Parliament as to which sections of the Commons' list would actually be written up and preserved on the enrolled record of an assembly'.[52] In the course of this process, other supplications might be added that the clerk considered to have met the criteria to qualify as a common petition. It is important not to overstate the subversive intentions of royal servants, but the shift to enrolment was undoubtedly an important factor in bringing the supplicatory agenda of the Commons within the overall purview of the Crown.

By the time of the next major constitutional crisis of 1376 it is apparent that an important change had occurred in the way in which the Commons chose to articulate their requests (or demands) for reform from the Crown, and these, I suggest, related in part to the developments that have just been outlined. For, whereas in 1340 the demands of the Commons had been presented as *written* common petitions, in 1376 the Commons instead elected a Speaker – Sir Peter de la Mare – who engaged in dialogue with the king's ministers and articulated the Commons' political demands orally.[53] Much attention has been given to the course of this

[49] For discussion, see Dodd, *Justice and Grace*, pp. 140–1.

[50] The classic statement is by D. Rayner, 'The Forms and Machinery of the "Commune Petition" in the Fourteenth Century', *EHR*, 66 (1941), 198–233, 549–70, esp. pp. 204, 570.

[51] W. M. Ormrod, 'On – and off – the Record: The Rolls of Parliament, 1337–1377', in L. Clark (ed.), *Parchment and People: Parliament in the Middle Ages* (Edinburgh, Edinburgh University Press, 2004), pp. 39–56 (p. 46).

[52] Ibid., p. 46.

[53] As indicated in the *Anonimalle Chronicle*'s account of the parliament, translated (from French) in J. Taylor, *English Historical Literature in the Fourteenth Century* (Oxford, Clarendon Press, 1987), pp. 300–13.

parliament.[54] In addition to the appointment of the Speaker, the assembly also, notably, witnessed the impeachment of a number of unpopular courtiers and financiers, the appointment of a reform council, and the presentation of a record number of common petitions – 126 altogether. The petitions raised a vast array of different topics. Many were of a new type of localised petition that MPs now 'sponsored' on behalf of the original petitioners.[55] But none pushed for reform to central government in the way MPs had attempted by using the common petition format in 1340. Instead, these reforms were stipulated through the speeches and hard-bargaining of de la Mare during the course of Parliament. It is my contention that the advent of the Commons' Speaker in 1376 was in part a symptom of, and reaction to, the changed status of the common petition. In effect, the Commons found it expedient to articulate their demands orally rather than in writing, because this gave immediate effect to their reform agenda and because it required the Crown to provide answers and commitments to their proposals well before Parliament ended. The problem with written petitions was that they could be deferred, lost, or simply rejected – with no chance of any comeback. Crucially, by using the Speaker in this way the Commons had found a way of negating some of the procedural advantages enjoyed by the king when he linked the reception of common petitions to grants of taxation.

But in articulating demands for reform orally, now apparently through the mouth of one individual, the Commons risked losing an element that made the written common petition so powerful politically and procedurally: unanimity. In 1397, as we have seen, the Commons were vulnerable when their agenda was still at the point of formulation and when, quite probably, there was no universally felt 'ownership' amongst MPs of a collective supplicatory agenda. Possibly aware of the dangers, as well as the possibilities, of more free-flowing dialogue with the Crown, the Commons in 1376 were careful to set out their expectations of the shared responsibilities of their members. Early in the assembly the *Anonimalle Chronicle* recorded that:

> on the second day all the knights and Commons aforesaid gathered and went into the chapter house and sat around, each close to the other, and they began to talk of the substance of the causes of parliament, and they said that it would be desirable at the beginning to be sworn one to the other, to hold counsel as to what was spoken and ordered among them, and loyally to treat and ordain for the welfare of the kingdom without concealing anything; and to this they all unanimously assented and took an oath to be loyal one to the other.[56]

What was important was that MPs spoke honestly about the problems experienced within the realm, and that they should do so without fear of being betrayed by their colleagues. The oath they took to be loyal to each other was a striking assertion of the need to remain united and strong, and has led one historian to characterise the Commons

[54] The most detailed account is G. Holmes, *The Good Parliament* (Oxford, Clarendon Press, 1975).

[55] Dodd, *Justice and Grace*, pp. 143–55.

[56] Taylor, *English Historical Literature*, p. 302.

of 1376 as a 'sworn confederacy'.[57] It was, perhaps, also a sign of the increased vulnerability of the Lower House to informants and turncoats, now that its opposition programme was being formulated within a less rigid or regulated environment. The crucial principle of collective responsibility was also articulated in the assertion that 'what one of us says, all say and assent to'.[58] As for the Speaker, it was vital that his authority to articulate demands on behalf of his colleagues be widely recognised, but also that he should act exclusively as the mouthpiece of his colleagues: not of anyone else, nor for that matter solely for himself. Hence, 'it was decided among [the MPs] that … what Sir Peter spoke by their advice, all should assent to and should maintain'.[59] De la Mare himself noted that where circumstances warranted he would 'subject … [himself] to the correction and amendment of … [his] colleagues'.[60]

Unanimity could be maintained, but anonymity could not, at least for the Speaker. Indeed, one of the more ignominious acts of the Gaunt-led regime, once Parliament had ended in 1376, was the imprisonment of de la Mare for six months for his contumacy as Speaker: he was finally set free in June 1377, shortly after Edward III died.[61] The Speaker could not avoid the political limelight, but he could be protected. When de la Mare acted as Speaker for a second time in October 1377 he was careful – for understandable reasons – to establish his freedom to speak without fear of recrimination:

> …if there was anything to say he would say it not of his own accord, but by the will, consent, and express wish of all the commons there present: and if he should depart from their intent, or if he should say anything which had not been agreed by his companions, that he might be corrected by his same companions there as soon as possible, and before they had left that place.[62]

Not able to rely on anonymity, the Speaker thus achieved immunity by stressing his indivisibility with the whole body of MPs. It was an approach that worked: de la Mare was the first and last medieval Speaker to suffer the consequences of making life difficult for the Crown.

Conclusion

In 1397 Richard II took the highly unusual step of defining as off limits all discussion about the size and finances of his household within Parliament. This was a forlorn attempt to redefine the subject as a matter pertaining exclusively to the

[57] Ormrod, 'The Good Parliament of 1376', p. 175.

[58] Taylor, *English Historical Literature*, p. 305.

[59] Ibid., p. 304.

[60] Ibid., p. 306.

[61] J. S. Roskell, 'Sir Peter de la Mare, Speaker for the Commons in Parliament in 1376 and 1377', *Nottingham Medieval Studies*, 2 (1958), 24–37 (p. 32).

[62] *PROME*, parliament of October 1377, item 15. For general discussion of the Speaker's 'protestation', see J. S. Roskell, *The Commons and Their Speakers in English Parliaments, 1376–1523* (Manchester, Manchester University Press, 1965), Chapter 2.

royal prerogative. If the episode demonstrates the particular paranoia of this king, it also illuminates very clearly how and why petitions mattered in the 14th century, especially those presented by the Commons in Parliament. Petitions presented in the name of the Commons carried a degree of immunity, as a result of their anonymity, which allowed the political community to probe into the affairs of the king far more obtrusively than if the petitions had been presented by named individuals. When the successful outcome of common petitions was explicitly made the condition of grants of taxation, as happened in 1340, the power this gave to the wider political community could be immense. But at the same time written petitions could be inflexible, overly reductionist, and open to manipulation. Over the course of the 14th century the Commons shifted their mode of addressing especially sensitive, contentious, or controversial subjects as the remit of common petitions opened up and threatened to swamp hard-edged programmes of political reform, and as they also increasingly came to be managed by the royal secretariat. I have suggested that the advent of the Commons' Speaker was in part a reaction to these new circumstances. Unanimity was no less important in these changed conditions to ensure that requests in the name of the Commons carried weight and authority, but new ways were sought to maintain the crucial element of immunity.

The Speakership offered a means of circumventing the weaknesses of the written common petition format, but in January 1397 it is possible that the Speaker – Sir John Bussy – was himself a threat to the Commons' reform agenda, for he was a stooge of the king and almost certainly would not have willingly conveyed the demands of his fellow MPs for household reform to Richard II. This might explain the distinct whiff of political intrigue that surrounds the whole Haxey incident, and the king's genuine alarm at what was afoot. Richard II successfully headed off this threat to his prerogative, but in seeking permanently to redefine what could, and could not, be petitioned about, he failed, and not just because he was deposed 18 months later. He failed because by the late 14th century a remarkably permissive petitionary culture was too firmly established within the DNA of the late medieval English parliament to be expunged at the whim of an oversensitive and overbearing monarch. Richard's failure to curb the freedom of the political community to express its concerns – through written or verbal requests – was to achieve an explicit statement in 1399 when Thomas Haxey sought Henry IV's affirmation of the pardon he had been granted in 1397.[63] In a process that appears, somewhat ironically, to have mirrored what had happened in 1397, Haxey initially presented a bill of his own, before it was then taken up and endorsed by the Commons.[64] In his supplication, Haxey stated that he had presented his bill in 1397 'for the honour

[63] Chris Given-Wilson suggests that Haxey was motivated to appeal to Henry IV primarily to ensure that the stigma of his treason conviction was entirely removed from his name, not having any adverse impact on his heirs: *Henry IV* (New Haven, CT, Yale University Press, 2016), p. 444.

[64] *PROME*, parliament of 1399, items 90, 104. The original of the bill Haxey presented in 1399 is The National Archives, Kew, SC 8/22/1066. The process was not quite identical: in 1399, Haxey addressed his bill to the king and the Lords; in 1397 his initial complaint was addressed to the Commons.

and advantage of [Richard II] and of the whole realm', and that his conviction as a traitor had been 'contrary to right and to the procedure that had previously been followed in parliament'. In their subsequent endorsement, the Commons repeated Haxey's sentiment about his conviction, but added that his treatment had also been 'to the ruin of the customs of the commons', and they furthermore called on Henry IV's good graces 'for the protection of the liberties of the said commons'. The MPs were acutely aware of the enormous constitutional issues at stake after the high-handed actions of their former king, and they recognised the vital importance, now that a new regime had been installed, of affirming the principle that they ought to feel free to question misgovernance without fear of repercussion or retribution. This was, in a sense, an early affirmation of the principle of political freedom of speech, and petitions remained at the very forefront of this stated principle.

This discussion has focused on one type of petition, in one particular historical and geographical context. My intention, in the first instance, was to demonstrate that the notional separation of petitioning between a premodern era – where petitions were used for narrow individualistic ends in a way that upheld the power and authority of the rulers – on the one hand, and later periods – where petitions might be used to challenge structures of authority and resist abuses of power – on the other hand, requires some modification. Richard II considered petitioning to be potentially so threatening to his authority that he redefined the laws of treason to encapsulate those whose requests he considered to be unconscionable. Medieval common petitions – or petitions from the Commons – were not used as a mode of *popular* protest, but they were certainly used as a means of protest, and were capable of holding rulers and officials to account, of challenging unpopular policies, and influencing the shape of government as much as later modes of petitioning. In seeking to qualify broader narratives of petitionary development, however, it should be acknowledged that England in the Middle Ages was a special case: in no other European context was petitioning quite so deeply embedded in the political dialogue between the ruler and his subjects. This owed much to the distinctive attributes of the English polity and the particular place of Parliament within it. It was the fusing of Parliament's legislative and fiscal functions, on the one hand, with a strong tradition of broad-based representation and participation in government by townsmen, clergy, and above all, lesser landowners (i.e. gentry), on the other hand, that created the circumstances in which English kings faced the intensely politicised petitions of their subjects.[65]

Many of the questions I have considered also, however, have a wider chronological and geographical application. In this discussion I have emphasised the importance of thinking about petitions not simply as 'requests' or 'supplications' – terminology that can attribute an unduly passive or deferential role to the petitioner – but also as 'complaints', and even 'demands', in which petitioners assumed a far

[65] J. Watts, *The Making of Polities: Europe, 1300–1500* (Cambridge, Cambridge University Press, 2009), pp. 233–8; Maddicott, *The Origins*, Chapter 7.

more critical and combative relationship with higher authority. It is an approach that diminishes the apparent disparity in power between those who petitioned and those who received these petitions, by underlining the point that rulers were not always free to respond to the requests made of them as they might have wished: petitioners, though cast in the role of mere supplicants, had many means at their disposal to exert pressure and elicit a favourable outcome. It was the claim of representativeness that gave the requests of the Commons in the late medieval English Parliament such persuasive power. At the same time, the processes that governed when and how petitions were presented to rulers could influence how those petitions were received. I have suggested that in written form a petition possessed certain attributes that could act to help and/or hinder its chances of success. In writing (or in print), a petition exuded formality and legitimacy, it could act as a rallying point for mobilising broad-based support, and it could influence how the adjudicating authority responded (for example, by suggesting forms of words to be used in a resulting edict, pronouncement, or law); but at the same time, a 'hard-copy' petition might be more easily discarded, it was more easily subsumed into long-winded bureaucratic processes, and it could not respond to rapidly changing circumstances as part of ongoing negotiation. For the petitioner, judging how to present a request or complaint, and when to do so, could be just as important as the language used to frame it, and the nature of the supplication itself, in determining its eventual fate.

Appendix: The Bill of Thomas Haxey, 1397

Plese a les comunes d'Engleterre en cest present parlement considerer les tres grandes coustages nostre seignur le roi deins sa meson, si bien del multitude des evesques et dames ove leur meynie, et la poeple queaux appent, autrement q'ad este en temps de ses progenitours et ent ordegner due remede, que les ditz evesques de cy en avant ovesque leur meignie demoergent sur leur seignuries, si bien en descharge nostre seignur le roy et son poeple, come en eide et salvacion des subgitz des ditz evesques, et pur autres biens q'ent purront avender. Et auxi de consider coment lui Seint Pierre fist imposicion du clergie de la diocise de Caunterbirs de quatre deniers de la livere l'an darrein, quel imposicion estoit expressement encountre la regalie nostre seignur le roi, a grand damage et destruction de la clergie et de la comunes d'Engleterre, et adnullement de les droitz de la corone nostre dit seignur le roy, et ent ordener due remede en salvacion nostre dit seignur le roy et son roaume, pur Dieu, et en oevre de charitee.[66]

May it please the commons of England in this present parliament to consider the very great costs of our lord the king in his household, as well as the multitude of bishops and ladies with their followers and people attached to them, which is not

[66] *Rot. Parl.*, Vol. III, pp. 407–8.

as it was in the time of his progenitors; and to ordain due remedy for this, so that the aforesaid bishops with their households shall in future remain in their lordships, which will not only alleviate the burden on our lord the king and his people, but will also be of benefit and salvation to the subjects of the said bishops, as well as bringing other advantages. Also, may they consider how last year the Holy Father imposed a charge of four pence in the pound on the clergy of the diocese of Canterbury, which imposition was expressly contrary to the regality of our lord the king, to the great damage and destruction of the clergy and commons of England, and the annulment of the rights of the crown of our said lord the king; and to ordain a due remedy for this, for the salvation of our said lord the king and his realm, for God and by way of charity.[67]

[67] *PROME*, parliament of January 1397, Appendix, item 1.

12

Negotiating Citizenship through Petitions in Late Medieval Italy

MARTA GRAVELA

In Italy, as in most European countries since the late Middle Ages, petitions were increasingly used by people at various levels of society to present grievances, plead for mercy, and demand favours and privileges.[1] Petitionary practices were not a new form in the late medieval period;[2] nevertheless, in the 14th and 15th centuries, following the model of petitions to the pope, this form of request became ubiquitous and widespread.[3] Individuals, groups, and communities addressed huge numbers of oral and written petitions to authorities, which proved increasingly willing to receive them; their content could range from individual economic and legal concerns, to more complex judicial matters, to the expression of collective social and political dissent.

Despite the undeniable abundance of late medieval and early modern petitions in Italian archives, it is only from the end of the 1990s and early 2000s that they

[1] Essential references in C. Nubola, 'Supplications between Politics and Justice: The Northern and Central Italian States in the Early Modern Age', in L. Heerma van Voss (ed.), *Petitions in Social History*, Supplement 9 of *International Review of Social History*, 46 (2001), 35–56; M. Vallerani, 'La supplica al signore e il potere della misericordia: Bologna 1337–1347', *Quaderni storici*, 131 (2009), 411–41; and S. Cerutti, 'Travail, mobilité et légitimité: Suppliques au roi dans une société d'Ancien Régime (Turin, XVIIIe siècle)', *Annales: Histoire, Sciences Sociales*, 65 (2010), 571–611. For a comparison with the transalpine area, see A. Würgler, 'Suppliche e "gravamina" nella prima età moderna: La storiografia di lingua tedesca', *Annali dell'Istituto storico italo-germanico in Trento*, 25 (1999), 515–46; A. Würgler, 'Shaping the "I" and the State? Petitions in Early Modern Europe', in B. Waddell (ed.), *Addressing Authority: An Online Symposium on Petitions and Supplications in Early Modern Society* (2016), https://manyheadedmonster.com/2016/11/03/shaping-the-i-and-the-state-petitions-in-early-modern-europe/ (accessed 10 February 2024).

[2] G. Koziol, 'The Early History of Rites of Supplication', in H. Millet (ed.), *Suppliques et requêtes: Le gouvernement par la grâce en Occident (XIIe–XVe siècle)* (Rome, École française de Rome, 2003), pp. 21–36.

[3] L. Schmugge, 'Suppliche e diritto canonico: Il caso della Penitenzieria', in Millet, *Suppliques et requêtes*, pp. 207–31; and the other essays in the same volume.

Proceedings of the British Academy, **262**, 239–253,

have received considerable attention from scholars, and that their social and political significance has been adequately acknowledged. By taking into account the various forms of requests submitted, and the procedures to present them, several studies have examined the use of petitions and their impact on the relationship between governments and subjects. Beyond the distinction between individual and collective requests, the numerous and multifarious types of petitions can be broadly divided into two categories: judicial and patronage petitions.[4] The former included petitions related in various ways to court proceedings, embracing all sorts of appeals for judicial mercy, as well as requests for justice, with particular reference to *ex officio* procedures, faster and cheaper than the ordinary, and therefore more accessible.[5] The latter – patronage petitions – involved applications to do or obtain something in spite of legal constraints: use of inheritances and possessions beyond restrictions, concession of gifts, favours, offices, and privileges, even when lacking the essential requirements.[6]

Researchers have highlighted the role of both individual and collective petitions as a means of initiating the negotiating process with the authority: from requests for judicial mercy or fiscal exemption to political *gravamina*, petitions engaged rulers and subjects in a process that could provide new and partially shared solutions.[7] This process could entail a varying degree of reciprocity, implying that subjects could play an active role not only in reshaping specific situations, but also in inducing legal changes. Other studies, focusing on petitions from a 'socio-legal' perspective, have insisted on how this form of request informed the relationship between the law and the individual case: petitions made it possible to act within the gaps and ambiguities of the existing law; to suspend temporarily a norm for particular reasons; and finally to question the general nature of a rule and its local application, leading to the 'construction dialectique d'un univers normatif'.[8]

Finally, from the late Middle Ages petitions played a crucial part in the construction of political power. Drawing on the pontifical model, in the 14th and 15th centuries newly established authorities used petitions as a tool of government. Petitions enabled a lord who had recently gained power to act as the warrant of justice and equity, or to become the merciful protector of the weak and the poor, thereby providing the ideological basis for a power that still lacked

[4] I adopt here the distinction proposed by N. Covini, 'La trattazione delle suppliche nella cancelleria sforzesca: Da Francesco Sforza a Ludovico il Moro', in Nubola and Würgler, *Suppliche e 'gravamina': Politica, amministrazione, giustizia in Europa (secoli XIV–XVIII)* (Bologna, Il Mulino, 2002), pp. 107–46, esp. pp. 108–9.

[5] S. Cerutti, *Giustizia sommaria: Pratiche e ideali di giustizia in una società di ancien régime (Torino XVIII secolo)* (Milan, Feltrinelli, 2003).

[6] S. Cerutti and M. Vallerani, 'Introduction', in S. Cerutti and M. Vallerani (eds), *Suppliques: Lois et cas dans la normativité de l'époque moderne, L'Atelier du Centre de recherches historiques*, 13 (2015), http://journals.openedition.org/acrh/6545 (accessed 10 February 2024).

[7] Nubola, 'Supplications between Politics and Justice', p. 31; Würgler, 'Suppliche e "gravamina"'; as well the essays collected in Nubola and Würgler, *Suppliche e 'gravamina'*.

[8] Cerutti and Vallerani, 'Introduction'.

either official acknowledgement or firm recognition by subjects.[9] This was particularly true for 14th-century city lords (*signori*) who still ruled through extant communal institutions and usually did not have an established and incontestable power, such as Taddeo Pepoli in Bologna, or the Della Scala in Verona, to give a couple of examples.[10] Petitions were equally useful for 15th-century dukes in need of wider consent in an age of continuous conflict and internal factionalism, such as the Sforza dukes of Milan,[11] and rural lords who had just acquired their fiefs, such as the Borromeo when they started constructing their lordship on Lake Maggiore in the 1430s.[12] Urban, rural, and regional lords required a renewed image of power; the authority had to be perceived by its subjects as close and capable of acting like a 'protective father': by providing a direct link between the centre of power and its subjects and thus granting legitimacy to a new sovereign power, petitions proved functional to the construction of the princely state, which explains why they were increasingly adopted in late medieval and early modern polities.[13]

Petitions were also common in city states that had preserved a 'republican' government, such as Venice, Siena, or Genoa, a study of the last of which forms the core of this chapter.[14] Even though urban political institutions remained in place,

[9] Vallerani, 'La supplica al signore'; M. Vallerani, 'La pauvreté et la citoyenneté dans les suppliques du XIVe siècle', in Cerutti and Vallerani, *Suppliques*.

[10] Vallerani, 'La pauvreté et la citoyenneté'; G. Orlandelli, *La supplica a Taddeo Pepoli* (Bologna, R. Patron, 1962); G. M. Varanini, '"Al magnifico e possente segnoro": Suppliche ai signori trecenteschi italiani fra cancelleria e corte. L'esempio scaligero', in Nubola and Würgler, *Suppliche e 'gravamina'*, pp. 65–106. The author also offers a broad summary of the studies and surviving series of petitions to Italian 14th-century lords; G. Albini, '"Civitas tunc quiescit et fulget cum pollentium numero decoratur": Le concessioni di cittadinanza in età viscontea tra pratiche e linguaggi politici', in A. Gamberini, J.-P. Genet, and A. Zorzi (eds), *The Languages of Political Society: Western Europe, 14th 17th Centuries* (Rome, Viella, 2011), pp. 97–120.

[11] Covini, 'La trattazione delle suppliche'; N. Covini, 'Pétitions et suppliques pendant la domination des Visconti et des Sforza au XVe siècle : Exception, dérogation et formes simplifiées de justice', in Cerutti and Vallerani, *Suppliques*. For *gratie* granted also by the Visconti see N. Covini, '*De gratia speciali*: Sperimentazioni documentarie e pratiche di potere tra i Visconti e gli Sforza', in M. Vallerani (ed.), *Tecniche di potere nel tardo medioevo: Regimi comunali e signorie in Italia* (Rome, Viella, 2010), pp. 183–206. For further analysis of petitions to the Sforza, see G. Giudici, 'Petitions, Information and Governance in 15th and Early 16th-Century Sforza Milan', in Waddell, *Addressing Authority*.

[12] F. Del Tredici, 'La giustizia dei Borromeo: Suppliche e costruzione di un piccolo stato signorile nel tardo medioevo', *Archivio storico lombardo*, 145 (2019), 71–103. For an early modern example, see B. Forclaz, *La famille Borghese et ses fiefs: L'autorité négociée dans l'état pontifical d'ancien régime* (Rome, École française de Rome, 2006), pp. 59–77.

[13] Nubola, 'Supplications between Politics and Justice'. For a comparison with the kingdoms of England and France, see G. Dodd and S. Petit-Renaud, 'Grace and Favour: The Petition and Its Mechanisms', in C. Fletcher, J.-P. Genet, and J. Watts (eds), *Government and Political Life in England and France, c. 1300–c. 1500* (Cambridge, Cambridge University Press, 2015), pp. 240–78.

[14] D. Romano, '"Quod sibi fiat gratia": Adjustment of penalties and the exercise of influence in early Renaissance Venice', *Journal of Medieval and Renaissance studies*, 13 (1983), 251–68; A. Barlucchi, 'Le "petizioni" inviate dalle comunità del contado al governo senese (secoli XIII–XV)', in Millet, *Suppliques et requêtes*, pp. 265–79.

Renaissance Genoa experienced significant political instability, which caused frequent and long-lasting periods of subjection to external powers, such as the French king or the lord of Milan.[15] Local officers, aldermen (*Anziani*), and governors (*dogi*) had always received petitions of various sorts, from individual judicial petitions to petitions of subject communities of the region. However, the phenomenon reached unprecedented proportions in the 15th century; it is thus important to assess the impact of external authorities on petitioning practices to verify how petitions were critical to the legitimation of authority.

This chapter scrutinises a corpus of roughly 400 petitions from the archival series of the *Diversorum*. These petitions asked for citizenship rights or alternative forms of membership, and were submitted in the first half of the 15th century, under French, then Genoese, and finally Milanese governors.[16] The next section will discuss the question of late medieval citizenship and uses of petitions to apply for this status, while the third section will further explore Genoese petitions to shed light on the question of when and why petitions mattered both for petitioners and authorities. The aim of the chapter is to reconsider late medieval petitions highlighting not only how they served the authorities' purposes, but also how subjects used them to reshape their legal and fiscal condition from below.

Petitions and Citizenship in Late Medieval Italy

Late medieval and early modern citizenship did not have a univocal meaning, unlike modern citizenship, which implies – theoretically, at least – that citizens are automatically entitled to benefits within a system of civil and political rights. Both in Italian cities and in large parts of Europe, in the late Middle Ages the content of citizenship could vary radically from city to city, and even within the same urban community, depending on one's legal status, and during one's life.[17] Not only was personal status bound to change when people moved from one place to another (from being a citizen, one became a foreigner in the new city and

[15] For recent studies on late medieval Genoa and its institutional organisation, see C. Shaw, 'Genoa', in A. Gamberini and I. Lazzarini (eds), *The Italian Renaissance State* (Cambridge, Cambridge University Press, 2012), pp. 220–36; and C. E. Beneš (ed.), *A Companion to Medieval Genoa* (Leiden and Boston, MA, Brill, 2018).

[16] Two main archival series collected the various forms of petitions received by the city government of Genoa: the *Diversorum* (registers) and *Diversorum Communis Ianue* (single documents bound in *filze*), both now preserved in Archivio di Stato di Genova, Archivio segreto (hereafter: ASGe, AS).

[17] M. Prak, *Citizens without Nations: Urban Citizenship in Europe and the World, c. 1000–1789* (Cambridge, Cambridge University Press, 2018). The most recent studies on citizenship in medieval Italy are collected in S. Menzinger (ed.), *Cittadinanze medievali: Dinamiche di appartenenza a un corpo comunitario* (Rome, Viella, 2017), though a broad analysis focusing on late medieval citizenship is still missing. For a first comparative attempt see M. Gravela, 'Frammentare l'appartenenza: Suppliche di cittadinanza a Genova e Venezia (XIV–XV secolo)', *Quaderni storici*, 161 (2019), 137–70.

possibly a citizen again), but also – as we will see – when people wanted to adjust their rights and duties to their current needs; moreover, multiple status existed (*forenses*, *habitatores*, *conmorantes*, etc.) beyond the distinction between citizens and foreigners.

In the 12th and 13th centuries admission to the citizenry was straightforward to a certain extent. New inhabitants could become citizens by acquiring a house and paying all direct taxes. However, from the late 13th century, procedures for citizenship became more complicated, and requirements more heterogeneous and difficult to meet.[18] In the 14th and 15th centuries, across postcommunal Italy, people had to obtain a privilege from the authority in order to be 'made citizens' (*cives facti privilegio*). However, a large part of the population of foreigners living in a city gave up on the prospect of gaining this new status. As a consequence, citizenship increasingly became an exclusive condition that concerned only a small number of people, who were mainly seeking to obtain economic privileges (the right to buy possessions, trade without particular restrictions, invest in the urban public debt, and so on) or establish political and diplomatic links.

Applications for citizenship rights had to be submitted by means of a petition, a form of request that made it possible not only to derogate from the law, thus applying for the *civilitas* even if lacking the main requirements established by local norms, but also to adjust the norm to the individual case by creating 'partial' forms of citizenship to meet individual needs. The earliest examples are from 14th-century Florence, where petitions were used precisely to acquire the privilege of citizenship by getting around the limitations of local rules or gaining a significant fiscal arrangement.[19] In Venice, given the thorough reorganisation of procedures and requisites for citizenship regularly taking place since 1305, petitions were essential not only as a means for derogation, but also for ordinary requests, as they enabled petitioners to gain access to different types of citizenship.[20] In some places, such as Venice or Genoa, inhabitants asked city authorities to adjust their status and regulate their situation. In other cities, such as Siena, urban governments prompted

[18] P. Grillo, 'Da diritto a privilegio: La cittadinanza nell'età comunale', in B. Del Bo (ed.), *Cittadinanza e mestieri: Radicamento urbano e integrazione nelle città bassomedievali (secc. XIII–XVI)* (Rome, Viella, 2014), pp. 25–46. On the link between citizenship and tax payment, see S. Menzinger, 'Fisco, giurisdizione e cittadinanza nel pensiero dei giuristi comunali italiani tra la fine del XII e l'inizio del XIII secolo', *Quellen und Forschungen aus italienischen Archiven und Bibliotheken*, 85 (2005), 36–73; and the essays collected in M. Vallerani (ed.), *Fiscalità e cittadinanza*, special issue of *Quaderni storici*, 147 (2014).

[19] P. Gualtieri, *Il comune di Firenze tra Due e Trecento: Partecipazione politica e assetto istituzionale* (Florence, Olschki, 2009); L. De Angelis, 'La cittadinanza a Firenze (XIV–XV secolo)', in Del Bo, *Cittadinanza e mestieri*, pp. 141–57.

[20] Among the many studies devoted to Venetian citizenship by Reinhold Mueller, see at least R. C. Mueller, '*Veneti facti privilegio*: Les étrangers naturalisés à Venise entre XIVe et XVIe siècle', in J. Bottin and D. Calabi (eds), *Les étrangers dans la ville: Minorités et espace urbain du bas Moyen Âge à l'époque moderne* (Paris, Éditions de la Maison des sciences de l'homme, 1999), pp. 171–81, and his most recent *Immigrazione e cittadinanza nella Venezia medievale* (Rome, Viella, 2010).

people who spent part of the year in the city and part in the countryside to choose definitively a fiscal domicile.[21]

Private petitions thus became the universal tool to negotiate citizenship rights and corresponding duties. As the following analysis will show, these petitions were employed to request an exception to the rule owing to the specificity of an individual case, and thus to apply for peculiar civic conditions with only limited rights, but also very few obligations towards the city government and the community.

Citizens *pro tempore* and *Conventionati*: When and Why Genoese Petitions Mattered

It is not always simple to analyse the rate, chronology, and substance of petitions for citizenship rights, since in some cities they were entirely lost, or provisions in response included only a few traces of their content.[22] Despite the fact that in most cases original petitions were not preserved, as they were most probably returned to petitioners or presented orally, their texts were copied or transcribed into the resulting privileges and *gratie*, which enables an in-depth analysis of their content and rhetoric.[23] This was also true in Genoa, where the vast majority of petitions were submitted orally to a committee formed by the aldermen (*Anziani*) and the governor of the city (*doge*), and subsequently written down by the city chancery together with the response, as suggested by the introductory clauses: 'audita supplici requisicione coram eis exposita', 'audita humili petitione coram eis verbo narrata' ('after listening to the humble request presented/humble petition expressed before them'), 'humiliter supplicatur et exponitur pro parte … cuius requisicionis tenor talis est' ('it is petitioned and expressed humbly by … the content of whose request is as follows').[24] Petitions were thus transcribed into the registers and single

[21] G. Piccinni, 'I "villani incittadinati" nella Siena del XIV secolo', *Bullettino senese di storia patria*, 82–3 (1975), 158–219; G. Piccinni, 'Differenze socio-economiche, identità civiche e "gradi di cittadinanza" a Siena nel Tre e Quattrocento', *Mélanges de l'École française de Rome – Moyen Âge*, 125 (2013), http://journals.openedition.org/mefrm/1304 (accessed 10 February 2024).

[22] Hardly anything is known for petitions submitted in Rome, but see I. Ait, '"...concivi nostro carissimo": Il privilegio di cittadinanza concesso dai Conservatori di Roma a Francesco Tommasi, mercante senese', in P. Maffei and G. M. Varanini (eds), *Honos alit artes: Studi per il settantesimo compleanno di Mario Ascheri*, Vol. II, *Gli universi particolari: Città e territori dal medioevo all'età moderna* (Florence, Firenze University Press, 2014), pp. 153–60. Only the provisions are available for Milan: Albini, 'Civitas tunc quiescit'; B. Del Bo, 'La cittadinanza milanese: Premessa o suggello di un percorso di integrazione?', in Del Bo, *Cittadinanza e mestieri*, pp. 159–80; B. Del Bo, *Le concessioni di cittadinanza nel quadro dei provvedimenti di politica economica di Filippo Maria*, in F. Cengarle and M. N. Covini (eds), *Il ducato di Filippo Maria Visconti, 1412–1447: Economia, politica, cultura* (Florence, Firenze University Press, 2015), pp. 211–30.

[23] This occurred in Verona with petitions addressed to the Della Scala, but also in Ferrara with the Este and Padova with the *gratie* granted by the da Carrara; see Varanini, 'Al magnifico e possente segnoro'.

[24] ASGe, AS, *Diversorum*; *Diversorum Communis Ianue*.

documents then collected in *filze*, which reported the various steps of the procedure to grant citizenship or alternative membership forms.

In 15th-century Genoa petitions became a tool to get around the local norms regarding the acquisition of citizenship and either obtain its main privileges without the associated duties, or obtain another form of membership within the civic community that was not laid down in law. It is hard to find a coherent series of norms concerning citizenship in Genoese statutes, as the only two surviving rules were ambiguous in regulating applications for citizenship and its essential criteria. The key rule – dating back to the 12th century and which had seemingly fallen out of use – was that a certain number of years of residence in Genoa, depending on the applicant's provenance, be taken as the main prerequisite for citizenship. The rule thus disregarded several specific situations and the actual procedure, and was quite vague.[25] However, a second norm – without any clear links with the former – specified which social groups were entitled to take part in the committee in charge of establishing the fiscal burden for new citizens.[26] Surprisingly, this rule was not copied in the latest collection of Genoese laws promoted in 1399 by the French governor Collart de Colleville and completed in 1403 by the successor Jean Le Meingre, also known as Boucicaut. This appears even more striking if we consider that all subsequent petitions for citizenship requested an exception to this second rule.

The procedure to obtain citizenship in Genoa was thus created in practice through petitions, which derogated from norms by making a separate deal between the petitioner and the authority. As we will shortly see, this resulted in the creation of two new forms of urban membership – the *civilitas ad tempus* and the *conventio* – which granted a temporary and revocable status, but most of all assured petitioners an annual fixed fiscal deal, thus exempting them from the numerous impositions of direct taxes.[27]

Petitioners

In order to grasp better when and why petitions for citizenship rights mattered, it is essential to look at petitions from the perspective of individuals and authorities. The first fundamental question to be addressed concerns the identity of petitioners. In late medieval Genoa, petitions could be submitted by any adult regardless of social

[25] *Historiae patriae monumenta*, Vol. XVIII, *Leges genuenses*, col. 611 (article 'de his qui habitaculum Ianue iuraverint').

[26] ASGe, *Manoscritti membranacei*, Vol. I, article 'de non recipiendo aliquem in civem Ianue nisi modo infrascripto', fo. 130r; see R. Savelli, '*Capitula, regulae* e pratiche del diritto a Genova tra XIV e XV secolo', in R. Savelli, *Politiche del diritto e istituzioni a Genova tra medioevo ed età moderna* (Genoa, n.p., 2017), https://www.academia.edu/34681992 (accessed 10 February 2024), pp. 5–60 (pp. 15–16).

[27] These types of membership were first examined by G. Petti Balbi, 'Cittadinanza e altre forme di integrazione nella società genovese (secc. XIV–XV)', in Del Bo, *Cittadinanza e mestieri*, pp. 95–140; now see also Gravela, 'Frammentare l'appartenenza'.

standing, gender, or wealth. Nevertheless, personal acquaintance with a member of the elite willing to sponsor the petition provided a procedural short-cut and a higher chance of success for the petitioner. Petitions for citizenship rights, however, were largely submitted by men, since they were household heads and acted therefore on behalf of their families, if they had any.[28] Among the 400 petitions examined, very few were submitted by women, usually widows of recently admitted citizens who requested further fiscal exemptions because of their husbands' deaths; none of them applied for a renewal of citizenship rights, thus suggesting that they did not find it necessary to keep living in the city. As we will see, citizenship rights (some in particular) proved convenient to a limited number of inhabitants, which apparently did not include women.[29]

The second crucial question regards the 'timing' of petitions: at what stage of social integration did petitions for citizenship play a relevant role? It is a general assumption that foreigners applied for citizenship when they first arrived in a new city, in order to benefit from legal protection offered by urban institutions and to gain access to local economic and social networks. This was certainly true in some cases, given that petitioners could present their requests immediately after moving to Genoa if they decided to settle down with their families and economic activities. In 1404 Pietro Tanzi from Milan presented a petition stating that he intended to relocate to Genoa ('Ianuam accedere et in ibi conmorari') together with his own family and his brother's, as well as his in-laws, and that he aspired to the privileges and safeguards enjoyed by proper citizens.[30] For this reason, he requested that he be admitted to citizenship, provided that he could be assured a series of exceptions.

However, petitions were not only used by foreigners willing to formalise their new situation: more often than not they were employed by medium or long-term inhabitants, who had never previously asked for official recognition, when they wanted to change or confirm their status, possibly in response to new fiscal policies.[31] Worried about the prospect of excessive taxation, people who had been living in Genoa without any sort of certification for years – sometimes over a decade – petitioned local authorities in order to be registered for the first time as citizens with a fixed fiscal deal, as Antonio Pini did in 1404.[32] Explaining that he

[28] A significant exception was the petition submitted by Eleonor of Arborea, wife of a prominent Genoese citizen, to obtain a safe conduct. It is to be noted that she never applied for citizenship. ASGe, AS, *Diversorum*, Vol. 497, fos 90v–91v.

[29] This did not exclude women from collective life entirely, as argued by J. Kirshner, 'Nascoste in bella vista: Donne cittadine nell'Italia tardo-medievale', in Menzinger, *Cittadinanze medievali*, pp. 195–228. See also J. Kirshner, *Marriage, Dowry, and Citizenship in Late Medieval and Renaissance Italy* (Toronto, University of Toronto Press, 2015).

[30] ASGe, AS, *Diversorum*, Vol. 501, fos 92v–93v, 95v.

[31] Similarly in Milan: Del Bo, 'La cittadinanza milanese'.

[32] ASGe, AS, *Diversorum*, Vol. 501, fos 99r–100v. On *Anthonius Pinus*, see also G. Casarino, 'Rappresaglie o privilegi? Dai debiti mercantili alla co-promozione industriale: I Lucchesi a Genova tra Tre e Quattrocento', in G. Petti Balbi (ed.), *Comunità forestiere e 'nationes' nell'Europa dei secoli XIII–XVI* (Naples, Liguori, 2001), pp. 299–324 (pp. 318, 321–4).

had been living in Genoa for over 17 years, he said he wanted to join the citizenry and become one of them ('vellet se aggregare numero civium Ianue et civem Ianuensem fieri'). He asked the aldermen and the governor of the city to establish the sum he ought to pay in direct taxes. As a result, he received 10-year citizenship with a deal to pay 12 *lire* and 10 *soldi* every year. It is clear that Antonio used the petition in a specific moment and for a specific purpose. He applied for citizenship not when he first moved to Genoa, but several years later: possibly when new taxes were introduced in order to fund the military expenses of the wars brought about by the French governor, or when new laws raised taxes on non-Genoese inhabitants. It is hard to say whether he really meant to be a citizen; rather, his priority seems to have been to avoid the burden of excessive and unpredictable taxation.

Likewise, recently admitted citizens could petition the city government more than once to ask for renewal of their position for a few years, since they wanted neither to give up on their benefits, nor to pay direct taxes entirely. Pietro Maiolino from Pisa, a temporary citizen, together with his family and merchant partners since 1403, petitioned again Genoese authorities in 1416 to obtain an extension of his privilege, which he received for another five years and with a fiscal arrangement of 20 *lire* a year.[33] The same could apply some years later to petitions for *conventiones*, attested since the 1420s: petitions could either be submitted before or soon after moving to Genoa, in order to avoid inclusion in the urban fiscal lists, as Perino de Vigenio explained ('ipse velit venire cum eius familia ad habitandum Ianuam, sed … timet ne aggravetur in avariis et oneribus comunis').[34] Timing was also essential when approaching the expiry date of the *conventio*, as people had to submit another petition to avoid losing this status: in 1436, 15 petitions for extension of the *conventio* were transcribed only in the chancery register, without counting the *filze*.[35]

Petitions thus played a crucial role in enabling inhabitants to reconsider their legal and social condition at different stages of their life and in different moments of their process of inclusion, mainly depending on their economic and financial needs as well as their plans to live, work, and trade in Genoa. However, the importance of petitions was not limited to when they enabled a change or confirmation of status, but also lay in the sort of status to which they provided access and the extent of the exception they granted.

Given that petitions offered the opportunity to start a process of negotiation between individuals and authorities, they were employed by petitioners to apply for different forms of urban membership. Even though other Italian cities had also introduced various 'degrees' of urban citizenship,[36] the peculiarity of the Genoese

[33] ASGe, AS, *Diversorum*, Vol. 505, fos 73v–75r.

[34] ASGe, AS, *Diversorum Communis Ianue*, Vol. 3022, n. 158.

[35] ASGe, AS, *Diversorum*, Vol. 518.

[36] For instance, two types of naturalised citizenship were created in Venice: *civilitas de intus* or *de extra*, which entailed different requisites, but also different commercial rights; see Mueller, '*Veneti facti privilegio*'.

case lay precisely in the fact that these different statuses existed outside local norms and were created through exceptions. The law recognised two categories of citizenship: *cives originarii* – born and raised in Genoa – and naturalised citizens, i.e. foreigners who met the requirements to be equated with the former (years of residence and payment of taxes). The latter option, however, turned out to be too restrictive for inhabitants who could not meet the prerequisites or, more often, were not interested in acquiring all rights and duties connected to citizenship. In particular, applicants aiming at gaining fiscal discounts on direct taxes, and sometimes commercial privileges, as well as legal protection for themselves and their goods, were uninterested in acquiring the full political rights that citizenship implied because they had no intention to engage in the political life of the city.[37] In a word, they only aspired to certain prerogatives of citizenship and therefore sought to minimise their obligations as citizens.

Since petitions made it possible to request an exception to the rule on account of the specificity of an individual case, petitioners used them to present their peculiar situation and the reasons why the general rule could not be applied. As in other types of petitions – such as judicial ones – the vast majority of petitioners had recourse to the leitmotif of poverty as a way to legitimise their request. Regardless of the actual socio-economic status of applicants, poverty became the model to be adopted by petitioners in order to present themselves as socially weak individuals who deserved the authorities' mercy, and thus to justify the request of an exception.[38] No other recurring models appear to have been used. Despite the fact that Genoa certainly attracted inhabitants and workers from various parts of the Mediterranean, petitioners never mentioned cultural, religious, or language differences that could hinder their opportunities to establish and work in the city. Poverty was the main rhetorical strategy used by petitioners when making their case for special treatment.

As a result, two main forms of membership emerged from petitions in the first decades of the 15th century: *civilitas ad tempus* and *conventio*. Both were aimed at obtaining the right to live, work, and possibly trade in Genoa for a few years, and – key point – obtain a fixed annual fiscal deal. The former created citizens *sicut cives originarii* – like the native citizens – but deprived of political rights; the latter *conventionati* – inhabitants of lower social level – who were presumably also deprived of legal protection. These two options were functional to the petitioners' needs and economic strategies, since they both granted a temporary and revocable status, and a certain sum of money to be paid every year in exchange for exemption from most unpredictable direct taxes.

The *civilitas ad tempus* was mostly required by merchants and wealthy entrepreneurs who aspired to benefit from the same economic privileges and opportunities, as well as legal protection, enjoyed by native citizens: by petitioning for this new intermediate status, they showed their willingness to settle for 10 years and contribute to Genoa's economic life, also accepting to pay an annual sum

[37] Taking part in political offices was not a priority for Genoese citizens either: Shaw, 'Genoa'.

[38] Vallerani, 'La pauvreté et la citoyenneté'.

ranging from 10 to 40 *lire* on average. In the aforementioned petition submitted in 1404, Pietro Tanzi from Milan declared he aimed to enjoy the benefits of proper citizenship ('gaudere beneficiis concessis civibus'), though he could not afford to pay all direct taxes.[39] Accordingly, he asked the urban government to admit him to citizenship by establishing a certain amount of tax that took into consideration his family's actual condition ('attenta facultate et possibilitate ipsorum'), as he was not as wealthy as others: clearly a rhetorical device, considering that he had recently been listed among the richest citizens of Milan.[40] The aldermen and French governor accepted his petition and granted him and his extended family a 10-year privilege of *civilitas*, provided they would pay all indirect taxes and 37 *lire* and 10 *soldi* a year for direct tax, which was still a considerable amount of money. This new status, which entailed all the rights of the *cives originarii* but political participation, was granted in spite of the law and by adopting a 'legal fiction': for the 10 following years local institutions would treat them as if they had been born in Genoa ('ac si ipsi supplicantes superius nominati et eorum quilibet forent originarii proprii dicte civitatis Ianue').[41] At the end of that period, Pietro and his relatives would have had to submit another petition to renegotiate their situation and possibly ask for renewal of their privilege.

While petitions for *civilitas ad tempus* gradually decreased, the second type of local membership – the *conventio ad habitandum* – is evident from the 1420s. It did not replace temporary citizenship, as it was aimed at people of different social level. Dozens of petitions were presented every year to apply for this status, which only lasted three-to-five years and brought with it limited rights, but required a much smaller fiscal burden. In one of the dozens of requests for *conventio* submitted in 1426, for instance, the tailor Filippo from Milan declared that, after exercising his craft in his hometown, he had wandered around and finally decided to settle in Genoa. However, being 'pauperrimus' he doubted that he would be able to stay for long if he did not get a fiscal deal. After assessment of his situation, his petition was approved and the offices established a five-year agreement for 30 *soldi* a year.[42] Another Milanese, the barber Pietro, similarly explained he had nothing but his hands with which to work ('nichil habens nisi manus') and obtained a five-year deal for the sum of 2 *lire* and 10 *soldi* a year.[43] While some petitioners actually belonged to a higher social level, such as textile entrepreneurs like Filippo and Pietro who

[39] ASGe, AS, *Diversorum*, Vol. 501, fos 92v–93v, 95v.

[40] F. Del Tredici (ed.), 'I 120 maggiori estimati milanesi', in *Lombardia nel Rinascimento: Repertori, materiali e indici*, https://lombardianelrinascimento.it/repertori-materiali-e-indici/118/ (accessed 10 February 2024). Similar petitions were submitted by Vincentius Aymarus and Laurencius de Callorio, rich textile entrepreneurs from Piedmont, who were assigned to pay 'only' 10 and 20 florins a year respectively: ASGe, AS, *Diversorum*, Vol. 501, fos 96v–98v, 102v–104v.

[41] Privilege granted 'non obstantibus aliquibus capitulis, ordinibus vel decretis comunis Ianue aliter disponentibus, generalibus vel specialibus et generaliter capitulo posito sub rubrica de non recipiendo aliquem in civem nisi in modum infrascriptum'.

[42] ASGe, AS, *Diversorum Communis Ianue*, Vol. 3023, n. 224.

[43] Ibid., n. 175.

aimed at starting a business in Genoa, others were artisans and workmen who did not have their own workshop and were employed as wage earners. As a result, these petitions only focused on the fiscal agreement petitioners sought, once again individually established and usually ranging between a few *soldi* and 8 *lire*.[44]

Both petitions for temporary citizenship and for this 'residence permit' focused on describing the individual case and providing a suitable justification to appeal for an exception. This type of petition, which might be classified as seeking a form of patronage, did not aim at changing the legal framework in any way. Even though the chancery often produced standard texts, petitioners always insisted on the need for individual measures that were tailored to their peculiar situation. Despite the numerous petitions for *conventio* and the undeniable impact they had on urban fiscal arrangements, no normative changes were made in the following decades so far as citizenship and its alternatives were concerned.[45] While subsequent provisions and reorganisation of Genoese law involved various matters, such as the administration of justice, inheritance law, or the organisation of political offices, the rules of citizenship remained completely untouched.[46]

Authorities

Needless to say, petitions mattered not only for petitioners, but also for the authority that received them and used them as a tool for government, as studies on late medieval urban lords have shown.[47] In this respect, it is essential to consider when and why petitions for citizenship rights were introduced and even encouraged by rulers. When looking at rates of petitions for citizenship and related types of requests, two important concentrations can be observed: the former regards the applications for *civilitas ad tempus* in the early 15th century, whose peak lies in the period 1404–9, under the governorship of Jean Le Meingre (1401–9); the latter concerns the requests for *conventio ad habitandum*, which were strikingly numerous in the 1420s when Genoa passed under the dominion of the duke of Milan, Filippo Maria Visconti (1421–35).[48]

Even though more than a few late-14th-century sources have survived, no petitions for citizenship rights seem to have existed before the early 15th century.[49]

[44] Ibid., Vols 3022ff. See Gravela, 'Frammentare l'appartenenza'.

[45] Gravela, 'Frammentare l'appartenenza'.

[46] Savelli, '*Capitula, regulae* e pratiche del diritto'.

[47] See nn. 9–11.

[48] On the Milanese rule, see R. Musso, 'Le istituzioni ducali dello "Stato di Genova" durante la signoria di Filippo Maria Visconti', in L. Chiappa Mauri, L. De Angelis Cappabianca, and P. Mainoni (eds), *L'Età dei Visconti: Il dominio di Milano tra XIII e XV secolo* (Milan, Edizioni La Storia, 1993), pp. 65–111; and F. Somaini, 'Filippo Maria e la svolta del 1435', in Cengarle and Covini (eds), *Il ducato di Filippo Maria*, pp. 107–66.

[49] Four registers drafted between 1382 and 1399 still exist, as well as one *filza* containing more than 200 documents produced from 1375 onwards; ASGe, AS, *Diversorum*, Vols 497–500; ASGe, AS, *Diversorum Communis Ianue*, Vol. 3021.

This absence cannot be simply reduced to a mere dispersal of sources; rather, it suggests that at the end of the 14th century petitions were not employed to apply for citizenship because they were not necessary, as all applicants met the essential prerequisites, or – more probably – because the city government did not accept such remarkable exceptions to the rule, either in terms of rights or of fiscal discounts. Alternatives to 'proper' citizenship apparently did not exist.

The subjection of Genoa to external authorities and the establishment of foreign governors radically changed the context for Genoese citizenship, especially under the French governor Jean Le Meingre.[50] Not only did he complete the reorganisation of local laws started by his predecessor, Collart de Colleville – an action with strong symbolic significance, as it was meant to mark the beginning of the new dominion – he also bypassed the power of Genoese political institutions by making decisions with a French council and replacing or combining ordinary judicial procedures with summary judgements based on his will.[51]

In this context, petitions for *civilitates ad tempus* were first introduced, presumably as another means for governing by resorting to individual exceptions, in clear parallel with the governmental actions of most 14th-century urban lords.[52] This style of government, which among other things shaped an innovative type of citizenship, was based on a contractual approach that assured Jean Le Meingre of a degree of consent in Genoa for a few years, until his military defeats finally earned him the hostility of the local elite and the reputation of a tyrant.[53]

These sorts of petitions, which had not been particularly numerous previously – about 20 have been tracked in the French period – gradually disappeared in the following years. This type of petition resurfaced again towards the mid-15th century in the form of citizenship granted *ad honorem* to people who had played, or were likely to play in the future, a crucial role for Genoa on economic, financial, or political grounds.[54]

Other options were more successful. From the 1420s petitions were used to introduce another unprecedented type of membership to the community, the *conventio ad habitandum*: the former temporary type of citizenship was not appealing to all immigrants and inhabitants, given the fiscal burden it entailed, but also the privileges it bore, which were not necessarily desirable at different social levels. Nevertheless, during these decades governments had to face a dramatic demographic decline as a result of the subsequent waves of plague and continuous wars that affected northern

[50] F. Levy, *La monarchie et la commune: Les relations entre Gênes et la France, 1396–1512* (Rome, École française de Rome, 2014).

[51] F. Levy, 'Gênes au XVe siècle, dominations étrangères et esprit civique', in M. Schnettger and C. Taviani (eds), *Libertà e dominio. Il sistema politico genovese: Le relazioni esterne e il controllo del territorio* (Rome, Viella, 2011), pp. 55–88.

[52] On this, see especially Vallerani, 'La supplica al signore'; and the other studies in n. 10.

[53] Levy, 'Gênes au XVe siècle', pp. 77–81.

[54] ASGe, AS, *Diversorum*, Vols 536–7; Petti Balbi, 'Cittadinanza', pp. 115–22.

and central Italy;[55] at the same time, Genoa was starting to become a new textile-manufacturing centre, alongside Venice, Florence, and Lucca.[56] In the attempt to avoid depopulation due to the fiscal pressure brought about by military expenses and to foster settlement of entrepreneurs as well as workmen,[57] Milanese governors created a new type of membership that was far less burdensome in terms of taxes, and at the same time granted fewer civic privileges. The *conventio* met the demand of a much larger part of Genoese population than the *civilitas*, therefore providing a tool to encourage immigration and to certify their presence in the city, assuring a minimum fiscal contribution at the same time.

Conclusion

In late medieval Italian cities petitions were the universal tool to acquire citizenship, an exclusive status mostly accessible through extraordinary measures. Requests for exceptions usually insisted on partial fiscal exemptions and derogation from the rules concerning the rights of new citizens. However, 15th-century Genoese petitions did much more than that. They enabled petitioners to go beyond the mere bypassing of legal constraints, by creating innovative forms of urban membership. *Civilitas ad tempus* and *conventio* became convenient alternatives to full-fledged citizenship, certainly more appealing to merchants, entrepreneurs, artisans, and workmen living and trading in Genoa. The suspension of the law envisaged by petitions not only made these options feasible, but also offered the possibility of demanding them at various stages of life, depending on personal needs and intentions.

First introduced by foreign rulers, both temporary citizenship and resident permits were subsequently adopted by Genoese authorities. Accepting and encouraging petitions for citizenship rights had multiple purposes. On the one hand, it enabled governors, especially during the French domination, to enhance the contractual approach of their government and boost their consent by displaying the merciful and benevolent face of power. On the other, it met the economic and demographic needs of the city by encouraging merchants and artisans to settle in the city in times of serious crisis and fiscal pressure.

Petitions were thus a tool used to negotiate individual rights and duties, in which both rulers and subjects were involved. However, while petitioners strongly influenced the construction of new membership forms, the same bottom-up process did not concern the normative sphere, as Genoese petitions did not have any impact on formal rules. Studies have often insisted on the fundamental contribution given

[55] M. Ginatempo and L. Sandri, *L'Italia delle città: Il popolamento urbano tra Medioevo e Rinascimento (secoli XIII–XVI)* (Florence, Le Lettere, 1990); G. Alfani, A. Carbone, B. Del Bo, and R. Rao (eds), *La popolazione italiana del Quattrocento e Cinquecento* (Udine, Forum, 2016).

[56] Casarino, 'Rappresaglie o privilegi?', p. 302.

[57] On the fiscal impact of wars in the 1420s and 1430s, see Somaini, 'Filippo Maria e la svolta del 1435', p. 151.

by the petitioning process to readjusting rules and making new laws, a process especially – but not exclusively – concerning collective petitions; this sometimes occurred also with individual patronage petitions for citizenship rights in late medieval Italy (e.g. in Venice, where citizenship laws went through continuous revision on the basis of demographic and economic needs, as well as the features and requirements of petitioners). Nevertheless, the same did not occur in late medieval Genoa: Genoese petitions were aimed at creating exceptions rather than rules.

13

Petitioning Soldiers, the Power of the Patient, and the Provision of Military Welfare in 17th-Century England and Wales

ISMINI PELLS

The English Civil Wars, fought between 1642 and 1651, were a series of conflicts between the supporters of the king and Parliament over their authority and capacity to govern the three kingdoms of England and Wales, Ireland, and Scotland. The wars resulted in the trial and execution of King Charles I in 1649 and the establishment of a republican government, before the restoration of Charles II to the throne eleven years later. During the Civil Wars, pensions and other financial payments were made available to wounded soldiers on an unprecedented scale and, for the first time in English history, to soldiers' family dependants through a petitionary process. There are possibly as many as 4,000 petitions and supporting documents from Civil War claimants to military welfare in county record offices and other archives across England and Wales.[1] These documents are, of course, just the ones

[1] The material has been gathered for the AHRC-funded 'Conflict, Welfare and Memory during and after the English Civil Wars, 1642–1710' project, run among the Universities of Leicester, Nottingham, Southampton, and Cardiff; see www.civilwarpetitions.ac.uk (accessed 10 February 2024). This chapter is based on the petitions gathered by the 'Conflict, Welfare and Memory' project to date, which are drawn from the quarter sessions and county committee records for the following counties: Buckinghamshire, Caernarfonshire, Denbighshire, East Sussex, Essex, Gloucester/Gloucestershire, Herefordshire, Hull, Leicestershire, Lincoln/Lincolnshire, Northamptonshire, North Riding of Yorkshire, Northumberland, Nottingham/Nottinghamshire, Oxfordshire, Somerset, Staffordshire, Warwickshire, Westmoreland, West Riding of Yorkshire, Worcester/Worcestershire, and York. This represents a total of 952 petitions and supporting documents. However, the analysis in this chapter is only based on those relating to maimed soldiers and has excluded those from war widows. No petitions survive for the following areas (though many of these have records of payments made as a result of petitions): Berkshire, Breconshire, Bristol, Coventry, Dorset, Durham, East Riding of Yorkshire, Hampshire, Isle of Wight, Newcastle, Poole, Rutland, Shropshire, and Southampton. Some major towns and cities such as Hull were regarded as counties in their own right and had their own quarter sessions.

Proceedings of the British Academy, **262**, 254–267, © The British Academy 2024.

that have survived, and therefore the evidence presented in this chapter is representative of a much larger phenomenon.

However, before addressing these petitions, this chapter will begin by examining when and why petitions mattered to soldiers in their negotiations with Parliament to ensure the implementation of the military pension scheme during and after the Civil Wars. It will highlight the limitations as well as the power of these petitions. It begins with an evaluation of how historians have drawn attention to the scale and intensity of petitions to Parliament during the mid-17h century. The next section focuses on the petitions from actual claimants to military welfare. Framing veterans as medical patients, the chapter will argue that investigating when and why their petitions mattered also reveals broader patterns surrounding the ways in which wounded Civil War soldiers accessed and negotiated welfare at a local level. Indeed, in tackling both these first two points, it will emphasise that Civil War military welfare is a prime example of an occasion when the initiative for improvement came from lay people, rather than policy-makers or medical professionals. Third, a study of when and why petitions mattered in the context of Civil War military welfare sheds light on the varied ways in which petitioners/patients interacted with their local communities. The chapter will demonstrate that experiences of infirmity were not only a physical but also a cultural phenomenon, and that care was often linked to the social and political context in which the military pension scheme operated.

Petitions, Pensions, and Welfare: Context

Petitions mattered in Civil War military welfare, quite simply because, without a sustained petitioning campaign by Parliament's New Model Army throughout 1647, it is likely that there would have been little effective state-sponsored military welfare provision resulting from the Civil Wars. Wounded soldiers had been entitled to claim financial relief from the state since the 1593 Act for Relief of Soldiers had created a system of parochial taxation, which was administered by county treasurers and distributed by justices of the peace (JPs) at the quarter sessions.[2] This Act (and its subsequent revisions in 1598 and 1601) were developed alongside the Elizabethan poor relief legislation. Like other poor relief measures, the military pension scheme reflected contemporary attitudes towards the social order. Order was maintained both by the rulers' recognition of their responsibility to protect the ruled from economic and social insecurity, and an expectation from the ruled that their rulers would duly provide this protection.[3] However, veterans were

[2] G. Hudson, 'Disabled Veterans and the State in Early Modern England', in D. Gerber (ed.), *Disabled Veterans in History* (Ann Arbor, University of Michigan Press, 2003), pp. 117–44 (pp. 118–19).

[3] G. Hudson, 'Ex-Servicemen, War Widows, and the English County Pension Scheme, 1593–1679', DPhil thesis (University of Oxford, 1995), p. 43.

accorded a separate Act because they were viewed differently from the rest of the impotent poor. Elizabethan statesmen 'stated clearly that they believed that maimed soldiers, as distinct from the impotent poor, *merited* relief for good service'.[4] Under the military pension scheme, poverty on its own was not sufficient grounds for granting welfare; veterans were entitled to pensions on the basis of physical disability suffered in the service of the state.[5] Such sentiments about military welfare would continue to shape both the language of the legislation and soldiers' petitions during the Civil Wars.

On 24 October 1642, the day after the first major encounter of the Civil Wars at the Battle of Edgehill, Parliament passed an ordinance reaffirming its commitment to 'provide competent Maintenance and Allowance' to those 'in the Service of the Parliament, in the present War' who were 'maimed, and thereby disabled by their Labour to provide for themselves, their Wives, their Children, as formerly they did'.[6] In addition, in a new departure from the Elizabethan legislation, Parliament promised that if any in their service were slain, Parliament would make provision for the soldier's wife and children out of the 'Respect they [Parliament] bear to the Memory of those who have spent their Lives in Service of the Church and Commonwealth'.[7] However, by the closure of the first round of hostilities in 1646, the amount of money being collected for this purpose was wholly inadequate for the numbers of casualties. In addition, war-weariness throughout the country and in Parliament had generated an increasing apathy and, at times, outright hostility towards soldiers and military matters, meaning that the political will to uphold Parliament's earlier promises towards its wounded veterans was generally lacking.

In February 1647, Parliament voted to disband their army without any assurances regarding arrears of pay and indemnity from prosecution for acts committed during the war. Consequently, draft petitions to Parliament began circulating among the rank-and-file. These were eventually published on 2 April as *The Petition of the Officers and Souldiers in the Army*. Article 4 of this document demanded:

> That such in this Army as have lost their limbs, and the wives and children of such as have been slain in the service, and such Officers or souldiers as have sustained losses, or have been prejudiced in their estates, by adhereing to the Parliament; or in their persons by sickness or imprisonment under the Enemy, may have such allowances and satisfaction, as may be agreeable to Justice and equity.[8]

Eventually, after sustained pressure from the army and negotiations between the officers and Parliamentary commissioners, Parliament passed an ordinance on

[4] Ibid., p. 11.

[5] Ibid., p. 17.

[6] S. Rait (ed.), *Acts and Ordinances of the Interregnum, 1642–60* (*A&O*), 3 vols (London, His Majesty's Stationery Office, 1911), Vol. I, p. 36.

[7] Ibid., Vol. I, p. 36.

[8] T. Fairfax, *The Petition of the Officers and Souldiers in the Army, under the Command of His Excellency Sr. Thomas Fairfax* (London, 1647), [p. 2].

28 May 1647 that increased the levels of taxation used to fund the monetary awards made to veterans and their families.[9]

Petitions to Parliament during the mid-17th century have attracted the attention of numerous historians, most notably David Zaret, Jason Peacey, and Derek Hirst. These scholars have all drawn attention to the ways in which, in Peacey's words, petitions were submitted to Parliament on an 'unprecedented scale' and petitioning 'took on a new intensity' during the Civil War years.[10] However, it would only be right in a consideration of when and why petitions matter to acknowledge the limits of the power of petitioning and when petitions ceased to matter. Despite the apparent success of the New Model Army's petitioning campaign, only a limited time was given in the new legislation for JPs to raise the rates of taxation required to fund more military pensions, and little was done by the authorities in the counties to enforce this. Following another 10 weeks of tension between the army and Parliament, it was not until the army marched on London in a show of force that Parliament passed another ordinance on 10 August extending indefinitely the time for the JPs to raise the rates to ensure compliance.[11] In this instance, the petitioning campaign needed to be backed up with military force to be effective.

The army's march on London is an extreme example of the escalation of tactics that, Peacey has argued, resulted from frustrations over parliamentary delay, and which illustrated that contemporaries viewed petitioning as only one method in a '*spectrum* of tactics' through which to participate in political affairs.[12] Petitioning might be viewed as a form of negotiation precedent to more affirmative political action. Nevertheless, the army's petitioning campaign had played an important role in ensuring that military welfare did not drop off the political agenda, and this is important from a medical history perspective as an example where the impetus for improvement came not from medical practitioners or policy-makers, but from prospective patients. The historiographies of petitioning and medicine are linked by the question of agency. Historians of petitioning, especially scholars working on the poor relief system alongside which the military pension scheme developed, have stressed that even pauper petitioners were not completely powerless. As it will be shown later in the chapter, the power of petitioners should not be overemphasised, but in many cases, it was the

[9] *A&O*, Vol. I, pp. 938–40.

[10] D. Zaret, 'Petitions and the "Invention" of Public Opinion in the English Revolution', *American Journal of Sociology*, 101 (1996), 1497–555 (pp. 1503–4); D. Zaret, *Origins of Democratic Culture: Printing, Petitions, and the Public Sphere in Early-Modern England* (Princeton, NJ, Princeton University Press, 2000), p. 220; J. Peacey, *Print and Public Politics in the English Revolution* (Cambridge, Cambridge University Press, 2013), pp. 270–1; J. Peacey, 'To Every Individual Member: The Palace of Westminster and Participatory Politics in the Seventeenth Century', *The Court Historian*, 13 (2008), 127–47 (p. 138); D. Hirst, 'Making Contact: Petitions and the English Republic', *Journal of British Studies*, 45 (2006), 26–50 (p. 27).

[11] *A&O*, Vol. I, pp. 997–8.

[12] Peacey, *Print and Public Politics*, p. 297.

underprivileged who took the initiative in the petitioning process and they had a wide range of strategies at their disposal.[13] Likewise, the medical historian Roy Porter famously contended that 'In medicine's history, the initiatives have often come from, and power has frequently rested with, the sufferer, or with lay people in general, rather than with the individual physician or the medical profession at large.'[14]

Petitions, Pensions, and Welfare: Process

The military pension scheme that was established in 1647 remained in place for the next 13 years. During this period, only those who had fought for Parliament were entitled to financial awards. In 1660, the monarchy was restored and royalist veterans started to make their own claims. Two years later, parliamentarians were officially barred from accessing the scheme when the 'Act for the releife of poore and maimed Officers and Souldiers who have faithfully served His Majesty and His Royal Father in the late Wars' was passed.[15] This legislation was, in part, also the result of a petitioning campaign led by royalist veterans in May 1661, largely directed to the Privy Council and Charles II. Surprisingly, although one petition was published as *An humble Representation of the sad Condition of many of the King's Party*, it was not presented to Parliament. Geoffrey Hudson has plausibly suggested that this was because the organisers of the petition were 'sensitive to any imputation that they were acting in the same manner as parliamentarian servicemen in 1647'.[16] The 1662 Act was almost identical to the parliamentarian legislation, with the exception that the amount of money collected in taxation was again increased and that claimants had to demonstrate that they had been in 'the Service of his said late Majesty or his Majesty that now is during under the late Warrs … and not deserted the same by taking up Armes against his said late Majesty or his Majesty that now is'.[17] The Act lapsed in 1679, and while the Elizabethan legislation was still in force, the increased rates were no longer legal. The pension scheme thus became largely ineffectual, though some Civil War soldiers continued to petition and receive pensions into the beginning of the 18th century.[18]

[13] S. Hindle, *On the Parish? The Micro-Politics of Poor Relief in Rural England c. 1550–1750* (Oxford, Oxford University Press, 2009), pp. 445–9.

[14] R. Porter, 'The Patient's View: Doing Medical History from Below', *Theory and Society*, 14 (1985), 175–98 (p. 175).

[15] D. Appleby, 'Unnecessary Persons? Maimed Soldiers and War Widows in Essex, 1642–1662', *Essex Archaeology and History*, 32 (2001), 209–21 (p. 216); *Journals of the House of Lords* (n.p., n.d.), Vol. X (1 August 1648), p. 405; Hudson, 'Disabled Veterans', p. 122.

[16] Hudson, 'Ex-Servicemen', pp. 147–8.

[17] J. Raithby (ed.), *Statutes of the Realm*, Vol. V, *1628–80* (London, Dawsons, 1819), pp. 389–90.

[18] Hudson, 'Disabled Veterans', p. 122.

Throughout the operation of the Civil War pension scheme, petitions mattered directly to wounded veterans as the vehicle by which they might claim the scheme's benefits. To obtain a pension, maimed soldiers had to present a petition at the court of quarter sessions in their home county, held four times a year. Petitioners had to appear in person before the court and defend their claims under questioning from the magistrates, which is a reminder that there was a significant oral aspect of the petitioning process that has been largely lost to posterity. Petitioners are likely to have been acutely aware of the power of performance, and to have made strong emotive appeals that were aimed both at the magistrates and the watching members of the public.[19] The oral aspects of petitioning had a long tradition in England, in part as a legacy of a time when the official language of the courts (French) was different from the native language of the petitioners (English).[20] It is also highly likely that the spoken word continued to be important in many areas of Wales during the time of the Civil Wars, where the official English language of the court would have been unintelligible to Welsh-speaking petitioners and where bilingualism on the part of the magistrates was a key skill.[21] Indeed, some petitions may not have been 'lost' but were perhaps never written down in the first place.

After hearing the petition and interrogating the petitioner, the presiding JPs determined whether to award a payment.[22] If they deemed a soldier to be deserving, he would receive a pension. This regular payment was given for as long as the JPs allowed, and potentially for the rest of the soldier's life. If he was not so fortunate, he would receive a gratuity, in the form of a one-off payment. Most petitions were submitted to the quarter sessions, although some claimants appealed to borough corporations, the county committees set up to co-ordinate Parliament's war effort, military governors, or even leading figures such as Oliver Cromwell or Charles II. Such petitioners were either granted money from revenues under these authorities' control or were referred back to the relevant county quarter sessions, usually with a note of endorsement. This highlights the fluidity of petitions as a medium and the range of options available to petitioners, who could strengthen their hand by approaching multiple sources of relief and playing one authority off against another.

[19] For a more in-depth discussion of this aspect of Civil War veterans' petitions, see I. Pells, 'Soliciting Sympathy: The Search for Psychological Trauma in Petitions from Seventeenth-Century Maimed Soldiers', in E. Peters and C. Richards (eds), *Early Modern Trauma: Europe and the Atlantic World* (Lincoln, University of Nebraska Press, 2021), pp. 128–50.

[20] Q. Verreycken, '"En nous humblement requerant": Crime Narrations and Rhetorical Strategies in Late Medieval Pardon Letters', *Open Library of Humanities*, 5 (2019), 1–31 (p. 8).

[21] S. Howard, *Law and Disorder in Early Modern Wales: Crime and Authority in the Denbighshire Courts, c. 1660–1730* (Cardiff, University of Wales Press, 2008), pp. 32–4.

[22] *A&O*, Vol. I, pp. 938–40; D. Appleby, 'Unnecessary Persons?', p. 210; Hudson, 'Disabled Veterans', p. 122.

Rhetoric, Performance, and Community

Civil War veterans did not only care about petitions because they were the practical mechanism through which they claimed relief. The traditional literary forms and conventions used in supplications for relief may have emphasised the humility of the petitioner, but these also provided them with a form of public empowerment. As Diane Purkiss notes, war created anxieties about masculinity, not least because the broken bodies of the wounded were visible reminders that the male body was not the ideal of invincibility but vulnerable and open to mutilation.[23] Alexandra Shepard likewise questions if physically disabled veterans who were dependent upon the state for a large part of their living retained much of a claim to patriarchal manhood.[24] However, as Shepard argues so well, historians must be careful not to equate masculinity with patriarchy, as men who did not live up to patriarchal imperatives still found ways to assert their manhood. Scholars must pay attention to the different varieties of early modern manhood and the ways in which manhood was worked out between men.[25] Despite different emphases, most moral theorists defined manhood broadly in terms of discretion, reason, moderation, self-sufficiency, strength, self-control, and honest respectability.[26]

Long-established petitioning tropes provided wounded veterans with the vehicles by which to emphasise these criteria. First, petitions for military welfare provided veterans with the opportunity to highlight the masculine criteria of strength and self-sufficiency in their pasts by discussing their former employment. Of the petitions collected by the Civil War Petitions project, around 65 per cent reference former employment or trade, or note that the soldier's injuries prevented him from working. Of course, it was a requirement of the legislation that claimants demonstrate they were 'disabled in body for work'.[27] However, the focus on employment provided veterans with the opportunity to make assertions about the industriousness of their labour prior to military service, which were customarily used to distinguish the deserving from the idle poor.[28] For example, Richard Roberts told the Denbighshire quarter sessions that although he was now 'somew[ha]t vncapable to follow his Trade' as a result of an uncured gunshot wound in his shoulder, he formerly 'by his hard industry, & sweat of his browes, hath mayntayned his wife & children w[i]thout being trowblesome to any'.[29] John Brooks similarly

[23] D. Purkiss, *Literature, Gender, and Politics during the English Civil War* (Cambridge, Cambridge University Press, 2005), pp. 35–8. I am very grateful to Bethany Parker for this and the next reference, and for her helpful discussions on the negotiation of masculinity.

[24] A. Shepard, *Meanings of Manhood in Early Modern England* (Oxford, Oxford University Press, 2003), p. 214.

[25] Ibid., p. 6.

[26] Ibid., p. 9.

[27] *A&O*, Vol. I, p. 939.

[28] A. Shepard, *Accounting for Oneself: Worth, Status, and the Social Order in Early Modern England* (Oxford, Oxford University Press, 2015), pp. 166, 181.

[29] Petition of Richard Roberts, 28 April 1663, National Library of Wales, Chirk Castle MS, B86/14.

told the Leicester Borough Corporation that he had 'betooke himselfe to his trade, & laboured very hard, to the utmost of his power' until he was 'unable to p[er] forme worke as formerly' as a result of 'coulds, & wounds, received in the said warr'.[30] Second, the petitions enabled veterans to draw attention to the masculine criteria of moderation, self-control, and honest respectability in their present lives. Henry Norton of Turf House, near Hexham in Northumberland, for example, claimed that he had always 'liued Commendably of himselfe' until 'age seized upon him'.[31]

Assertions of industriousness and honesty may seem unremarkable as features commonly used in petitions for relief, while historical scholarship has consistently emphasised how supplicants were well aware of the self-fashioning necessary for a successful petition.[32] It is also likely that the scribes who wrote the petitions assisted the veterans in this matter. Few petitions were written by the soldiers themselves. Most were drafted for a fee by either the clerk of the peace or literate neighbours, such as parish clergy or schoolmasters, who were educated men and familiar with the classical format required for petitions by virtue of their grammar school education.[33] These scribes reordered and refocused what petitioners told them into a coherent argument that included all the deferential formulae that may appear hollow to modern readers, but would have been a huge breach of etiquette if forgotten.[34] Such petitions have been described as 'hybrid voices', between petitioner and scribe, 'influenced by the experiences of the petitioner, the cultural worlds of the scribe and ... a broad idea of what it was thought justices wanted to hear'.[35]

Nevertheless, it must be remembered that petitioners were required to appear in person before the court, which not only comprised the magistrates but also members of the local community who watched proceedings from the public areas.[36] In requiring veterans to defend their petitions in open court, the petitioning process gave them the power to stand before their peers as well as their superiors and assert their claims to manhood. The granting of a pension was interpreted as a public validation of such claims. For example, Phillipp Jones submitted a petition to the Hereford Borough Corporation in 1680, requesting either a place in an almshouse or parish relief after his county pension had been removed the previous year with

[30] Petition of John Brooks, 1681, Leicestershire and Rutland Record Office, BR IV/1/10.

[31] Petition of Henry Norton, 12 July 1710, Northumberland Archives, QSB 32/28.

[32] Hindle, *On the Parish?*, pp. 383–6; G. L. Hudson, 'Arguing Disability: Ex-Servicemen's Own Stories in Early Modern England, 1590–1790' in R. Bivins and J. V. Pickston (eds), *Medicine, Madness and Social History: Essays in Honour of Roy Porter* (Basingstoke, Palgrave Macmillan, 2007), pp. 105–17 (p. 117); Appleby, 'Unnecessary Persons?', p. 215.

[33] Appleby, 'Unnecessary Persons?', p. 211; R. Houston, *Peasant Petitions: Social Relations and Economic Life on Landed Estates, 1600–1850* (Basingstoke, Palgrave Macmillan, 2014), p. 73.

[34] Houston, *Peasant Petitions*, pp. 77–8; Appleby, 'Unnecessary Persons?', p. 213.

[35] J. Healey, *The First Century of Welfare: Poverty and Poor Relief in Lancashire, 1620–1730* (Woodbridge, Boydell, 2014), p. 93.

[36] Appleby, 'Unnecessary Persons?', p. 212.

the lapse of the 1662 Act. Jones clearly believed that his county pension had been granted in recognition of his respectability. He maintained that:

> yo[u]r poore pet[itione]r hath served severall p[ar]ties of Creditt w[i]thin the s[ai]d Cittie, and ever demeaned himself Civilly in his service as a true servant ought to doe in any trust that was reposed in him to doe for his Masters or M[ist]r[es]s whom hee served vnder besides he w[as] a true Denison borne of the s[ai]d Citty, and hath served his Ma[jes]tie Charles the first of ever blessed memorie in his service as a true Subiect or Souldier, where for testimony whereof he is admitted vnto a smale penc[i]on of 4or nobles a yeare.[37]

Jones's claims were not the empty boasts of a man trying to justify his position, as it seems that contemporaries agreed that granting welfare represented an acknowledgement of the recipient's good character. Neighbours were certainly quick to complain when pensions were granted to perceived idle and immoral persons. The inhabitants of Tenbury protested to the Worcestershire JPs against the pension granted to one Nathaniell Maund, who:

> hath for these many yeares wholely declin'd his trade, giving himself alltogether to begging, both in ye Town & Country, comitting what he gains thereby, to sale; and ye money he very oftens converts to drunkenesse. and he is a common drunkard; a Railer, & will abuse any of ye Town or parish with most base & opprobrious language. In brief, he is of ye most vicious life & conversation of any person in ye Countrey.[38]

Likewise, in Lincolnshire, the inhabitants of Skillington petitioned their local magistrate, the earl of Lindsey, that John Walpole 'did Falsly informe this honorable Court, that by reason of his Age he was past his worke, and Could get none For that little he could doe (when in truth he refused A seruice, through lasines) and said he Could get more by the halfe by beging'. The Skillington inhabitants could not even find the words to describe Walpole's bad character, calling him 'A turbulent Crosgrained [blank space]'.[39] Men such as William Ebrall in Warwickshire discovered that the courts were not afraid to remove pensions for behaviour that was adjudged to be lazy or bad. In Ebrall's case, he was deprived of his pension because he had 'lately run out of the Countrey w[i]th the wife of John Hancox of Beusall reputed a Com[m]on Harlott'.[40]

The assertions of industriousness and honesty used by maimed soldiers to negotiate with authorities for relief also make petitions a significant source for medical historians, as these documents are a reminder of two important points that Porter was at pains to stress: first, that patients had a sense of agency and should not be

[37] Petition of Phillipp Jones, 1680, Herefordshire Archive and Records Centre, BG 11/5/44, 1680 file, petitions bundle, no. 9.

[38] Petition against Nathaniell Maund, 1680, Worcestershire Archives and Archaeology Service, 110/1/136/24.

[39] Petition against John Walpole, 1683, Lincolnshire Archives, KQS/A/2/2 KSB/1683, fo. 110.

[40] Warwickshire Quarter Sessions Order Book, 1650–7, Warwickshire County Record Office, QS40/1/3, fo. 266v.

viewed as victims; and second, that health matters were not only a physical but also a cultural phenomenon, in which medical practitioners might only have a peripheral role.[41] Indeed, less than 5 per cent of the petitions collected to date make any reference to treatment by medical practitioners. Most of these cases emanate from soldiers not yet or recently disbanded during the years of the Civil Wars themselves, such as Tobye Gabran of Gloucester. In November 1643, he informed Gloucester's governor, Edward Massey, that he had been shot while serving as a matross[42] when the city had been besieged in August/September, 'and thereby constrainde to lye vnder the Surgeons hands to be cured (this sixe weekes)'.[43]

Although soldiers might have received treatment from regimental medical staff in the immediate aftermath of their wounding, the petitions from widows whose husbands had initially survived suggest that the responsibility for longer-term veteran care rested with the wounded soldiers' families. For example, Elizabeth Newum told the Nottinghamshire county committee that she had racked up fees of more than £4 with the surgeon and apothecary while caring for her husband Nathaniel before his death. The practitioners were now hounding her for the money, which she had no idea how to pay 'unless I bee forct to sell up all that I have and soe I and my poor infant shall bee forced to beg'.[44] As Newum's petition demonstrates, wives sometimes sought professional medical help in caring for their husbands. Yet, in the longer term, wives took on much of the care of wounded veterans themselves. Few petitioners describe their day-to-day care regime, but there are hints that wounded veterans required assistance in performing their daily functions. In Warwickshire, William Steane of Brinklow had had 'his Chinne ... shott off and alsoe a greate part of his under iawe which disables him for receiveing any foode, but only liquid things and that by the helpe of an other'.[45] John Thomas of Hereford required a guide after he had lost his sight 'by hard dures & drifts of seruice'.[46]

Neither Steane nor Thomas appears to have had a family to assist him. Paid assistance required money (Thomas bemoaned the fact that he did not have enough money to 'succour his poore guide'), but using a family member as a carer also had an impact on the household income by restricting their time for paid employment.[47] While a few veterans, such as Habell Stepney in Sussex or Robert Ashorst of Marsh Baldon in Oxfordshire, explained how their wife's physical frailty prevented them from taking on work to compensate for their own inability to provide for their

[41] A. Bacopoulos-Viau and A. Fauvel, 'The Patient's Turn: Roy Porter and Psychiatry's Tales, Thirty Years On', *Medical History*, 60 (2016), 1–18 (pp. 4, 6); Porter, 'The Patient's View', pp. 175, 182.

[42] A gunner's assistant.

[43] Petition of Tobye Gabran, 17 November 1643, The National Archives (TNA), SP 28/228/II, fo. 345.

[44] Petition of Elizabeth Newum, 10 December 1645, TNA, SP 28/241/I, fo. 78.

[45] Warwickshire Quarter Sessions Order Book, 1665–82, Warwick County Record Office, QS40/1/5, fo. 197.

[46] Petition of John Thomas, c. 1662–3, Herefordshire Archive and Records Centre, BG11/5/38, 1662–3 folder, 1662–3 file, no. 12.

[47] Ibid.

families, not one petition from a wounded soldier collected so far mentions the impact that caring for them had on their wife's ability to carry out paid work.[48] This resonates with Shepard's work on witnesses in church court cases, where she discovered that male witnesses consistently ignored or downplayed the contribution made by their wives towards their household income.[49]

Paid assistance or using a family member as a carer thus put pressure on limited family finances, but when households or individuals failed to cope with such pressures, care became a community matter. Wounded soldiers often recognised in their petitions the burden they placed on their neighbourhood by resorting to private charity or parish relief. Humphrey John William of Pwllheli in Caernarfonshire claimed that he had 'nothing wherevpon to subsist but the Charitable benevolence of his loving neighbours and other good disposed people your peticoner not desirous to bee ouer chardgable vnto them any further'.[50] Consequently, the wounded soldiers' petitions were of importance to their local community as well as to themselves. While the local community would have still contributed to the wounded soldier's maintenance through the taxation that funded the pension scheme, the cost of his upkeep would have been more widely spread if he could be moved off private charity or parish relief and on to a county pension.

The financial benefit to local societies in moving former soldiers on to a county pension is reflected in the enthusiasm with which some communities supported their veterans' petitions. Oliver Bonden's petition to the Essex quarter sessions on behalf of his son, who had been wounded at the second Battle of Newbury, was endorsed with the signatures of no fewer than 28 inhabitants of Springfield.[51] Between 1670 and 1675, the inhabitants of Barwick in Elmet in the West Riding of Yorkshire supported the claims of five different veterans.[52] As Robert Houston has argued, petitioning was often a cooperative, even social activity. Petitioners probably talked over their case with family, friends, and local officials. The voice in the petition was that of the supplicant but the end product was a work of collaboration, in which the petitioner's relief met a wider group objective as much as satisfying the individual's need.[53] Amanda Whiting has even gone so far as to say that the search for a single author of a petition is pointless as well as futile: this only serves to add to the list of achievements and activities of the putative 'author'. Especially,

[48] Petition of Habell Stepney, 7 October 1670, East Sussex Record Office, QR/167/34; petition of Robert Ashorst and his wife, 1688, Oxfordshire History Centre, QS/1688.Ep M5.

[49] Shepard, *Accounting for Oneself*, pp. 226–30.

[50] Petition of Humphrey John William, 10 July 1660, Gwynedd Archives, Caernarfonshire Record Office, XQS/1660/62.

[51] Petition of Oliver Bonden, 1646, Essex Record Office, Q/SBa2/61.

[52] Certificate for Martin Prince, 1670, West Yorkshire History Centre, QS 1/9/2/6/24; petition of Robert Prince, 1672, West Yorkshire History Centre, QS 1/11/7/6/1; petition of George Bollands, 1674, West Yorkshire History Centre, QS 1/13/4/6/3; certificate for Martin Hague, 1675, West Yorkshire History Centre, QS 1/14/5/6/3; petition of Thomas Cowpland, 1675, West Yorkshire History Centre, QS 1/14/6/6/2.

[53] Houston, *Peasant Petitions*, p. 86.

but not only, in cases where petitions were explicitly collective projects, the search for a single author 'risks foreclosing enquiry into the agency of the petitioners as subscribers, supporters, and presenters'.[54] Such roles were elided in interpretations of what it meant to be a petitioner, particularly as those who penned the paper document may have had little control over the verbal and physical self-expression of those who presented it.[55]

The involvement of the local community in wounded soldiers' petitions demonstrates that soldiers' experiences of infirmity were shaped by the socio-cultural context in which the pension scheme operated. This context was similar to other forms of poor relief but, as has been shown, what set the military pension scheme apart from other forms of poor relief was that entitlement to welfare was based on service to the state rather than simply poverty. In this situation, petitions mattered as the instrument by which wounded soldiers were able to assert their loyalty to the state power in whose cause they had been injured to emphasise the worthiness of their case and set them apart from other competing claims. The royalist veteran Robert Wrigglesworth of Little Thirkleby in the North Riding of Yorkshire claimed that he 'was allwayes Faithfull and Loyall never revolting'.[56] Claims of loyalty became particularly important at times of political change, which put intense pressure on the pension scheme. For example, numbers of claimants skyrocketed when the scheme was first overhauled in 1647, and again in 1662 when royalists were first officially able to access pensions. Petitioners stood to gain by emphasising their own loyalty at the expense of others. In 1648, Matthew Thackwray was awarded a pension of £2 by the West Riding of Yorkshire quarter sessions as a reward for denouncing George Thackwray and Henry Lee for formerly being in royalist service.[57]

Although petitions denouncing recipients of welfare on moral grounds (as in the cases of Maund, Walpole, and Ebrall) have commonly been discussed by early modern historians, denunciations based upon political considerations have received much less attention.[58] This is perhaps because in other forms of poor relief, loyalty and service to the state were not the key criteria for relief. Nevertheless, the significance of political denunciations has been more widely acknowledged among scholars working on modern petitions. Shelia Fitzpatrick argued that denunciations should be viewed as a form of political participation that is revealing of both public opinion and the relationship between state and society. Denunciation petitions mattered because 'denunciation was genuinely

[54] A. Whiting, *Women and Petitioning in the Seventeenth-Century English Revolution: Deference, Difference, and Dissent* (Turnhout, Brepols, 2015), pp. 263–4.

[55] Ibid., pp. 266, 283.

[56] Petition of Robert Wrigglesworth, 6 October 1685, North Yorkshire County Record Office, QSB/1685/264.

[57] West Riding of Yorkshire Quarter Sessions Order Book, April 1647–August 1649, West Yorkshire History Centre, QS10/2, fo. 142.

[58] Hindle, *On the Parish?*, pp. 397–8; Healey, *The First Century of Welfare*, pp. 105–6.

conceived as a civic duty', and 'morally repugnant though it may be, [denunciation] is actually one of the quintessential forms of individual agency and participation' within the state.[59]

With this in mind, historians must not assume that petitioners only emphasised their loyal service as part of a cynical ploy to increase their chances of securing a pension. Protestations of loyalty could be more than a mask of deference used by wounded soldiers to appeal to the political preferences of the presiding magistrates or the powers that had appointed them to the county bench. As Andy Wood argues, paternalism and deference were 'genuine impulses' in the early modern period because power was contested and social relations dynamic.[60] As Wood puts it, 'Paternalism maintained a set of dominant interests; and yet it gave subordinates room for manoeuvre, handing to them a tool which, if used carefully, could win important concessions. Sometimes, this dialectical dance was cynically self-aware; alternatively, one or both sides might place genuine faith in the exchange.'[61] Many petitioners may have taken sincere pride in their service and, as we have seen that as petitions were often a community matter, the loyal service of the soldier may also have been used to reflect the loyalty of his neighbourhood. All sides got something out of this arrangement.[62] The petition mattered because the soldier got his money, the community got the veteran off the parish and on to county relief, and the local authorities got the protestations of loyalty that could be used to reinforce law and order and to underline their own legitimacy as rulers. This last was especially important when considering that many new JPs were appointed from the late 1640s and throughout the 1650s. These men, selected for their parliamentarian political reliability, were often drawn from a lower social rank than their predecessors had been. While the Restoration may have witnessed the return of JPs drawn from the families who had traditionally served in this role, the security of the new regime was never far from these men's minds, and some remodelling of the county benches in relation to political partisanship continued into the 1670s.[63]

Conclusion

This interaction between popular politics and the state, where petitions act as a 'point of contact' between the governed and the government, brings us back to the point where this chapter started, with the petitioning campaign that helped establish

[59] S. Fitzpatrick, 'Editor's Introduction: Petitions and Denunciations in Russian and Soviet History', *Russian History*, 24 (1997), 1–9 (p. 7).

[60] A. Wood, 'Deference, Paternalism, and Popular Memory in Early Modern England', in S. Hindle, A. Shepard, and J. Walter (eds), *Remaking English Society: Social Relations and Social Change in Early Modern England* (Woodbridge, Boydell, 2013), pp. 233–53 (p. 237).

[61] Ibid., p. 238.

[62] Ibid., p. 243.

[63] A. Fletcher, *Reform in the Provinces: The Government of Stuart England* (New Haven, CT, Yale University Press, 1986), pp. 15–22.

the military pension scheme.[64] Petitions are, after all, as Mark Knights has reminded historians, demonstrative of a participatory political culture; they engaged different voices in public dialogue and negotiation over both local and national issues, where the distinction between the two was often eroded.[65] This is why petitions matter in the history of military welfare. Petitioning helped Civil War soldiers both to pressurise Parliament into instituting an adequate pension scheme and to access this welfare in their locality once it was established. Petitions provided the tools by which soldiers might negotiate their notions of manhood and honest respectability with both their local governors and their local community. Simultaneously, petitions provided the means by which local communities could be relieved of the direct burden of providing for disabled veterans and by which the state might elicit loyalty and order. From a medical history perspective, the wounded soldiers' petitions enable historians to investigate the extent and nature of patients' agency in determining the care they received from others. The petitions also reveal the often marginal role played by practitioners in the wider picture of patient care. Patient agency and the marginal role of medical practitioners in patient care were both subjects advocated by Porter as worthy of further investigation. However, the petitions enable us to study these subjects in more depth and on a wider scale than has often been possible in many case studies, especially those focusing on the early modern period.[66] In contrast to many other case studies of 'medical history from below', this chapter has been reliant neither upon a small number of disparate or local case studies, nor upon sources relating to literate elites.

At the same time, we should not overemphasise the power of petitions. The intervention required by the New Model Army in 1647 or the approval by a JP required to secure financial aid are reminders that both national and local governors were quite capable of ignoring petitions that did not suit them. As Faramerz Dabhoiwala has argued, 'Every act of petitioning attests to the agency of the supplicant, the transformative potential of writing, the ability of scribe to help turn suffering into happiness. Yet ultimately it was always the agency of those being petitioned that determined the outcome.'[67] However, this did not mean that petitions did not matter. The ruled maintained remarkable faith in the petitioning process in spite of the risk of an unsuccessful outcome, not least because they understood that their petitions conferred some benefit upon their rulers as well as upon themselves. It was only when this faith was lost, as the New Model Army's march on London showed most dramatically, that petitions failed to matter. The public loss of faith and the resultant show of force shocked contemporaries; but contemporaries were shocked because this was the exception, rather than the rule.

[64] R. W. Hoyle, 'Petitioning as Popular Politics in Early Sixteenth-Century England', *Historical Research*, 75 (2002), 365–89 (p. 366).

[65] M. Knights, *Representation and Misrepresentation in Later Stuart Britain: Partisanship and Political Culture* (Oxford, Oxford University Press, 2005), p. 110.

[66] Bacopoulos-Viau and Fauvel, 'The Patient's Turn', p. 12.

[67] F. Dabhoiwala, 'Writing Petitions in Early Modern England', in M. Braddick and J. Innes (eds), *Suffering and Happiness in England 1550–1850: Narratives and Representations* (Oxford, Oxford University Press, 2017), pp. 127–48 (p. 147).

14

Petitions above Party: Congressional Representation by Petition, 1789–1950

MAGGIE BLACKHAWK AND DANIEL CARPENTER

POLITICAL THEORY HAS long recognised the centrality of parties to representative democracy, even going so far as to claim that 'parties created democracy' and to call 'modern democracy unthinkable save in terms of the parties'.[1] Given this apparent centrality, the empirical study of political parties has birthed its own subfield in political science and has inspired a vast literature on the role of political parties in democracy. The investigation of representation as a phenomenon related to but distinct from partisan democracy has, however, has been underdeveloped in the literature.[2]

One exception is found in the work of Nadia Urbinati who, in exploring the relationship between representation and partisanship, identified that 'representative democracy is an original form of government that is not identical with electoral democracy'.[3] Rather, in a representative democracy, we expect the ability to judge representatives not only at the end of their electoral mandate, but throughout the electoral term. In this way, representation is not simply an idea to be collapsed into the process of electoral accountability, but is a 'political process' in its own right and one that 'transforms and expands' politics, as well as being essential to a democracy.[4] Drawing upon the work of Benjamin Constant, Urbinati builds on the helpful distinction between 'representation of people's opinion (the will regularly expressed in elections)' and 'representation in the durée' ('those changes in public opinion that might [occur] between one election and the next').[5] Both petitioning

[1] E. E. Schattschneider, *Party Government* (New York, Holt, Rinehart, and Winston, 1942), p. xxvii; N. Rosenblum, *On the Side of Angels: An Appreciation of Parties and Partisanship* (Princeton, NJ, Princeton University Press, 2008), p. 3.

[2] H. Pitkin, *The Concept of Representation* (Berkeley, CA, University of California Press, 1967).

[3] N. Urbinati, *Representative Democracy: Principles and Genealogy* (Chicago, IL, University of Chicago Press, 2006), p. 223.

[4] Ibid., p. 37.

[5] Ibid., p. 51.

Proceedings of the British Academy, **262**, 268–283, © The British Academy 2024.

and partisan politics offer a means to represent changes in the public opinion that might occur between elections or in the durée. It bears further note that, in a context of a non-universal franchise, beyond capturing opinion between elections, representation in the durée might also offer a means to represent the unenfranchised and those excluded entirely from electoral representation, as a number of historical studies of petitioning have shown.[6] The representative role and functions of petitions and petitioning are an important reason why these practices have mattered in the modern era.

According to Urbinati, the heart of representation in the durée is formed by political institutions that offer three different functions in terms of representation: First, they foster deliberation among the public beyond electoral deliberation.[7] Second, they ensure the *representivity* or adherence of the representative to her constituency through the alignment of ideology and other forms of relationship.[8] Last, they afford the public a means for *advocacy* to further ensure representative accountability.[9] In allowing the public to render judgement of elected leaders, their policies, and their process beyond the point of election, these institutions essentially serve as 'a substitute for revolution'.[10] One of the paradigmatic representative institutions in the United States to serve as a site of deliberation and as a means to ensure representativeness is, no doubt, that of the political party – the function of which 'is above all that of "integrating the multitude" by unifying people's ideas and interests' into matters that are general and of national interest.[11]

Far less attention has been paid to other institutions of representation that foster a form of representation in terms of advocacy – most notably, the petition – and to how political parties have operated within the broader landscape of representative institutions operating within the durée. In the United States, petitions served from the Founding period onwards as a vital mode of representation through advocacy and a mode of representation that operated wholly within the durée, including the notable feature that they allowed representative advocacy especially but not only for populations that were unenfranchised.[12] Despite a growing literature on

[6] M. Knights, *Representation and Misrepresentation in Later Stuart Britain* (Oxford, Oxford University Press, 2005), pp. 103–62; M. Knights, 'Participation and Representation before Democracy: Petitions and Addresses in Premodern Britain', in I. Shapiro, S. C. Stokes, E. J. Wood, and A. S. Kirshner (eds), *Political Representation* (Cambridge, Cambridge University Press, 2009), pp. 35–57; H. Miller, *A Nation of Petitioners: Petitions and Petitioning in the United Kingdom, 1780–1918* (Cambridge, Cambridge University Press, 2023), pp. 229–52.

[7] Urbinati, *Representative Democracy*, pp. 47–8. See also D. Woodly, *The Politics of Common Sense: How Social Movements Use Public Discourse to Change Politics and Win Acceptance* (New York, Oxford University Press, 2015); and D. Woodly, *Reckoning: Black Lives Matter and the Democratic Necessity of Social Movements* (Oxford, Oxford University Press, 2021).

[8] Urbinati, *Representative Democracy*, pp. 49–52.

[9] Ibid., pp. 44–8.

[10] Ibid., p. 14.

[11] Ibid., p. 38.

[12] D. Carpenter and C. D. Moore, 'When Canvassers Became Activists: Antislavery Petitioning and the Political Mobilization of American Women', *American Political Science Review*, 108 (2014),

this political institution in the United States, little has been written about how petitioning practice coevolved with partisan political shifts – and, thus, how these two distinctive forms of representation interacted over time.

This chapter aims to highlight the distinctiveness of American petitioning histories from that of political parties and begin to fill this gap by drawing upon an original database of all petitions submitted to the US Congress from the Founding until 1950.[13] In documenting over 500,000 petitions submitted to the US Congress during this period, the Congressional Petitions Database (CPD) reveals a prodigious and vital political institution and form of representation that operated within Congress for the first century-and-a-half following the creation of the American Congress and the federal government.[14] But, importantly, petitioning offered a form of representation centred on advocacy – a form that stood in contrast to the function of political parties, and which centred on fostering deliberation and ensuring the continued representativeness of elected officials between elections.

The CPD offers a rare view of advocacy in the aggregate and the even rarer view of the responsiveness of formal branches of government to that advocacy. It aggregates this responsiveness by tracking the number of 'introductions' – the process in which a member of Congress brought a petition to the floor of a chamber of Congress, thereby entering it into the formal record – of petitions over time. Over the course of roughly 16 decades (1789–1949), the volume of petitions introduced to Congress experienced a number of peaks, most notably once in the antebellum (or pre-Civil War) era and another in the late 19th century, before declining steadily in the early 20th century. In the years following the Second World War, the vestiges of the petition system in Congress were effectively dismantled by a series of federal laws, and the number of petitions declined to near zero levels.[15] An important question, yet unanswered in the literatures on American politics and history, is whether these aggregate currents of advocacy and responsiveness by Congress corresponded in any detectable way to party system transformations and representation offered by parties.

Our examination of temporal patterns suggests that petitioning advocacy and representation followed rhythms quite different from partisan institutional

479–98; M. McKinley, 'Lobbying and the Petition Clause', *Stanford Law Review*, 68 (2016), 1131–205; M. McKinley, 'Petitioning and the Making of the Administrative State', *Yale Law Journal*, 127 (2018), 1538–637; D. Carpenter, Z. Popp, T. Resch, B. Schneer, and N. Topich, 'Suffrage Petitioning as Formative Practice: American Women Presage and Prepare for the Vote, 1840–1940', *Studies in American Political Development*, 32 (2018), 24–48; M. Blackhawk, 'Equity outside the Courts', *Columbia Law Review*, 120 (2020), 2037–128; M. Blackhawk, D. Carpenter, T. Resch, and B. Schneer, 'Congressional Representation by Petition: Assessing the Voices of the Voteless in a Comprehensive New Database, 1789–1949', *Legislative Studies Quarterly*, 46 (2021), 817–49; D. Carpenter, *Democracy by Petition: Popular Politics in Transformation, 1790–1870* (Cambridge, MA, Harvard University Press, 2021).

[13] Blackhawk et al., 'Congressional Representation by Petition', pp. 819–20, 823–5.

[14] https://dataverse.harvard.edu/dataset.xhtml?persistentId=doi:10.7910/DVN/JMOXQI (accessed 15 February 2024).

[15] McKinley, 'Petitioning and the Making of the Administrative State', p. 1548.

evolution in American national politics. While we do not claim full independence of petitioning representation and partisan representation, the discordance between these histories, both before and after the Civil War, suggests that petitioning followed energies that were both non-partisan and occasionally anti-partisan, as petitioners attempted to leverage advocacy to improve representation between elections and to place on the agenda important issues that the parties had ignored.[16] However, despite the importance of petitioning to representation within the United States and the growth of the political parties over the long 19th century, the peaks and valleys in the volume of petitions do not appear to bear a relationship to major shifts in party during the same historical period. Although these related institutions share commonalities in that they both reinforce representation between elections, they seemingly reinforce representation distinctively, or are, at the very least, drawn on at different times by the populations that rely on those institutions.

The lack of an apparent relationship between petitions and party stands in stark contrast to the deep enmeshment and volatility seen between parties and other institutions of representation, including, most obviously, the electoral process. We show, in contrast, that there does not appear to have been a period where the party in power or the party system reigning at the time resulted in significant transformations, such as a broadening or narrowing of petitioning practice. While it is well known that the Whig Party experienced some of its original growth in early anti-Jackson petitioning campaigns, these petitioning campaigns predated the party and did not depend upon electoral organisation.[17] Even the height of antebellum petitioning in response to the 'Gag Rule' in the House focused more substantively on the battle over slavery than the regnant issue cleavages of the second party system.[18] This chapter will show that petitions served a vital – and independent – function of representation within the Congress seemingly above party for over 100 years.

Contours of Representation by Petition

Our research efforts, in collaboration with other scholars, have produced several large databases of petitions sent to the US Congress.[19] Figure 14.1 reports the total number of petitions introduced to Congress over the course of American history from 1789 to roughly 1950, where the aggregates are divided by population. After

[16] D. Carpenter, 'Agenda Democracy', *Annual Review of Political Science*, 26 (2023), 1–20.

[17] Carpenter, *Democracy by Petition*, pp. 271–93; D. Carpenter and B. Schneer, 'Party Formation through Petitions: The Whigs and the Bank War of 1832–1834', *Studies in American Political Development*, 29 (2014), 213–34; M. F. Holt, *The Rise and Fall of the American Whig Party: Jacksonian Politics and the Onset of the Civil War* (Oxford, Oxford University Press, 1999), p. 27.

[18] Carpenter and Moore, 'When Canvassers Became Activists', pp. 482–5; Carpenter, *Democracy by Petition*, pp. 311–26.

[19] Blackhawk et al., 'Congressional Representation by Petition'; Carpenter et al., 'Suffrage Petitioning as Formative Practice'; Carpenter and Moore, 'When Canvassers Became Activists'.

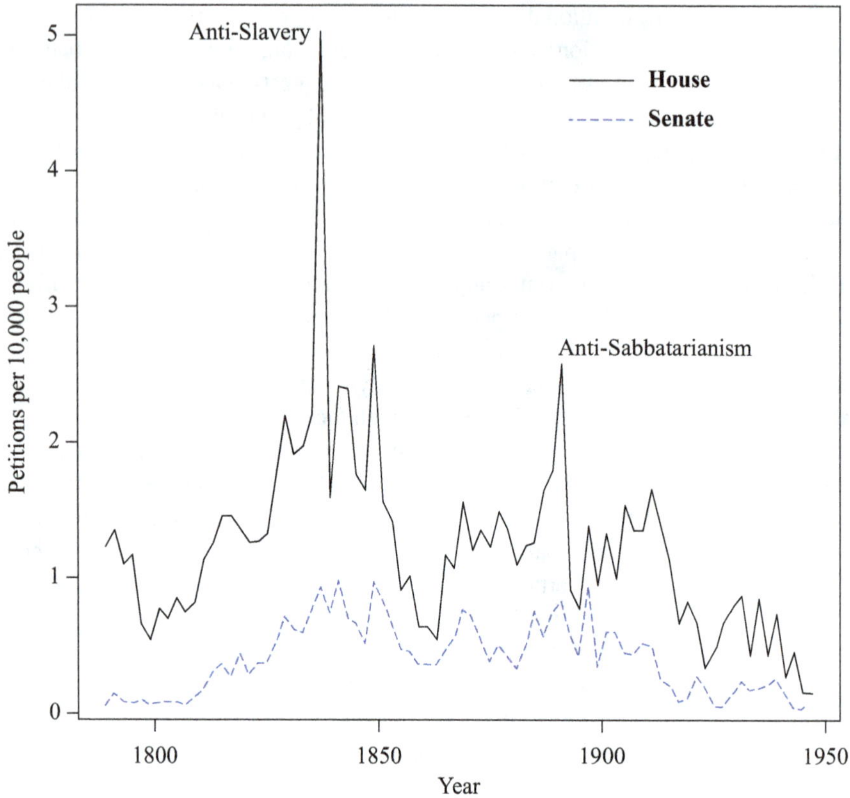

Figure 14.1 Petitions per 10,000 people for the House of Representatives and Senate, 1789–1950. Congressional Petitions Database.

a slight decline, there is a steady rise from 1800 to 1850, with important peaks in the 25th Congress (1837–9) and the 30th Congress (1847–9). In the run-up to the Civil War, aggregate petitioning declined but then remained at about one to one-and-a-half petitions introduced to the House per 10,000 residents from the Reconstruction period (1865–77) to the First World War. Petitions to the Senate add roughly another half petition per 10,000 American residents.

The first thing to note about these aggregate trends is that the clearest explosions of popular petitioning (1837–9 and 1891–3) occur not at times of partisan transformation but during relative party system stability. The issues that occasioned these mass petitioning peaks are also issues on which the parties did not heavily diverge at the time. Slavery in the 1830s and Sabbatarianism in the 1890s were, if anything, 'second-dimension' issues, far lower on the hierarchy of American party political debate than tariffs, for example. At the very time that partisan conflict over slavery became most intense (the 1850s), petitioning fell to historic lows. The second thing to note about the time series is that after the First World War the drop off of petitioning is such that it aggravates hypothesis testing. There are many reasons for this, including the establishment of alternative channels for petition introduction – innovative commissions, boards, and agencies – in response to earlier petition campaigns, as well as potential changes in the method of petition introduction and process in Congress.[20] But the rise of opinion polling, primary elections, and interest group lobbying as alternative sources of information for politicians also surely provides critical context.[21] We therefore confine our attention to developments before the First World War and split the antebellum period from the post-Civil War to 1914.

The Antebellum Era: Petitions Moving without Parties and Parties Moving without Petitions

Petitioning was ubiquitous in the early 19th century and substantially higher than had been experienced in the early US Republic.[22] The explosion of mass petitioning to legislatures was indeed a continental and global phenomenon, occurring in Canada and the British West Indies as well as in Britain and in Europe.[23]

These broad patterns underscore an important point. The most striking discordances between a shift in partisan representation and a shift in representation by petition come in those times when petitioning peaks and when the party systems

[20] McKinley, 'Petitioning and the Making of the Administrative State', pp. 1574–628. See also the chapter by Huzzey and Miller in this volume about the decline of petitions to national legislatures in a number of countries in the early 20th century.

[21] J. M. Hansen, *Gaining Access: Congress and the Farm Lobby, 1919–1981* (Chicago, IL, University of Chicago Press, 1991); T. Skocpol, *Diminished Democracy: From Membership to Management in American Civil Life* (Norman, University of Oklahoma Press, 2006).

[22] McKinley, 'Petitioning and the Making of the Administrative State', 1571–2; Blackhawk et al., 'Congressional Representation by Petition', 826; Carpenter, *Democracy by Petition*, pp. 60–86.

[23] See D. Carpenter and D. Brossard, '*L'éruption patriote*: The Revolt against Dalhousie and the Petitioning Explosion in Nineteenth-Century French Canada', *Social Science History*, 43 (2019), 453–85; C. Wilton, *Popular Politics and Political Culture in Upper Canada, 1800–1850* (Montreal, McGill-Queen's University Press, 2000); Carpenter, *Democracy by Petition*, Chapter 6; Miller, *A Nation of Petitioners*. See also M. D. da Cruz (ed.), *Petitioning in the Atlantic World, c. 1500–1840: Empires, Revolutions, and Social Movements* (Basingstoke, Palgrave, 2022); H. Miller, 'Introduction: The Transformation of Petitioning in the Long Nineteenth Century (1780–1914)', *Social Science History*, 43 (2019), 409–29; B. Agnès, *L'appel au pouvoir: Les pétitions aux parlements en France et au Royaume-Uni (1814–1848)* (Rennes, Presses universitaires de Rennes, 2018); C. Lipp and L. Krempel, 'Petitions and the Social Context of Political Mobilization in the Revolution of 1848/49: A Microhistorical Actor-Centred Network Analysis', *International Review of Social History*, 46 (2001), 151–69; D. Palacios Cerezales, 'Embodying Public Opinion: From Petitions to Mass Meetings in Nineteenth-Century Portugal', *E-Journal of Portuguese History*, 9 (2011), 1–19; D. Palacios Cerezales, 'Re-Imagining Petitioning in Spain (1808–1823)', *Social Science History*, 43 (2019), 487–508; J. Oddens, '"The Greatest Right of Them All": The Debate on the Right to Petition from the Dutch Republic to the Kingdom (c. 1750–1830)', *European History Quarterly*, 47 (2017), 634–56; and Würgler's chapter in this volume.

shift. Petitions peaked (exploded in short periods of time) when party systems were not changing. And when party systems did change – whether in 1800 or 1828 – there were not generally petitioning surges or fall-offs.

In 1837 a global economic panic shook the United States, which soon descended into an economic depression, and a petitioning explosion also commenced (Figure 14.1). It is likely, though not certain, that the global economic crisis contributed to this petitioning surge, as the disruption of work and widespread outrage at political elites led to greater willingness to challenge established representative institutions. Yet the relationship between economic crisis and petitioning is far from simple. For one, the core issue that led women and men across the northern United States to petition was not an issue related to the economic crisis but instead the spread of the slave system, and especially proposals to contain it by abolishing enslavement and the slave trade in the District of Columbia.[24] Second, the American party system did not change immediately in the aftermath of the Panic of 1837. It took until 1840 for a national Whig candidate to ascend to the presidency, and another year for state legislatures, in 1841, to choose their Senators and cement the Whigs' long-awaited majority. By contrast, the petitioning explosion of the 25th Congress (1837–9) came at a time when the Democrats' dominance in Congress and the executive branch had been well established by three successive electoral cycles.

Two developments show the irreducibility of the representation offered by petitioning and that offered by parties. First, the antebellum period saw both a broad antislavery campaign and a civil rights movement.[25] While these campaigns were critical in building new, third-party organisations (the Liberty and Free-Soil Parties, especially in places such as Ohio),[26] and in eventually challenging the ideological structure of the Whig Party and facilitating the rise of the Republican Party,[27] they did not coincide with, nor were they caused by, immediate developments in the Democrat–Whig binary of the second party system. Petitioning facilitated the rise of new party organisations and civic associations associated with the issue of slavery, but party organisations and their instability did not directly give rise to petitioning.[28]

Nor did established party organisations, whether dominant or ascendant, appear to have organised petitioning campaigns in the antebellum United States.

[24] Carpenter, *Democracy by Petition*, pp. 304–12, 318–19, 321–2; S. Zaeske, *Signatures of Citizenship: Petitioning, Antislavery, and Women's Political Identity* (Chapel Hill, NC, University of North Carolina Press, 2003), pp. 33, 45–6, 47, 49–50, 52–3, 69–71, 88–9.

[25] M. Sinha, *The Slave's Cause: A New History of Abolition* (New Haven, CT, Yale University Press, 2016); K. Masur, *Until Justice Be Done: America's First Civil Rights Movement* (New York, Knopf, 2021).

[26] Masur, *Until Justice Be Done*.

[27] E. Foner, *Free Soil, Free Labor, Free Men: The Republican Party before the Civil War* (New York, Oxford University Press, 1970); W. Gienapp, *The Rise of the Republican Party, 1852–1856* (New York, Oxford University Press, 1987); Holt, *The Rise and Fall*.

[28] Carpenter, *Democracy by Petition*, pp. 271–5; D. Carpenter, 'Recruitment by Petition: American Antislavery, French Protestantism, English Suppression', *Perspectives on Politics*, 14 (2016), 700–23.

This absence of relationship stands in stark contrast to the deep enmeshment of political parties and elections during the long 19th century.[29] During the same period that political parties formed into a 'parallel government' and a 'colossal … pyramid' that provided funding, infrastructure, routinisation, and formalisation to the electoral process, political parties initiated no similar relationship with the institution of petitioning – at least not at the national level.[30] Political parties had formed and filled the breach left by the reluctance of state and local governments to engage in election administration. Petitioning had no similar breach to fill with private administration at the national level, because Congress was somewhat more responsive in building out administration of the petitioning apparatus into innovative commissions, boards, and agencies when volume exceeded its own internal capacity.[31]

The second development of the antebellum period that involved both petitions and parties, less commonly noticed, was the Bank War of 1832–4. The Second Bank of the United States had been reauthorised by Congress in 1816 and was set for possible reauthorisation in 1836. President Andrew Jackson vetoed the reauthorisation bill in 1832, and that year his Treasury Secretary Roger Taney began withdrawing deposits from the Bank. Opponents of Jackson, led by Henry Clay of Kentucky, seized on the deposit withdrawals to mount a campaign that started as a defence of the Bank but morphed quickly into a protest against overweening executive power, producing tens of thousands of signatures on petitions to Congress within a few months. These petitions anticipated the development of Whig Party voting two years later and in the decades to come, as well as being indicative of state Whig party strength in the ensuing decade.[32] Yet the fact that the Bank War and its associated petitioning campaigns came before the Whig Party even existed means that the rhythms of petitioning shaped the contours of the party system in this critical period. While petitioning tended to focus on issues that the major two parties neglected or wished to suppress (such as slavery) – providing a window into how the party system and petitioning interacted – it remains the case that petitioning politics was irreducible to broad partisan and electoral transformations.

These patterns can be discerned in aggregate analysis using the CPD, which suggests that there was no consistent monotonic relationship between party system

[29] G. Gerstle, *Liberty and Coercion: The Paradox of American Government from the Founding to the Present* (Princeton, NJ, Princeton University Press, 2015), pp. 149–81.

[30] J. Bryce, 'Preface', in M. Ostrogorskii, *Democracy and the Organization of Political Parties*, 2 vols (London, Macmillan, 1902), Vol. I, p. xlii, and M. Josephson, *The Politicos, 1865–96* (New York, Harcourt Brace, 1938), p. 69, both cited by Gerstle, *Liberty and Coercion*, pp. 159–60.

[31] McKinley, 'Petitioning and the Making of the Administrative State', pp. 1574–628. For the similar hiving off of petitioning into separate administrative processes in the British context, see R. Huzzey and H. Miller, 'The Politics of Petitioning: Parliament, Government, and Subscriptional Cultures in the United Kingdom, 1780–1918', *History*, 106 (2021), 221–43 (p. 227).

[32] Carpenter and Schneer, 'Party Formation', pp. 229–33.

transformation and petitioning. We code a party system shift in two ways, first by following standard accounts in the American politics literature,[33] which locates these shifts in 1800 and 1828, and second by using party categories in Congress when both of the top two parties in Congress were different from the top two parties in the previous Congress, in either chamber. Such changes occur seven times in the period before the Civil War. For instance, in the First Congress the top parties were named Pro-Administration and Anti-Administration, but by the Fourth Congress these party titles had changed to Federalist and National Republican. To simplify, a majority shift does not suffice to create a party system change. New parties must emerge at the top, both in the first (plurality or majority) and second positions. Such transformations do not occur after the Civil War but occur frequently before it.

Table 14.1 shows that such changes occurred for seven congresses in the antebellum period, but that the differences in aggregate petitioning across these congresses did not. It is well known that majority shifts are associated with changes in congressional voting, and of course it is true that a shift in majorities in either

Table 14.1 Changes in petition levels and one-year changes across moments of party transformation, 1789–1861

House of Representatives

	Congresses	Mean number of petitions	Standard error
No shift	28	1,966.536	297.5713
Shift	7	2,778.143	917.4957
Combined	35	2,128.857	298.4372
Difference[a]		**811.6071**	**744.0177**

[a] T-test with unequal variances: $t = 0.8414$ ($p = 0.4268$)

Senate

	Congresses	Mean number of petitions	Standard error
No shift	28	684.3214	129.0883
Shift	7	836.2857	210.9088
Combined	35	714.7143	110.7477
Difference[b]		**151.9643**	**279.7852**

[b] T-test with unequal variances: $t = 0.6145$ ($p = 0.5514$)

[33] J. Sundquist, *Dynamics of the Party System* (Washington, DC, Brookings Institution Press, 1983).

chamber reflect changes in popular voting beforehand (or, in the Senate before popular election, shifting majorities in state legislatures or coalitions of legislators within those state chambers).[34]

Changes since the Civil War: The Weak Partisan Nature of Suffrage Petitioning

The United States has been governed by a stable 'party system' since the Civil War, when the dominant two-party regime of Democrats and Republics was cemented. While a few enduring third parties emerged in the United States after the Civil War (the Socialist Party, the Greenbackers, the Populist Party, among others), they have not been consistent competitors for dominance of the national legislature or the presidency.[35] In Congress, the dominance of majority parties has been a function of their ability to control procedures.[36]

Before turning to aggregate statistics it is worth documenting two simple facts. First, the major party transformation of this era, which occurred in the election of 1896,[37] did not coincide with an unusual rise or decline in petitioning (see again Figure 14.1). Moreover, the monetary policy issues central to that campaign and to populist agitation did not contribute a large share of petitions to Congress.[38]

Second, the campaigns that brought the most petitions or the most heavily signed petitions to Congress in this period – Sabbatarianism, temperance, or prohibition, and the women's suffrage issue – did not split the two major parties.[39] One sees, if anything, an absence of large-scale petitioning on some of the economic issues that divided the two major parties, such as tariffs and distributive benefits.[40]

The suffrage movement provides one of the most powerful examples of this phenomenon (see Figure 14.2). Suffrage petitioning was often aimed at state

[34] K. Poole and H. Rosenthal, *Ideology and Congress: A Political Economic History of Roll-Call Voting* (New York, Cambridge University Press, 2006).

[35] Sundquist, *Dynamics of the Party System*, pp. 31, 38, 313–16.

[36] G. W. Cox and M. D. McCubbins, *Setting the Agenda: Responsible Party Government in the US House of Representatives* (New York, Cambridge University Press, 2005).

[37] Sundquist, *Dynamics of the Party System*, pp. 154–60.

[38] E. Sanders, *Roots of Reform: Farmers, Workers, and the American State* (Chicago, IL, University of Chicago Press, 1999); R. F. Bensel, *Passion and Preferences: William Jennings Bryan and the 1896 Democratic Convention* (Cambridge, Cambridge University Press, 2008); R. F. Bensel, *The Political Economy of American Industrialization, 1877–1900* (Cambridge, Cambridge University Press, 2000), pp. 355–456.

[39] McKinley, 'Petitioning and the Making of the Administrative State', p. 1574; A. M. E. Szymanski, *Pathways to Prohibition* (Durham, NC, Duke University Press, 2003); C. McConnaughy, *The Woman Suffrage Movement in America: A Reassessment* (New York, Cambridge University Press, 2013); Carpenter et al., 'Suffrage Petitioning as Formative Practice'.

[40] F. E. Lee, 'Patronage, Logrolls, and "Polarization": Congressional Parties of the Gilded Age, 1876–1896', *Studies in American Political Development*, 30 (2016), 116–27; Bensel, *The Political Economy*, pp. 457–509.

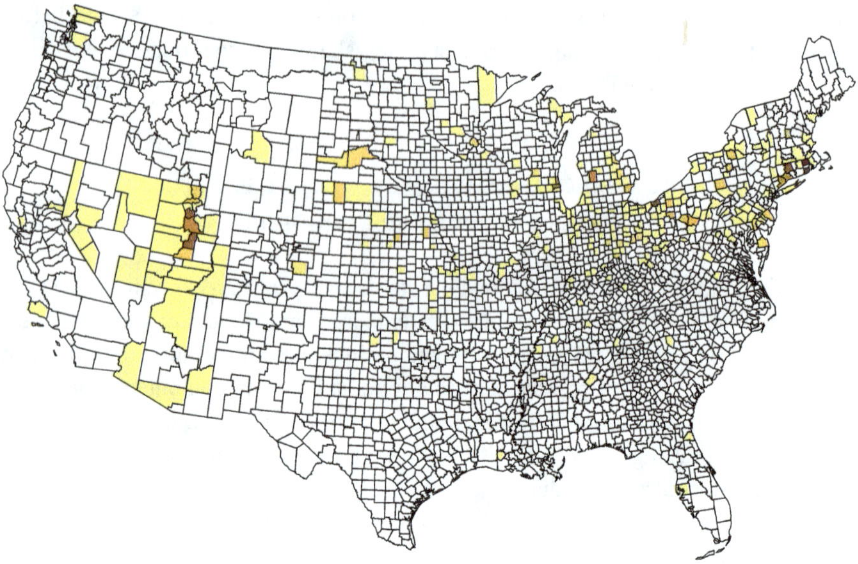

Figure 14.2 Heat map of women's suffrage petitions to the US Congress, 1900–10. Congressional Petitions Database.

Note: The heat map measures the intensity of suffrage petitions within US counties with the heat colours running from a minimum of zero to a maximum of 7.37 suffrage petitions per 10,000 population. The mean of the variable across all counties is 0.08 suffrage petitions per 10,000 population, and the mean for all counties with one or more suffrage petitions during this period is 0.80 petitions per 10,000 population.

legislatures, as women's suffrage did not split the national parties. And where issues of national suffrage petitioning were involved, petitions poured into Congress mostly from the west, where women were contesting their place in the public sphere and were in some cases already voting and even holding office. The south saw few suffrage-related petitions in the run-up to the 19th Amendment, and the campaigns for women's suffrage largely occurred in states that had reliably Republican voting patterns.

The timing of suffrage petitioning does suggest a weak connection to elections, in the sense that general election years saw a much larger petitioning average on suffrage issues related to the year after the general election.[41] Yet, again, many of these petitions were coming from people who could not vote, and from states that were not pivotal to the electoral college contest. It is more likely that general election years provided, especially for suffrage petitions, a context in

[41] Carpenter et al., 'Suffrage Petitioning as Formative Practice', pp. 36–9. On women's petitioning before the suffrage campaign, see two new fascinating and original treatments: J. Beatty, *In Dependence: Women and the Patriarchal State in Revolutionary America* (Chapel Hill: University of North Carolina Press, 2023); and S. Chatfield, *In Her Own Name: The Politics of Women's Rights before Suffrage* (New York: Columbia University Press, 2023).

which claims for voting rights were all the more concrete both to petitioner and to officeholder, and thus more likely to motivate a petitioning campaign calling for suffrage.

Did Shifts in Majorities Induce More Petitioning?

Whether changes in party systems can explain the peaks and valleys of American petitioning over the *longue durée*, then, seems doubtful. It is worth asking, though, whether moments of partisan replacement, the ousting of one partisan majority by another, led to changes in the volume of petitioning. There are theoretical reasons to believe this may be an explanation, as petitioners were usually petitioning not merely to a disembodied sovereign but to a set of officeholders whom they might have hoped to hear and respond to their grievances.[42]

The CPD again allows for aggregate tests of this hypothesis. Simple statistical comparisons across congresses from the CPD (see Table 14.2) suffice to show that partisan shifts did not move petitioning aggregates. In general, petitioning aggregates to a chamber were unmoved when that chamber witnessed a new partisan majority. We do not rule out the possibility that the issue-based mix of petitions changed – this is a subject best left for another study – but in terms of overall petition introductions, the rhythms of petitioning were separable from those of partisan politics.

Petitions, Parties, and Democracy

Our aggregate portrait is one that presents the institution of petitioning as a form of representation that stood alongside electoral and partisan systems for centuries and that was irreducible to those institutions. We do not claim full 'independence' of petitioning and partisanship, for several reasons. First, we have actively claimed that in some cases petitioning movements facilitated the organisational development of new parties.[43] Second, it is often the case that when parties offered clear ideological markers to voters on certain issues, contestation and advocacy were done within electoral and partisan institutions, and petitions played less of a role.[44] Where fault lines developed in the American party system – such as the active suppression of slavery- and race-related issues, as well as those relating to Indian removal, from the second party system of Democrat–Whig contestation – petitioning campaigns

[42] McKinley, 'Petitioning and the Making of the Administrative State'; Carpenter, *Democracy by Petition*, pp. 29–30, 55–8.

[43] Carpenter and Schneer, 'Party Formation', pp. 229–33. The point that petitions can facilitate the formation of parties is also evident in other historical contexts: M. Janse, '"What Value Should We Attach to All These Petitions?": Petition Campaigns and the Problem of Legitimacy in the Nineteenth-Century Netherlands', *Social Science History*, 43 (2019), 509–30 (pp. 525–6).

[44] Carpenter, 'Recruitment by Petition', pp. 702–3, 705–6.

Table 14.2 Petitioning across shifts in partisan majorities in US Congress, 1789–1950

Antebellum House (pre-1860)

	Congresses	Mean petitions by Congress	Standard error
No majority shift	20	1714.8	274.0343
Majority shift	15	2680.933	575.0791
Combined	35	2128.857	298.4372
Difference[c]		**966.1333**	**637.0328**

[c] T-test with unequal variances: $t = 1.5166$ ($p = 0.1448$)

Antebellum Senate (pre-1860)

	Congresses	Mean petitions by Congress	Standard error
No majority shift	26	679.8077	132.1937
Majority shift	9	815.5556	207.9446
Combined	35	714.7143	110.7477
Difference[d]		**135.7479**	**246.4065**

[d] T-test with unequal variances: $t = 0.5509$ ($p = 0.5898$)

House after 1860

	Congresses	Mean petitions by Congress	Standard error
No majority shift	34	6971.647	512.4936
Majority shift	10	8416.5	1462.241
Combined	44	7300.023	515.7446
Difference[e]		**1444.853**	**1549.451**

[e] T-test with unequal variances: $t = -0.9325$ ($p = 0.3706$)

Senate after 1860

	Congresses	Mean petitions by Congress	Standard error
No majority shift	35	2330.8	247.9781
Majority shift	9	1984.333	360.6176
Combined	44	2259.932	209.9525
Difference[f]		**346.4667**	**437.6508**

[f] T-test with unequal variances: $t = 0.7917$ ($p = 4398$)

often arose *en masse* to attempt to place those issues on the national agenda.[45] As Robert A. Dahl, Elmer E. Schattschneider, John Kingdon, and other theorists have maintained, the ability of the people to shape the agenda is a core feature of any democracy.[46]

Beyond this, petitioning as an institution of representation has been embedded in US constitutional understandings from the Founding onwards.[47] Recognition of the right to petition as fundamental helped shape the formal Constitution, most notably in the drafting and ratification of the First Amendment. But it also helped shape Article I, as well as helping to guide Congress's powers of statecraft as it built the American state and reinforced the right to petition and the forms of representation it protected.[48] Petitioning was fundamental and sacrosanct to the understanding of representation in the early United States, especially as visions of representation shifted from direct to more republican forms of government under the Articles of Confederation.[49] Petitioning provided for representation within the durée and, importantly, it offered an institution of representation that turned on advocacy. But it also allowed a channel for advocacy that was translated into the context of republican government. It offered representation that included formal process and the promise of response, without reducing petitioning to a form of direct democracy – thereby conflating the moment of petitioning with the force of elections, as the institution of instruction once had done.[50]

Beyond representation in the durée, petitioning has also served as a 'substitute for revolution' in other ways – especially in the context of a representative democracy that denied universal suffrage.[51] Petitioning allowed those without the vote, or those who could vote formally but whose incorporation into the party system was weak, to aggregate and organise their voices in another manner, one that carried with it the expectation of a response. Rather than turn to separatism and secession, excluded communities could use petitions to advocate for and begin to shape the

[45] Carpenter, *Democracy by Petition*, pp. 43–4, 476–7.

[46] R. A. Dahl, *Democracy and Its Critics* (New Haven, CT, Yale University Press, 1989); J. Kingdon, *Agendas, Alternatives, and Public Policies* (Washington, DC, CQ Press, 1984); E. E. Schattschneider, *The Semisovereign People: A Realist's View of Democracy in America* (Fort Worth, TX, Harcourt Brace Jovanovich, 1975).

[47] R. J. Krotoszynski Jr, *Reclaiming the Petition Clause: Seditious Libel, 'Offensive' Protest, and the Right to Petition the Government for a Redress of Grievances* (New Haven, CT, Yale University Press, 2012), pp. 104–35; Blackhawk et al., 'Congressional Representation by Petition'; McKinley, 'Petitioning and the Making of the Administrative State', pp. 1551–68; McKinley, 'Lobbying and the Petition Clause'.

[48] McKinley, 'Petitioning and the Making of the Administrative State'.

[49] Ibid., pp. 1618–19; McKinley, 'Lobbying and the Petition Clause', pp. 1148–52; B. Schneer, T. Resch, M. Blackhawk, and D. Carpenter, 'The Popular Origins of Legislative Jurisdiction: Petitions and Standing Committee Formation in Late Colonial Virginia and the Early US House', *Journal of Politics*, 84 (2022), 1727–45; G. S. Wood, *The Creation of the American Republic, 1776–1787* (Chapel Hill, NC, University of North Carolina Press, 1969), esp. pp. 189–91.

[50] McKinley, 'Lobbying and the Petition Clause', pp. 1147–52.

[51] Urbinati, *Representative Democracy*, p. 14.

terms of their inclusion.[52] But it is also worth further exploration to understand how these mechanisms fostered revolution, in addition to serving as an alternative to it. Petitioning not only allowed groups at the margins to advocate for inclusion, it also allowed them the ability to drive national agendas towards issues disregarded by electoral and partisan politics, including, paradigmatically, the institution of human enslavement.[53]

As seen during the antebellum era, the highest peak of petitioning volume per capita occurred over the issue of human enslavement—an issue that neither party was willing to address. The introduction of petitions *en masse*, even in the face of a hostile Congress and the questionably constitutional 'Gag Rule', allowed people at the margins and without political power to maintain national attention on abolition through their advocacy – in so doing, demonstrating the vital distinction between the forms of representation offered by parties and petitions as complementary, but dissimilar, institutions.

The irreducibility of petitioning politics to partisan politics implies that not only do we need to place other institutions of representation alongside elections in our understanding of American democracy and, indeed, democracy more generally; we need better to theorise and envision representation within the durée, as multiple institutions of representation operate and interact between elections.[54] This theorisation of the *longue durée* will probably also require distinguishing the representative institutions that maintain the relationship between representative and represented through passive means such as ideology, and those, like the petition, that require advocacy.[55]

As both an ideal of political equality and a system of governance, democracy demands literal accountability in the communication between citizen and officeholder.[56] Accounts of generalised 'inclusive institutions' also provide important room for petitioning, not merely as social movement practice or mobilisation, but also as a system of complaint and response.[57] While a substantial literature

[52] Masur, *Until Justice Be Done*; Beatty, *In Dependence*; Chatfield, *In Her Own Name*.

[53] Carpenter, 'Agenda Democracy'; Carpenter, *Democracy by Petition*, pp. 298–340. On the broader relationship between petitioning and political change, including revolution, see R. Huzzey, M. Janse, H. Miller, J. Oddens, and B. Waddell, introduction to this volume.

[54] See Miller, *A Nation of Petitioners*, pp. 229–52, for the United Kingdom case.

[55] Urbinati, *Representative Democracy*.

[56] C. Pateman, *Participation and Democratic Theory* (New York, Cambridge University Press, 1970); B. Barber, *Strong Democracy: Participatory Politics for a New Age* (Berkeley, CA, University of California Press, 1984); Dahl, *Democracy and Its Critics*; S. Macedo, *Diversity and Distrust: Civic Education in a Multicultural Democracy* (Cambridge, MA, Harvard University Press, 2000); A. Gutmann and D. Thompson, *Why Deliberative Democracy?* (Princeton, NJ, Princeton University Press, 2004); D. Allen, *Talking to Strangers: Anxieties of Citizenship since Brown v. Board of Education* (Chicago, IL, University of Chicago Press, 2004); D. Allen, *Education and Equality* (Chicago, IL, University of Chicago Press, 2016); P. Pettit, *On the People's Terms: A Republican Theory and Model of Democracy* (New York, Cambridge University Press, 2012); C. Calhoun, D. P. Gaonkar, and C. Taylor, *Degenerations of Democracy* (Cambridge, MA, Harvard University Press, 2022).

[57] D. Acemoglu and J. Robinson, *Economic Origins of Dictatorship and Democracy* (New York, Cambridge University Press, 2006).

has arisen around the concept of social movements to express some of this citizen voice,[58] the fact remains that petitions are often constitutive of such movements and have rarely been reducible to movements themselves. The institution of the petition offers a means of advocacy to maintain representation between representative and represented that could be fostered by social movement organisation but does not require it – and it could allow for alternative forms of organisation directed towards advocacy also, as well as no formal organisation whatsoever.[59] The institution of petitioning promised formal, equal, and transparent process, regardless of the political power of the petitioner or the number of petitioners.[60]

As we begin better to theorise representation in the *longue durée*, then, we can envision that petitions moved above parties not in a hierarchical way, but in the particular sense that for much of American national political history petitioning observed its own rhythms, stoking contests and raising issues that the party system had forgotten, and emphasising voices left aside in American electoral politics.[61] The decline of congressional petitioning does not mean that these alternative, non-electoral energies of American politics have disappeared – supplanted by other institutions that promised representation between elections. It means, instead, that they have taken new and different forms, and that our understanding of democracy must better encompass a range of forms of contestation outside votes and their counting.[62] Representation in the *longue durée* could comprehend an even more robust and complex form of representation than that described in the context of elections – including, but not limited to, the institution of the petition.

[58] L. J. Disch, 'Toward a Mobilization Conception of Democratic Representation', *American Political Science Review*, 105 (2011), 100–14; D. McAdam, S. Tarrow, and C. Tilly, *Dynamics of Contention* (New York, Cambridge University Press, 2001); H. Kitschelt, 'Social Movements, Political Parties, and Democratic Theory', *Annals of the American Academy of Political and Social Science*, 528 (1993), 13–29; K. Forrester, 'Feminist Demands and the Problem of Housework', *American Political Science Review*, 116 (2022), 1278–92; S. Tarrow, *Power in Movement: Social Movements and Contentious Politics*, 4th edn (New York, Cambridge University Press, 2022); Woodly, *The Politics of Common Sense*.

[59] McKinley, 'Lobbying and the Petition Clause'.

[60] Ibid.; Blackhawk et al., 'Congressional Representation by Petition'.

[61] Carpenter, 'Agenda Democracy'.

[62] McKinley, 'Petitioning and the Making of the Administrative State'; McKinley, 'Lobbying and the Petition Clause'; Krotoszynski Jr, *Reclaiming the Petition Clause*.

15

Petitioning the Soviet 'President': Mikhail Kalinin's Reception Office, 1919–1946

LARA DOUDS

BOTH THE TSARIST and Soviet states generally circumscribed petitioning as a mechanism of broad political and social collective expression, yet, individual, supplicatory requests and complaints remained a crucial form of interaction and communication between government and governed for five centuries.[1] The persistence of authoritarian politics in Russia from medieval times to the present has seen the preservation and expansion of the traditional form of personal petitioning even across revolutionary divides and radical regime change.

Petitions were a ubiquitous feature of the political landscape under the tsars and the Bolsheviks. The pervasiveness of this practice is illuminated by the plethora of subgenres of 'letters to power' in the Russian case, from the more supplicatory 'request' (*proshenie*), 'plea' (*khodataistvo*), 'statement' (*zaiavlenie*), and 'appeal' (*obrashchenie*) to the 'denunciation' (*donos*) and 'complaint' (*zhaloba*) and the more assertive 'demand' (*trebovanie*) or the loan word *petitsiia*. Elena Bogdanova, a leading specialist on 'complaints' in modern and contemporary Russia, has warned that labelling all applications to the authorities as 'petitions' translates the phenomenon for western audiences and obscures important culturally distinctive nuances.[2] On the other hand, categorising these genres into a strict taxonomy misses the overlaps between them and hides the remarkable scale and breadth of citizen approaches to the authorities.

[1] On collective peasant petitions demanding broad political change, see A. Verner, 'Discursive Strategies in the 1905 Revolution: Peasant Petitions from Vladimir Province', *Russian Review*, 54 (1995), 65–90. On collective, explicitly political petitions from soldiers, see M. Ferro, 'The Russian Soldier in 1917: Undisciplined, Patriotic, and Revolutionary', *Slavic Review*, 30 (1971), 483–512.

[2] E. Bogdanova, *Complaints to the Authorities in Russia: A Trap between Tradition and Legal Modernization* (Oxford, Routledge, 2021), p. 22. See also E. Bogdanova, 'Obtaining Redress for Abuse of Office in Russia: The Soviet Legacy and the Long Road to Administrative Justice', *Communist and Post-Communist Studies*, 51 (2018), 1–12; and E. Bogdanova, 'Religious Justifications of Complaints Addressed to the President in Contemporary Russia', *Laboratorium*, 6 (2014), 55–79.

Proceedings of the British Academy, **262**, 284–302, © The British Academy 2024.

With the opening of Soviet archives in the 1990s, historians discovered that letters to the authorities, including petitions, were among the most voluminous type of material preserved there. It became clear that all sorts of Soviet citizens wrote to all levels of the state: leaders such as Stalin; central state and Communist Party agencies including the secret police; regional, local party, and state officials; and newspapers, which published snippets in their pages and often forwarded them to the authorities for action.[3] A rich literature has developed over the past three decades that has used petitions as a source on daily life in Soviet society to shed light on discrete topics of complaint or request.[4] Some historians working on Stalinist society have wondered what these 'letters to the authorities' say about state–society relations, and a consensus is growing that they had a stabilising effect on the system, although precisely how they did so remains a matter of debate.[5] Alexei Tikhomirov has argued that in writing petitions to leaders in emotional, personal language, Soviet citizens talked themselves into 'trusting' the regime.[6] Letter writing was a stabilising force for the Soviet regime and a means by which people 'learned to feel Soviet'. On the other hand, Alexander Livshin and Igor Orlov have taken a more pragmatic view, suggesting that 'in the Soviet period, in the absence of forms of communication and interaction between the state and the population inherent in a democratic society ... a petition to those in power through appeals, complaints, [and] denunciations was a surrogate substitute for feedback.' They further argue that

[3] S. Fitzpatrick, 'Supplicants and Citizens: Public Letter Writing in Soviet Russia in the 1930s', *Slavic Review*, 55 (1996), 78–105: M. Lenoe, 'Letter-Writing and the State: Reader Correspondence with Newspapers as a Source for Early Soviet History', *Cahiers du monde russe*, 40 (1999), 139–69.

[4] Examples include G. Alexopolous, *Stalin's Outcasts: Aliens, Citizens, and the Soviet State, 1926–1936* (Ithaca, NY, Cornell University Press, 2003); K. Ironside, '"I Beg You Not to Reject My Plea": The Late Stalinist Welfare State and the Politics of One-Time Monetary Aid, 1946–1953', *Journal of Social History*, 51 (2018), 1045–68. See also C. Doucette, 'Soviet Letters', in G. Gilbert (ed.), *Reading Russian Sources: A Student's Guide to Text and Visual Sources from Russian History* (Oxford, Routledge, 2020). See also collections of published primary sources (consisting largely of petitions) with useful introductions: M. D. Steinberg, *Voices of Revolution, 1917* (New Haven, CT, Yale University Press, 2001); L. H. Siegelbaum and A. Sokolov (eds), *Stalinism as a Way of Life: A Narrative in Documents* (New Haven, CT, Yale University Press, 2008); C. J. Storella and A. K. Sokolov, *Voice of the People: Letters from the Soviet Village, 1918–1932* (New Haven, CT, Yale University Press, 2013); I. B. Orlov, O. V. Khlevniuk, and A. Ia. Livshin (eds), *Pis'ma vo vlast', 1917–1927: Zaiavleniia, zhaloby, donosy, pis'ma v gosudarstvennye struktury i bol'shevistskim vozhdiam* (Moscow, Rosspen, 1998); I. B. Orlov, O. V. Khlevniuk, and A. Ia. Livshin (eds), *Pis'ma vo vlast', 1928–1939: Zaiavleniia, zhaloby, donosy, pis'ma v gosudarstvennye struktury i sovetskim vozhdiam* (Moscow, Rosspen, 2002); and G. L. Freeze, *From Supplication to Revolution: A Documentary Social History of Imperial Russia* (Oxford, Oxford University Press, 1988).

[5] See the pioneering work by Sheila Fitzpatrick on petitioning in Russian and Soviet history, especially the special issue she edited for: *Russian History*, 24:1/2 (1997).

[6] A. Tikhomirov, 'The Regime of Forced Trust: Making and Breaking Emotional Bonds between People and State in Soviet Russia, 1917–1941', *Slavonic and East European Review*, 91, (2013), 78–118; A. Tikhomirov, 'The State as a Family: Speaking Kinship, Being Soviet and Reinventing Tradition in the USSR', *Journal of Modern European History*, 15 (2017), 395–418. See also A. Livshin, 'Bridging the Gap: Government–Society Dialogue via Letters', *Slavonic and East European Review*, 91 (2013), 57–77.

such letters between state and citizens 'can be analysed as a form of implementation of a power contract. Both parties to this contract accepted the unspoken rules of the game and followed a coherent model of behaviour.'[7]

Viewing Russia's petitioning practices in a comparative context provides insights into why petitions have mattered in authoritarian systems where other forms of political expression are limited. For example, work on contemporary China has emphasised the extent to which petitions function as 'useful complaints' for authorities, providing information about popular grievances, and abuses by local officials, that facilitate 'decentralized authoritarianism'.[8] In her examination of state–society relations in the German Democratic Republic, Mary Fulbrook highlights the importance of the practice of the *Eingaben* (citizens' communication), arguing that petitioning can be viewed as an alternative route to democratic participation in which individual East Germans could feel 'their voices heard' while also 'informing the character and direction of the domestic political agenda', an approach that offers interesting parallels with the Soviet case.[9]

With this framework in mind, this chapter focuses on the 'Priemnaia', or 'Reception Office', of Mikhail Kalinin, the Chairman of the Presidium of the Central Executive Committee of Soviets, and official head of state of the Soviet Union, from 1919 to 1946. This institution was a main government designated channel for receiving petitions.[10] Over the course of 27 years, Kalinin's Priemnaia received millions of petitions and was inundated on a daily basis with *khodoki*, petitioners in person.[11] The Priemnaia was an important pillar of 'Soviet democracy'. The earliest years of Soviet government saw a period of experimentation in the nature of authority. Soviet leaders believed that they were constructing a superior democratic system, but they were unsure of the particular forms that this new government should take. Marx had taught them to be wary of the 'bourgeois parliamentary democracy' of late-19th-century Europe, which amounted to nothing more, in Lenin's words, than the oppressed majority being 'allowed once every few years to decide which particular representatives of the oppressing class shall represent and repress them in parliament!'.[12] Yet Soviet leaders had no concrete programme of what the postrevolutionary government of the transitional phase of the 'dictatorship of the proletariat' should look like.

7 Orlov et al., *Pis'ma vo vlast', 1917–1927*, p. 7.

8 J. Chen, *Useful Complaints: How Petitions Assist Decentralized Authoritarianism in China* (Lanham, MD, Lexington, 2016).

9 Mary Fulbrook, *The People's State: East German Society from Hitler to Honecker* (New Haven, Yale University Press, 2005), p. 271.

10 Another crucial central institution for receiving petitions was the 'Complaints Bureau' set up in April 1919 under the People's Commissariat of State Control (from 1920 the People's Commissariat of Workers' and Peasants' Inspection, or Rabkrin). See E. A. Rees, *State Control in Soviet Russia: The Rise and Fall of the Workers' and Peasants' Inspectorate, 1920–34* (London, Palgrave Macmillan, 1987).

11 On the presence of premodern Eurasian petitioners, see D. Zaret, 'Petition-and-Response and Liminal Petitioning in Comparative/Historical Perspective', *Social Science History*, 43 (2019), 431–52.

12 V. I. Lenin, *State and Revolution* (London, Lawrence and Wishart, 1947), p. 103.

While the Bolsheviks rejected 'bourgeois parliamentary democracy', this did not mean that they immediately embraced a repressive party-state dictatorship. An important element of 'genuine' democracy was economic equality, but in politics too institutional choices had to be made, at least until the state began to 'wither away' under the future socialist society. Rather than adopting liberal representative institutions criticised by Marx, the Reception was conceived (alongside elected workers and peasants' soviets or councils, and a vanguard party) as a means of erasing the gap between state and society and making government responsive to the masses.

In this context, petitioning was reimagined by the new state builders as a 'living link' to public concerns. Accordingly, the practice of sending personal petitions was promoted by the revolutionary regime from its earliest months, and Soviet citizens quickly took it up as a major avenue of engagement with the authorities. As we shall see, petitioning was seen to offer communication and accountability in the absence of multiparty elections, civil society freedoms, and other outlets for expression.

The Russian Revolution and the Establishment of the Reception

Dating back to the Middle Ages, petitioning, alongside violent protest, was one of the most significant forms of popular political agency in Muscovite and Imperial Russia. Requests and complaints were directed at various levels of authority, but corruption and inefficiency at lower levels meant that petitions were frequently directed to the top. A central pillar of the legitimising 'myth of the Tsar' was the notion of the benevolence of the ruler, who would intervene to protect his lowly subjects from abuses of the boyars. In the 16th century a special chancellery, the Chelobitnyi Prikaz, was created to deal with petitions to the tsar in person and in letter form. Although it was dissolved in the late 17th century, the state retained a bureaucracy for processing petitions thereafter. By the turn of the 20th century the tsarist 'Petitions Chancellery' was receiving more than 65,000 petitions annually.[13]

[13] Sometimes referred to as the Chelobitennyi Prikaz, on which see P. Brown, 'Muscovite Government Bureaus', *Russian History*, 10 (1983), 269–330 (pp. 294–5); A. Kleimola, *Justice in Medieval Russia: Muscovite Judgment Charters (Pravye Gramoty) of the Fifteenth and Sixteenth Centuries* (Philadelphia, PA, American Philosophical Society, 1975), p. 11; V. A. Kivelson, *Autocracy in the Provinces: The Muscovite Gentry and Political Culture in the Seventeenth Century* (Stanford, CA, Stanford University Press, 1996), pp. 11, 32, 52–3, 80, 89–90, 112, 137–40, 180–82, 199–201, 211236, 242–63; S. O. Schmidt, 'Chelobitennyi prikaz v seredine xvi stoletiia', *Izvestiia akademii nauk SSSR: Seria istorii I filosofii*, 7 (1950), 445–59; N. P. Eroshkin (ed.), *Istoriia gosudarstvennykh uchrezhdenii dorevoliutsionnoi Rossii* (Moscow, Vysshaia shkola, 1968), p. 45; and L. Douds, 'Lenin's "Living Link": Petitioning the Ruler across the Revolutionary Divide', in L. Douds, J. Harris, and P. Whitewood (eds), *The Fate of the Bolshevik Revolution: Illiberal Liberation, 1917–41* (London, Bloomsbury, 2020), pp. 63–76.

In consolidating their new revolutionary government, Soviet leaders had to cater to popular expectations of state power shaped by the existing political system. The impetus to establish the Reception therefore came from below: its creation was an *ad hoc* response to the deluge of expectant petitioners accustomed to exercising this mechanism of request or complaint. As one of the institution's secretaries remarked, the early weeks of the revolution were 'a time of uncontrollable pilgrimage to Lenin. Every day from morning till night I found dozens of people who came to see Vladimir Ilich from their localities. They sat for hours in the waiting room of the Council of People's Commissars, patiently waiting for the Reception.'[14] Revolutionary upheaval and instability only intensified the popular desire to petition the centre, and a huge quantity of petitions, as well as visitors, arrived at the government's headquarters.[15]

The first Priemnaia, or Reception Office, had been hastily put together by Lenin's staff shortly after the October Revolution. The new government's first headquarters, at the Smolny Institute, accommodated the large numbers of workers, soldiers, and peasants descending daily.[16] From all over the former Russian empire, peasants in particular, nominated by their local community and travelling on funds assembled by the village communes, came to meet with the 'head Bolshevik'.[17]

The Council of People's Commissars Priemnaia was open from noon on Tuesdays and Thursdays in the first year after the move to the Kremlin for visitors to submit petitions.[18] Reception staff heard the requests and complaints of all petitioners and noted them down. After their day's work, the staff reported to Lenin on all 'interesting and socially important visits'. He read the written reports prepared by Reception staff, gave directions on tasks arising, and demanded that their implementation be followed up.[19] During the first six months of Soviet power the Priemnaia received more than 6,000 petitions.[20] Lenin's work leading the new government was weighed down under the avalanche of petitions and

[14] M. N. Skrypnik, 'Krest'iane-khodoki y Il'icha v smol'nom', in *Vospominaniia o Vladimire Il'iche Lenine*, Vol. II (Moscow, Institut Marksizma-Leninizma pri TSK KPSS, 1957), pp. 89–92.

[15] V. D. Bonch-Bruevich, *Izbrannie sochineniia v trekh tomakh*, Vol. III (Moscow, Izdatel'stvo akademii nauk SSSR, 1963), p. 166. See also A. F. Ilyin-Zhenevskii, *The Bolsheviks in Power: Reminiscences of the Year 1918*, trans. B. Pierce (London, New Park, 1984), pp. 7, 28.

[16] 'Trebovatel'naia vedomost' na bydachu zhalovaniia sluzhashchim Upravleniia delami Sovnarkoma', 25 October 1917–1 March 1918, State Archive of the Russian Federation (GARF), fo. 130, op. 1, d. 99. Also see E. K. Koksharova, 'V. I. Lenin v sovnarkome v 1917 godu', in E. K. Koksharova, *Lenin v 1917 godu: Vospominaniia* (Moscow, Izdatelstvo Politicheskoi Literaturi, 1967), p. 291; and Bonch-Bruevich, 'Pervye dni sovnarkomovskogo apparata' in Koksharova, *Lenin v 1917 godu*, p. 275.

[17] M. N. Skrypnik, 'Krest'iane-khodoki y Il'icha v smol'nom', in *Vospominaniia o Vladimire Il'iche Lenine*, Vol. II, p. 76.

[18] Bonch-Bruevich, *Izbrannye sochineniia*, Vol. III, p. 167.

[19] Ibid., Vol. III, p. 166.

[20] L. A. Fotieva, *Iz zhizni V. I. Lenina* (Moscow, Izdatel'stvo politicheskoi literatury, 1967), p. 90.

he soon attempted to channel them towards the head of state, Kalinin, who was effectively the Soviet 'president'. The new Priemnaia of the All-Russian Central Executive Committee of Soviets became, from April 1919, the government's preferred central channel for receiving requests, complaints, and other letters from the public, and soon absorbed the original Priemnaia of the Council of People's Commissars.

Kalinin and the Reception Office

In March 1919, Kalinin was appointed as the new chairman of the All-Russian Central Executive Committee of Soviets, making the new Soviet 'president' a softer, more tolerant figure than the previous incumbent. His appointment demonstrated accessibility on the part of the Soviet government, since it played on his carefully cultivated persona. Although the future 'all-union village elder' was born in 1875 into a peasant family in the village of Verkhnyaya Troitsa, about 150 miles north of Moscow, he left aged 14. Thereafter he worked as a house servant for General Mordukhai-Boltovsky in St Petersburg and later trained as a factory carpenter in the city.[21] Although he was only in his early 40s, Kalinin's public image presented him as an old rural elder: his goatee, tarpaulin boots, and crumpled jacket would sometimes be completed by a stick and glasses, which were essentially props, given that he did not need them. His presentation as 'village elder on an all-Soviet scale' made him one of the most well-known figures in early Soviet Russia, promising a sympathetic response to the peasantry. From 1919 he was a constant presence in the Soviet press in photographs and news articles, as well as in film footage and on postage stamps.[22]

On 25 April 1919 the government newspaper *Izvestiia* marked the official opening of Kalinin's Priemnaia. A notice announced that 'Comrade Kalinin, Chairman of the All-Russian Central Executive Committee, will receive petitioners on Saturday 26 April from 10 a.m. to 12 p.m. in the Fourth House of Soviets, 7 Mokhovaia Street, third floor, apartment four.'[23] This location became the permanent headquarters of the Reception, staffed by six officials and secretaries. Situated on the corner of Vozdvizhenka and Mokhovaia Street in central Moscow, it was an imposing, mint-green building, which had previously been a hotel. In spring 1919, security concerns had led the Presidium of the All-Russian Central Executive Committee to resolve, 'in order to make the reception of petitioners to the Presidium … more accessible to the general masses, to take them outside of

[21] A. Dementyev and A. Pyanov, *Mikhail Kalinin* (Moscow, Novosti, 1975), pp. 5–11.

[22] P. Kenez, *The Birth of the Propaganda State* (Cambridge, Cambridge University Press, 1985), p. 61.

[23] *Izvestiia*, no. 87, 25 April 1919, p. 1.

the Kremlin walls'.[24] As one enthusiastic visitor at this time, the American socialist Louise Bryant, observed:

> To get into the Kremlin requires too much red tape. Therefore, while the President (Kalinin) eats in the Kremlin dining-room … and sits in the Council of the People's Commissars, he receives his army of callers in an ordinary building in the heart of the city. One needs no pass or credentials to get in; one needs simply to walk up a flight of stairs, open a door and emerge into a large bare reception room full of noisy peasants.[25]

Kalinin's first years as Chairman of the Central Executive Committee consisted of an extended 'meet and greet' across the Soviet Republic as civil war raged. Soon after his appointment, he boarded the *October Revolution* agit-train and set out for the eastern front tasked with rallying popular support for the new government. In 1919–20, Kalinin's *October Revolution* made twelve long journeys and would acquire a nickname as the 'All Russian Central Executive Committee on rails.'[26] As well as being equipped with political, information, editorial, and newspaper offices and a cinema, the train had its own Priemnaia. This mobile Reception dealt with petitions on the spot. In 1919, Kalinin hosted 753 meetings and 400 gatherings of other kinds.[27] His extended tour attempted to consolidate Soviet authority across the country, and echoed premodern practices in Europe where monarchs received petitioners on their progresses around their kingdoms.

In Kalinin's absence, the Presidium of the Central Executive Committee decided on 4 June 1919 to appoint officials from among its members to receive petitioners in Moscow. They included the prominent statesman V. I. Nevsky, People's Commissar for the Railways. Even as Kalinin was traversing the country on his agit-train, written petitions continued to arrive at the Reception headquarters in Moscow. Many of these petitions were set out in the formulaic and supplicatory prerevolutionary style, with the traditional heading 'Proshenie'. Others began with the new greeting 'Respected Comrade', demonstrating how quickly the public shifted to mimic the language of the revolutionary regime in order to inspire a sympathetic response.[28]

Petitions preserved in the archival file 'Letters to Kalinin, April–December 1919' run to hundreds of pages and contain a varied range of requests for assistance with employment and housing, for grants to relieve hardship, or to present complaints about local issues. For example, citizens complained that they had not been compensated for animals confiscated by the Red Army, or that *razverstka*, or grain requisitioning, had been implemented too harshly. Other requests were

[24] GARF, fond 1235, op. 36, d. 35, l. 4.

[25] L. Bryant, *Mirrors of Moscow* (New York, Thomas Seltzer, 1923), p. 98.

[26] Lidiia Maksakova, *Agitpoezd 'Oktiabr'skaia Revoliutsiia' 1919–1920* (Moscow, Nauka, 1956), pp. 7–10.

[27] Ibid, p. 8.

[28] Russian State Archive for Socio-Political History (RGASPI), f. 78, op. 1, d. 22, l. 44.

for amnesties or pardons from arrest and imprisonment.[29] Indeed, as Golfo Alexopoulos's important work on 'Stalin's outcasts' has demonstrated, petitions for the pardon or restoration of rights of *lishentsy* (those deprived of rights because of origins or behaviour alien to the new Soviet values) became an integral part of the Soviet system of revolutionary justice and a means for socially 'undesirable' people to claim their Soviet credentials.[30]

In July 1919 Kalinin's Reception Office received a petition from 'the peasants of the Vladimir province, Vyaznikovsky district, Denisovsky volost through a Red Army peasant agitator in the city of Kimry, Tver province, Mikhail Vilkov'. Vilkov wrote:

> I ask for your response on the voice of the peasants mentioned above ... I, as an agitator of the RSFSR, was the other day in my volost in the villages at work ... and I chatted with the peasants mentioned above. They welcome my agitation, but according to them, on the ground, the volost, and district executive committees undermined trust among the population ... the peasants say 'we pay, contribute and they take from us and we fulfil all the requirements, but we don't know, we don't see where everything is going, since the executive committee gave not one report to the population, but if we start talking at meetings, then they treat us impudently, and say that the peasants are embittered against the authorities'. In view of this, the dark peasants, through me, ask you to come to our volost and district to buoy the spirit of the peasantry in view of the grain accounting, since the counterrevolutionaries are frightening them that this year the authorities will take away grain without mercy.[31]

The question of literacy and petitioning presented by this interesting example has not yet been fully explored, but traditional means of letter writing to the authorities in rural areas (where literacy rates across the countryside of the Russian empire have been roughly estimated in 1917 at 53.2 per cent for men and 22.6 per cent for women), included the local *pisar'*, or scribe, and the mostly literate peasant elders.[32] When these traditional channels for letter writing were disrupted because of revolutionary upheaval, it seems that peasants made use of the Communist Party's own officials to communicate their requests to the central authorities. This obstacle was reduced by the Soviet government's push to eradicate illiteracy, which boosted the literacy rates for rural men and women to 92 and 77 per cent respectively by 1939.[33]

Meanwhile, as civil war receded in 1921 and Kalinin returned to Moscow, he continued to cultivate his image as a sympathetic 'man of the people' in order to appeal to ordinary petitioners – particularly to the peasant population, as 'one of their own'. Louise Bryant (a sympathetic contemporary who reflected the

[29] RGASPI, fond 78, op. 1, dd. 22–4.

[30] G. Alexopoulos, *Stalin's Outcasts: Aliens, Citizens, and the Soviet State, 1926–1936* (Ithaca, NY, Cornell University Press, 2003).

[31] RGASPI, fond 78, op. 1, d. 22, l. 44.

[32] B. Mironov, 'The Development of Literacy in Russia and the USSR from the Tenth to the Twentieth Centuries', *History of Education Quarterly*, 31 (1991), 229–52 (p. 241); C. Gaudin, *Ruling Peasants: Village and State in Late Imperial Russia* (Dekald, Northern Illinois University Press, 2007), pp. 63, 69–73, 78.

[33] Mironov, 'The Development of Literacy', p. 242.

government's rhetoric) wrote of Kalinin at this time that 'the remarkable thing is that when he gets back to Moscow he makes no effort to shake the dust of the provinces from his boots, he rather makes a point of remaining distinctly a villager. He receives you in his Moscow office wearing the same old mended spectacles, the same threadbare coat and, I am sure, the same heart and mind.'[34]

When Kalinin discovered that local authorities sometimes hindered the issuing of passes for travel to Moscow for petitioners he ordered that officials must issue the required paperwork. In April 1920, for example, Kalinin's secretariat wrote to the chairman of the Galich executive committee in Kostroma province: 'I ask you, comrade, to issue an appropriate order to the Kostroma volost so that the delegates of this volost are allowed to go to the centre to the Chairman … to clarify the needs of the volost … this is what the central authority exists for, to clarify all the misunderstandings that arise in the localities.'[35]

In July 1921, Soviet leaders enacted further measures to strengthen the mechanism of petitioning the centre. An article entitled 'Combating Arbitrariness' appeared in *Izvestiia* complaining that people who wrote petitions to Moscow were often threatened with arrest and repression by the very local officials about whom they complained.[36] To counteract this, the article insisted upon active assistance from regional and rural soviets to organise trips to the capital, as well as tough action from the centre against local repression of petitioners, and further recommended that all appeals should be considered within three to seven days.

For the next 25 years Kalinin led the work of the Priemnaia and oversaw its expansion and bureaucratisation. In the final year before his death in 1946, Kalinin's Priemnaia received 324,424 petitions.[37] According to a report of 30 March 1945 by P. A. Savelyev, head of the Reception Office, Kalinin and his assistants had received about 1 million petitioners in person and about 3 million petitions by post since it was established in 1919.[38]

The Reception Office registered and recorded petitions arriving by letter and in person, before sending them on to relevant departments to respond to each petitioner. By the late 1920s, detailed monthly and annual *obzor*, or summary reports, were compiled for circulation within government, providing a close statistical analysis of how many petitions were received and what proportion were individual or collective, classified by topic (such as tax, land, education) and region.[39]

[34] Bryant, *Mirrors of Moscow*, p. 96.

[35] Fond Muzeia M. I. Kalinina, Inv. Kn. 3, Inv. 119, l. 3, cited in B. M. Rudiak, 'Materialy priemnoi M.I . Kalinina: Istochnik dlia izucheniia istorii sovetskogo obshchestva', *Voprosy istorii*, 28 February 1957, p. 124.

[36] *Izvestiia*, no. 144, 5 July 1921, pp. 2, 63; Orlov et al., *Pis'ma vo vlast', 1928–1939*, pp. 8–9.

[37] GARF, 'Report on the work of the Reception of the Supreme Soviet USSR', OP. 65, D. 592, L.3.

[38] Report of P. A. Savelyev (Head of the Reception Office of the Chairman of the Presidium of the Supreme Soviet of the USSR) on the 25th anniversary of the Reception Office of M. I. Kalinin, 30 March 1945, fond of the M. I. Kalinin Museum, Inv. Kn. 2, Inv. 6985, l. 7, cited in Rudiak, 'Materialy priemnoi', p. 125.

[39] GARF, fond 7523, op. 65, d. 592, ll. 5–51 (1946); and RGASPI, fond 78, op. 1, d. 423, ll. 179–84.

One upsurge in petitions to Kalinin, the peasant-president and 'All-Union Village Headman', occurred as a result of Stalin's drive for the collectivisation of agriculture.[40] A deluge of petitions flooded Kalinin's Reception Office in the wake of this disruptive and transformative policy from 1928. One example of a petition that exploited Kalinin's public persona came from Petr Afanasev Polin in September 1928. He wrote:

> Dear comrade Mikhail Ivanovich Kalinin, convinced that you will answer the majority of letters from the population, I am turning to you with a request [*pros'ba*] ... I, a citizen of the village of Kremenets ... of the Zhizdrinsky district of the Bryansk province ... have a family of 21 people ... The family consists of me, an old man of 67 years old, my wife of the same age, and 5 sons with their wives and young children.

Polin gave precise details of the amount of land his household had under cultivation as well as listing their animals, and stated that the agricultural tax imposed upon him in that year came to 275 rubles, 85 kopecks. Again, exploiting the Soviet regime's own representation of Kalinin as a peasant-elder, Polin implored:

> Dear comrade Kalinin, you yourself are from the peasants by origin and therefore you will understand how hard on your hands the work is when you are excessively imposed upon and counted among the kulaks. They say that now they are putting pressure on the kulaks and liberating the poor and middle peasants. But it's a shame when a neighbour with an approximately good farm, with the same allotted land norm, pays 5 10 rubles, and I pay 275 rubles, 85 kopecks ... Think, Mikhail Ivanovich, if we, like the rest of the citizens, split up [via collectivisation], then owing to the lack of living quarters and the lack of livestock, and the youth of the children, we would have six farm labourers, from whom they wouldn't take anything ... the government calls for a collective, and on the other hand, the local authorities push for this collective, ordering: 'Split up, and then you yourself will be farm labourers and will not pay the government' ... The family ... splits up, believing that then we will be protected by the local authorities. But will the government be better off as a result of this? ... I am not able to pay the imposed tax: the penalties will increase and the farm will go bankrupt. Why? Only because the income tax of 25 per cent was erroneously charged to me. I believe that such pressure ... on large families is unfair, and you, comrade, as head of the leading legislative body, should take this into account and help bring relief to my large, essentially poor household. Dear comrade Mikhail Ivanovich Kalinin, I humbly request your honour to reduce the tax in kind. Please do not abandon our request.[41]

The various persuasive techniques at play in this document demonstrate how a petition could function as both a private forum for implicit criticism of general government policy (and of the local officials in implementing it) and as a plea for merciful individual assistance. Polin's letter was one of 3,307 petitions

[40] S. Fitzpatrick, *Stalin's Peasants: Resistance and Survival in the Russian Village after Collectivsation* (Oxford, Oxford University Press, 1994), pp. 15–16, 232–2, 238, 299, 329–30.

[41] RGASPI, fond 78, op. 1, d. 308, ll. 88–9.

received by Kalinin's Priemnaia relating to land issues, and among 2,182 specifically on collectivisation, in September 1932, which according to monitoring by departmental statisticians had decreased from the peak of collectivisation-related complaints and requests, which had numbered over 10,473 a few months earlier in July that year.[42]

The scale of petitioning was very significant, but why did the Soviet government invest such a great deal of time and energy into cultivating petitioning, and monitoring and processing these requests and complaints? The next section considers why petitions mattered, from the point of view of both the state and its citizens.

Petitions and the Soviet State: Information-Gathering and Legitimation

From the state's perspective, citizens' petitions helped the government to overcome the 'dictator's dilemma': how, in the absence of free and competitive elections or a free press, an authoritarian regime is left uncertain about the real level of popular support it enjoys among its citizens. Experts on petitioning in modern China have argued that '[c]itizens' specific grievances are revealed in petitions and if addressed can placate them and generate acceptance of the regime'.[43] Similarly, Martin Dimitrov's work on communist Bulgaria has argued that authoritarian governments produced internal assessments of the quality of governance in order to identify and address problems before they threatened regime stability. Even more so than in liberal democracies, complaints and requests served as information-gathering channels in communist systems and a means 'to monitor the level of popular trust in the regime'.[44]

In the Soviet case, petitioning was only one part of a wider project to gather information on the public 'mood' (*nastroenie*), a significant 'consultative' impulse by the 1930s, which also included police and party *svodki* (surveillance reports), and circulated questionnaires on social and cultural issues.[45] Indeed, Evgeny Dobrenko, in his study of Stalin-era reading culture via library questionnaires, has suggested that the state's seeking out of public opinion went

[42] RGASPI, fond 78, op. 1, d. 423, ll. 179–81.

[43] Chen, *Useful Complaints*, p. 13; C. F. Minzner, 'Xinfang: An Alternative to Formal Chinese Legal Institutions', *Stanford Journal of International Law*, 42 (2006), 103–79 (p. 117).

[44] Chen, *Useful Complaints*; M. K. Dimitrov, 'Vertical Accountability in Communist Regimes: The Role of Citizen Complaints in Bulgaria and China', in M. K. Dimitrov (ed), *Why Communism Did Not Collapse: Understanding Authoritarian Regime. Resilience in Asia and Europe* (Cambridge, Cambridge University Press, 2013), pp. 276–302.

[45] See P. Holquist, '"Information Is the Alpha and Omega of Our Work": Bolshevik Surveillance in Its Pan-European Context', *Journal of Modern History*, 69 (1997), 415–50: S. Davies, *Popular Opinion in Stalin's Russia* (Cambridge, Cambridge University Press, 1997); and E. Zubkova, *Russia after the War: Hopes, Illusions, and Disappointments, 1945–1957* (Armonk, NY, M. E. Sharpe, 1998).

beyond consultation and was tantamount to an active mobilisation that required for forging of the 'New Soviet Person'.[46]

Petitioning offered the Soviet government a means of gathering information about the situation on the ground and of hearing the 'authentic voice of the land', as Lenin remarked, and also functioned as a means to draw citizens into the active participation required by the new regime.[47] Kalinin extolled the informational function of the petitioning system when he told journalists from the *Sotsialisticheskoe zemledelie* newspaper in 1945 that 'I can always tell by petitions to my Reception Office which issues are now acute.'[48] Kalinin considered that the petitions represented an informal consultation with the population. But for what purpose was this information used?

Information gathered from petitions was used by central government staff to monitor local officials in terms of policy implementation, goods provision, and corruption. This allowed the central state to police its bureaucracy in the periphery and punish malpractice, with a view to improving the performance of local administration and winning support from those citizens with grievances. Sovietologist Alex Inkeles suggested that this mechanism of popular oversight must have provided 'the citizenry with the satisfaction of at least feeling that it exercises some public control over officials', and more recently Elena Bogdanova has argued that 'the opportunity to file a complaint against a bureaucracy and knowing that something will be done about it were in effect the only civil rights Soviet citizens consciously possessed'.[49] Soviet leaders treated petitioning as a form of public oversight from below, preferred for its flexibility compared to what was understood as the legal red tape of bourgeois states.

Both internal and public official documents promoted Kalinin's Priemnaia as a tool of popular *kontrol* over state institutions in order to create a system of accountable, responsive 'proletarian democracy'. The internal government regulation 'Outline of the Rules of Management of Soviet Institutions' declared in December 1918 that 'to combat red tape and successfully expose abuses, as well as to eliminate dishonest officials who have penetrated Soviet institutions … in every Soviet institution the days and hours of reception of the public should be hung not only inside the building, but outside so that they are accessible to all without any passes'.[50]

[46] E. Dobrenko, *The Making of the State Writer: Social and Aesthetic Origins of Soviet Literary Culture* (Stanford, CA, Stanford University Press, 2000). See also E. Wood, *The Baba and the Comrade: Gender and Politics in Revolutionary Russia* (Bloomington, Indiana University Press, 1997), p. 7, on the necessity of active participation of Soviet citizens.

[47] Bonch-Bruevich, *Izbrannye sochineniia*, Vol. III, p. 166.

[48] 'Besedy M. I. Kalinina s korrespondentom gazety', *Sotsialisticheskoe zemledelie*, 29 December 1945, in RGASPI, fond 78, op. 1, d. 32, l. 6.

[49] E. Bogdanova, 'Sovetskaia traditsiia pravovoi zashchity, ili v ozhidanii zaboty', *Neprikosnovennyi zapas*, 1:39 (2005), 76–83. For an East German parallel, see P. Betts, *Within Walls: Private Life in the German Democratic Republic* (Oxford, Oxford University Press, 2012), pp. 175–90.

[50] 'Nabrosok pravil ob upravlenii sovetskimi uchrezhdeniiami', 12 December 1918, in V. I. Lenin, *Polnoe sobranie sochinenii*, 5th edn, Vol. XXXVII (Moscow, Izdat. Politicheskoi Literatury, 1963), pp. 366–7.

From 1919 the Reception Office became ever more closely intertwined with the concept of state *kontrol* as a participatory, democratic lever. *Kontrol* (meaning 'checking' or 'supervision' in a general sense, like the English term 'comptroller') would enable the 'labouring masses' to monitor bureaucrats, until such time as the proletariat could take over the work of administration themselves.

Lenin's own preoccupation with petitioning as a tool to combat bureaucracy and unaccountability is demonstrated in the decree 'On the Elimination of Red Tape' of 30 December 1919.[51] According to Lenin, this 'living link' was a vital tool of his revolutionary proletarian-democratic government.[52] In a letter of 3 December 1921 to state officials who dealt with complaints from petitioners to the government, Lenin wrote 'in handling complaints and petitions, it is clear that serious and urgent cases have demonstrated the usefulness of the Reception as a living link [*zhivaia sviaz'*]'.[53] Kalinin echoed this opinion of petitioning as a unique form of accountability before the people when some Soviet leaders called for the closing of the Reception. In a 1938 speech to the chairmen of the presidiums of the Supreme Soviets of the Republics, Kalinin categorically opposed such proposals and highlighted the legitimising force of petitioning: 'You must, at least once a week, appear in front of the people. You say that we have the most democratic parliament in the world, the most democratic power in the world, yet you want to liquidate the reception room so that it would be very difficult to get to a representative of the authorities.'[54] These examples make clear that the openness, accessibility, and responsiveness of the government to citizens supposedly afforded by the work of the Priemnaia remained central to notions of Soviet democracy.

For Soviet leaders, the accountability delivered through petitioning was a force to stabilise and legitimise their regime. Kalinin was aware of the usefulness of successfully resolved petitions in spreading support for the regime beyond the immediate petitioner. He tried to ensure that the Reception responded promptly and 'politically correctly' to as many petitions as possible. In a speech to the national Assembly of Complaint Bureaus in July 1933 he commented that

> [i]f you need to be able to apply politics anywhere, it is precisely in the issue of considering complaints, because in our conditions every decision is a policy … It is better to refuse than to throw a person around like a ball … A dozen correct decisions in the district is like a rally of 10,000, after all. Do you think the right decision remains only in one village? It extends to 10 or even 15 kilometres, because the masses themselves act here as agitators … and this decision will be discussed 10 times at dinner, in the evening, etc. … Consideration of complaints is one of the important conductors of communism.[55]

[51] Dekreta SNK RSFSR, 'Ob ustranenii volokity', 30 December 1919, *Dekrety sovetskoi vlasti*, 7, 10 December 1919–31 March 1920 (Moscow, 1975).

[52] Fotieva, *Iz zhizni V. I. Lenina*, pp. 89–91.

[53] Lenin, *Polnoe Sobranie Sochinenii*, Vol. XLIV, p. 268.

[54] GARF, fond. 7523, op. 9, d. 112a, l. 66.

[55] RGASPI, fond. 78, op. 1, d. 434, ll. 58–63.

Scholars have also suggested that when many individual petitions made the same complaint or request, they could set the agenda for policy in order to maintain social order.[56] Historians of early modern Europe have argued that patterns of petitioning sometimes played a role in legislative and administrative reforms.[57] This dynamic, to a degree, also applied in the Soviet case. Receiving petitions allowed Kalinin not only to feel the pulse of the popular mood but to reflect it to other policy-makers. L. S. Braun, an American priest in Moscow, suggested that Kalinin insisted religion was still popular when the party elite considered reviving the Orthodox Church to promote morale during the Second World War, citing many petitions that had included requests for churches not to be closed or to be reopened. As Chairman of the CEC of Soviets and a full member of the Politburo from 1926, Kalinin participated in weekly meetings of Stalin's cabinet and was well placed to act as a conduit for the petitioners he met in the Reception Office.

Petitions and the Soviet Citizen: Grievances, Assistance, and Trust

But why did petitioning matter from the point of view of Soviet citizens? It could be argued, as scholars have suggested for other places and periods, that the petition functioned as a 'safety valve'.[58] In this way, the petition provided a source of legitimation for the regime and channelled and neutralised dissatisfaction into discrete channels that forestalled more significant unrest.[59]

Certainly contemporary observers of the Reception Office remarked on its pacifying effect on petitioners. On her visit to Kalinin in the early years of the regime, Bryant reflected the government's line that '[a]ll day long he receives the never-ending string of peasants in the manner of a village priest, giving consolation and advice – and something more solid and satisfying than a prayer, for he is obligated to make an immediate decision in each case on hand or a promise that it shall be taken up through his office'. She added that 'It was known all over the country that he made it a point to give heed to their grievances … Many of them felt they had obtained a favour simply by talking with him.'[60]

[56] M. Almbjär, 'The Problem with Early-Modern Petitions: Safety Valve or Powder Keg?', *European Review of History*, 26 (2019), 1013–39.

[57] B. Kümin and A. Würgler, 'Petitions, *Gravamina*, and the Early Modern State: Local Influence on Central Legislation in England and Germany (Hesse)', *Parliaments, Estates and Representation*, 17 (1997), 39–60; P. Loft, 'Involving the Public: Parliament, Petitioning, and the Language of Interest, 1688–1720', *Journal of British Studies*, 55 (2016), 1–23; P. Loft, 'Petitioning and Petitioners to the Westminster Parliament, 1660–1788', *Parliamentary History*, 38 (2019), 342–61.

[58] Almbjär, 'The Problem with Early-Modern Petitions', p. 1015.

[59] Ibid.

[60] Bryant, *Mirrors of Moscow*, pp. 98–9.

As well as the routine airing of grievances, the dramatic nature of some in-person petitioning suggests that the Reception could be used as a public arena for the performative expression of dissatisfaction. Natal'ia Veselovskaia, an emergency doctor, noted an occasion when she was called to Kalinin's Reception. When her medical team arrived, they were met by one of the Reception officials who explained that a citizen had arrived with exorbitant demands for help, 'expressing himself in an aggressive tone, with threats and reproach'. The citizen, exclaiming that they 'would not let him speak' and that they were 'gagging his mouth', grabbed a hammer and nailed his tongue to a plywood suitcase. Veselovskaia saw a young man 'holding a suitcase on his knees, on which lay his long tongue with a nail sticking out'. She recalled that 'The crowd around gasped and were indignant.' When he refused treatment, Veselovskaia took him to the local psychiatric hospital, with suitcase still attached. There the duty doctor attended and 'in a fast and unexpected movement, grabbed the tongue at the tip and took it off the nail. It turned out that in the tongue there was an old hole with calloused edges and the man used it for the sake of influencing those he appealed to: the hammer was only for effect!'[61]

This incident is not the only example of theatrical protest and public self-harm in the Reception Office. Veselovskaia mentioned a similar incident involving an amnestied gulag inmate who had petitioned for the rights of an innocent returnee, including living space and a job in Moscow. He was dissatisfied with his treatment by the Reception Office of the Sokolniki District Executive Committee, and reportedly,

> [w]ishing to bring attention to himself, he took off his pants, mounted a large tree and nailed his scrotum to it with a hammer and nail. This was all accompanied by loud ranting about the injustice of the authorities. He insisted that the chairman of the district executive committee had done this to him. The public, attracted by his cries, gathered in a considerable number.[62]

The Reception was a convenient location for this kind of protest. It was a space where government officials were accessible, and also offered a captive audience of other petitioners from all over the country who might spread the word about what they witnessed far and wide. The idea that the protest was holding the state to its own promises of responsiveness, thereby confirming the existing order while mocking it, smacked of the carnivalesque. Finally, the demonstration of physical self-harm by some petitioners seems to have been calculated to attract attention while avoiding the serious retribution that was meted out to overtly political protest.

Petitioning was also useful to citizens as a channel through which they could seek the redress of wrongs and alleviate material hardship. Sheila Fitzpatrick's work on Soviet petitions in the 1930s offered an estimated response rate of 15–30 per cent

[61] Natal'ia Konstantinovna Veselovskaia, *Zapiski vyezdnogo vracha skoroi pomoshchi* 1940–53 (Moscow, АИРО-XXI, 2010) pp. 59–60.

[62] Veselovskaia, *Zapiski vyezdnogo vracha skoroi pomoshchi*, p. 60.

to public complaints directed towards the central authorities in this period.[63] Internal reports compiled by Kalinin's Priemnaia on the scale and types of petitions received suggest that the Soviet government did attempt to engage with petitioners. Even if responding to all petitions proved impossible, the authorities consistently aimed to reply and to pursue actions to deal with complaints.[64] Surviving documents suggest that the Reception referred petitions to other government departments and that state officials internally discussed responses to petitions.[65]

While in some ways petitions in the early Soviet period functioned as a safety valve, the overall impact was more complicated. Petitioners who did not receive their desired response could be further alienated rather than placated. The memoirs of Julius Margolin, a Belarussian gulag inmate during the early 1940s, demonstrate the sense of cynicism generated by the experience of a failed petition.[66] Margolin wrote a petition after he was seized by the Red Army during their 'liberation' of Poland and was sent to the gulag. He explained that:

> [i]n Soviet camps, prisoners have ample opportunity to write complaints. Alongside the ordinary box for letters in the office, another special box is hanging; it bears the inscription 'For Complaints and Petitions to the commander of the camp, the Presidium of the Supreme Soviet [Kalinin's Priemnaia], or the Chief Prosecutor of the USSR'. A month after it is deposited in the box, the zek will receive an official notice that his request is being processed. In another six or nine months the long-awaited response will arrive from Moscow.

Margolin recalled how during their first months in the camp new inmates from outside Russia 'wrote an unbelievable number of complaints, appeals, and requests for pardons to Kalinin and other officials. The Russian zeks made fun of their contents. Wise from bitter experience, they did not write. Writing petitions is something like measles – the childhood disease of every inmate in his first year of imprisonment.'

Margolin petitioned for a review of his case in order to be freed as 'a peaceful, progressive person who never wronged the Soviet Union, never crossed its borders legally or illegally'. The answer arrived six months later on a generic printed form, and to his dismay Margolin lamented that

> [c]learly neither Kalinin nor the Chief Prosecutor had read my appeal. It had gone from their offices to a lower one, then to a third and fourth and it finally arrived in Pinsk at the office of the prosecutor who had been responsible for my arrest. The prosecutor took a printed form, put my name on it, signed and sent it back with the standard format 'Upon review of the complaint of so and so … it is noted that the punishment was meted out correctly, according to his deeds.'[67]

[63] Fitzpatrick, 'Supplicants and Citizens', pp. 101–2.

[64] GARF, fond 7523, op. 65, d. 592, ll. 5–51.

[65] See for example the correspondence between Kalinin and Nadezhda Krupskaia in Siegelbaum and Sokolov, *Stalinism as a Way of Life*, pp. 286–91.

[66] All quotes in this paragraph are from J. Margolin, *Journey into the Land of the Zeks and Back: A Memoir of the Gulag*, trans. S. Hoffman (Oxford, Oxford University Press, 2020), pp. 136–7.

[67] Ibid., pp. 136–7.

Margolin had been imprisoned as a 'socially dangerous, suspicious element', rather than for having actually done anything, so the response was both inaccurate and disappointing. He recognised, however, that 'it was difficult to demand that Soviet justice examine the personal circumstances of every one of the millions of camp inmates. In the course of a year, Kalinin received so many appeals from the camps that neither he nor his staff were able to read them had they sincerely wished to do so.'[68]

Margolin recalled another unsuccessful attempt at petitioning Kalinin. This time the case related to a fellow zek, Yulich. This former factory director was arrested during the purges, and his wife managed to reach the camp and meet her husband a few years later. She told him of her efforts to appeal to Kalinin for his release:

> she went to Mikhail Kalinin himself, to plead on her husband's behalf… She obtained an audience with the 'All-Russian elder' … After the first words, Kalinin jumped up from his seat. The Soviet apostle of humanism in golden glasses and with a grey goatee hastily asked the woman: 'Where is your husband?' 'In the Ertsevo camps'. 'Aha' rejoiced Kalinin, 'that's really marvellous. Those are our best camps! A real sanatorium! How happy I am for your husband. He'll be fine there. Marvellous, marvellous, marvellous!' Grabbing the dumbfounded woman by the shoulder, without letting her say a word, he pushed her to the door and led her out in the wink of an eye … the entire audience lasted three minutes.[69]

The reality of this petitioner's experience was at odds with the state's public image of the Reception as the embodiment of the Soviet state's responsiveness to its citizens.

The language of petitions might also contribute to diffusing tension and promoting trust in the authorities. Writing of early modern Britain and Ireland, Rab Houston has argued that '[l]anguage uses people as much as they use language': 'someone who employs deferential forms becomes deferential; by the same token, an expression of paternalism makes it harder … to treat an inferior in ways that are other than fatherly'.[70] Thus, the use of the customary supplicatory language of petitions showed 'an implicit acceptance of social, economic and political inequality with the hope of making this inequality work to the petitioners' benefit.'[71] In the Soviet case, Tikhomirov has argued that writing letters to party and state authorities was a mechanism for producing trust that ensured the legitimacy and stability of the political order. Tikhomirov suggested that 'This logic of letter writing explains the fact that a lack of trust in anonymous, impersonal, and usually ineffective institutions was compensated for by interpersonal, personalized trust as an effective way of reinforcing reciprocity, predictability and a sense of security in

[68] Ibid., p. 137.
[69] Ibid., p. 368.
[70] R. A. Houston, *Peasant Petitions: Social Relations and Economic Life on Landed Estates, 1600–1850* (Basingstoke, Palgrave Macmillan, 2014), pp. 271–3.
[71] K. J. Kesselring, *Mercy and Authority in the Tudor State* (Cambridge, Cambridge University Press, 2007), pp. 203–7.

everyday life.' For Tikhomirov, the resulting 'regime of forced trust' allowed the state to obtain the population's confidence by personifying politics and setting up channels for communicating with leaders directly, enabling the 'emotional mobilization' of the people.[72] He argued that letter writing acted as a stabilising force for the Soviet regime and as a mechanism through which people 'learned to feel Soviet', rather than for the more prosaic reason that they received a helpful response to their petitions.[73] Certainly written petitions served as a platform for Soviet citizens to construct approved discourse that displayed their revolutionary credentials, their ability to 'speak Bolshevik', as the influential Soviet subjectivities paradigm introduced by Stephen Kotkin asserted, although the relationship between authentic feelings and public expression is complex.[74]

While Tikhomirov's emphasis on the performance of citizenship through petitions is fascinating, one may reasonably doubt how far these pleas should be regarded as authentic expressions rather than a calculated and even cynical device to elicit a sympathetic response from the authorities. Indeed, in his classic analysis of naïve monarchism, James C. Scott argued that contact between the powerless and powerful is laden with deception. The powerless feign deference as a mechanism to realise their objectives without summoning the wrath of the authorities through open resistance or criticism. Subordinates construct public (loyal) transcripts in dialogues with power, and hidden (disloyal) transcripts 'spoken behind the back of the dominant'.[75] It might be more useful to view the Soviet petitions in a similar way to the 16th-century pardon requests described as 'fiction in the archives' by Natalie Zemon Davis when she considers the discursive strategies employed by petitioners, rather than their authentic emotional attachment to the regime.[76] What is even more difficult to discern is how far the petitioners were treated critically by the authorities or accepted as 'reality', shaping the state's perception of and reaction to events and popular mood.

Conclusion

Overall, petitions served as a barometer of popular mood for a government eager to gather this kind of information in order to 'manage' it. The Soviet government's display of responsiveness to requests and complaints was a means of cultivating

[72] A. Tikhomirov, 'The Regime of Forced Trust', 92, 107

[73] Ibid., pp. 98, 111.

[74] S. Kotkin, *Magnetic Mountain: Stalinism as a Civilization* (Berkeley, University of California Press, 1995). For a critique, see J. Waterlow, 'Speaking More than Bolshevik: Humour, Subjectivity, and Crosshatching in Stalin's 1930s', in M. Neumann and A Willimott (eds), *Rethinking the Russian Revolution as Historical Divide* (London, Routledge, 2017), Chapter 9.

[75] J. C. Scott, *Domination and the Arts of Resistance* (New Haven, CT, Yale University Press, 1990), p. xii.

[76] Natalie Zemon Davis, *Fiction in the Archives: Pardon Tales and Their Tellers in Sixteenth-Century France* (Stanford, CA, Stanford University Press, 1990).

a sense of legitimacy. It was a tool to police the functioning of a vast and underadministered state where a large proportion of petitions concerned abuses of local officials. Yet, the processing of petitions by the Soviet authorities did not always function as a 'safety valve' to reduce the dissatisfaction of citizens and promote support of the regime in a predictable and straightforward way. The massive volume of requests and complaints made it impossible to satisfy every case. More often than not, petitioners did not receive the desired solution, and so might be left more alienated by the process. Even a successful result did not guarantee automatic 'support' for the state more broadly. The state's promotion of petitioning preserved a sense of citizens' rights to redress. When the parameters of permissible public criticism were widened, such as in the Gorbachev era in the 1980s, an avalanche of critical letters of complaint and request overwhelmed government and society. Through their petitions, Soviet citizens had long been active and seasoned 'complainers'; the deluge of critical public opinion that shook the regime during glasnost was not due to something brand new: its roots lay in the pervasive and persistent practice of petitioning.

Conclusion: And Your Petitioners, &c.

HENRY MILLER

PETITIONS HAVE BEEN a ubiquitous form across the polities, places, and periods surveyed in this volume. While the absence of records means that it is not always possible to quantify the scale of petitions in a given era or territory, there is enough other evidence to indicate their pervasiveness. If petitioners have often been disappointed with the outcome of their requests to power, this has not seemingly deterred their recourse to petitioning. This is for a number of reasons. Petitions – and petitioning – have proven to be highly adaptable, mutable, and ambiguous forms of interaction with power, which goes a long way to explaining their popularity across very different political and social contexts. Petitions are adaptable, in that while they have often been regulated by officials or authority, there remains considerable scope for creativity, not least in terms of the language of the text, the material form of the petition, and the associated rituals that accompany it. This leads to a second point. Petitions are highly mutable as a form of political activity as they can mutate into other forms: a signatory list, as is now well-established, is a resource that is foundational to other forms of collective action; to give another example, the origin of political parties and movements is not infrequently traceable to a landmark petition. The fluidity of petitions and petitioning explains the interconnectedness with various other forms of political activity, from riots and revolts to more conventional forms of participation, such as letter writing to elected representatives. At times, petitioning may underpin a wider repertoire of collective action; in other instances it may form one element among other forms and not necessarily the most important. Finally, the ambiguity of petitions, often superficially deferent to the authority to which petitioners were appealing combined with a more assertive subtext, was a strength rather than a weakness of the genre. It explains why petitions remained an unstable, dynamic, and unpredictable form of interaction between people and authority, and more often a 'powder keg' than a 'safety valve'.[1] While

[1] M. Almbjär, 'The Problem with Early Modern Petitions: Safety Valve or Powder Keg?', *European Review of History*, 26 (2019), 1013–39.

Proceedings of the British Academy, **262**, 303–309, © The British Academy 2024.

the chapters in this volume have reflected different disciplinary and methodological persuasions, they share a perspective that considers petitions and petitioning as practices and processes, stressing their interactive quality rather than offering a top-down or bottom-up account.

Our volume has sought to chart the chronologies of petitioning, the peaks and troughs, continuities and transformations, over a long period of time. Shifts in petitioning, including during and after moments of revolutionary change, often coexisted alongside deep continuities. Changes and transformations were rarely linear; while we might expect a trend away from individual, private petitions to public, collective mass petitioning over time, it is possible to find examples of collective petitions in the medieval period on affairs of state, and examples of individuals complaining about personal grievances in the 20th century. Rather than a shift from one type of petitioning to another, change might be better framed as shifts in the balance between different categories of petition. At the same time, there was a trend from petitioning being used for a wide range of different requests (including for employment, patronage, or personal status, many of which were hived off into specialised processes or were superseded by other categories, such as application forms) with the consequence that the meaning of petitions in the modern era has become more specific, referring to practices that are typically linked to representative and political institutions.[2]

The volume has emphasised many reasons why petitionary practices have mattered, for both authorities and the people who appeal to them. For various reasons, including legitimation, information-gathering, containing and channelling criticism, and entrenching authority, petitions have been useful tools for rulers, states, political elites, and officials. From the other end of the petitionary process, petitions have been valuable for claiming general rights and citizenship, but also, more specifically, for claiming exemptions, legal and financial privileges, and personal benefits. Petitioning has been a widespread practice on account of its many uses, but it has been especially valuable for those groups and individuals who have been marginalised or lacking in political and legal rights, or social, economic, and cultural capital. For such groups, petitions have provided an accessible way of making contact with the state or authority compared to other avenues, and allow petitioners to mobilise numbers or other claims to consideration when they could not rely on personal connections, wealth, or status.

In summarising the volume's key arguments in the broadest possible terms we hope to make clear the significant implications of this book for a wide audience of scholars across the humanities and social sciences. The study of petitionary practices should be integrated more systematically and deeply into accounts of political and social history, especially as it offers new perspectives on historical processes, structures, and lived experiences. As themes, petitions and petitioning

[2] See R. Huzzey and H. Miller, 'The Politics of Petitioning: Parliament, Government, and Subscriptional Cultures in the United Kingdom, 1780–1918', *History*, 106 (2021), 221–43.

also have much to contribute to the social and political scientific analysis of topics such as power and authority, state and citizenship, democracy and democratisation, collective action and popular contention, and participation and representation, to give just a few examples.

Having distilled some of the key arguments from this book, the conclusion finishes by considering some of the future directions that studies might take in this field. We might classify these potential lines of enquiry as addressing different questions: where, when, what, how, and who?

In terms of geography, or 'where', future studies examining different places within Europe and North America will usefully test the extent to which the cycles of continuity and change identified here follow the same chronology. Moreover, an even broader geographical range of research will reveal the importance of different national contexts in shaping variations in both the nature of petitions and the trends of petitioning over time. Beyond this, there is a need to place analyses of petitions and petitioning in Europe and North America in a global perspective. This would bring the analysis offered in this volume into conversation with the expanding and rich literature on other parts of the globe, including colonial Spanish America and postindependence Central and South America;[3] 19th- and 20th-century Africa;[4] and modern South

[3] A far from exhaustive list includes W. Fowler, *Independent Mexico: The Pronunciamiento in the Age of Santa Anna, 1821–1858* (Lincoln, University of Nebraska Press, 2016); A. Masters, *We, the King: Creating Royal Legislation in the Sixteenth-Century Spanish New World* (Cambridge, Cambridge University Press, 2023); B. Premo, 'Before the Law: Women's Petitions in the Eighteenth-Century Spanish Empire', *Comparative Studies in Society and History*, 53 (2011), 261–89; A. Slemian, 'Petitions to the Courts of Appeal in Portuguese America and the Protection of Rights (c. 1750–1808)'; and A. Caso Bello, 'Petitions to Correct Revolutionary Rumours: The City Council of Santafé Bogotá and Madrid's *Agentes de Indias*, c. 1780–1795', in M. da Cruz, *Petitioning in the Atlantic World, c. 1500–1840* (Cham, Palgrave Macmillan, 2022), pp. 65–84, 85–104; J. Sanders, 'Indigenous Citizens and Black Republicans: Continuities and Evolutions of Subalterns' Political Visions and Repertoires in Post-Independence Columbia and Mexico', in J. Pollmann and H. te Velde (eds), *Civic Continuities in an Age of Revolutionary Change, c. 1750–1850: Europe and the Americas* (Basingstoke, Palgrave, 2023), pp. 171–96; S. Albiez-Wieck, *Taxing Difference in Peru and New Spain (16th–19th Century)* (Leiden, Brill, 2022); T. Herzog, *Defining Nations: Immigrants and Citizens in Early Modern Spain and Spanish America* (New Haven, CT, Yale University Press, 2003); C. Ireton, 'Black Africans' Freedom Litigation Suits to Define Just War and Just Slavery in the Early Spanish Empire', *Renaissance Quarterly*, 73 (2020), 1277–319; A. Masters, 'A Thousand Invisible Architects: Vassals, the Petition and Response System, and the Creation of Spanish Imperial Caste Legislation', *Hispanic American Historical Review*, 98 (2018), 377–406; K. McDonough, 'Indigenous Rememberings and Forgettings: Sixteenth-Century Nahua Letters and Petitions to the Spanish Crown', *Native American and Indigenous Studies*, 5 (2018), 69–99; M. A. Valerio, 'The Spanish Petition System, Hospital/ity, and the Formation of a Mulato Community in Sixteenth-Century Mexico', *The Americas*, 78 (2021), 415–37; and M. Fernández Peña, 'Liberalismo y política popular: El derecho de petición en el Perú de 1860', *Boletín Americanista*, 86 (2023), 177–96.

[4] Studies of petitions or accounts that draw heavily on petitions include B. Alozie, '"Female Voices on Ink": The Sexual Politics of Petitions in Colonial Igboland, 1892–1960', *Journal of the Middle East and Africa*, 10 (2019), 343–66; T. Decker, 'Handwritten in Lagos: Selfhood and Textuality in Colonial Petitions', *History in Africa*, 48 (2021), 355–82; G. Wasambo Kayira, 'Petitioning the State: Group Councils and the Development of Political Consciousness in Malawi, 1940s–1950s', *Journal of Southern*

Asia, among other places.[5] Such a dialogue would be fruitful in terms of assessing the relationship between the importation or imposition of petitions alongside other mechanisms of colonial rule, and indigenous and customary forms of complaints, and indeed the hybridity of these forms within and between empires. A further strand of research might consider the practice of petitions and petitioning as part of a historical process in which rights for citizens in the imperial metropole developed alongside the deprivation of rights of colonised peoples, as Josep Fradera has argued in his comparative study of empires.[6] For example, while Britons made increasing use of petitioning, in effect to democratise an oligarchic polity in the long 19th century, colonised peoples appealing to the 'imperial Parliament' were more constrained in their ability to do so and their petitions were often impeded, or received with indifference or hostility.[7]

The international and transnational dimension to petitioning might also be examined more fully. In earlier centuries, the papacy attracted petitions from across Christendom as an authority that transcended the jurisdictions of temporal rulers and states.[8] In the 20th century, during the late colonial period and era of

African Studies, 47 (2021), 1045–60; C. J. Korieh, *Nigeria and World War II: Colonialism, Empire, and Global Conflict* (Cambridge, Cambridge University Press, 2020); C. Leonardi and C. Vaughan, '"We Are Oppressed and Our Only Way Is to Write to Higher Authority": The Politics of Claim and Complaint in the Peripheries of Condominium Sudan', in E. Hunter (ed.), *Citizenship, Belonging, and Political Community in Africa: Dialogues between Past and Present* (Athens, Ohio University Press, 2016), pp. 74–100; H. Mokoena, 'Vigilance: Petitions, Politics, and the African Christian Converts of the Nineteenth Century', in S. Comyns and P. Fermanis (eds), *Worlding the South: Nineteenth-Century Literary Culture and the Southern Settler Colonies* (Manchester, Manchester University Press, 2021), pp. 327–45; and E. Vezzadini, *Lost Nationalism: Revolution, Memory, and Anti-Colonial Resistance in Sudan* (Woodbridge, Boydell, 2015).

[5] Relevant work in this field includes S. T. Connors, 'Mass Petitioning, Education Reform, and the Development of Political Culture in Madras, 1839–1842', *Historical Journal*, 65 (2022), 393–414; R. De and R. Travers (eds), *Petitioning and Political Cultures in South Asia*, special issue of *Modern Asian Studies*, 53:1 (2019); J. Jaffe, 'The Languages of Petitioning in Early Colonial India', *Social Science History*, 43 (2019), 581–98; M. Hull, *Government of Paper: The Materiality of Bureaucracy in Urban Pakistan* (Berkeley, University of California Press, 2012); J. Saha, *Law, Disorder, and the Colonial State: Corruption in Burma, c. 1900* (Basingstoke, Palgrave, 2013), pp. 72–96; R. Travers, *Empires of Complaints: Mughal Law and the Making of British India, 1765–1793* (Cambridge, Cambridge University Press, 2022); and F. Cody, 'Inscribing Subjects to Citizenship: Petitions, Literacy, Activism, and the Performativity of Signature in Rural Tamil India', *Cultural Anthropology*, 24 (2009), 347–80.

[6] J. Fradera, *The Imperial Nation: Citizens and Subjects in the British, French, Spanish, and American Empires* (Princeton, NJ, Princeton University Press, 2018). See also A. Curthoys and J. Mitchell, *Taking Liberty: Indigenous Rights and Settler Self-Government in Colonial Australia, 1830–1890* (Cambridge, Cambridge University Press, 2018), for the dynamic of expanding rights for white settlers as part of a process in which indigenous peoples were simultaneously dispossessed.

[7] Compare R. Huzzey and H. Miller, 'Petitions, Parliament, and Political Culture: Petitioning the House of Commons, 1780–1918', *Past & Present*, 248 (2020), 123–64, and R. Huzzey and H. Miller, 'Colonial Petitions, Colonial Petitioners, and the Imperial Parliament, c. 1780–1918', *Journal of British Studies*, 61 (2022), 261–89.

[8] P. Zutshi, 'Petitions to the Pope in the Fourteenth Century', in W. M. Ormrod, G. Dodd, and A. Musson (eds), *Medieval Petitions: Grace and Grievance* (York, York Medieval Press, 2009), pp. 82–98; D. Palacios Cerezales, 'Catholic Transnational Repertoires in the Nineteenth Century: Signatures, Newspapers, and Organisation', in D. Palacios Cerezales and O. Luján (eds), *Popular Agency and Politicisation in Nineteenth-Century Europe: Beyond the Vote* (Cham, Palgrave, 2022), pp. 235–58.

decolonisation, petitions became a vehicle for claim-making in the international arena, especially in terms of asserting a right to self-determination and independent statehood, as shown by case studies of particular places or moments.[9] But a broader analysis of the international dimension of petitions and petitioning, in this or earlier periods, remains to be written.

Considering the 'when' of petitions and petitioning, the transition (while acknowledging important continuities) between the early modern era and the new forms that emerged during the 'age of revolutions' in the long 19th century has been increasingly well documented.[10] However, some significant gaps in the long history of petitioning still remain, including the evolution between classical antiquity and the medieval development of petitions, particularly perhaps outside England and France, which have been the subject of significant study.[11] While the decline of petitions to national legislatures in the 20th-century era of universal suffrage seems to be a trend, or at least evident, in the UK, the USA, and France,[12] this era in which petitioning became an everyday but largely unrecorded form of political participation would repay further research, especially in terms of understanding how these shifts played out on the ground and in different polities. The transition from colonial petitions systems to the use (or indeed the abandonment) of petitioning in newly independent states in the era of decolonisation would also be interesting in terms of understanding the shifting relationship among power, authority, and legitimacy. In this vein, future work might consider whether the historical use of petitions as a legitimation device for regimes was still relevant, or whether states, be they democratic or authoritarian, increasingly used elections as the main instrument for claiming popular endorsement.[13]

[9] L. Walker, 'Decolonization in the 1960s: On Legitimate and Illegitimate Claims-making', *Past & Present*, 242 (2019), 227–64; S. Pedersen, 'Samoa on the World Stage: Petitions and Peoples before the Mandates Commission of the League of Nations', *Journal of Imperial and Commonwealth History*, 40 (2012), 231–61; J. McQuade, 'Beyond an Imperial Foreign Policy? India at the League of Nations, 1919–1946', *Journal of Imperial and Commonwealth History*, 48 (2020), 263–95; A. B. Lorca, *Mestizo International Law: A Global Intellectual History, 1842–1933* (Cambridge, Cambridge University Press, 2014), pp. 225–62; E. Kluge, 'West Papua and the International History of Decolonization, 1961–69', *International History Review*, 42 (2020), 1155–72; A. V. Burra, 'Petitioning the Mandates: Anti-Colonial and Anti-Racist Publics in International Law', PhD thesis (University of Michigan, 2017).

[10] D. Carpenter, *Democracy by Petition: Popular Politics in Transformation, 1790–1870* (Cambridge, MA, Harvard University Press, 2021); H. Miller, *A Nation of Petitioners: Petitions and Petitioning in the United Kingdom, 1780–1918* (Cambridge, Cambridge University Press, 2023); B. Agnès, *L'appel au pouvoir: Les pétitions aux parlements en France et au Royaume-Uni (1814–1848)* (Rennes, Presses universitaires de Rennes, 2018); J. Oddens, *Op veler verzoek: Inclusieve politiek in Nederlands (1780–1860)* (Amsterdam, Boom, 2023).

[11] G. Koziol, *Begging Pardon and Favor: Ritual and Political Order in Early Medieval France* (Ithaca, NY, Cornell University Press, 1992); G. Dodd, *Justice and Grace: Private Petitioning and the English Parliament in the Late Middle Ages* (Oxford, Oxford University Press, 2007).

[12] See the chapter by Huzzey and Miller in this volume.

[13] For considerations of the role of petitions and elections in modern authoritarian systems, see J. Gandhi and E. Lust-Okar, 'Elections under Authoritarianism', *Annual Review of Political Science*, 12 (2009), 403–22; and H. Lueders, 'Electoral Responsiveness in Closed Autocracies: Evidence from Petitions in the Former German Democratic Republic', *American Political Science Review*, 116 (2022), 827–42.

Conceptually, or 'what' are petitions, another way of thinking about these almost universal practices in a way that allows comparison with other modes of politics and social activity would be to think of them as enabling technologies. The petition, and more particularly the signatory list, has been analysed as a 'technology' of political recruitment and organisation in the modern era.[14] We might extend this insight to other periods, but also think critically about how the uses of petitions and petitioning have been and still are shaped by various technologies, such as manuscript, print, telecommunications, and the internet and digital systems. Borrowing from scholars working on e-petitions in contemporary politics,[15] we might seek to reconstruct the 'petitions systems' operating in other historical contexts. Moreover, we might probe the relationship between official forms of petitioning prescribed by and to some extent controlled by authority, and the more informal and often unpredictable modes of subscriptional culture that have always existed alongside them.

Methodologically, or 'how' future scholarship might study petitions and petitioning, research could profitably apply a number of approaches, including drawing on the development of the digital humanities. The mapping of petitions and signatures using geographical information systems or equivalent software would usefully reveal spatial patterns that would otherwise be difficult to reconstruct. Such methods would allow the broader analysis of the relationship between petitions, place, representation, and identity. Where records allow, counting petitions or using quantitative methods would be valuable in tracking trends across time and in connecting petitioning to broader patterns in political development, or showing the independence of petitions from other trends, including partisanship.[16] In some cases, it may be possible to connect a series of records from different periods to trace the flows of petitions to a particular institution such as the English, later British, and UK Parliament, over the *longue durée*. The close reading of petitions as texts and their generic conventions has been a feature of existing work. Such accounts have revealed the structures of petitions as well as examining the use of rhetoric.[17] The development of digital humanities, including corpus linguistics and other techniques,[18] offers further opportunities for analysing the language of petitions on a scale beyond the

[14] D. Carpenter, 'Recruitment by Petition: American Antislavery, French Protestantism, English Suppression', *Perspectives on Politics*, 14 (2016), 700–23.

[15] See the chapter by Leston-Bandeira in this volume.

[16] See the chapter by Blackhawk and Carpenter in this volume.

[17] G. Khan, 'The Historical Development of the Structure of Medieval Arabic Petitions', *Bulletin of the School of Oriental and African Studies*, 53 (1990), 8–30; S. Zaeske, 'Signatures of Citizenship: The Rhetoric of Women's Antislavery Petitions', *Quarterly Journal of Speech*, 88 (2002), 147–68; Y. Akin, 'Reconsidering State, Party, and Society in Early Republican Turkey: Politics of Petitioning', *International Journal of Middle Eastern Studies*, 39 (2007), 435–57; L. Bowen, 'Genre, Authorship, and Authenticity in the Petitions of Civil War Veterans and Widows from North Wales and the Marches', in B. Waddell and J. Peacey (eds), *The Power of Petitioning in Early Modern Britain* (London, UCL Press, forthcoming).

[18] The application of such methods to historical election speeches by MPs and candidates in the British context gives an indication of what could be done: L. Blaxill, 'Quantifying the Language of British Politics, 1880–1910', *Historical Research*, 86 (2013), 313–41; L. Blaxill, *The War of Words: The Language of British Elections, 1880–1914* (Woodbridge, Boydell, 2020).

capacity of a lone scholar. Tracing the similarities or variations of petitionary rhetoric and structures in different languages would be another interesting line of enquiry, especially in states and empires that received petitions in multiple languages.

Finally, this volume has generally focused on the what, when, and where of petitions and petitioning, rather than the 'who': the petitioners. This was a conscious choice, as many excellent case studies of the use of petitions by different groups in various periods, places, and polities existed already, but important definitional and chronological questions had received less attention. Yet the agency of petitioners, signatories, and organisers in shaping both petitions and the practices of petitioning has been a significant theme in this volume. As we have seen, petitioners skilfully repeated back official rhetoric to the authorities to which they appealed, and frequently exploited moments of upheaval and revolutionary change to press their claims on new institutions or rulers seeking to establish their legitimacy. As well as more case studies of different categories of petitioners (including those with social, political, and economic capital, such as mercantile elites,[19] as well as those for whom petitions were a 'weapon of the weak'), scholars might consider the relationship between petitioners and collective identity formation more broadly. The use of petitions by children and young people – groups often lacking formal citizenship, political rights, and other forms of accessing power – would also be interesting.[20] Moreover, future research might shed further light on the scribes, brokers, sponsors, and officials who so often mediated petitions. Beyond examining different groups of petitioners, researchers might consider the polyphonous[21] sound of petitioners, and what this sounded like to the recipients of their requests. For instance, what was it like for 19th-century members of the political elite to be confronted with the cacophonous sound of petitioners? While rarely permitted in legislatures at this time,[22] petitioners could nevertheless make their voices heard through the presenting and reading out of their petitions. New studies might reflect further on the importance of the 'voice' of petitioners, not least in giving credibility to their representative claims.

In examining the characteristics, chronology, and effects of petitions and petitioning in Europe and North America over several centuries, this volume's ambition has been to emphasise the broader importance of these practices. These wonderful and fascinating documents, as well as the practices that accompanied them and the stories behind them, illuminate many of the varieties of the human experience, past and present. In this spirit, we hope that the essays offered here, rather than being the final word, are considered as an opening gambit, with the aim of stimulating a rich and ongoing conversation in the years to come.

[19] A. S. Overkamp, 'Maintaining Order in Revolutionary Times: The Political Practices of a Mercantile Elite in the Rhineland, 1770–1830', in Pollmann and Te Velde, *Civic Continuities*, pp. 145–70.

[20] For a case study, see H. Peck, '"For the Dead Fathers Sake"? Orphans, Petitions, and the British Civil Wars, 1647–1679', in Waddell and Peacey, *The Power of Petitioning*.

[21] Here I am borrowing a term used by the late Aaron Graham.

[22] H. Miller, 'Introduction: The Transformation of Petitioning in the Long Nineteenth Century (1780–1914)', *Social Science History*, 43 (2019), 409–29 (p. 419).

Index

www.ingramcontent.com/pod-product-compliance
Lightning Source LLC
Chambersburg PA
CBHW060008280326
42015CB00003B/119

* 9 7 8 0 1 9 7 2 6 7 7 2 1 *